E 184, G3 E46 1995

EMIGRATION AND SETTLEMENT PATTERNS OF GERMAN COMMUNITIES IN NORTH AMERICA

Edited by

Eberhard Reichmann
LaVern J. Rippley
Jörg Nagler

D1501449

COASTAL BEND COLLEGE LIBRARY
3800 CHARCO ROAD
BEEVILLE, TEXAS 78102
(512) 354-2740

Max Kade German-American Center
Indiana University-Purdue University at Indianapolis

Max Kade German-American Center
Indiana University-Purdue University at Indianapolis

Deutsches Haus-Athenaeum, 401 East Michigan Street
Indianapolis, Indiana 46204

Eberhard Reichmann, Editor-in-Chief

Volume 8

© 1995 by Max Kade German-American Center
All rights reserved
ISBN 1-880788-04-7

Printed in the United States of America
by Indiana University Printing Services

Produced and Distributed by
NCSA LITERATUR
430 South Kelp Grove Road, Nashville, IN 47448

The Cover utilizes the departure and arrival motifs on the certificate for honorary membership in the "Nationalverein für deutsche Auswanderung und Ansiedlung," a 19th-century emigration association with branches throughout Germany.

In Memoriam

Günter Moltmann (1926-1994)
Peter Assion (1941-1994)

Contents

PREFACE

The present volume contains articles based on papers delivered at the conference on "Emigration and Settlement Patterns of German Communities in North America," held at New Harmony, Indiana, on Sept.28—Oct.1, 1989. The year of the conference coincided with the 175th anniversary of the founding of New Harmony by Johann Georg Rapp and his Swabian millenarians. It was the perfect place for bringing together, from both sides of the Atlantic, leading and promising younger scholars from the growing field of German-American Studies. The blend of emigration/immigration historians, sociologists, linguists, folklorists and other specialists allowed for a multidisciplinary approach to the overarching theme.

Primarily responsible for the conceptual and organizational aspects on the American side were Ruth and Eberhard Reichmann (Max Kade German-American Center, Indiana University-Purdue University at Indianapolis), and Jörg Nagler (German Historical Institute, Washington, D.C.).

Their counterparts in Germany were Antonius Holtmann (University of Oldenburg) and the late Günter Moltmann (University of Hamburg).

The breadth and depth of this international conference would not have been attainable without the generous support of: The Max Kade Foundation, The German Historical Institute, The Indiana German Heritage Society, The Robert Lee Blaffer Trust, and the Jasper, Indiana donors: The Arnold F. Habig Foundation, The United Cabinet Foundation, The Dubois County Bank Foundation, and The Welcome World Committee. Our sincere thanks to all who extended a helping hand.

We mourn the loss of two distinguished colleagues and friends:

Günter Moltmann, who had been honored with the Outstanding Achievement Award of the Society for German-American Studies, truly advanced the field of emigration/immigration research, both as a scholar and a mentor. Delighted with the success of the New Harmony conference model, he suggested that similarly organized symposia be held at not too distant intervals.

Peter Assion (University of Marburg) was one of Germany's leading folklorists and one of the few colleagues across the Atlantic with a keen interest in German-American folklore and history.

We dedicate this book to their memory.

INTRODUCTION

On both sides of the Atlantic scholarly research on German emigration to North America and the processes of assimilation and integration into the societies of the New World has been showing an acceleration similar to the one witnessed in the now immensely popular area of genealogy. The years of 1976 (American Bicentennial) and 1983 (German-American Tricentennial) were particularly instrumental in sending appropriate signals of historical and "roots" awareness to researchers and the general public.

The New Harmony Conference sought to provide first-hand exchange between European and North American researchers and to strengthen cooperation on topics and methods relevant to the many aspects of migration research.

Keynoter Günter Moltmann reiterated Marcus Lee Hansen's position (1920s) that called for contextuality, i.e. the necessity of incorporating the causative cultural and socio-economic force fields from which, and into which, migrants moved. The "separate study" of parts (emigration/ immigration) cannot be expected to yield the results of what Moltmann calls "integrated studies." His carefully considered outline of the research field will be part of his legacy to the profession. With Ernst Bloch, Moltmann also points to the migrant's continued cultural identity that cannot be readily traded in—despite John Quincy Adams' demands, despite Nativism and the Americanization movement.

The pressure to Americanize found, and still finds, its equivalent in the historiographical diminution and frequent disregard of the German element, the largest ethnic group in the U.S.A. (1990 Census). In this respect, Gerhard Bassler (VII.20) shows striking similarities between Canadian and American historiographic deficiencies: standard textbooks and acclaimed histories do little in presenting significant ethno-German aspects of Canadian history— despite readily accessible pre-World War I documentation from both German-Canadian and English-Canadian primary accounts. The "WW I effect" and nativist principles of Americanization and Canadianization policies have influenced generations of historians. There are, however, unmistakable signs that ethnographic aspects of North American history can no longer be ignored.

Over a span of more than 300 years, millions of emigrants from German-speaking areas experienced the process of being uprooted and transplanted. While motives for emigration and ways of settlement were brought about by diverse circumstances, we can nevertheless discern a specific set of reasons for leaving. We can identify "push" and "pull" factors and note the shifting of motives and numbers of emigrating individuals, groups and classes, during certain historical periods and from specific geographic regions.

The title of our book subsumes all these aspects under the term *patterns*. As these patterns evolved they made explicit similarities and differences in the experience of migrant groups and their descendants. We call them *communities*, using this term's broadest range of meanings, from religious communities to communities of interest such as music societies (Bohlman). *Community* is understood as a natural phenomenon in the sense of *Gemeinde* and *Gemeinschaft* (Ferdinand Tönnies) and emphasizes the cohesion of experiences and cultural values that ties people together. It shaped much of the 19th-century immigration process and thus includes towns or rural areas in which people from certain regions settled; it includes those who flocked together, bound by religious or political commitment, or by bonds of class or gender; it includes groups who arrived as a result of pre-planned strategies for clustering immigrants in specific areas in order to preserve their faith, their German language and their cultural heritage.

Demographics and Documentation (I) begins with Aaron Fogleman's new methodological approach to the growth of the colonial society in 18th-century America. While James Henretta in his influential book, *The Evolution of American Society, 1700-1815*, finds 18th-century immigration to be significant, he nevertheless attributes the phenomenal growth of the American population primarily to natural increases. Fogleman challenges this assumption by a more accurate calculation of the overall numbers involved. He constructed a table showing decennial immigration by ethnic group. His calculation of German immigration in particular is more precise than any others done before. The "immigrant factor"—Fogleman's new term in his population projections, comprising immigrants and their descendants—must now be seen as predominant for demographic growth during colonial times. By 1776 over half of the population were in this category.

George F. Jones (I,2) tackles the historiographical deficit on German-speaking immigrants in Georgia by pointing to the availability of "copious documentation," much of which does, of course, require a good working knowledge of German and "old German script."

America became an important destination for **Religious Minorities...** (II) Donald F. Durnbaugh (II,3) and Jonathan J. Andelson (II,4) provide theological and demographic perspectives for this particular type of immigration and community formation. Durnbaugh surveys the many dedicated groups of "Radical Pietist" persuasion from the Germanies of the 18th and 19th centuries. Freedom of religion and available land promised the realization of their dreams for more perfect communities as they awaited the Second Coming of Christ. The Radical Pietist foundation of the groups who established communitarian settlements in North America rests largely on the writings of Jacob Böhme (1575-1624). His mystical thought was communicated to later generations by Gottfried Arnold and Johann Georg Gichtel.

The case of the "Community of True Inspiration," coming to upstate New York in 1843, is presented by Andelson. His paper examines the demographic character of the Inspirationists at the time of their immigration and during the first decades of their existence in America. They adopted the corporate name "Ebenezer Society" and, in search for more land and more isolation from "worldly" neighbors, they founded a new settlement around Amana, Iowa, were they have been living ever since.

Church and Community (III) formed the central constellation not only for religious minorities but for the members of traditional churches as well, i.e. for the vast majority of German immigrants. Wolfgang Grams (III,5) examines the split of Cincinnati German Lutherans along ethnographic boundaries. The North Germans had to have their own *"plattdeutsche Kirche."* Ethno-linguistic separation from the South Germans provided for expression of the faith and unhindered communication in the familiar dialect band of Low German. Mindful of the fact that at the heart of community is communication, the North/South split—usually lamented as typical German disunity—must be seen as coming from a psychological need for a cultural and social safety net during the difficult process of acculturation.

Antonius Holtmann (III,6) follows the North German Cincinnati Protestants to their pioneer settlement in Indiana, examining the question of clergy or lay supremacy at the White Creek (1840-1905) via close reading of the *Protokollbücher* and the constitution of St. Johannes Kirche. He shows that the congregational assembly was the primary decision maker in matters of organization, discipline, church rules and on details concerning mutual obligations of pastor and congregation, including decisions against pastor and synod. Not until the 1890s did matters of administration move gradually into the pastoral domain.

A Catholic counterpart to Protestant settlement patterns and congregation building is depicted in the portrait of Father Kundek's far-reaching missionary/colonizing activities in Southern Indiana (III,7). Heiko Muehr, Angela Sasse, Mary Kenneth Scheessele and John Schipp show how patriarchal dynamism of an extraordinary priest created a lasting legacy of parishes, monasteries and towns built on the principle of ethno-religious homogeneity, here: German and Catholic.

Bettina Goldberg's study of cultural change in Milwaukee's Missouri Synod congregations and their schools, 1850-1930, focuses on the gradual shift from German to English (III,8). The author shows that although German as a medium and subject of instruction was given up in most of the schools during the anti-German climate of World War I, the war had functioned only as a catalyst, not as the cause for abandoning German.

Rob Kroes (III,9) examines the Dutch-American experience of ethnic and religious clustering in Montana. Parallel to what German settlements experienced, the language of the Dutch pioneers retreated and surrendered to English, but intra-group marriage is still common. What has kept them together and what is valued as the source of cohesion and catalyst of heritage appreciation is their church, the Christian Reformed Church. This nationwide denomination has a membership that still is almost exclusively of Dutch descent.

The counterpart to settlement patterns of religious minorities and church-centered community formation and life is found in **Secular Settlements...**" (IV). Stefan von Senger und Etterlin (IV,10) offers an insightful and well-documented overview on concepts and realities of various emigration societies (1820-1860). A colonialist political movement among liberal and patriotic German intellectuals sought to channel emigration into particular areas or "colonies" which would then become magnets for future emigrants. While all of the nationally-minded group emigrations dispersed soon after arrival, many of their members contributed to the concentration of German settlers in the Midwest and Texas.

Far removed from any nationalist and religious leanings were the socialist-oriented German workers and freethinkers who founded New Ulm, Minnesota. Jörg Nagler (IV,11) presents the ideological thrust and the background that led to the founding of the only Turner town in America. In his portrayal of the difficult initial phase (1854-1859) he shows how reality tested their concepts and resolve.

Ethnic homogeneity, as in the case of New Ulm, was of no concern to the New Llano Cooperative Colony near Los Angeles (1914). This socialist utopian experiment was moved to Louisiana backwoods in 1917/18. Hartmut Keil (IV,12) feels that an *inter-ethnic* perspective, such as provided by New Llano, might be increasingly important for understanding American social developments in the first half of the 20th century. A sizable minority of the fluctuating New Llano membership were so-called "radicals" of German origin, some of them with long records of participation in workers' organizations, others sons and daughters of immigrants, disillusioned by xenophobia and the persecution of radicals and their organizations during the first "Red Scare."

Continuities and Discontinuities of Regional Affinities" (V) are documented for certain periods of immigration to New Jersey (Peter Winkel; Annemieke Galema), Texas (Lauren Ann Kattner) and St. Louis, Missouri (Walter Kamphoefner). In all cases chain migration played a role. In fast developing Trenton no neighborhood was entirely dominated by either the Germans or the Irish; nevertheless, one could identify certain ethnic clusters.

Winkel's research (IV,13) on 85 Hessian men, immigrants from 1848-1860, shows that they married mostly non-Hessian women, and that the willingness to marry outside the ethnic environment reached 25% among single men and women. The author warns that the results of the Trenton study must not be used for generalizations. The Hessian experience in other New Jersey cities was different.

Little is known about Frisian migration to the U.S., says Annemieke Galema (IV,14), for this ethnic group is normally subsumed under the labels of "Dutch" and "German." Dutch/Frisian individualism is reflected in preferential settlement patterns based on regional, not national, origin. Her study of the Frisians in Paterson, NJ (1880-1914) shows great changes in employment patterns experienced by largely rural immigrants attracted to a city of rapid industrial growth.

In her study on "Land and Marriage...," (IV,15) Lauren Ann Kattner uses rigid analysis of tax, civil, church and census records, along with maps, letters, family stories and architectural histories. Regional identification influenced a variety of settlement patterns and resultant housing and marital choices among mid-19th century Texas-Germans in Galveston, New Braunfels, Yorktown, and Fredericksburg.

For the study of urban population recruitment and migration paths, Walter Kamphoefner (IV,16) found the thoroughness of a St. Louis census taker (1860) useful. The man had recorded the birth places of most Second Ward residents on the heavily German south side. The St. Louis data, combined with similar information on rural Missouri Germans, throws light on factors that influenced choice among various locales. Among several urban/rural contrasts, Kamphoefner documents that urban immigrants, despite some evidence of regional clustering, were of more heterogeneous origins. What also became apparent is that Southwest Germans often located temporarily on the East Coast before continuing to St. Louis, while Northwest Germans tended to come directly to the Gateway City.

In **Aspects of Ethnic Culture** (VI) Philip Bohlman examines the
function of "...Music in the Multi-Religious German-American Community"
(VI,17). Communal by nature, music brought together the diverse German
elements. It served, moreover, as a means of expressing the commonness of
German culture by bridging regional, linguistic, and religious differences.
Repertoires came to form an aesthetic core that the community redefined and
shaped through performance. Bohlman's case study was done in Bonduel,
Wisconsin, a small town settled almost entirely by Germans.

Agnes Bretting (VI,18) takes a look at "Women's Lives in New York
City..." around 1900 by analyzing the women's pages of the city's two most
important German-language papers. For different reasons the conservative,
middle-class-oriented *New Yorker Staats-Zeitung* and the socialist *New Yorker
Volkszeitung*—the official organ of the Socialist Labor Party—persevered in
the traditional female role models. Both papers responded to their female
readers' daily concerns, which were—regardless of class differences—
primarily based on the difficult processes of acculturation. While the *StZ* saw
a woman's assignment and fulfillment in the *Hausfrau* role, the *VZ* saw
drudgery in house work and stressed socialist class consciousness.

Carolyn S. Blackwell reviews both the question of "German Jewish
Identity and German Jewish Emigration to the Midwest" (VI,19). Central to
the question of Jewish identity has always been the ethno-religious continuity
of a dispersed people forming scattered minorities that were subjected to
restrictions, rejections, and persecutions. With the era of Enlightenment had
come the promise of acceptance and the possibility of reaching equality
through educational achievement (*Bildung*). However, the European wave of
19th-century nationalism, frequently coupled with racism, developed a new
anti-Semitic component that perpetuated certain discriminatory practices and
attitudes. This contributed to the psychological and practical sides of the
identity question, of assimilation and/or existence as a separate group, and to
decisions to emigrate. Memoirs, private and public documents are used to
illustrate the German Jewish experience and achievements in the Midwest.

The concluding chapter, **"Emigration and Immigration in Context..."** (VII), provides examples for the **"Pros and Cons"** of migration
and settlement processes, of acceptance and rejection on the basis of
ethnicity and achievement, of cultural comparison, and of Old World wrath
and New World praise.

Gerhard Bassler's study of "German-Canadians in English-Canadian
Perspectives" (VII,20) has already been referred to at the beginning. The
author's critique of these perspectives scores an important point: when
historiography blends out an ethnographically significant component of a

population, the accuracy of history and the credibility of historians are at risk.

Like the U.S. panorama of German ethnicity, Canada shows strong denominational and ethnolinguistic divisions, largely based on regional origin. Unlike the U.S., however, *Reichsdeutsche* comprised a much smaller number than Germans from regions of Eastern Europe with a strong Mennonite component. The uniting factor for all groups is their German heritage. Language and culture maintenance before World War I was quite natural. Today's political acceptance of ethnic diversity holds some promise for the preservation of the German-Canadian heritage.

Horst Rössler (VII,21) examines the typically negative position of Germany's socialist elites on questions of emigration and colony formation in the New World. Like the British Chartists, these elites felt that emigration was not the solution to 19th-century social problems caused by the shift to a "modern money economy and capitalist industrialization," both accompanied by the beginning of overpopulation and a declining agricultural mode of production. The solution envisaged by communist/socialist leaders could only come through the process of organizing the masses for the "inevitable class struggle." But all the ideological appeals did not stop thousands of socialists from heading for America.

Wolfgang Helbich (VII,22), well known for his extensive work on immigrant letters, goes into 19th-century German immigrant judgment and prejudices of the Anglo-Americans and their society, as conveyed in letters. He finds explicit judgments that are virtually unanimous (stereotypes) and others that differ considerably on a given phenomenon. The emphasis of the study is on the descriptive validity or the source value of the opinions ex-pressed by the immigrants. Comparatively, Helbich probes into the differences between the perceptions of the "common immigrant" and the "trained observer." Traditionally the writings of educated foreign travelers about America and Americans have been accepted as valuable source material for U.S. social history. Helbich adds the record left by "untrained observers."

Eberhard and Ruth Reichmann (VII,23) give "...A Tribute to the 175th Anniversary of New Harmony, Indiana" with observations on the two sides of possibly contradictory perspectives of the emigration/immigration process. The Harmonists, religious dissidents who broke with the "Evangelische Landeskirche," earned bitter scorn in their home communities for disturbing the peace and order of these traditionally homogeneous villages. In America, on the other hand, they were highly praised and admired for their astonishing economic success. New Harmony, their second town, became known as "the wonder of the West"—the first German "economic miracle." Only in our time, through Sister City friendship bonds, have the Harmonist pioneers been exonerated "back home." They are now a source of pride for their achievements in distant America.

Much of German Americana still needs to be discovered and rediscovered, too. We trust that this book can be a part of this ongoing process.

The Editors

"When People Migrate, They Carry Their Selves Along"—Emigration and Settlement Patterns of German Communities in North America

Günter Moltmann, *Universität Hamburg*

Migration is a global and timeless phenomenon. It concerns all of us, whether directly as individuals or indirectly as a part of the total human experience. This paper deals with Germans who have come to the U.S. and settled here, like so many other nationalities. The *Harvard Encyclopedia of American Ethnic Groups* includes articles on some 70 different building blocks of the American ethnic mosaic.[1] Indeed, America is the preeminent nation of immigrants. But elsewhere in the world migratory processes have been continuing as well. While Mexicans and Haitians head for the U.S., Germans from Eastern Europe and huge numbers of asylum seekers come to the Federal Republic of Germany, Jews from the former Soviet Union to Israel and the U.S., Turks from Bulgaria to Turkey, Vietnamese "boat people" to Hongkong, Tamils from Sri Lanka to Canada, Sudanese to Ethiopia. In addition to group migration we have increased spatial mobility of individuals who change places and countries, look for work here or there, and move their belongings wherever they think they can prosper.

One is even tempted to attribute normalcy to migration and consider settlement to be the actual transitory occurrence. Do people change their living quarters the way they change their clothes? Has it come true what the *Essex Register* of Salem, Mass., predicted as early as August 1816?

> The business of Emigration is so great, that it threatens to introduce a new era in the manners of mankind. Every family, like that of Abraham, will take a view at its settlement of the habitable globe, to find the place where laws are most mild, the economy of government is best observed, and the habits are most congenial.[2]

This perception, I suspect, is too simple. Most people migrating from one country to another do not shake off their old clothes in a hurry and put on new ones suited to their future environment—at least not immediately upon arrival. John Quincy Adams once said that immigrants "must cast off the European skin, never to resume it. They must look forward to their posterity, rather than backward to their ancestors."[3] But who can do that? Most people carry their past along. As the philosopher Ernst Bloch said in his *Tübinger Einleitung in die Philosophie: "Ein Mensch nimmt sich mit, wenn er wandert"* (People carry their selves with them when they migrate).[4] Along with the things necessary for their physical existence, the immigrants' baggage includes their cultural heritage, their mother tongue, their ways of life, their personal concepts, their value systems and preconceived plans for the future, their hopes and expectations.

The German ethnographer Ina-Maria Greverus, in her book *Der territoriale Mensch*, describes a custom of 19th century European emigrants who, when departing for America, went to the village cemetery for a last visit to the graves of their ancestors. There they took a bit of the soil, filled it into a bag, and carried it to America with the intention of having that soil from home on their own graves when their time would come to be buried in the New World.[5] Several paintings and drawings by the 19th century artist Carl Hübner, member of the Düsseldorf school of realist painters, depict such scenes in German cemeteries. There is also a poem describing this ritualistic act.[6]

One might be inclined to discard that custom as being nostalgic and sentimental—but, as Greverus convincingly explains, there was the question of identity involved. Those emigrants exercising the custom wanted to make sure they would still be the same human beings in a different environment and not be uprooted and lost in a world of anonymity.

What bearing has all this on our topic? Migration is a complex thing. It can't be neatly divided into its components for separate study: *emigration* there—*immigration* here, exodus from the country of origin—settlement in the country of destination, uprooting in the Old World—integration in the New World.

Historians interested in migrations should investigate all phases of such processes and consider them as parts of integrated studies. They should look at the conditions of the old country, the nature of the decision of people to

leave, and the procedures of migration. They should also study the arrival of
the immigrants in the New World, the reception, the immigrant experience
while entering a society strange to them, their dispersion over the country
and, finally, settlement and adjustment. Migrants have to go through all these
phases. They have to cope with very specific difficulties in each of them.
They have to adapt to changing situations. But, essentially, they remain the
same people. If social history is devoted to real human beings and their
experience, historians should not break this experience into unrelated pieces.

In the 1920s, immigration historian Marcus Lee Hansen pointed at the
importance of integrated studies:

> America was a huge magnet of varying intensity drawing to itself the people of
> Europe from those regions where conditions made them mobile and from which
> transportation provided a path. . . Accordingly, both Europe and America are the
> field for research. How extensive these researches must be may be understood from
> the suggestion that emigration has been connected with as many phases of European
> life as immigration has of American life.[7]

Since Hansen's article in *The American Historical Review*, migration
research has produced a more complete picture of migratory movements. But
the task of integrating these studies remains to be completed. Little pieces
have yet to be put together into mosaics before we will be able to perceive the
whole picture.

For a better understanding of migrations certain correlations have to be
considered. An obvious correlation, for instance, can be seen between
preconceived images of the country of destination and reactions to reality
after actual settlement. If expectations had been modest, satisfaction with life
in the new environment was likely. Disappointment, however, was
unavoidable when expectations had been unrealistically high. Immigrant
letters can be quite revealing in this respect, although one can also easily be
misled. For immigrants who left their homes with dream-like notions of life in
the future often did not want to admit that they had been wrong. For this
reason one may find more fictitious success stories in those letters than meets
the eye.

This leads directly to another correlation. Societal attitudes toward
emigration should be compared with attitudes of the receiving society toward
immigration. To be sure, on both sides those attitudes can be rather
ambivalent. Seeing people leaving home forever, makes those who stay
behind either sad or happy—if they are not indifferent. They may be
saddened by the severance of human ties, a personal loss or, in broader
terms, they may bemoan the losses in the (cheap) labor force, or even the loss
of financial means needed for the home economy. On the other hand, some

may have been relieved to see certain emigrants leave—people they didn't like. This was certainly also the case when there was a labor surplus or, if there were not enough provisions to feed everyone, and, not to forget, when "radicals" departed who, in times of social crisis, threatened the existing *Ordnung*.

This spectrum of reactions to the *emigration* phenomenon has its equivalent in the country of *immigration*. Immigrants were and are welcomed as long as they are useful. But if they flood the labor market and thereby lower the wages, their arrival is met with protest. If they are paupers or have any kind of mental or physical drawbacks or, worse, are regarded as dangerous to law and order, dislike can quickly turn into hatred, and xenophobia can even enter political platforms. The reception of migrants can vary greatly, depending on social circumstances. Those who are disliked or considered superfluous in the old country may be welcomed in the new. Migrants may be equally disliked on both sides. To understand that, the socio-economic context in both countries or areas must be taken into consideration.

More correlations invite scrutiny. Let us take, for example, the occupational expectations of the emigrant and the chances for their realization. How did people intend to make a living and how did they really do it over time? Did adventurers find rewarding adventures? Did gold-diggers become rich? Did prospective artisans or peasants get the workshop or the farm which fulfilled their dreams? Were scientists, artists, doctors, teachers and academics of all kinds able to find work in their respective fields? If not, in what way and to what extent did they change their plans? Could they stay, or did they return? Career possibilities in a new country may differ greatly from "back home," but there would seem to be some kind of correlation between the former occupation and the later one(s).

Furthermore, the life of immigrants has always been influenced by the alternatives of *individual* or *group* migration. When one discusses the settling of newcomers and the ways settlements were founded and developed, it is important to know whether and, if so, how communal projects had already been conceived in the Old World. Were they carried forth by people with common interests and with plans for pursuing their aims cooperatively? This question will be dealt with later. And there is another related element that should be mentioned here: chain migration. This phenomenon cannot be understood without studying the communities both in the country of origin and in the receiving country. Walter Kamphoefner's book, *The Westphalians: From Germany to Missouri*, is a fascinating example of such dual-focus research.[8]

Finally, there are such elements as accustomed life styles, housing, food, climate and natural environment—all of which have an impact upon the future life of immigrants, their adaptability to new environmental conditions, and the selection of places where to go and settle.

In sum, migration should not be studied in chronological or geographical isolation. Exodus and integration, departure and arrival, old roots and new sprouts, give and take, each of these combinations is intimately interwoven and should be viewed as such, if one tries to understand spatial mobility.

In 1836, Karl Follen, a German liberal and intellectual in the U.S., visited with his fellow countryman Georg Rapp, the founder of the Harmony Society. This body of religious dissenters from Württemberg had established their third communal settlement, Economy, 18 miles from Pittsburg. As had its forerunners, Harmony (Pennsylvania) and New Harmony (Indiana), Economy provided Rapp and his followers an opportunity to live according to their millenarian expectations. This intrigued Follen and, at first look, he was highly satisfied: ". . .the community, by their labor, earned not only enough to support them in comfort, and even luxury, but there must be a large surplus."[9] His encounter with George Rapp, however, was disappointing. Eliza Follen, who had accompanied her husband, related the following story in her *Life of Charles Follen*:

> He was the finest looking old man I ever saw. He looked like a Prophet; his white curling locks fell gracefully on his shoulders; he must have been more than six feet in height, and he had an eye like an eagle's. When Dr. Follen expressed his great pleasure at the abundance of the crops, and the proof which his success gave of the advantage, in respect to economy, of such a community, he said, coldly, "Yes, it was very well." Dr. Follen expressed the wish that others might imitate such an example, and reap advantage from his experiment. Rapp answered, that their prosperity arose entirely from their separation from the world and the world's people. Dr. Follen replied, "that Jesus did not separate himself from his fellow-men; that he lived in the midst of the world, among sinners; and that he thought that he was the true model for reformers." The color mounted in the old man's face; his fresh and yet youthful complexion was actually red with displeasure; he looked away, and made no answer. Dr. Follen then asked, if this community did not earn more than they consumed? Mr. Rapp made an evasive answer, and presently he said that he must go into the house (which was close by) to take some refreshment after his ride. He did not ask us to go in, but left us in the heat at mid-day; it was evident he disliked the close questions of his countryman.[10]

Karl Follen, who certainly was very intelligent, was also an opinionated man. He did not grasp the concept behind this settlement, but rather viewed it as an economic enterprise and, as such, a model for others. Furthermore, Follen, a Unitarian, thought isolation from the world was wrong. He did not perceive that he was arguing against the very nerve of the community. The Harmonists went to America to be closer to God at the time when He was to return to the world on the last day of judgment. They wanted to be isolated in their holy experiment and really disliked being measured by worldly success and their "abundance of crops." If Follen had been better acquainted with their background in Germany and the spiritual reasons for their coming to America, he might have had a more rewarding conversation with George Rapp.

Of course, only a small number of German settlements in North America were inspired, planned, built and governed like those of the Harmonists. However, the total number of settlements is staggering. Not a few of them still exist today and can be identified as such. Others have disappeared from the map or have lost their German identity long ago. There are also places which can be discerned as former German settlements still showing traces of their origin. But having become multi-ethnic or just plain Americanized, an interested visitor would hardly describe them as being German-American.

Roughly, German-American settlements can be divided into two not wholly distinct categories. On the one hand there are preconceived and designed communities, on the other those which emerged in North America without specific plans and schemes. Let me call the first group "colonies" and the second one "neighborhoods." The first group, the colonies, included settlements like Germantown (Pa.), Ephrata and Bethlehem (Pa.), Salem (N.C.), Ebenezer (Ga.), New Harmony and Ferdinand (Ind.), Ebenezer (N.Y.), the Amana settlements in Iowa, Zoar (Oh.), Frankenmuth (Mich.), Teutopolis (Ill.), New Ulm (Minn.), Hermann (Mo.) New Braunfels and Fredericksburg (Tex.). The second group, the neighborhoods, included rural areas with a heavy German population like the Mohawk Valley (N.Y.), the Shenandoah Valley (Virg.), southeast Pennsylvania, areas in the so-called "German Belt," reaching from New York State through Pennsylvania, Ohio, Indiana and Illinois to Wisconsin, branching out into Michigan, Minnesota and the Dakotas, Iowa and Nebraska, Missouri, Kansas and Arkansas, small areas also in Louisiana, California, Washington, Oregon and Montana. Furthermore, it included German quarters, often called "Little Germanies," in cities like New York, Philadelphia, Baltimore, Charleston, New Orleans, Cincinnati, Chicago, Milwaukee and St. Louis. Around 1900, German neighborhoods were to be found in almost every state of the Union, often intermingled with other ethnic neighborhoods and surrounded by Anglo-American-dominated areas.

"Colonies" had their origin in rational colonization schemes, drafted in Germany or in centers of German-Americans where the need for a second move, usually farther west, was felt. Colonization schemes were collectively conceived or, perhaps more often, they were developed by individuals who qualified for leadership, or by big and small pretenders. Small circles founded colonization societies and recruited followers who trusted them. Promoters were expected to have the know-how to organize groups, give directions, collect the financial means neccessary for the move, arrange for transportation, find and buy land in America, and lead the people to their destination, either personally or by commissioners or agents. Ultimately, the driving force behind such enterprises, however, was the collective resolve and will power of the participants to make the move and build a settlement in accordance with the intention and purpose of the original scheme.

The non-German prototype of such settlement development was, of course, Plymouth Plantation, founded by the Pilgrim Fathers in accordance with the Mayflower Compact. The German-American model, in many ways different from Plymouth Plantation, was Germantown, Pa., inspired by the promotional activities of William Penn, conceived by a circle of Pietists in Frankfurt/Main, prepared by the Frankfurt Land Company, and established under the guidance (if not leadership) of Franz Daniel Pastorius.

Colony-settlements were marked by diverse objectives and backed by asserted interests. Prime movers of group experiments were religious institutions, often also organized religious dissenters observing specific doctrines. But, there were others as well, adherents of secular ideologies, socialist utopians, promoters of vague schemes for the founding of German culture colonies, and companies of capitalists and stockholders. Then there were the pragmatic societies who saw group migration as a means through which to alleviate the hardships of travel and a way to find new homes, but without adhering to specific beliefs or principles.

Group ventures attracted many people because they promised the fulfillment of common goals. Life in a free society, economic prosperity, unmolested devotion to religious doctrines, the realization of secular ideologies, the transfer of culture concepts—all this could be better achieved in cooperative endeavors. The will power of many people working together seemed to insure success, while individual migration promised lonesome struggles against all sorts of obstacles and, ultimately, perhaps even despair. Group membership provided a safety net. Many colonization societies were actually early mutual aid societies; they were similar to organizations which were expressly formed as mutual aid societies among immigrants who had settled in American cities and discovered that cooperation and association enhanced their existence immensely.

Group migration and settlement also meant organization. Knowledgeable persons had to do the planning and recruiting. Proposals for the move and the settlement had to be worked out; by-laws had to be drafted so that every participant knew his rights and duties. Often emissaries and explorers were sent out first to the port of embarkation and across the ocean to clear everything possible in advance. The history of group migrations is documented in numerous blueprints, compacts, drafts and plans, worked out before departure from Germany, during the trip, or after arrival and settling in America.

A fine example is Frankenmuth, a small but thriving Michigan town with ca. 3,000 inhabitants. The early history of this place, taken from Warren Washburn Florer's *Early Michigan Settlements*, reads as follows:

> Founded—August, 1845. / By—Fifteen German immigrants: Pastor August Craemer and wife . . . [then follow names of thirteen young Frankonian peasants of both sexes]

> Object—Indian Mission, Colonization. / Planned by—Reverend Wilhelm Loehe, Neuendettelsau, Bavaria, Germany. / Colonists—Lutherans from Altmuehltal and Rosstal, Bavaria. / Arrived—About August 15, 1845 on Banks of the Cass. / First Abode—Log Cabin, completed August 25, 1845. Size—20 feet by 30 feet. / Location—On grounds of Old Cemetery. / Church—Dedicated December 25, 1846. Size—26 feet by 42 feet. / Fruits of Indian Mission—Baptism of 3 Indian children on December 27, 1846. / First White Child—Johann Pickelmann, Baptized July 30, 1846. / New Immigrants—One hundred Bavarians from same area. / Arrived—Day after Ascension 1846.[11]

More details on the founding of Frankenmuth can be found in a report in Pastor Löhe's *Kirchliche Mittheilungen aus u. über Nord-Amerika*, 1850.[12] This report shows, among other things, that missionary activities of Lutherans among American Indians were the main purpose of the colony. The young Frankonian colonists subscribed to that and provided for the minister to carry on his missionary work. In the year before their departure, an emissary of Pastor Löhe had gone to Michigan and established contacts with the Lutheran Michigan Synod which helped to find a place for the new settlement.

Two years after its founding, a community charter was written and signed by 51 male adult members. The charter was to provide solutions for civic problems that had arisen. Its headline: *"Gott ist ein Gott der Ordnung: Gemeindeordnung der Gemeinde Frankenmuth"* (Our Lord is a Lord of Order: Charter of the Community of Frankenmuth). The name "Frankenmuth" means "Franconian Courage" and reflects the self-image of the settlers as well as a kind of elevated language, very common in the 19th century. The cooperative spirit of the Frankenmuth people was clearly manifest in the charter. Every member of the community was obliged to burden sharing with communal work and common expenses, such as assisting in the construction of churches, schools, roads and bridges. Disputes were to be settled by elected trustees. Through this procedure lawsuits in unfamiliar court settings could be avoided—or at least limited to severe cases. Other paragraphs in the charter dealt with thoroughfares, fences, compensation for damages, etc.[13] The missionary activities continued, although in later years shifted to the Pine River Indian Settlement (north of St. Louis, Mich.), to which place the Indians had apparently been removed.[14] It is said that the cooperative spirit of Frankenmuth still exists today.

Many other German-American colonies developed in a similar way. However, early concepts and preplanning were no guarantee for success. If organizational skills were lacking, if financial misjudgment occurred, if fraud and bad treatment befell the group, if the communal spirit was not strong enough to hold the members together, then failure was imminent. There are many stories about groups that fell apart when misfortune occurred, when leaders proved to be too weak, when economic security could not be achieved, when zeal and enthusiasm diminished. We might generalize: the greater the devotion to common goals and, at the same time, the more pragmatic the colonists were in dealing with daily affairs, the better the prospects were for lasting success. Vagueness of schemes, illusions about future achievements, mistakes in management, and financial incompetence often led to the collapse of colonies, if they came into existence at all.

Some failures are well known. The colony projects inspired by Gottfried Duden's enthusiastic report on conditions in Missouri are among them. At least three societies were founded: the Berlin Society, the Solingen Society, and the Giessen Society. All three dissolved either before their members reached their destination or shortly afterwards. The leaders of the Giessen Society, Friedrich Münch and Paul Follen—a brother of the above mentioned Karl Follen—had the grand scheme of building a German republic in the backwoods of North America—not independent from the U.S., but rather cooperating with it in promoting liberty throughout the world.[15] Karl Follen had cherished a similar scheme as early as 1819. In view of reactionary political trends in continental Europe he had proposed to establish a "German educational institution in North America," serving as an asylum for oppressed liberals as well as an aid society supporting distressed German emigrants.[16] Utopian schemes like these were doomed to failure because they lacked sober judgment and were conceived without first-hand knowledge of the real American world.

In this same context another enterprise should be mentioned, the Society for the Protection of German Immigrants to Texas. Its scope was huge. In 1842, in the town of Biebrich, twenty-one members of the higher nobility— two ruling princes, one prince from a sovereign house, thirteen *Standesherren* of various ranks (nobles from houses recently deprived of sovereign rights), five counts from non-sovereign houses, and a banker founded this association in order to organize and carry out a large-scale migration program. Major objectives were: the support and protection of thousands of immigrants, the founding of a unified German settlement overseas, the development of shipping trade with North America, the prevention of potential social unrest in Germany, the provision of operating facilities for an ambitious German nobility, and the securing of economic gains for the members of the association.

Thousands of German peasants found the project attractive and went to America. New Braunfels and Fredericksburg were founded, but the association was unable to handle the self-arranged mass exodus—like the sorcerer's apprentice in Goethe's poem, *Der Zauberlehrling*, who could not stop the floods he had witched. They could not satisfy the demands of the settlers, having vastly underestimated the costs and having run into increasing debts. In the spring of 1847 the commissioner-general at New Braunfels declared bankruptcy.[17] By that time many immigrants had perished, others had deserted. But those remaining formed the nucleus of a prosperous German-American settlement in the Texas Hill Country. Thus, the scheme had failed, but settlements remained and grew steadily. Actually, in our classification these settlements rather belong to the second category, the neighborhoods. What the German-Texans did after the collapse of the society was individual self-help, which was typical for many immigrants who had not come to America under the auspices of an organization.

Neighborhood settlements were more common than colony settlements. However, the numerical proportion of German-Americans in neighborhoods and in colonies is difficult to establish. There are no appropriate statistics, and the borderline between the two categories is somewhat unclear. Colonies which fell apart often continued as neighborhoods. On the other hand, it happened that in neighborhoods the idea sprang up to found a colony elsewhere in the U.S. New Ulm, Minn. is such an example. Workingmen from Chicago moved there to escape the labor market and unsatisfactory living conditions in the city.

Group migration was more typical for the 18th century than for the 19th, when many Germans flocked to America simply on their own or with only minimal assistance by emigration agencies and ship companies. During the second half of the 19th century, state authorities, private institutions and the churches offered some protection. Sometimes small groups were organized just for the time of traveling, but they dissolved as soon as the American shore was reached. Not a few individual or family migrants entered the American mainstream right away, with and without difficulties. However, most of them began their new life in the neighborhood of fellow immigrants which made adjustment to the new culture less painful.

To be sure, persons who had come alone or with their families and settled in neighborhoods also "carried their selves along" (Ernst Bloch). The American journalist Charles Dawson Shanly presented the following observations in "Germany in New York," an article published by *Atlantic Monthly* in 1867:

> They carry their country along with them when they emigrate, just as they carry their cherished household goods. A patch from the banks of the Rhine, the Oder, or the Main can be found anywhere in the heart of New York, or in the country for ten miles around it. This burly and honest person who keeps a restaurant, or salon, in Broadway, on the German plan, flitted hither a dozen years ago from the borders of the Black Forest. He loved that romantic district and its traditions so well that he brought them away with him in his capacious heart, and set them up in his back yard, which thenceforward became a *Garten Wirtschaft*,—a sort of Occidental "Gulistan" of sausage and lager bier. There the traits of his boyhood's home are represented by small pine-trees, arranged in tubs full of earth. But if the presence of these is not sufficient to keep fond memory wide awake, then he employs a scenic artist to decorate the walls of the yard with views representing sombre stretches of pine-land, lighted up fitfully with wild gushes of water manufactured out of indigo and flake-white. Sometimes a wild boar appears in the foreground, slaking its thirst at a cascade of these refreshing pigments; and this imparts truth and character to the scene, besides being suggestive of Westphalia ham and *Weissbier*, both of which are to be had in the establishment. A castle frowns over all, from a lofty pinnacle of rock. To bring the pleasant *Garten Wirtschaft* of his native land yet more vividly before him, the portly vintner sets along the walls numerous earthen pots with climbing plants in them; and should these imbecile exotics display any lack of energy in scaling the masonry, then a requisition is again made upon the scenic artist, who, beginning with his magic pencil where the trailer struck work, continues it *ad libitum*, carrying its leaves and tendrils in mellow distemper over any given area of wall surface.[18]

As wide-spread and cherished as this ambience may have been in German-America, the correlation between pre- and post- migration life of neighborhood residents differed from that of colony settlers. The moving force behind them was not a collective idea, but individual aspirations for better living. The catch-phrase, *"Amerika, das Land der unbegrenzten Möglichkeiten"* (America, the land of unlimited opportunities)—derived from Ludwig Max Goldberger's book with the same title (1903)—corresponded very well to the expectations of independent migrants. Individuality was the great idea of the 19th century. Not discipline and self-restraint, but adventurism and need for personal freedom caused so many people to migrate.

Yet individual courage often crumbled when newcomers learned that America was not exactly a rose garden. There came the culture shock, hard work, and sometimes humiliation. Need for support was felt. Who could offer that in the absence of earlier group cooperation? Fellow immigrants from the *Vaterland* seemed best suited. Immigrants with similar experiences and problems moved closely together to help each other. For immigration historians there lies an interesting field to be studied. Rural German-American neighborhoods, their lifestyles and developments have been less investigated than their urban counterparts, perhaps with the exception of southeast Pennsylvania. For the urban experience some excellent books on "Little Germanies" have been written, e.g. Kathleen Conzen's monograph on *Immigrant Milwaukee*, Agnes Bretting's *Soziale Probleme der deutschen Einwanderung in New York City*, or Hartmut Keil's anthologies on the German workers in Chicago.[19]

In a way, people in neighborhoods tried to achieve the advantages of the pre-planned colonies. They developed a community spirit and shaped their quarters in accordance with their accustomed life styles. The German language was prevalent. In German-American sections of the cities shops offered German food and other goods. German restaurants provided *Gemütlichkeit*. German churches and schools were built, also German hospitals, theaters and libraries. German club life was revived. German societies and mutual aid societies, voluntary fire and militia organizations were founded. German-language newspapers were printed, German books written and published. Turners and singers, marksmen's associations and music bands made German-speaking immigrants feel at home. However, as deeply felt as the German ways may have been in these urban neighborhoods, it was of a transitory character. Most people who had moved there did not intend to stay there forever. Rather they thought that they could use a familiar neighborhood as a safe starting point for further stages of their immersion into American life. But what was perhaps meant to be an interim abode sometimes turned out to be a long or even permanent one. There was a constant turnover of residents. Once acclimated, many moved farther into the country, and new German-speaking "greenhorns" swelled the ranks again.

Urban "Little Germanies" have sometimes been compared with decompression chambers where people could eventually overcome adjustment problems connected with the culture shock and—with the help of others—get used to life in a different culture. Ethnic historians have focused their research on effective Americanization of newcomers and long-lasting ethnic separateness. They might well focus their interest also on the phenomenon of symbiosis. That is what mainly happened in German settlements in North America—more accelerated in urban centers, more delayed in rural neighborhoods, and in lengthy and protracted processes in colony settlements. One can still perceive both the pace and the results of such faster or slower symbiotic processes by comparing German-American life in Cincinnati's "Over-the-Rhine" with the Texas Hill Country and religious communities in Pennsylvania.

Speaking of different time spans in symbiotic processes in different kinds of settlements does not mean that urban centers were always short-lived, or that rural neighborhoods endured longer, and that colonies were most stable. Settlement endurance depended on other factors too, the most important ones being chain migration with waves of new immigrants going to the same places. Kitchener in southeast Ontario, a city which grew out of a settlement founded by Mennonites from Pennsylvania in 1800, attracted many German immigrants and was called Berlin before 1916. In the course of time its German-American character faded, but it was revived three times: during the 1850s, after the First World War, and again after the Second World War. The history of this place, as presented by the late Gottlieb Leibbrandt, shows the ups and downs of German immigrant culture. It is, on the whole, a story about consistency, but in detail one of repeated infusion of newcomers.[20]

The endurance of German-American settlements was determined by geographic factors too. "Little Germanies" prospered at distribution centers of immigration. Boston, New York, Philadelphia, Baltimore, Charleston, New Orleans, Galveston / Houston, and San Francisco were the major ports of arrival for ships from Europe. Immigrants had to pass through these ports. For obvious reasons there were always some who remained at the points of entry. There were other distribution centers within the country and with the same effect on immigrants, for example, Cincinnati, Chicago, St. Louis, and Memphis—all with "Little Germanies" that emerged and endured. That New Orleans and Memphis were among them is particularly remarkable because their climate was not at all attractive for Germans. Besides excessive heat and humidity, yellow-fever epidemics occurred there, adding up to a bad reputation for these places. But as distribution centers they still attracted people.

Most German immigrants, however, settled in regions with more moderate climates. As Walter Kamphoefner has shown in a 1983 issue of *Geographische Rundschau*, the "German Belt" was roughly bound in the west by the annual average precipitation line of 610 mm, which runs through Minnesota, South Dakota, Nebraska, Kansas, Oklahoma and Texas. In the north it was bound by the average December-to-February temperature line of 14°F (–10°C), which runs through the Great Lakes and slightly to the north of them. In the south it was bound by the average December-to-February temperature line of 36°F (2°C), which runs through southern Kansas,

Missouri, Kentucky and along the Appalachians, through Virginia to Maryland.[21] The climate of the "German Belt" corresponded a bit more with the climate in Germany. Here again, a correlation between pre- and post-migration conditions can be observed. To understand why Germans preferred the "German Belt" for their settlements one has to consider climatic aspects.

It was preferably within such regions of more familiar weather that Germans built their new homes. There was compromise in the way they constructed their town and farm houses. Timber frame work was applied here and there, but—as a rule—more often American construction methods and architectural designs were used. With regard to farming techniques and crop production, also to artisanship and mechanical devices, Germans made adjustments to American prototypes. The processes of symbiosis began to work.

Complete adaptation was necessary as far as the physical layout of real estate was concerned. Germans had to adhere to the grid pattern of the American land acts of 1785 and 1796 which provided for the rectangular survey system in the spatial layout of townships, sections, quarter sections and building lots. Therefore, German-American neighborhoods and settlements were different from those in the old fatherland. In buying a farm, in clearing the land, in the daily way of life and in thinking and prospecting—the Germans had to change. Unavoidably, they had to adjust to straight roads, north-south and east-west, intersecting at right angles with a cross road every mile. On a smaller scale this was the same in towns. Streets and housing blocks, all were designed in accordance with a simple rational system. German-Americans could forget about European patterns where roads and the location of houses were determined by natural and historical circumstances, bent and crooked, winding and meandering, which means changing and picturesque perspectives.

Thus, settling in America was usually both: clinging to cherished traditions and adjusting to strange modes of life. Migrants go through different worlds. Physically and mentally, this might be difficult to accomplish, but, at the same time, it is a challenge and a great opportunity. Again, and in closing, the words of Ernst Bloch may be recalled. He himself was a migrant, who changed his country of residence three times. He said:

> *Ein Mensch nimmt sich selbst mit, wenn er wandert. Doch ebenso geht er hierbei aus sich heraus, wird um Flur, Wald, Berg reicher. Auch lernt er, buchstäblich, wieder kennen, was Verirren und was Weg ist, und das Haus, das ihn am Ende empfängt, wirkt keineswegs selbstverständlich, sondern als erreicht.*

> When people migrate, they carry their selves along. Yet at the same time they come out of their shell, they enrich themselves through experiencing plains, forests and

mountains. Also, they literally learn again what it means both to go astray and to find a way; and the house which welcomes them in the end is not at all a foregone conclusion—it has to be earned.[22]

NOTES

[1]*Harvard Encyclopedia of American Ethnic Groups*, Stephan Thernstrom, ed. (Cambridge, Mass., 1980).

[2]*Essex Register*, vol. 16, no. 67 (Aug. 21, 1816): 4, col. 3; repr. in *Aufbruch nach Amerika: Die Auswanderungswelle von 1816/17*, Günter Moltmann, ed. (Stuttgart, 1989), 306f.

[3]Letter from U. S. Secretary of State John Quincy Adams to Baron Moritz von Fürstenwärther, June 4, 1819; repr. in *Niles' Weekly Register*, April 29, 1820; also in *Aufbruch nach Amerika*, 243ff.

[4]Ernst Bloch, *Tübinger Einleitung in die Philosophie*, Gesamtausg., vol. 13 (Frankfurt/M, 1970), 49.

[5]Ina-Maria Greverus, *Der territoriale Mensch: Ein literatur-anthropol. Versuch zum Heimatphänomen* (Frankfurt/M, 1972), 182f.

[6]Carl Hübner's first painting on this subject, "Deutsche Auswanderer" (1846), is owned by the National Gallery in Oslo, Norway. Hübner was inspired by Müller von Königswinter's poem, "Grüsst Land und Dorf zum letzten Mal," publ. in *Rheinische Zeitung* (1842), no. 205; cit. W. v. Kalnein, ed., *Die Düsseldorfer Malerschule*, exhib. cat., Kunstmuseum Düsseldorf (Mainz, 1979), 345ff.

[7]Marcus Lee Hansen, "The History of American Immigration as a Field for Research," *American Hist. Review*, 32 (1926/27): 500-518, esp. 501.

[8]Walter D. Kamphoefner, *Westfalen in der Neuen Welt: Eine Sozialgeschichte der Auswanderung im 19. Jh.*, Beiträge zur Volkskultur in Nordwestdeutschland (Münster, 1982), 26; Engl. ed.: *The Westphalians: From Germany to Missouri* (Princeton, 1987), 28.

[9]Eliza Follen, *The Life of Charles Follen* (Boston, 1844), 269f.

[10]Ibid., 270.

[11]Warren Washburn Florer, *Early Michigan Settlements*, 3 vols. (Ann Arbor, 1941-1953), vol. II, p. III.

[12]*Kirchl. Mittheilungen aus u. über Nord-Amerika* (Neuendettelsau, 1850), No.4; repr. in Florer, vol. II, 30-33, esp. 30.

[13]Text of "Gemeinde-Ordnung," ibid., vol. II, 10.

[14]The church register of Frankenmuth reports that 12 more Indian children were baptized in 1847, 6 in 1848, and 10 in 1849, among them 5 children of the Indian chief Pamarike, ranging from 2-6 years; see facsimile repr., ibid., vol.II, 21f.

[15]See Kamphoefner, *The Westphalians*, 94-96.

[16]See Helmut König, ed., *Dt. Nationalerziehungspläne aus der Zeit der Befreiungskriege*, (Berlin, 1954), 36-48; repr. of Follen's scheme, ibid., 305-317.

[17]For details see Rudolph Leopold Biesele, *The History of the German Settlements in Texas, 1831-1861* (Austin, 1930), chaps. IV and V; Wolf-Heino Struck, *Die Auswanderung aus dem Herzogtum Nassau (1806-1866)*, in series *Geschichtl. Landeskunde*, vol. IV (Wiesbaden, 1966), chap. III.

[18]*Atlantic Monthly* 19 (Jan.-June 1867): 555-564, esp. 556, "Gulistan" (rose garden), as described by the Persian poet Saadi.

[19]Kathleen Neils Conzen, *Immigrant Milwaukee, 1836-1860: Accommodation and Community in a Frontier City* (Cambridge, Mass., 1976); Agnes Bretting, *Soziale Probleme dt. Einwanderer in New York City 1800-1860* (Wiesbaden, 1981); Hartmut Keil and John B. Jentz, eds., *German Workers in Industrial Chicago, 1850-1910: A Comparative Perspective* (DeKalb, Ill., 1983); Hartmut Keil and John B. Jentz, eds., *German Workers in Chicago: A Documentary Hist. of Working-Class Culture from 1850 to World War I* (Urbana, Ill., 1988); Hartmut Keil, ed., *German Workers' Culture in the U.S., 1850 to 1920* (Washington, D.C., 1988).

[20]Gottlieb Leibbrandt, *Little Paradise: The Saga of the German Canadians of Waterloo County, Ontario, 1800-1975* (Kitchener, 1980).

[21]See Walter D. Kamphoefner, "300 Jahre Deutsche in den USA," *Geograph. Rundschau*, 35 (1983): 169-173, esp. 171.

[22]See fn. 4.

I.
DEMOGRAPHICS AND DOCUMENTATION

1 | Immigration, German Immigration and 18th-Century America

Aaron S. Fogleman, *University of South Alabama*

Immigration to America calls to mind images of millions of Europeans crowding into eastern port cities, struggling to get ahead, to escape the slum and carve out a better life, either in the city itself, or in the countryside, perhaps on the frontier. While it is self-evident that the immigrants sought opportunity, and that many also sought some kind of freedom, the degree to which they left behind the Old World or brought some of it with them is debated. When did they become Americans? Or did America become them?

Most Americans have encountered these images or questions in one way or another, but for most the center of their attention has been the century 1815 to 1914, when some 38 million immigrants arrived. In this century, much of what we think of as "America" came to be and the immigrants were vital in its shaping. After World War I, immigration continued at a significantly slower pace until the renewed wave of Spanish-speaking and Asian immigration in our time. But, of course, the story begins before 1815.

Historians are increasingly realizing the importance of studying the movement of hundreds of thousands of people from Europe and Africa to colonial America as "immigration" rather than "colonization." The difference is important. Colonization better describes the 17th century, when the first settlers arrived from England and elsewhere to begin the struggle for a foothold in what was for them a new continent. They extended the European economic system to new frontiers—one that was alien to the inhabitants who had been living there for centuries. They carved out communities, societies, even utopias in the wilderness. For many years it was not even clear if individual settlements, perhaps the movement as a whole, would succeed. "Immigration," on the other hand, more appropriately describes an influx of people into a land that is already well-populated and developed by a relatively similar culture. They contribute to that culture (as opposed to overcoming the culture that was already there), and by their presence and activity cause it to expand.

Sometime between Jamestown and Lexington, the movement of people from Europe and Africa to North America became immigration rather than colonization. The transition varied in nature and timing from colony to colony, but, in general, immigration better characterizes the massive influx of peoples into British North America during the 18th century. The outer edges of this rapidly expanding collection of societies, however, more closely resembled 17th-century "colonization": White settlers, sometimes bringing African slaves, quickly settled deep in the backcountry among Native American peoples, then expanded their societies to such a degree that they overwhelmed the cultures already present, replacing them with something new. Yet in the 18th century, immigrants came first to flourishing, prosperous societies in the East. Virtually all of them landed at the important port cities of New York, Philadelphia, Baltimore, Annapolis, Charleston and Savannah. Many remained in the cities; some moved to the surrounding countryside; and others moved into the backcountry, or to the frontier.

It is, of course, impossible to establish with accuracy the volume of 18th-century immigration to the 13 colonies. The only detailed, individual records kept over a long period of time for any ethnic group are the ship lists maintained in Philadelphia for Germans arriving between 1727 and 1808. So historians have struggled to arrive at usable estimates of total immigration, employing a number of different methodologies.[1]

One method which corroborates some earlier estimates, yet yields information on immigration in a more usable form, is to make use of the best, most recent immigration estimates by historians of each ethnic group (i.e., Africans, northern and southern Irish, Germans, Scots, English, Welsh, and others), then present those estimates in a single table. Earlier, such estimates were vague and rarely based on what quantitative data is available for the 18th century. More recently, historians of ethnic groups, using information on ship departures and arrivals, along with samples of how many immigrants different kinds of ships could carry (and other indicators), have arrived at estimates that are somewhat more accurate. Furthermore, these new estimates give some indication of how immigration varied over time and between ethnic groups in the 18th century, something other estimates have not done. A composite of what appears to be the best estimates by the ethnic-group historians is presented in Table 1.[2]

Table 1 suggests a best estimate for all white immigrant groups together of 307,400 for the years 1700 to 1775. The figure falls within the range established by Henry A. Gemery (278,400 to 485,300 for 1700 to 1780) but is at the lower end of that range. This reflects a recent trend among ethnic-

Table 1   Estimated Decennial Immigration by Ethnic Group into the Thirteen Colonies, 1700-1775

Decade	Africans	Germans*	Northern Irish	Southern Irish	Scots	English	Welsh	Other	Total	Prop
1700-09	9,000	(100)	(600)	(800)	(200)	<400>	<300>	<100>	(11,500)	.02
1710-19	10,800	(3,700)	(1,200)	(1,700)	500	<1,300>	<900>	<200>	(20,300)	.03
1720-29	9,900	(2,300)	(2,100)	(3,000)	800	<2,200>	<1,500>	<200>	(22,000)	.04
1730-39	40,500	13,000	4,400	7,400	(2,000)	<4,900>	<3,200>	<800>	(76,200)	.13
1740-49	58,500	16,600	9,200	9,100	(3,100)	<7,500>	<4,900>	<1,100>	(110,000)	.19
1750-59	49,600	29,100	14,200	8,100	(3,700)	<8,800>	<5,800>	<1,200>	(120,500)	.20
1760-69	82,300	14,500	21,200	8,500	10,000	<11,900>	<7,800>	<1,600>	157,800	.27
1770-75	17,800	5,200	13,200	3,900	15,000	7,100	<4,600>	<700>	67,500	.12
Total	**278,400**	**84,500**	**66,100**	**42,500**	**35,300**	**<44,100>**	**<29,000>**	**<5,900>**	**(585,800)**	**1.00**

* "Germans" refers to German-speaking peoples, many of whom came from areas outside the modern borders of Germany, esp. Switzerland and Alsace.

Note: Figures in Table 1 were rounded to the nearest one hundred immigrants. The estimates in the table are divided into three categories: most accurate (no demarkation), less accurate ( ), and least accurate < >.

Source: Aaron S. Fogleman, "Migrations to the Thirteen British North American Colonies, 1700-1775: New Estimates," *Journal of Interdisciplinary History*, 22 (1992), 691-709, here 698.

group historians to lower the estimates by their perhaps more filiopietistic predecessors, and suggests an increased reliability in this method of calculating immigration, though undercounting certainly is not impossible. Even 300,000 immigrants, arriving in an area whose base population in 1700 was only about 175,000 white inhabitants, suggests the scale of the redefinition implied by their arrivals.[3]

But total numbers are only a beginning. What the more precise immigrant-group data permit as well is a new estimate of the relative size of each group's arrivals and so its impact. Africans were by far the largest group of immigrants in the 18th century.[4] The largest European immigrant group may have been the Germans, not the "Scots-Irish", as many have believed.

The estimates in Table 1 also suggest that the timing of each ethnic-racial group's immigration more or less followed the general pattern of all immigrants together: gradual but significant increases until the 1730s, then a sudden take-off in that decade, which continued until the end of the colonial era. King George's War (1740-1748) and especially the French and Indian War (1754-1763) interrupted the flow of immigrants into the colonies, but in each case the volume reached new heights after the close of hostilities. The only deviation from this general pattern occurred with the German-speaking immigration, which peaked in the 1740s and 1750s and then declined until the end of the colonial period.

The figure for total immigration in Table 1 (585,800) may seem low. Indeed, it is only as good as the secondary sources upon which it is based, but I would suggest that even using this figure as a minimum indicates that immigration in 18th-century America was extremely high and had a tremendous impact on the overall demographic growth of what was one of the fastest growing populations in the world. Strangely, some historians who have accepted *higher* figures of total immigration than those presented in Table 1 have minimized its impact on colonial population growth and implicitly on colonial American culture. For example, James Henretta presents one of the higher estimates of immigration (400,000 whites alone), yet concludes that natural increase was the dominant cause of the phenomenal American growth rate before 1776.[5] Strictly speaking, this is true. The population grew from 250,000 in 1700 to 2,500,000 in 1775, yet only about 585,000 immigrants arrived in the interval. What Henretta ignores, however, is that much of the implied "natural increase" is in the reproduction of immigrant families.

The impact of immigration on 18th-century population growth was more significant than previous historians have realized. The sheer demographic effect of the immigrants *and their progeny* can be approached by several indices of this event. The simplest "immigration index" is arrived at by dividing the number of immigrants in a time period by the total population at the beginning of the time period.[6] This gives a crude measure of the impact of immigrants in proportion to the initial size of the society. In the case of colonial America, the small base population of 250,000, and the substantial total immigration of 585,000, yield a ratio, or index, of 2.3, which suggests a dramatic effect. Comparing this with the same index for 1800-1875 (1.7) or 1840-1915 (1.8), one can see that the overall demographic repercussions of immigration on American society actually turn out to be higher in the 18th century than in the 19th. Table 2 shows the immigration index for selected 75-year intervals, along with more conventional measures of population growth:

Table 2   **The Immigration Index and Other Measures of Population Growth in the U.S. in Selected 75-Year Intervals**

(A) Year	(B) Population	(C) Percent Increase	(D) Immigration in Interval	(E) Immigration Index D/B*	(F) Natural Increase in Interval	(G) D/D+F, or % Growth from Immigration
1630	5,000	5600%				
1705	285,000		215,000	43.0	65,000	77%
1700	250,888					
1775	2,500,000	900	585,800	2.3	1,668,000	26
1800	5,308,483					
1875	45,000,000	748	9,100,333	1.7	30,591,184	23
1840	17,069,453					
1915	100,000,000	486	31,168,025	1.8	51,762,521	38
1900	75,994,575					
1975	214,000,000	182	28,285,532	0.4	109,719,893	20

* population at the beginning of the interval

Sources: *Hist. Statistics of the U.S.*, Part 1, 105-106; U.S. Bureau of the Census, *Statistical Abstract of the U.S., 1984* (1983), 88; and Table 1. The 1630-1705 immigration figure was calculated from Henry A. Gemery, "Emigration from the British Isles to the New World, 1630-1700: Inferences from Colonial Populations," *Research in Economic Hist.*, 5 (1980), 179-231, here 204, which indicates that 155,000 arrived from the British Isles during this period, Galenson, *White Servitude*, 216-217 (ca. 25,000 blacks, 1650-1700), my own estimation of 30,000 other whites for 1630-1700, and Table 1 (5,000 total for 1700-05). 207,000 immigrants were estimated for 1800-1820 (from Hans Jürgen Grabbe, "European Immigration to the U.S. in the Early National Period, 1783-1820," in Susan E. Klepp (ed.), *The Demographic Hist. of the Philadelphia Region, 1600-1860*, vol. 133, n. 2 of *Proceedings of the American Phil. Soc.* (June, 1989), 190-214. 1871-75 immigration = .5(1871-1880).

Columns C and G show traditional measures of population growth and immigration. They demonstrate the extremely high growth in their respective areas throughout most of American history and incredible levels for the 17th century. These measures are very misleading for early periods of settlement, however. The population doubled because of "immigration" as soon as the second man disembarked at Jamestown. Population growth in the first interval in Table 2 was due more to colonization (as distinguished earlier from immigration) and does not make for a good comparison with later periods. By the 18th century, however, society had developed to the point where immigration best describes the movement of people into the colonies and the measures in the table become more meaningful. The percentage of growth due to immigration (column G) was highest from 1840 to 1915 (38%) when it reached its peak in real numbers. But this does not show how growth due to immigration compared to the population that was already there. The immigration index shows this relationship and better indicates how important immigrants had been to the make-up of the population at the end of the different intervals.

Table 2 demonstrates that, after the period of initial settlement, the immigration index was at its highest point in American history during the first three quarters of the 18th century, higher even than in the 19th century. Immigration has always been an important element of American political, social, economic, and demographic history, but in this respect it was most important during the century in which it has received the least attention from historians—the 18th. Though in real numbers 18th-century immigration equalled only a tiny fraction of what it did in the following centuries, it was then a much more important factor in determining the growth of the American population than it ever was later. In the first three quarters of the 19th century nearly 9,000,000 immigrants arrived and the population increased 748%. From 1840 to 1915, 31,000,000 immigrants came. But in both cases immigrants made up a lesser proportion of the population that was already there and hence had less influence on subsequent population growth than they did from 1700 to 1775.

The demographic impact on 18th-century America was so great, in fact, that a hypothetical glimpse at the level and make-up of the population in 1776, had there been no immigration in the preceding 75 years, reveals a very different kind of society than the one which fought the Revolution. What would the population of 250,000 in 1700 have looked like by 1775, if the nearly 600,000 immigrants had never come? First of all, it would have been overwhelmingly of English descent, just as it was in 1700. The Middle and Southern Colonies would have resembled New England in this respect. African slavery would have been important, but numerically much smaller, and perhaps easier to deal with by some of the founding fathers as they struggled with notions of liberty and equality after the Revolution—had there even been a revolution.

After approximating the continuous annual growth rate for the population in the 18th century without immigration, it is possible to project the population of 1700 to see how large the population would have been in 1775. Projecting the population in this manner allows us to determine how much of the population in 1775 was either immigrant or descended from 18th-century immigrants, as opposed to having descended by natural increase from the 17th-century population—a more accurate measure of the total impact of immigration. The continuous annual rate of natural increase for the population from 1700 to 1775 was 2.3%. At this rate of increase, the population of about 250,000 in 1700 would have only equaled about 1,400,000 by 1775 (instead of 2,500,000). Thus nearly half (1,100,000 or 44%) of the population in 1775 was either immigrant or descended from 18th-century immigrants. That is, only about 56% was the result of the natural increase from the base population of some 250,000 in 1700.[7]

Immigration to New England in the 18th century was minimal. Some Scots-Irish and Germans did settle in Maine, New Hampshire and Massachusetts, however. After making slight adjustments in the immigration figures to take this into account, it follows that only 45% of the population of the Middle and Southern Colonies in 1775 was descended from the base population living there in 1700, and the majority (55%) was either immigrant or descended from 18th-century immigrants.[8]

The sudden take-off in immigration in the 1730s indicates that the phenomenon of large-scale immigration became increasingly important in the decades before the Revolution, but that it was a long-term trend, not a sudden surge beginning in 1760 as Bernard Bailyn and Barbara DeWolfe suggest. They place too much emphasis on the short-term effects of immigration and its relationship to the Revolution. Bailyn and DeWolfe refer to immigration in the 15 years before Lexington and Concord as an "explosion," and stress that it represented about 10% of the total population in 1776. This represented a new experience which had important implications during the escalating imperial crisis, both for Americans occupying an expanding frontier, and for British officials trying to develop a rational western policy.[9]

In reality, recent immigrants (those arriving within the previous decade) made up a much larger proportion of the population in 1740 and 1750 than in 1770 or 1775, though their relative numbers were still significant in the 1770s. The 76,200 immigrants who arrived from 1730 to 1739 equalled over 8% of the nearly 1,000,000 people in the colonies in 1740. Ten years later, immigrants of the previous decade equaled over 9%. However, by the 1770s, when Bailyn and DeWolfe suggest that immigration had reached its highest relative impact on the population already living in the colonies, that impact was actually beginning to decline: immigrants arriving in the 1760s made up only slightly over 7% of the population in 1770 and those arriving from 1770 to 1775 equalled less than 3% of the total inhabitants living in 1775 (see Table 3).[10]

Table 3   Recent Immigrants as a Proportion of the Total Population in Colonial America 1700-1775

Decade	Population	Immigrants	Proportion
1700-09	331,711	11,500	.035
1710-19	466,185	20,300	.044
1720-29	629,445	22,000	.035
1730-39	905,563	76,200	.084
1740-49	1,170,760	110,000	.094
1750-59	1,593,625	120,500	.076
1760-69	2,148,076	157,800	.073
1770-75	2,500,000	67,500	.027

Sources: For the population figures, see U.S. Bureau of the Census, *Hist. Statistics of the U.S., Colonial Times to 1970* (Washington, D.C., 1975), Pt. 2, Series Z2-17, 1168. Figures for immigrants are from Table 1.

How conscious were these newly-arrived ethnic groups of their identity? Do they, for example, appear to have settled together? To the extent that they did, they pose in most dramatic form the issue of a growing society trying to absorb the various subcultures occupying its landscape. Several historians have maintained that, even though there was *de facto* clustering of ethnic groups, a "liberal" climate of individualism and self-aggrandizement were the crucial factors in determining settlement patterns. Highly mobile immigrants and others chose where they would settle and resettle based on their perception of their personal situation at any given time. Date of arrival, location of the nearest unoccupied land, land prices, access to courts and markets, soil types, and topography were important factors influencing settlement, and there was little or no correlation between ethnicity and these factors. More recent historians have emphasized that broad settlement patterns in America reflected the origins of immigrants in Europe. The volume of trans-Atlantic communication was significant, and speculators, officials, and others in America and England knew where to find certain kinds of emigrants in Europe. The purpose for which they hoped to use prospective settlers in America determined in which areas they concentrated their recruiting activities and, ultimately, where the immigrants settled in the colonies.[11]

A question looming over this long historiographical debate is just how mixed or distinct settlement patterns of the different ethnic groups actually were. If there was little or no clustering into ethnic enclaves—if the landscape of, for example, Pennsylvania consisted of Germans, English, Irish, Welsh, and others living not in separate regions but interspersed among each other, then clearly "ethnicity" had little to do with determining broad settlement patterns of immigrants and their descendants. On the other hand, if the Pennsylvania landscape was one in which different ethnic groups did settle and live in distinct regions, mixing only minimally with others, then "ethnicity" must have played some role in determining these patterns.

The important questions, then, are what percentage of the German, English, Irish, etc. populations settled in areas that were ethnically mixed and what percentage settled in areas that were not mixed. If the percentage of those settling in ethnically distinct areas is large enough, can "ethnicity" legitimately be excluded from the factors which determined settlement patterns? Thomas Purvis' surname analysis of the 1790 federal census helps answer these questions. Purvis has developed the best technique to date for handling the old, familiar problem of identifying nationality by surname when names were frequently changed, often beyond recognition, after arrival in America. His impressive, excruciatingly difficult analyses, used in other ways by Purvis himself to demonstrate the importance of ethnicity in the early American population, make it possible to provide a rough measure of ethnic segregation in settlement patterns by county in some states.[12]

Demographers have developed the "Index of Dissimilarity" to measure the degree of segregation in residence patterns among ethnic groups. It measures the difference in the distribution of two population groups within the same area and indicates what the lowest proportion of either population is that would have to be shifted in order to achieve an equal distribution for both groups. In other words, people of a given ethnic group who move into an area have two choices: They can either cluster with other members of their group, or they can settle the way everyone else does. The index measures the degree to which the results of these two choices are similar or "dissimilar." If

15% of the population of Pennsylvania in 1790 was Scots-Irish and 15% of every *county* in Pennsylvania was Scots-Irish, then the Index of Dissimilarity would be 0.0—meaning that the way the Scots-Irish settled was exactly the same as the way everyone else settled at the county level. A high Index of Dissimilarity means that the Scots-Irish pattern was so "dissimilar" to the non-Scots-Irish pattern that large percentages of the total population would have to be moved in order for the Scots-Irish to live in a pattern "similar" to the others.

Table 4 shows the Index of Dissimilarity for each ethnic group versus the rest of the population in Pennsylvania. A measure of 0.0 means that both distributions in a given test were exactly equal (i.e., there was no segregation) and a measure of 1.0 means both groups resided completely separate from one another.

Table 4   **Ethnic Segregation in Pennsylvania by County in 1790**
The Index of Dissimilarity

Ethnic Group*	% of white population	Index of Dissimilarity
Germans	38.0	.431
English	25.8	.271
Scots-Irish@	15.1	.308
Scottish@	7.6	
Irish	7.1	.269
Welsh	3.6	.274
Dutch	1.3	.394
French	0.9	.368
Swedish	0.6	.410
	100.0	

* i.e., each group versus all others (Germans vs non-Germans, etc.)
@ Purvis was unable to distinguish Scots-Irish names from Scottish, thus they must be taken together when figuring the Index of Dissimilarity. He estimated that the Scots-Irish equaled about two-thirds of the total.
    Source: Thomas Purvis, "Patterns of Ethnic Settlement in Late 18th-Century Pennsylvania," *Western Pennsylvania Hist. Magazine*, 70 (1987), 107-122, here 115.

Table 4 shows that there was significant segregation in residence by county of all ethnic groups in Pennsylvania in 1790. After a century of immigration, Pennsylvania had become a society in which much of the population lived segregated in ethnic enclaves. In order to make the residence patterns of Germans and non-Germans equal, at least 43.1% of either population would have to be shifted. For Scots-Irish and Scots, 30.8% would have to be shifted, and for the English 27.1%. As high as these figures are, they may even be too low for the late colonial period. The Revolution disrupted many segments of society and drastically reduced the number of immigrants arriving. This snapshot of the Pennsylvania landscape in 1790 may reflect an ethnically diverse society that was beginning to intermix after the creation of the new nation.[13]

So in the 75 years before the Revolution nearly 600,000 Europeans and Africans immigrated through eastern ports and then settled the rural landscape in dispersed, but significantly ethnic, enclaves. Africans were the largest group, and Germans were probably the largest European group. A significant increase in immigration began in the 1730s and peaked in real numbers in the 1760s and early 1770s, though the peak period of immigration relative to the base population occurred in the 1740s and 1750s. The overall demographic impact of immigration on society was enormous: After the initial period of colonization, the immigration index reached its highest point in American history during these 75 years. By 1776, nearly half of the population was either immigrant, or descended from *18th-century* immigrants.

* * *

How different was the experience of German-speaking people—the only numerically significant non-British, white immigrant group in the 18th century? It is clear that Germans in Pennsylvania (where nearly 80% of the immigrants of that ethnic group initially landed) tended to be more segregated than other immigrant groups. Table 4 indicates that there was significant segregation for all ethnic groups, but that it was most significant for Germans. In fact, with the exception of the Dutch, French and Swedes, who together formed only 2.8% of the population, no other group was even close to the Germans, the Scots-Irish being the second highest at 30.8%.

Furthermore, measures of segregation between specific ethnic groups, rather than between one group and everyone else, show that even higher segregation in residence patterns by county existed in 1790, and that any combination involving Germans is the highest, even Germans vs Dutch (see Table 5). In other words, Germans tended to a large degree to live in different counties than either English or Scots/Scots-Irish. In 1790, about 85% of the population of Berks County was German, 72% of Lancaster County, 63% of Northampton, and 57% of Montgomery, while only about 11% of Delaware, 16% of Chester, and 17% of Cumberland were German. (All these were populous counties in older areas of settlement.) Many more Scots/Scots-Irish lived in different counties than the English, but the Index of Dissimilarity for these two groups while high (.281), is much lower than that for the Germans vs Scots/Scots-Irish (.466). All this suggests that non-British immigrants were less assimilable than British immigrants.[14]

Table 5   Index of Dissimilarity Measured by County for Selected Ethnic Groups in Pennsylvania in 1790

Germans vs Scots-Irish/Scots	.466
Germans vs English	.447
English vs Scots-Irish/Scots	.281
Germans vs Dutch	.481
English vs Welsh	.310

Source: Same as Table 4.

Ethnic clustering of Germans within counties where they represented only a small minority of the population was also significant. Township data available for northern Chester County in 1765 indicates a high degree of ethnic cohesion. Here the Index of Dissimilarity for Germans vs non-Germans is .450. If calculated for all townships in Chester County, instead of just those where Germans tended to settle, it would be much higher.[15]

Table 1 reveals the second way German immigration differed from other groups: They did not always come when other groups came. As indicated earlier, immigration increased gradually until the 1730s, then rapidly until the beginning of the Revolution, interrupted slightly by colonial warfare in the 1740s and significantly from 1754 to 1763. German immigration deviated from this pattern in that it was substantially larger than other European ethnic groups from 1740 to 1759, yet did not continue in such large numbers after the Treaty of Paris (1763), as did other groups. In the middle two decades of the century, 45,700 Germans arrived (55% of all who came before 1776), while 76,700 non-Germans arrived (only 34% of their total). After 1760, however, only 19,700 Germans arrived (23%), while 105,500 non-Germans came (47%).

German emigration to colonial America occurred in three phases, each with its own causes and character: 1683 to 1709, 1709-1714, and from about 1717 to 1775.

Religious persecution in central Europe and the pursuit of utopian experiments dominated the first phase, 1683-1709. Many small, well-organized German pietist groups, fleeing desperate conditions in central Europe, migrated together to their new asylum in Pennsylvania.[16] In addition to nearly continuous warfare, a renewed wave of religious intolerance and persecution against pietistic religious sects broke out in southwest Germany and Switzerland in the late 17th century. At the same time, William Penn and his agents traveled through these areas, making contacts with Mennonites and others, converting some to Quakerism, and getting others interested in the Holy Experiment. The groups led by Franz Daniel Pastorius, Johannes Kelpius, and Daniel Falkner were typical in this first phase, a period of colonization that many other settlements in North America also experienced. Though their numbers were small, perhaps about 300 by 1709, they left a legacy which endures to this day. This kind of religious immigration, motivated by persecution and/or utopian ideals, continued until the 1760s when the last groups of Moravians came to Pennsylvania and North Carolina. But beginning in 1709, a much larger and different kind of immigration overwhelmed and dominated German America.

In the second phase of German emigration to colonial America, from 1709 to about 1714, thousands of Germans, motivated by economic disaster in 1709 and an English settlement experiment, fled to New York and North Carolina in a single, mass emigration. The English government had been trying for years to recruit German settlers for the colonies to manufacture shipbuilding products on the Hudson River in New York. They published many pamphlets and books, but few immigrants responded. In 1709 a new appendix was added to one of these tracts: Queen Anne promised to pay the journey to America and support them upon arrival. To further ensure that the book would attract the attention of the many thousands of potential emigrants in southwest Germany, the Queen's picture was placed on the cover and the title page printed in golden color. The tract became known as the "Golden Book" and circulated widely in the Rhine Valley, just when one of the worst agricultural disasters of the century hit Europe.

The result was a massive rush of emigrants down the Rhine to the port city of Rotterdam, trying to take advantage of the Queen's offer. About 30,000 attempted to emigrate, but they so overwhelmed the English authorities with their numbers that only half made it across the Channel, many of whom were later sent home. Of those, about 2,400 sailed in ten ships to New York, while 650 settled New Bern, N.C.[17] As with the first phase, there was a sense of desperation in this emigration not present in later years. Most of the emigrants came from the Palatinate, or the immediately surrounding areas. The Palatinate suffered the most from warfare and depopulation in the late 17th and early 18th centuries. While many other areas in southwest Germany began recovering after 1650, conditions improved only minimally in the Palatinate. Overpopulation did not help cause the emigration of 1709, as is sometimes suggested, because the population there was still well below pre-1620 levels. Rapid population growth did not occur until after the conclusion of the War of the Spanish Succession in 1714. The English shipbuilding plan failed because of poor planning, lack of funds, and a new Tory government in London which disapproved of it, but the Germans stayed in America. For the first time they had come to the New World in large numbers. By 1714, most of them lived not in Pennsylvania, but in New York.

During the third phase of German emigration to colonial America, which began in the 1720s (perhaps as early as 1717) and continued until 1775, Pennsylvania once again became the dominant demographic and cultural center of Germans in the colonies, replacing New York. Tens of thousands of immigrants settled there and in the surrounding colonies, transforming the region. Well over 90% who came before 1775 arrived during this period and the vast majority landed in Philadelphia. Long-term conditions of overpopulation and scarcity of land in Europe, together with the active recruitment of Germans to settle in the colonies where labor was in short supply and land in abundance, combined to induce more than 80,000 German immigrants within about five decades to try their luck in the New World. Most of these were not desperately fleeing wars, religious persecution, or agricultural disasters (though the latter sometimes served as the final impetus). Instead they sought land and opportunity, because both seemed to be declining in Europe and were abundant in America. Emigration was a calculated risk, one of the few choices to escape their steadily deteriorating situation at home.

As noted earlier, German immigration declined significantly in the 1760s and 70s, during the latter portion of the third phase—another significant difference in the German experience. While the only choice for almost all British emigrants in the 18th century was to go to one of the British colonies in America, most Germans could and did emigrate to eastern Europe, not America. German-speaking emigration actually *increased* in the 1760s and 70s, just as British emigration to North America increased, but Germans went east, not west. In 1763 Catherine the Great began inviting Germans to settle in the southern Ukraine, along the Black Sea and the Sea of Azov. About 37,000 migrated in that direction. In fact, some 830,000 emigrated from southwest Germany during the entire 18th century (not just 1700-1775), but only about 125,000 (15%) went to the Americas. For centuries there had been a tradition of German migration to the east, which was renewed in record numbers as the Habsburgs, Russians, and the Hungarian nobility pushed back the Turks and Tartars. They vigorously sought loyal, industrious settlers to inhabit their newly won territories.[18]

As with any immigrant group, official and unofficial recruitment of Germans played a crucial role in determining the direction, volume and timing of their migrations. The best explanation for the relatively higher

German immigration in the 1740s and early 1750s (as opposed to non-German immigration), and relatively lower immigration in the 1760s and 1770s, is that American and British shipping and other interests, which had become highly organized and efficient in bringing over immigrants by mid-century,[19] were intensely interested in attracting Germans in the 1740s and 1750s, yet diverted their attentions elsewhere in the l760s and 1770s. Indeed, it was not until after 1815 that German immigration in America again achieved significant levels numerically, relative to other immigrant groups.

Thus the character of "18th-century" German immigration changed as the century progressed. Religious overtones were dominant early on, and though the religious immigration continued throughout this period, these immigrants represented only a small minority (about 5-6%) of the total after 1709.[20] Also, later immigrants did not flee Europe in desperation and in large groups, but tended to leave in smaller groups or as individuals, sometimes from a group of neighboring villages, as part of a chain migration. The majority left conditions of overpopulation and scarcity similar to those experienced by other European immigrants in America, though in southwest Germany and Switzerland these twin problems were more severe. It is important to understand this background of scarcity when looking at German attitudes toward landholding and internal migration in the colonies. How did they compare to other ethnic groups with a background of scarcity, and how did they compare to those Germans who came earlier under different circumstances?

The Germans were the largest, perhaps least assimilable of all European immigrant groups. They clustered together even more than did other ethnic groups, and they did not always come when the others came—other alternatives being available. Further, they were the only large, non-British, white immigrant group in the 18th century. Their status as aliens played an important role in their attempts to establish themselves and prosper in the colonies. Thus the experience of German-speaking immigrants and their descendants in the 18th century while similar, was in many important ways different from that of other ethnic groups in what was to a large degree an immigrant society.

* * *

In the 18th century, immigration fundamentally altered the make-up of American society. The population increased tenfold from 1700 to 1775 as a result of three factors: a high rate of natural increase among the base population in 1700, immigration, and the high rate of natural increase of the immigrants' descendants. By 1776, nearly half of the population—south of

New England more than half—was either born in Europe or Africa, or descended from Europeans and Africans who arrived during the previous 75 years. What this means is that the roots of the American population on the eve of the Revolution were as much in 18th-century Europe and Africa as in 17th-century America.

But the impact of the immigrants on 18th-century America went beyond their total numbers, large as they were. In 1700 a considerable majority of the population of the colonies was English or of English ethnic descent, but because of the immigration of so many different peoples during the subsequent 75-year period, the American population not only increased at an incredible rate, it also became ethnically diverse. By 1776, large numbers of Germans, Scots, Irish, and other "strangers" populated the colonies, not to mention hundreds of thousands of Africans and African Americans. The ethnic English population had become a minority.[21]

Closer scrutiny of the information in Table 1 reveals another striking characteristic: over 80% of all immigrants arriving from 1700 to 1775 were associated with some kind of servitude. The largest, most obvious group of servants were the African slaves, who constituted 48% of the total. Further, Roger Ekirch has found that some 50,000 British convicts were imported into the Thirteen Colonies from 1718 to 1775, or about 9% of the total. Also, Farley Grubb estimates that roughly half of the German-speaking immigrants entered servitude (as indentured servants or redemptioners) upon arrival in Pennsylvania, and Richard Dunn suggests the same percentage for British immigrants. If their estimates are close, then British and German servants together made up a further 23% of the total immigrant population. Thus, when some additions are made for the Welsh and other immigrant groups, at least 80% of all immigrants into the Thirteen Colonies in the 18th century were either slaves, convicts, or servants.[22]

Thus immigration had a dual impact on the fast-growing American population—it brought both opportunity and hardship, freedom and servitude. For many European immigrants it brought opportunity, but for Africans (nearly half of all immigrants) it meant perpetual slavery. Even for white immigrants there was a double effect. The phenomenal population growth caused scarcity in some areas, yet a constant infusion of new people making new beginnings, both in older areas of settlement and on the expanding frontier, provided opportunity to the immigrants themselves and to some degree their descendants. In this kind of climate many did succeed, but many others, especially servants, did not.

As the American colonies became more populous and ethnically diverse, they also became more difficult for the British authorities to manage. By 1776, America was to a large degree a complex collection of communities of immigrants and descendants of recent immigrants. It was not, however, the unprecedented numbers of *recently-arrived* immigrants who pushed the colonies and mother country toward conflict—something corroborated by William Nelson who found that Tories often tended to be immigrants.[23] The figures in Table 1 indicate that the watershed in the history of 18th-century immigration was in the 1730s, not 1760, as Bernard Bailyn and Barbara DeWolfe have suggested.

The Revolution ended this unique period of American history in which immigration played such a large role in population growth, and it was, in a way, a result of these demographic developments.[24] Immigration of a wide variety of peoples from Europe and Africa was a distinguishing feature of all the colonies in the Americas, but it was most extreme in the British colonies of North America—those that declared independence in 1776. For many reasons, England was unable to gain control of the colonies when it wanted to most (after 1763). Not the least of those reasons was the presence of a population which had grown phenomenally and, because of the diverse nature of immigration, had become more and more non-English in character. It was this populous, ethnically diverse society, created by decades of immigration and a phenomenal natural growth, which reacted violently and with fear toward perceived English encroachments after 1763 and was able to fight and win a long war.

NOTES

[1]The most comprehensive and best edited publication of these lists is Ralph B. Strassburger and William H. Hinke, eds., *Pennsylvania German Pioneers: A Publication of the Original Lists of Arrivals in the Port of Philadelphia from 1727-1808*, 3 vols. (Morristown, Pa., 1934). They list all males 16 years and older well enough to disembark upon arrival and sign oaths or affirmations of loyalty to the British king. Because the large majority of Germans landed in Philadelphia after 1726, these lists are the starting point for any estimation of German immigration into all ports during the colonial period. For a lengthy discussion of recent attempts to estimate total immigration into the Colonies during the 18th century see Aaron S. Fogleman, "Migration to the Thirteen British North American Colonies, 1700-1775: New Estimates," *Journal of Interdiscipl. Hist.* 22 (1992), 691-709, esp. 692-693.

[2]For a lengthy discussion of the sources used in compiling Table I, see Fogleman, "Migrations to the Thirteen British North American Colonies."

[3]For Gemery's estimates of White immigration, see "European Immigration to North America, 1700-1820: Numbers and Quasi-Numbers," *Perspectives in American Hist.* 1 (1984), 283-342, here 318.

[4]If immigrants are people who voluntarily leave their homeland to find a better life elsewhere, then African slaves are not immigrants. But in strictly demographic terms, immigrants are people who came from somewhere else, as opposed to being a product of the natural increase in the indigenous population. In this sense, everyone who came from

elsewhere was an immigrant, including slaves, transported convicts, and so forth. I have included Africans in Table 1 ("Immigration by Ethnic Group") because they contributed to early American demographic growth in the same ways as the other groups in the tables. The Africans actually came from a variety of different ethnic backgrounds, but taken together, their numbers more than triple those of the largest European group, the Germans. (On the importance of ethnicity among African slaves in the American colonies, see, e.g., Ira Berlin, "Time, Space, and the Evolution of Afro-American Society," *American Hist. Review* 85 (1980), 44-78.) In contrast to that of White immigration, estimates of the volume of African slave imports have actually been increasing. For a good summary of the sometimes bitter debate on the volume of the Atlantic slave trade, see David Henige, "Measuring the Immeasurable: The Atlantic Slave Trade, West African Population and the Pyrrhonian Critic," *Journal of African Hist.* 27 (1986), 295-313.

[5]After pointing out that the per annum growth rate from 1700 to 1775 was 3%, and that nearly 400,000 White immigrants arrived in the interval, Henretta states, "In the end foreign migration accounted for only about one-quarter of the expansion in the size of the White population. . . The greater part of the increment came rather from natural increase." See *The Evolution of American Society, 1700-1815: An Interdiscipl. Analysis* (Lexington, Mass., 1973), 11. Allan Kulikoff also emphasizes natural increase as opposed to immigration. See *Tobacco and Slaves: The Development of Southern Cultures in the Chesapeake, 1680-1800* (Chapel Hill, 1986).

[6]This "immigration index" is a measure I developed to make comparisons of the relative effects of immigration on overall population growth between different epics in American immigrant history.

[7]The continuous annual rate of natural increase was calculated by figuring the growth rate for each decade, less the immigrants from Table 1 (i_t), and then weighting each decadal rate by the population at the beginning of each decade (p_t):

$$r_t^* = \ln(p_t - i_t/p_{t-1}\circ) \div t$$

$$r^* = w_t \times r_t^* = .023 \ (2.3\%)$$

The formula $P_t = P_0(e^{r^*t})$ can be used to project the base population of 1700 for 75 years:

$$P_{1775}(\text{hypothetical}) = 250,888 \times e^{.023(75)} = 1,408,109$$

[8]Actual population in 1700: 158,125   in 1775: 1,817,289

$$P_{1775}(\text{hypothetical}) = 158,125 \times e^{.022(75)} = 823,341$$

$$823,341 \div 1,817,289 = 0.453 \ (45\%)$$

[9]Bernard Bailyn and Barbara DeWolfe, *Voyagers to the West: A Passage in the Peopling of America on the Eve of the American Revolution* (New York, 1986), see e.g. pp. 3-4, 28-66, and 358. For a fuller critique of Bailyn on this matter see my review article, "The Peopling of Early America: Two Studies by Bernard Bailyn." *Comp. Studies in Society and Hist.* 31 (1989), 605-614.

[10]Neither Bailyn and Dewolfe nor I mean to suggest that *all* immigrants arriving within any given period were living in the colonies at the end of the period. Some died and a few even

returned to Europe. But most who arrived during any given decade were still there at the end of the decade, so the measures given here do give one a sense of what proportion of the population at any given time may have been "new" immigrants.

[11]Much of the lit. emphasizing individualism in settlement patterns is from the 1970s. See e.g., James T. Lemon, *Best Poor Man's Country: A Geograph. Study of Early Southeastern Pennsylvania* (Baltimore and London, 1972); Stephanie G. Wolf, *Urban Village: Population, Community, and Family Structure in Germantown, Pa., 1683-1800* (Princeton, 1976); Robert D. Mitchell, *Commercialism and Frontier: Perspectives on the Early Shenandoah Valley* (Charlottesville, 1977). In the 1980s greater emphasis was placed on ethnicity and European origins. See e.g., David G. Allen, *In English Ways: The Movement of Societies and the Transferal of English Local Law and Custom to Massachusetts Bay in the 17th Century* (Chapel Hill, 1981); David Cressy, *Coming Over: Migration and Communication between England and New England in the 17th Century* (Cambridge, 1987); Bailyn and DeWolfe, *Voyagers to the West.*

[12]Purvis' work revising the long-accepted estimates of ethnic distribution by state in 1790 by Howard F. Barker and Marcus L. Hansen (American Council of Learned Societies, "Report of Committee on Linguistic and National Stocks in the Population of the U.S.," American Hist. Assoc., *Annual Report for the Year 1931,* I, Washington, D.C., 1932, 107-441), and the recent work of Forrest McDonald and Ellen Shapiro McDonald ("The Ethnic Origins of the American People, 1790," *William and Mary Quarterly* 37 (1980), 179-199), was publ. in his article, "European Ancestry of the U.S. Population, 1790," *William and Mary Quarterly* 41 (1984), 84-101. In this and other articles he explains his new, more accurate technique for surname analysis. He has done analyses by county for New Jersey, New York and Pennsylvania, and he has examined Germans in all states. See "The European Origins of New Jersey's 18th-Century Population," *New Jersey Hist.* 100 (1982), 15-31; "The National Origin of New Yorkers in 1790," *New York Hist.* 67 (1986), 133-153; "Patterns of Ethnic Settlement in Late 18th-Century Pennsylvania," *Western Pennsylvania Hist. Magazine* 70 (1987), 107-122; "The Pennsylvania Dutch and the German-American Diaspora in 1790," *Journal of Cultural Geography* 6 (1986), 81-99.

[13]Stanley Lieberson used the Index of Dissimilarity to measure segregation at the county level of 20th-century immigrants in Canada from the English- and French-speaking population of three provinces: New Brunswick, Quebec and Ontario—all with significant numbers of French-speaking inhabitants. He found .149 to be the lowest level of dissimilarity (between immigrants and monolingual speakers of English in New Brunswick and Quebec) and .827 to be the highest (between immigrants and monolingual speakers of French in Ontario). See Lieberson, *Language and Ethnic Relations in Canada* (New York: John Wiley & Sons, 1970), 59-61. A better comparison with Table 4 can be made simply by measuring residential segregation in Canada at the county level, instead of immigrants vs. French- or English-speakers. In New Brunswick, using the 1961 census reveals an Index of Dissimilarity of .604 for English vs. non-English, .620 for French vs. non-French, and .623 for French vs. English. (The source of data for these measures is Dominion Bureau of Statistics, *1961 Census of Canada,* series 1.2, Population—Official Language and Mother Tongue, Ottawa: Ministry of Trade and Commerce, 1963). This shows what a very high index is when measuring by county in an area where ethnicity and spatial distribution are known to be an extremely important part of a country's character.

[14]For percentages of ethnic groups by county in Pennsylvania, see Thomas Purvis, "Patterns of Ethnic Settlement in Late 18th-Century Pennsylvania," *Western Pennsylvania Hist. Magazine* 70 (1987), 107-122, here 115.

[15]The data on Chester County was compiled by Sara Mathews in "German Settlement of Northern Chester County," *Pennsylvania Folklife* 27 (1978), 25-32.

[16]Klaus Deppermann, "Pennsylvanien als Asyl des frühen dt. Pietismus," *Pietismus u. Neuzeit* 10 (1982), 190-212.

[17]Walter A. Knittle, *Early 18th Century Palatine Emigration: A British Government Redemptioner Project to Manufacture Naval Stores* (Philadelphia, 1937); Otto F. Raum, "Die Hintergründe der Pfälzer Auswanderung im Jahre 1709," *Dt. Archiv für Landes- u. Volksforschung* 3 (1939), 551-567; Hans Fenske, "International Migration: Germany in the 18th Century," *Central European Hist.* 13 (1980), 332-347, 336.

[18]The best short overview in English of 18th-century German emigration is still Fenske, "International Migration: Germany in the 18th Century." See his figures, 343-347.

[19]See Marianne Wokeck, "A Tide of Alien Tongues: The Flow and Ebb of German Immigration to Pennsylvania, 1683-1776," diss. (Temple Univ., 1983).

[20]For a discussion of the German-speaking Radical Pietist migrations of the 18th century, including estimates of their numbers, see Aaron S. Fogleman, "Hopeful Journeys: German Immigration and Settlement in Greater Pennsylvania, 1717-1775," diss. (Univ. of Michigan, 1991), 238-294; see also Donald F. Durnbaugh's essay in this volume.

[21]For a recent collection of studies on non-English-speaking peoples within the British Empire, see Bernard Bailyn, ed., *Strangers within the Realm: Cultural Margins of the First British Empire* (Chapel Hill, 1991).

[22]A. Roger Ekirch, *Bound for America: The Transportation of British Convicts to the Colonies, 1718-1775* (Oxford, 1987), 26-27; Farley Grubb, "German Immigration to Pennsylvania, 1709 to 1820," *Journal of Interdiscipl. Hist.* 20 (1990), 417-436, here 436; Richard S. Dunn, "Servants and Slaves: The Recruitment and Employment of Labor," in Jack P. Greene and J.R. Pole, eds., *Colonial British America: Essays in the New History of the Early Modern Era* (Baltimore, 1984), 157-194, here 159. Dunn estimates that 25,000 English servants and 70,000 Irish and Scottish servants (not convicts) arrived in the years 1701-75. He also estimates that 35,000 Germans were servants, but here I have chosen to use Grubb's figure, since he has studied this group more intensively. While Grubb's figure reflects only those Germans immigrating through Pennsylvania, this is where the large majority (ca. 80%) of all Germans did arrive, and his figure of "roughly half" of those arriving in that colony probably reflects that of the entire German immigrant population in all colonies.

[23]William N. Nelson, *The American Tory* (Oxford, 1961).

[24]From 1775 to the post-Napoleonic period immigration of all ethnic groups slackened substantially. See Thomas Archdeacon, *Becoming American: An Ethnic History* (New York, 1983), 57-84 for an enlightening discussion of the meaning of this lull in immigration.

2 | German Settlements in Colonial Georgia and Their Copious Documentation

George F. Jones, *University of Maryland*

During Georgia's fifty-year colonial period from 1733 to 1783, there were several German-speaking settlements in the young colony which a group of benevolent and idealistic gentlemen in London, known as the Georgia Trustees, had founded to give a home to down-and-out Englishmen and persecuted foreign Protestants, to procure raw materials, and to defend the British colonies in America from the Spaniards. The most important of these German-speaking settlements were Ebenezer and its dependencies, Bethany and Goshen; the Moravian congregation in Savannah; the "Dutch" villages of Acton and Vernonburg; and the German Village at Frederica near the Florida border.

Of these, Ebenezer alone lasted into the 19th century. The Moravians resided in Savannah only from 1735 to 1740, at which time they departed for Pennsylvania to avoid compulsory military service. The German Village at Frederica consisted largely of so-called "Palatines," who had been brought there to work on the fortifications and to provide crops for the garrison. As a result, it dissolved when the regiment was disbanded some eight years later. After the introduction of slavery, most of the inhabitants of Acton and Vernonburg gradually left for the up-country.

Although these settlements died young, they had served their purpose before their demise. They supplied labor and food for the infant colony and served as a bridgehead or staging area where new immigrants could work off their indentures while learning English, adapting themselves to the climate and frontier life, and earning money before moving to healthier and more fertile lands farther inland. Many promising English settlements along the Georgia coast were also soon abandoned.[1]

Most observers, including James Oglethorpe, John Wesley, and George Whitfield, attested to the success of the Georgia Salzburgers, mainly Protestants expelled by the Archbishop of Salzburg in 1731 and settled in 1734 at Ebenezer, some 25 miles northwest of Savannah.[2] Observers were favorably impressed by the Salzburgers' cattle raising, farming, silk production, and lumbering, and especially by their gristmills and sawmills, which were Georgia's first successful enterprises.[3]

The Salzburgers were first joined by individual Swiss and Palatines, later by three large transports of Swabians from the territory of the Imperial City of Ulm on the Danube. Some of the Swabians founded Bethany, five miles up the Savannah River from Ebenezer. At about the same time the Salzburgers spread south-eastward from Ebenezer to found the community of Goshen. Although Ebenezer was called a town, it hardly deserved the name, for the settlers, even the tradesmen, preferred to leave Ebenezer and settle on their own outlying plantations. Ebenezer remained what the Russians call an "inhabited area."

Because most of the English settlers of Savannah were townsmen with professions unsuited to the frontier,[4] the Trustees needed workers, dependable and accustomed to hard work. These they found among the so-called "Palatines"—most of whom were Swiss and Swabians. Some, particularly marriageable girls, were sent to Ebenezer, while others were bought by Oglethorpe for labor at Frederica. The larger part remained in Savannah to work for the Trustees or for private individuals. At the completion of their indentures, many of the Swiss were persuaded to accept land at two new German-language settlements named Acton and Vernonburg situated ten miles south of Savannah at the White Bluff on the Vernon River. By now the Red Bluff (Ebenezer), the White Bluff (Vernonburg), and the Blue Bluff (Bethany) were all German-speaking.

For scholars of German-American history, a major benefit from Georgia's German settlements was the voluminous documentation they engendered in both German and English.[5] These very detailed accounts can sometimes also throw light on the behavior and actions of other German settlers in America who are not so well recorded. The most important German treasure troves are at the Francke Foundation in Halle and the Moravian Archives at Herrnhut, while the Hessian archives at Marburg throw light on the lives and military participation of the Georgia Germans in the Revolution. The most important English documents are in the Colonial Office Papers of the Public Record Office in Kew and in the London archives of the Society for Promoting Christian Knowledge (SPCK).

Many of the reports and much of the correspondence of the ministers at Ebenezer that are housed in Halle were published contemporaneously by Samuel Urlsperger, the Senior of the Lutheran Ministry in Augsburg, who was a corresponding member of the SPCK. Unfortunately, Urlsperger greatly bowdlerized his edition of the reports, the *Ausführliche Nachrichten*, deleting everything he considered unsavory or discouraging.[6] These reports have been, and are being, translated and published as the *Detailed Reports*, with the deleted passages restored in some volumes.[7] One bit of suppressed material has survived: a secret diary by Johann Martin Boltzius, the senior Ebenezer pastor and author of most of the reports.[8] In this candid diary Boltzius tells how he confronted Oglethorpe and forced him to allow the Salzburgers to move from the sterile and inaccessible spot on which they had settled to a new location on the Red Bluff of the Savannah River.

Along with the reports in the *Ausführliche Nachrichten* is a vast quantity of letters. Although these, too, are badly bowdlerized, they do clarify certain points and identify certain individuals mentioned in the reports, often only as N. or N.N. Soon to be translated and published are the letters of Johann Driesler, the Lutheran minister at the German Village at Frederica.[9] The *Ausführliche Nachrichten* also contain a number of accounts and travelogues by German visitors, including two from Baron von Reck, leader of the first and third Salzburger transports.[10] Also informative are the travelogues of Johann Gottfried von Müllern, who conducted the fourth Salzburger transport to London, and of Johann Vigera, who conducted it the rest of the way to Georgia.[11]

The Moravian materials at Herrnhut have not been published but are available at the Unitätsarchiv.. These documents are unusually complete, often in duplicate and sometimes in triplicate, some copies being in French or Latin. Modern transcripts of these materials served Adelaide Fries for her still authoritative *The Moravians in Georgia, 1735-1740*.[12] One small item in this vast amount of material is an account of a journey made in 1765 from the Moravian town of Walachia in North Carolina to Savannah, which names many Germans on the route through the Carolinas and even describes Ebenezer. [13]

Most of the items pertaining to the Georgia Germans in the Colonial Office Papers in Kew were transcribed for, and edited by, Allen D. Candler in 39 volumes.[14] Items concerning the Georgia Germans' life during, and their participation in, the Revolution are found in Candler's *Revolutionary Records*.[15] The Salzburger correspondence at the SPCK has also been published.[16] Both informative and witty are the comments made by William Stephens, the Trustees' secretary and later President of the Council in

Savannah, who was especially concerned with the "Dutch" of Vernonburg and the "Dutch" militiamen.[17]

Because so many of the colonists in Georgia, both English and German, were indentured servants or were at least "brought over on the charity," extensive and precise records down to the farthing were kept for financial reasons.[18] Similarly detailed financial records are found among the previously mentioned records at Herrnhut. A leading Trustee, John Percival, the Earl of Egmont, maintained a personal journal of the Trustees' transactions, many of which deal with the recruitment, transport, and support of the Georgia Germans.[19] He also compiled a list of the English and German settlers up to the year 1741.[20] While the German names are often quite mangled, many can be corrected by comparison with the German reports of the ministers at Ebenezer.

Land grants and their recipients were carefully recorded,[21] and the *Cattle Brand Book* gives the names of all ranchers, many of whom were German-speaking.[22] Also instructive are the wills left by German settlers, which show how some poor indentured servants prospered and amassed modest fortunes in land, cattle, and slaves.[23] Of even greater cultural value are the inventories, which describe their tools, trinkets, and furnishings, for these give an intimate insight into the life styles of those who owned them.[24]

The ministers at Ebenezer diligently reported all births, baptisms, marriages, and deaths in the congregation to the SPCK. Unfortunately, all these reports have been lost, or at least lost sight of.[25] On the other hand, the vital records from 1754 to 1800 were kept in a church book at Ebenezer, which is now stored at the Library of Congress. This book has been translated and published.[26]

In addition to sources specifically about the Georgia Germans, there are many accounts of notable Georgians who happened to be German-speaking. Christian Gottlieb Prieber was a Saxon visionary who attempted to organize the Indians to defend themselves from European encroachment. Johann Gerhard de Brahm, who brought a Swabian transport to Georgia in 1751, was an expert surveyor and military engineer who wrote the first "History of Georgia." Johann Joachim Zubly was a reformed minister from Appenzell who represented Georgia at the Second Continental Congress. All these have been subjects of historical writings, but most of the authors used no German sources and were not greatly concerned with their subjects' European backgrounds or with their compatriots in Georgia.

Johann Christoph Bornemann of Göttingen, who founded New Göttingen on the Savannah River, wrote an interesting account of his journey to the New World.[27] Unfortunately, the surviving copy takes him only as far as the mouth of the Savannah River, but he did write some interesting letters to Albrecht von Haller in Bern.[28] Ebenezer was described by various visitors, such as the previously mentioned John Wesley and George Whitefield. Keen insights were recorded by Henry Melchior Muhlenberg when he revisited Ebenezer in 1774 to settle a dispute between the two pastors,[29] and one of these later published a volume of anecdotes, which remains undiscovered.[30]

The town of Ebenezer on the Red Bluff is perhaps the only German settlement in Colonial America that furnished any visual record of its actual founding. In 1976 Dr. Kristian Hvidt of the Royal Library of Denmark discovered a collection of drawings brought back from Georgia by Baron von Reck in 1736. Most of these depict the flora, fauna, and Indians of Georgia, with descriptions and explanations in German. One shows the building of the first two shelters and another gives a low-oblique view of the town, the latter having much in common with the well-known bird's eye view of Savannah which is often reproduced to show its city planning.[31]

Regrettably, so much of this valuable material has been ignored due to a still dominantly nativist and monolingual approach to American history.

NOTES

CRG = The Colonial Records of the State of Georgia.
GHQ = The Georgia Historical Quarterly.
[1]See Charles C. Jones, *The Dead Towns of Georgia.* Reprint (Bowie, MD., 1989).
[2]Their story is briefly told in George F. Jones, *The Salzburger Saga* (Athens, GA, 1984).
[3]See Gorge F. Jones, "Cattle Raising on the Early Georgia Frontier: A Salzburger Contribution," in *Fide et Amore: Festschrift for Hugo Bekker*, ed. Wm.C. McDonald and Winder McConnell (Göppingen, 1990), 173-184; "The Salzburger Mills," *Yearbook of German-American Studies* 23 (1988), 105-117.
[4]These professions are given in *A List of the Early Settlers of Georgia*," ed. E. Merton Coulter and Albert B. Saye (Athens, GA, 1949).
[5]The most complete bibliography is in George F. Jones, *The Georgia Dutch* (Athens, GA, 1992)
[6]Samuel Urlsperger, ed. *Ausführl. Nachrichten von den Saltzburgischen Emigranten* (Halle, 1735-51), 3 vols., 17 continuations. Continued as *Americanisches Ackerwerck Gottes* (Augsburg, 3 vols. 1751-54; 4th vol. 1759).
[7]George F. Jones, ed., *Detailed Reports on the Salzburgers who Settled in America* (Athens, GA, 1968 ff.).
[8]George F. Jones, ed., "The Secret Diary of Pastor Johann Martin Boltzius," *GHQ* 53 (1969): 78-110.
[9]Translating has just begun by this author.
[10] George F. Jones, "Baron von Reck's Travel Journal, 1734," *Bulletin of the Soc. for the Hist. of the Germans in Maryland* 31 (1963): 83-90; "Von Reck's Second Report from Georgia," *William and Mary Quarterly*, 3rd Series, 22 (1965): 319-33.
[11]George F. Jones, "The Fourth Transport of Georgia Salzburgers" *Concordia Hist. Institute Quarterly* 56 (1983): 3-26, 52-64.

[12]Winston Salem, N.C., 1967.

[13]George F. Jones, "Report of Mr. Ettwein's Journey to Georgia and South Carolina, 1765," *South Carolina Hist. Magazine* 91 (1990), 147-60.

[14]Allen D. Candler, ed., *CRG*], vols. 1-19, 21-26 (Atlanta, 1904-13). Later vols. ed. by Kenneth Coleman and Milton Ready (Athens, GA).

[15]Allen D. Candler, ed., *The Revolutionary Records of the State of Georgia*, 3 vols. (Atlanta, 1903).

[16]George F. Jones, ed., *Henry Newman's Salzburger Letterbooks* (Athens, GA, 1966).

[17]E. Merton Coulter, *The Journal of William Stephens*, 174f.(Athens, GA, 1958-59); also in *CRG,* vol.4, supplement.

[18]These appear throughout the *CRG.*

[19]*The Journal of the Earl of Egmont, 1723-38,* ed. Robert G. McPherson (Athens, GA, 1962). Vols. 2 and 3 appeared previously as vol. 5 of the *CRG.*

[20]See fn. 4.

[21]These grants appear throughout the *CRG* and most of them also appear in *Entry Claims for Georgia Landholders, 1733-55,* ed. Pat Bryan (Atlanta State Printing Office, 1975), and in *English Crown Grants in St. Matthew Parish in Georgia, 1755-75,* ed. Marion R. Hemperly (Atlanta, State Printing Office, 1974).

[22]*Records of the Register of Records and Secretary: Marks and Brands, 1755-1778, 1785-1793* (Dept. of Archives and History, Atlanta).

[23] *Abstracts of Colonial Wills of the State of Georgia, 1733-1777,* ed. Pat Bryant (Atlanta, State Printing Office, 1974). Reprint (Spartanburg, S.C., 1981); *Abstracts of Wills, Chatham County, Georgia,* ed. Mabel Freeman Lafar, (Savannah, GA, 1933).

[24]Book F, Colonial Estates Inventories 1754-1770. Record Group 49, Series 6.

[25]Because Egmont's journal and the last three years of Stephen's journal, long thought lost, have been found, there is reason to hope that these valuable records survive unknown somewhere in London.

[26]*Ebenezer Record Book* (Savannah, 1929) trans. A.G. Voigt. The LoC designation for the record book is *Jerusalem Church Records.* I have begun a revision with the help of Sheryl Exley, a descendant.

[27]A copy of Bornemann's travelogue with a translation by Bertha Reinert is in the archives of the Georgia Hist. Soc. in Savannah.

[28]See fn. 3

[29]*The Journals of Henry Melchior Muhlenberg,* ed. Theodore G. Tappert and John W. Doberstein (Philadelphia, 1942-1948), vol. II, 584-686.

[30]Christoph Friedrich Triebner, *Ebenezerische Todes-Thäler, oder Anekdoten einer 24-jähr. Amtsführung* (Lon, between 1786 and 1793).

[31]*Von Reck's Voyage,* ed. Kristian Hvidt (Savannah: Beehive Press, 1980), opposite pp. 66.

[32]See George F. Jones, "Peter Gordon's (?) View of Savannah," *GHQ* 70 (1986), 97-101; Rodney M. Baine and Louis De Vorsey, Jr., "The Provenance and. . . ," *GHQ* 73 (1989), 784-813.

II.
RELIGIOUS MINORITIES AND THEIR SETTLEMENTS

3 | Radical Pietism as the Foundation of German-American Communitarian Settlements

Donald F. Durnbaugh, *Elizabethtown College*

North America has been the promised land of those seeking to erect utopian commonwealths and communitarian settlements. The first planned communal colony was that of the Dutch Collegiant P. C. Plockhoy (1620?-1700?) on the Delaware shore in 1663. Since that time the combination of religious freedom and available land in the New World has attracted scores of adventurous and devout souls seeking to erect their New Jerusalems. The exact number of such establishments has not been determined, for previously-unknown experiments are occasionally still reported. Bestor recorded 130 through 1860; an overlapping number of those founded between 1787 and 1919 listed 270. Estimates on communes since 1945 range into the thousands.[1]

Some of these communities had political or philosophical theories as their basis, but a large majority had religious foundations. The religiously-based groups were by far the most successful, if longevity is taken as the standard of success. Rosabeth Moss Kanter has well described the social mechanisms contributing to this achievement; increasingly, however, there is substantial criticism of taking the length of life of a community as the criterion of success.[2]

Clearly, communities with a religious foundation are a characteristic element of American cultural history. Those with such orientation can be usefully subdivided into categories; most of them can be identified as belonging to the Radical (Anabaptist) Reformation, Radical Puritanism, or Radical Pietism. Others could be placed into a miscellaneous category which might be called Radical Christianity. (An appendix lists examples of these categories.)

This essay will focus on Radical Pietism; its thesis is that Radical Pietism provided the religious base for many communitarian settlements in North America from the late 17th through the early 19th centuries, especially those derived from German immigration. Although other shaping influences can be identified for some of these communities—e.g., in the case of the Ephrata Community—Radical Pietism was the predominant and formative influence. Following a brief statement of its character, the essay will sketch the formation of the leading German-American settlements, and then show their rootage in Radical Pietism.

Radical Pietism

Hans Schneider demonstrated in his extensive bibliographical survey that little basic agreement exists about the precise definition of Radical Pietism.[3] Since the divergent conceptions of Emanuel Hirsch and Martin Schmidt are there pointedly discussed, this is not the place to attempt to resolve the scholarly differences on that point. There is, however, general agreement that those individuals and movements usually reckoned in that camp derive primarily from earlier mystical spiritualism and the teachings of the theosophist shoemaker of Görlitz, Jakob Böhme (1575-1624). These dependencies are revealed in two basic ways; first, by specific citation of writers from the tradition of mystical spiritualism and of Böhme or his interpreters; second, by continual use of language and concepts derived from these movements. Such dependency, however, is not simply formal or theological; the actual practices of the communities reveal their Radical Pietist orientation. Two well-known figures active in the late 17th/early 18th centuries are particularly important for this topic: Johann Georg Gichtel (1638-1710) and Gottfried Arnold (1666-1714). Both served as important intermediaries in communicating the concepts of mystical spiritualism and Boehmism to the later communitarians. Arnold's voluminous writings served as source books for the emerging movements; Gichtel, who influenced Arnold, was a key disseminator of Boehmist thought from his vantage point in Holland, both through publications (among them the first complete edition of Böhme's writings in 1682) and through his extensive correspondence. Both men were repeatedly cited as authorities in the writings of German-American communitarians.[4]

Another formative characteristic of Radical Pietism is its stance of separatism from the church establishments (state churches). Whereas the churchly Pietism of P. J. Spener (1635-1705) and A. H. Francke (1663-1727) sought to reform the church from within, Radical Pietists were either expelled from the churches for their intransigence or left it in protest. They typically referred to the church as Babel or Babylon.

For the purposes of this paper, communities can be reckoned to Radical Pietism if they depend on mystical spiritualism and Boehmist writings, specifically referring to Arnold and Gichtel, and are separatist. Other characteristics such as primitivism (looking to the early church as a model), millennialism (expectation of the imminent Second Coming of Jesus Christ), or pacifism (usually referred to as non-resistance) could also be noted. They will be passed over here, not because of their unimportance, but because other radical Christian groups—not related to Radical Pietism—also claim them.[5]

We turn now to brief sketches of the leading German-American communitarian societies of Radical Pietist persuasion in North America.

Society of the Woman in the Wilderness

The two earliest American communal experiments were that of P. C. Plockhoy in Delaware (1663) and Bohemia Manor in Maryland (1683). The first had Dutch Collegiant and Mennonite background and the second Labadist orientation. Although both the Collegiant and Labadist movements had Radical Pietist connections, their ethnic character was not primarily German and so will be ignored here.[6]

Likely the most esoteric of the early American communities was the band of scholars who settled on the Wissahickon Creek near Germantown, Pa. in 1694. They had been gathered in Europe by the erudite Johann Jakob Zimmermann (1644-1693), famed for his accomplishments in theology, astronomy, and mathematics. For a time he had been a pastor in Württemberg and a celebrated professor at Heidelberg University, but his heterodox religious views kept him from a long tenure at any post. He was a strong advocate of and apologist for the teachings of Jakob Böhme.[7]

Zimmermann calculated that the millennium would occur in 1694. He reasoned that the pious should gather in the wilderness to prepare for this great event and therefore urged the faithful to travel to North America to await the Second Coming. In 1693 some 40 followers—almost all scholars—gathered in Rotterdam to take ship for Pennsylvania. One event Zimmermann had not foreseen: he died shortly before the group was scheduled to leave port. Despite this, those assembled decided to continue with their venture. They chose as Zimmermann's successor his protégé, Johannes Kelp or

Kelpius (1673-ca.1708). Kelp, only twenty years old at that juncture, was a graduate of Altdorf University and the author of several learned works.[8]

On the way to North America the society, now led by Kelp, sojourned for six months in England, where they had close association with members of the Philadelphian Society. This group, led by Jane Lead(e) (1624-1704), was devoted to propagating the thought of Jakob Böhme and had numerous contacts with Böhme's followers on the Continent.[9]

The delay in England meant that the Kelpians arrived in Philadelphia in late June, 1694. Once located in the Germantown area, they created rude shelters, partly in caves, and organized their semi-monastic society. The group called themselves the *Contented of the God-Loving Soul* or the *Chapter of Perfection,* but have come down through the pages of history under the name *Society of the Woman in the Wilderness;* this latter title is derived from the harbinger of the millennium cited in Revelation 12:6.

Tradition has it that members of the society spent a great deal of time observing the heavens, in their eagerness to discern the first signs of the final epoch of humankind. They also devoted their days to practicing medicine and conducting schools for the children of neighbors. It is known that they wrote prolifically, although only remnants of their literary production have been preserved, notably several hymns and a devotional treatise by Kelp, titled in English translation *A Method of Prayer* (1761, repr. 1951).[10]

The well-informed Quaker poet John Greenleaf Whittier (1807-1892) portrayed the life of Kelp and his colleagues in his poem "The Pennsylvania Pilgrim," in which reference is made to Böhme and to the millennialist Dr. Johann Wilhelm Petersen (1649-1727):

> Or painful Kelpius from his hermit den
> By Wissahickon, maddest of good men,
> Dreamed o'er the Chiliast dreams of Petersen.
> Deep in the woods, where the small river slid
> Snake-like in shade, the Helmstadt mystic hid,
> Weird as a wizard over arts forbid.
> Reading the books of Daniel and of John,
> And Behmen's Morning-Redness, through the Stone
> Of Wisdom, vouchsafed to his eyes alone. . .[11]

Although some newcomers were attracted to the society in America, the majority of the original body drifted away to follow more settled existences, or left the community to live as isolated hermits. Kelp died sometime around 1708 and the society ceased to exist.

Irenia

An offshoot of the Kelpian society along the Wissahickon was the little-known commune called Irenia (House of Peace). Its founder was the German scholar Henrich Bernhard Köster (1662-1749), who, with some other members of the Woman in the Wilderness, departed to set up his own community in 1695. These "Brethren in America" built a tabernacle at Plymouth Meeting, north of Germantown. Evidently because of Köster's polemical nature (despite the irenic name given to his group) the group soon quarreled and dissolved. The founder departed North America in 1699 and spent the rest of his long life in Germany, styling himself as a prophet from America.[12]

The Ephrata Community

The leader of the next group to be described had affinities with both Labadists and Kelpians. This was Conrad Beissel (1691-1768) from Eberbach/Neckar in the Electoral Palatinate. After expulsion from a baker's guild in Heidelberg for his Pietist activity, he lived among dissenters in the Wittgenstein and Marienborn areas; he was in touch there with two separatist movements, the New Baptists at Schwarzenau/Eder and the Inspirationists.[13]

In 1720 Beissel emigrated to Pennsylvania with the intention of joining the Kelpian community on the Wissahickon, only to find that the society had dispersed. After some time in Germantown, he entered with a small number of like-minded men a period of monastic seclusion in the "bush," that is, in the thinly-settled area of what is now Lancaster County. It was during this period that Beissel made a journey to Maryland to visit the Labadist colony of Bohemia Manor, then in its final years. He had some thought of joining them but was disillusioned by their lack of spiritual fervor.

Beissel was associated for a time with the Schwarzenau Baptists (Dunkers) of Germantown, who had organized themselves as a congregation in Pennsylvania in 1723, but soon broke away from them. The basic issues were his insistence on following his own revelations rather than relying on the authority of the Bible, his sabbatarian views, and his dependence upon the teachings of Böhme, mediated through the writings of Gichtel and Arnold.[14]

After 1732 Beissel organized his followers into a full-fledged monastic institution, with three categories of members: the Solitary Brethren (celibate men); the Solitary Sisters (celibate women); and the Householders (married couples, some with families). Members of the third group were held to be less highly developed spiritually than those living ascetic lives, even though some husbands and wives agreed to live together without marital relations. The community, often referred to as the Ephrata Cloister, adopted distinctive dress, kept the monastic hours of praise and work, and took new religious names. Beissel, known as the Superintendent, was called *Father Friedsam*.

Under his authoritative direction, the Ephrata Community flourished, numbering over 300 members at its zenith. Some converts came from Germany to augment its ranks, as news of its piety and spiritual attainments spread across the Atlantic. The community also developed a thriving economy, with a variety of mills and products. However, sensing that this activity brought members too much into contact with the world, the imperious Beissel led a concerted retreat from commercial activities. Cloister life was to continue as a stern regimen, devoted to the greater glory of God, not to the increasing comfort and well-being of the inhabitants.

There were several areas in which the brothers and sisters at Ephrata achieved unusual cultural attainments. These were especially calligraphy (*Fraktur*), choral music, and printing.[15] The arts of calligraphy and manuscript illumination were developed to an unprecedented height for America by the sisters at Ephrata. They created masterpieces of design and decoration; these now grace American museums, where they are considered rare, expensive, and coveted items for collection and display. Some of the most handsome were especially designed and ornamented as gifts to Beissel.

Other *Fraktur* pieces were created as music books for the choir. Visitors to Ephrata all commented on the unearthly beauty of the choral singing. The regimen of choir members was even more strict and narrow than that of the other residents in order, according to Beissel's admonition, that their purified bodies might be suitable vessels for the angelic choruses. Indeed, by contemporary account, the sounds they produced from their emaciated physiques were ethereal and transported the auditors to a higher realm. The music was composed and conducted after Beissel's own conception of musical annotation, complete with "master" and "servant" notes.[16]

Early Ephrata printing had been given to Benjamin Franklin in Philadelphia, but this proved unsatisfactory because it was done in Roman type. After the separatist Johann Christoph Sauer (1695-1758) started his printing shop in Germantown in 1738, Ephrata books (including its first hymnal) were published there. However, Sauer became unhappy at the degree of veneration accorded Beissel in the Ephrata manuscripts and soon refused to print for them.

This led to the development of printing and publishing by the Cloister itself. It began its activity in 1745 and already by 1748-1749 it was able to print the largest book in the history of colonial America; this was the folio volume of the *Martyrs' Mirror*, the first German translation of the original

Dutch editions of 1660 and 1682. For historians, the most important imprint issuing from the press at Ephrata was the *Chronicon Ephratense* (*Ephrata Chronicle*), published in 1786. Despite its glorification of Beissel, it is a marvelous historical source.[17]

After the death of Beissel in 1768, leadership at Ephrata devolved upon Peter Miller (Johann Peter Müller, 1709-1796), a well-educated former pastor among the German Reformed folk.[18] One of the compilers of the *Ephrata Chronicle*, Miller was a more balanced and more irenic leader than his predecessor but saw the fortunes of the Cloister decline under his guidance. This was caused in part by intensive settlement in the once isolated region around Ephrata, with its attendant worldly distractions, but also by the war impact of the American Revolution. Ephrata took in many American soldiers wounded at the battle of Brandywine Creek (1777); some of its members lost their lives while caring for their patients when a virulent camp fever swept through the improvised hospital. It is thought that several major buildings had to be burned to check the outbreak.

The last Ephrata celibates ended their lives in the 19th century, so that the Ephrata Community lives on only through some descendants of the householders; they call themselves the German Seventh Day Baptist Church. There are perhaps 100 members today, most of them related to a daughter colony of Ephrata known as *Snow Hill* (Quincy, Pa.). The so-called Snow Hill Nunnery was founded in 1798 as an offshoot of Ephrata along the Antietam Creek in Franklin County. Its name came from the founders, the Schneeberger family. Imitating the organization of the parent community, it had monastic orders of celibate brothers and sisters, and a third order of "outsiders" for those who lived in traditional families but worshipped with the celibates. Snow Hill never became large, having at its peak a membership of less than fifty. It perpetuated the style of singing and *Fraktur*-writing initiated at Ephrata but never matched the genius of the originals. By 1900 the last sister and brother had died and Snow Hill was perpetuated only as a congregation of the German Seventh Day Baptists.[19]

The Harmony Society

Just at the time that the Ephrata Community was waning in the late 18th century, a new movement with many similarities was forming in Württemberg. This was a group of religious separatists who found their leader in the weaver from Iptingen, Johann Georg Rapp (1757-1847). He taught that the Lutheran state church was apostate; true Christians should avoid contact with it. After 1785 his followers stayed away from worship services and communions, refused to have their infants baptized, their children confirmed, and also kept their children away from the schools and catechism classes. For a time, the rationalistic-minded state bureaucracy protected the Separatists from the wrath of the clergy. But when the "Rappites," as they were called, began to refuse military service and were reputed to look to the French upstart Napoleon Bonaparte as their deliverer, the government took strong action, fearing revolutionary ferment. Stubborn members of the sect were imprisoned.[20]

In 1803, "Father" Rapp decided that Württemberg should be abandoned and he proceded to look for an alternative home. After considering several possibilities, he concluded that an exploratory party should go to North America to seek a suitable site. The party of four was led by Rapp himself. After some months of exploration (and contact with the federal government to ask for special privileges) Rapp chose a location northwest of Pittsburgh in Butler County, naming it Harmony. In 1804 more than 650 separatists sold their possessions in Württemberg and made the difficult journey to the New World.

Although the group was not originally communal, through revelation it was decided that the Harmonists should pool their possessions in order to ensure their successful development in America. Early in 1805, members signed a covenant in which they renounced title to their property and pledged obedience to Rapp as their leader. Two years later the rule of celibacy was adopted, but there were still scattered instances of children born to families throughout Harmonist history.

By 1810, under Rapp's strict but inspiring leadership, Harmony had blossomed into a well-housed and well-financed undertaking; by 1814 there were few projects of construction or landscaping left to accomplish in Harmony. Some of the members began to think of the time when they could relax their stringent work schedule and begin to enjoy the fruits of their labor. In this they were proved mistaken, because Rapp decided that Butler County would no longer do as a site. The colony should push into the frontier, the distant Ohio valley in the Indiana territory.

The second Harmony was sited in Posey County in the extreme southwestern tip of Indiana, just north of the Ohio River along a tributary, the Wabash. In an orderly series of movements in 1814-1815 the members, goods, tools, and other property of the Harmonists were transported by boat to the new location. Here again, religious commitment, arduous labor, and good planning made for success. Despite loss of members to the various deadly illnesses encountered on the frontier, the Rapp-led group soon created a veritable paradise in the wilderness. Solid brick buildings, wide streets, vineyards, fields, flocks—all were united in the most attractive settlement west of Pittsburgh. The crowning achievement was the construction of a large cruciform church building in the middle of the town. The new Harmony was an impressive reality.

But once again, Rapp's volatile spirit could not rest on its laurels. He convinced his followers that the site was too isolated, too unhealthy, and not really suited to viticulture. They also came under some pressure from unfriendly neighboring settlers. So, in 1825 the much-tried community moved back to Pennsylvania to a location not far from the original site. The second Harmony village was sold to Robert Owen (1771-1858), a social reformer from Scotland.[21]

This time they settled on the Ohio River west of Pittsburgh in Beaver County and called their new community *Economy*. Once more the hardworking craftsmen built a model town, which to this day draws admiring visitors. The combination of agriculture, manufacturing (textiles), and shrewd leadership brought quick prosperity to Economy, which by the Civil War was estimated to be worth millions.

Rapp's death in 1847 robbed Economy of its charismatic leader, although his successors were able and efficient administrators. By the late 19th century the membership had dwindled drastically; the last assets were divided among the survivors in 1898 and the property was eventually taken over by the state as an historic site.[22]

Blooming Grove

Associated with the Harmonists was a little-known but fascinating colony of German origin called *Blooming Grove*, located near Williamsport, Pa.[23] Its founder, Dr. F. C. Haller (1753-1828), at one time a government official in Stuttgart, was one of the advance party of Rappites in 1803. During the period of search, he came upon the Dunkers or Brethren (the group with which Beissel had been related) in Maryland and Pennsylvania, was impressed by their practice of primitive Christianity, and joined their ranks. It is also thought that he had second thoughts about the emerging convictions on Rapp's part of the necessity of celibacy and Rapp's increasing authoritarianism.

A number of Rapp's followers shifted their allegiance to Dr. Haller. When he located a place of settlement in north central Pennsylvania, some fifty souls followed his lead and more joined later, some from German provinces and some from the Harmonists in Western Pennsylvania. Colonists erected a substantial log meeting house for the congregation, which became noted for its mellifluous singing. In the latter half of the 19th century,

Blooming Grove lost touch with the main Brethren group and became linked more closely with the German Baptist denomination planted by German-born missionaries.

Bethel and Aurora

Other segments of Harmonist membership found eventual affiliation with another Radical Pietist communitarian movement. This was created by "Dr." Wilhelm Keil (1812-1877). Originally a tailor in his home of Bleicherode near Nordhausen in Prussia, as a young man Keil associated with Pietist conventicles, where he became acquainted with the works of Böhme and Paracelsus. He pursued mystical and botanical studies and gained the reputation of having extensive medical knowledge. He migrated to the U.S. in 1831, coincidentally arriving in New York on the same steamer as John A. Roebling, the builder of the Brooklyn bridge.[24]

Keil soon moved to Pittsburgh, where he became known for his success as a physician; he adopted there the title "Doctor," which he used thereafter, without bothering to secure formal studies or state legitimation. Keil was converted in 1838 to Methodism (of the German-language variety) and quickly rose through the ranks as a class leader and lay preacher. His fiery genius and fervent preaching attracted many German-Americans throughout the Ohio Valley but brought tension with the Methodist leadership.

Keil taught separatism, maintaining that withdrawal from the world by true Christians was imperative; to make this a reality he decided to establish a colony along communitarian principles. This he effected in 1844 on land in Missouri along the North River in Shelby County. Many of the settlers came from former Methodist congregations of Western Pennsylvania and Eastern Ohio. A substantial group, however, were former Harmonists.

They had left the Rapp-led colony in Economy in the aftermath of a schism precipitated by the 1831-1832 visit—with entourage—of the so-called Count de Leon (1788-1834), whose real name was probably Bernhard Müller, a visionary and egocentric recent immigrant from Württemberg. The imperious visitor challenged the autocratic leadership of Father Rapp, who had at first been impressed by the claims of Müller. Fully a third of the Harmonists at Economy left with the count, who attempted to establish a new community ten miles away at Phillipsburg, Pa., which, however, soon foundered. The leader with some hardcore followers traveled in 1834 to Grand Encore, La., where the dream ended in illness and death. Most of the Phillipsburg colonists remained; it was members of this faction who were attracted to the new enterprise led by Keil. Some observers believe that Keil was introduced to communitarianism by them.[25]

Bethel, as the Missouri colony was named, prospered. By 1847 there were nearly 500 residents and three years later there were some 650 colonists on nearly 4,000 acres in Shelby and nearby Adair counties; several additional settlements had also been created. A variety of manufactured goods, from plows to leather goods, supplemented the agricultural base. In Bethel well-built houses and a solidly-built church edifice had been completed. Keil ruled absolutely in all areas of communal life—religious, economic, and social. Most traditional Christian ceremonies were abolished, such as the sacraments of baptism and confirmation. Observance of Easter, Christmas, and New Year, however, was perpetuated, and a "May Feast" was held around Pentecost. Keil's birthday (March 6) was a high celebration, as was the fall Harvest Season. An active musical life with both choral and instrumental groups enlivened the community's life and attained remarkable proficiency.[26]

The restless Dr. Keil was not satisfied with these accomplishments and, beginning in the early 1850s, sought new areas to conquer. Possibly the encroachments of new settlements in Missouri worried him. After scouts reported promising possibilities in Oregon Territory, 75 Bethel colonists under Keil's personal direction embarked in 1855 in a wagon train upon the grueling 2,000 mile trip to the far Northwest. Upon arrival Keil rejected the site chosen by the scouts, favoring a wooded location in the Willamette Valley, which he named *Aurora* (1856). After initial hardships, the new colony flourished. Its hotel and restaurant became famous in the Northwest region, as was the musical excellence of the colony's bands.[27]

For a time both Bethel and Aurora continued as one movement in two locations under Keil's tutelage, with a majority of the Bethel population moving over time to Oregon. Shortly after Keil's death in 1877, the two colonies decided to separate; the remaining 200 Bethel residents divided the common property. A final decree dissolving the communities was signed in Oregon in 1883.

The Society of Separatists of Zoar

Another separatist group from South Germany emerged shortly after the Rappite movement. Their original inspired leader was a Barbara Grubermann from Switzerland who met with secret conventicles in Württemberg in 1805. Despite harsh penalties imposed by the authorities—which included imprisonment, confiscation of property, and placing of children in orphanages—the movement persisted. Finally, in 1817, under the leadership of Joseph Michael Bäumler (1770-1845), in English *Bimeler*, a number of Separatists made their way to Philadelphia.[28]

Members of the Religious Society of Friends in that city helped the religious refugees and made it possible for them to purchase a large plot of land in Tuscarawas County in Eastern Ohio. The Separatists raised their first cabins there in 1817, naming the village *Zoar* (the place of refuge found by Lot after he escaped the destruction of Sodom and Gomorrah—Genesis 19: 22-23).

The pioneer situation, the heavy debt incurred for land, and the exigencies of survival pushed the colony to adopt a common ownership of goods. In 1819 the Zoarites entered into a formal contract to pool their possessions. They also agreed, to ease the financial burden, to limit the number of children. As was the case in other communitarian groups, economic success followed the adoption of the communal economy after the initial years of hardship. The combination of hard work, limited consumption, semi-celibacy, and shared goals brought economic and social progress. By 1852 the members at Zoar were thought to have a collective worth of one million dollars.

In 1853, however, Bimeler died—without having arranged for adequate succession in leadership. This led to a gradual decline in morale. In 1898, finally, there was an amicable division of the communal property among the remaining members. Zoar became another small rural village in Ohio.

Community of True Inspiration

The year 1817 had seen the creation of the Zoar Society; it also saw the revival of another Radical Pietist movement—the Community of True Inspiration. In its American incarnation it became known as the Amana Society. The Inspirationists had been organized in the Wetterau in 1714 under the leadership of the former Lutheran pastor Eberhard Ludwig Gruber (1665-1728) and the saddle-maker Johann Friedrich Rock (1687-1749).[29]

The roots of the Inspired go back to late 17th-century France and the Camisard movement, which resisted the forced recatholicizing of the French Reformed Church. Among the holdouts in the mountains, a fervent charismatic element emerged; some of its members escaped to England, where they became notorious as the "French Prophets." (A branch became known as the "Shaking Quakers," from which came Ann Lee and the important American communal movement of the Shakers.) A party of these French Prophets toured Pietist centers in the Germanies in 1711, finding some adherents but even more opponents among orthodox Protestantism.[30]

This is not surprising, because these prophets were given to extraordinary ecstatic utterances, which they understood as the very voice of God, hence, as binding revelations. Excited controversies followed their movements and a flood of polemical literature ensued. At Halle, the center of churchly Pietism, the initial response of the Pietist leadership was cautiously favorable, but this reaction soon turned negative. Nonetheless, some Hallensian students were caught up in the movement and carried it to other regions.

It was in this way that the Inspired reached the Wetterau, where it began its organized form in the Germanies. Both Gruber and Rock became effective spokesmen and trustworthy leaders. Gruber died just fifteen years after joining the group, but Rock provided many decades of devoted leadership. A long period of decline followed his death at mid-century, when members had to make do with reading and rereading the testimonies and prophecies of the earlier leaders (carefully taken down by scribes), in the absence of those with charismatic gifts.[31]

In 1817 two new prophets emerged, a young peasant woman from Alsace, Barbara Heinemann (1795-1883), and Christian Metz (1794-1867). Under the leadership of Metz, the scattered Inspirationists were brought together, with their major center at the Ronneburg castle near Büdingen. Their refusal to perform compulsory military service and insistence on holding their own religious services brought them into continual conflict with the religious and political authorities. Metz became convinced that they must leave Europe and they did so, moving between 1843 and 1846 to a site near Buffalo in Western New York state.

In 1854, in that colony (named *Ebenezer*), Metz received the revelation that they should have all things in common. The innovation proved to be successful, both economically and spiritually, but the growing density of population near Buffalo prompted a move to a more isolated region. This led to a final relocation to Iowa County, Iowa, accomplished between 1854 and 1864. The Inspired named their new home *Amana* ("remain true"). Soon, their 26,000 acres supported a colony of 1,800 settlers in seven villages. Financial prosperity blessed their hard work and craft skills. They became known for woolen goods, furniture, and foodstuffs.

No new prophets arose to replace Barbara Heinemann (who lost her gift after marriage) and Christian Metz, but watchful elders stayed true to the ancient revealed prophecies. Marriage was not forbidden, but it was considered to be a less spiritual state than celibacy. Childbearing was regarded as a lapse in faith, so new parents were relegated to the status of learners, along with the children.

Growing secular encroachments and economic adversity led in 1932 to the rejection of the communal economy. Property was divided among the Amana population under a joint stock corporation. The church society was reorganized as an independent body. In recent years Amana has become a popular tourist site and residents are generally well off financially. Many still adhere to the traditional church belief, although attendance is no longer compulsory.

This concludes the historical sketches of the German-American communitarian societies.

RADICAL PIETIST FOUNDATIONS

It was Emanuel Hirsch who first correctly noted in his magisterial history of Protestant theology that "with every attempt to comprehend any efficacious idea in Radical Pietism, one meets with amazing regularity the person of Jakob Böhme."[32] Hirsch's extended treatment was the first modern theological discussion of Radical Pietism. Recent studies have tended to underscore the accuracy of his judgment. C. David Ensign's doctoral thesis, unfortunately never published, is the best and most complete discussion of Radical Pietism in English. Ensign agrees completely with Hirsch about the centrality of Boehmist concepts.[33] Although F. Ernest Stoeffler, an authority on Pietism, confined his discussion of Radical Pietism to one brief chapter, he included Boehmist theosophy, along with Arndtian piety and Quietist mysticism, as its sources.[34]

As mentioned earlier, Johann Georg Gichtel and Gottfried Arnold are especially important in the transmission of Boehmism and mystical spiritualism. Many Boehmist concepts were conveyed to the Radical Pietist communitarians through Gichtel's publications; he had devoted his life in exile in Amsterdam to dissemination of the ideas of the shoemaker-philosopher. The voluminous writings of Gottfried Arnold were important to the communitarians for two reasons: first, they found there descriptions of the early Christians whose lives and religious practices they sought to emulate; and second, Arnold's works served to transmit to them much mystical literature from several national literatures. Arnold provided the fountains from which they drew the waters of their spiritual sustenance.

The importance of these two men—and of Boehmist vocabulary—is highlighted in a typical quotation from the *Chronicon Ephratense*, the chronicle of the Ephrata society, written to emphasize the genius of the community's "Superintendent," Conrad Beissel:

Before him [Beissel] the wisdom of God attempted to reveal the mystery of eternal virginity in the old countries through many precious instruments, of whom those dear men of God, Godfried Arnold and George Gichtel. . . may especially be mentioned. The latter's success was great, and I may well say that he had borne the light before the Superintendent [Beissel]; but he remained a virgin, nor did he attain to the secret nuptial couch of the Virgin Sophia, where children are born; still less did he reach the covenant household of Jesus Christ, but ended his life in a holy separateness.[35]

The peculiar and seemingly erotic language of Ephrata's members, so puzzling and offensive to their contemporaries, derived directly from the language of Böhme, communicated largely through Gichtel and Arnold, although some of the Ephrata community read Böhme's works directly.

The most systematic of Beissel's writings—*A Dissertation on Man's Fall*—was printed in English translation in 1765. In it he focused on the unity in the Godhead of fire and light, of the male and female principles. Through the workings of Lucifer, God was caused to divide all creation into the male and female "tinctures," although humans had originally been created in the image of the Heavenly Sophia as one androgynous being. Observing the pairing of animals, Adam fell into a spiritual sleep, during which Eve was formed. Through tasting of the fruit, the fall occurred and human lust began. Paradise was lost. It was only through the Second Adam, Jesus Christ, that the male and female tinctures were again perfectly united. In Christ is found an "exact balance of temper, where the male fire continually is clothing himself into water and light, and has crucified whatsoever is not mitigated therein." Therefore, concluded Beissel, "if I want to be united with the Virgin Sophia to heavenly fructification, I needs must in that body, wherein I am dressed, suffer with Jesus before the city-gate, where the reproach of Christ is my honorable garb, and his death my life." Bodily and spiritual virginity are both required for the union with the Heavenly Sophia.[36]

Beissel's successor, the former German Reformed pastor J. Peter Miller, summarized Beissel's teachings in clearer language:

There is a principle of light and one of darkness; their combination makes man, who, created in the image of the divine, resembles it therein. For God has a body which embraces everything. His goodness is the Virgin Sophia, the Holy Spirit. She was raped by the devil and should be cleansed in man; but he [Adam] desired a woman and fell.—After certain periods everything will be in order; even the devil will be saved—although not glorified, for a creature can lose that privilege by sin.—Everything is based upon humility and the sheltering protection of the Virgin Sophia.[37]

Contemporaries recognized the source of Beissel's doctrine. J. Christoph Sauer, the Germantown printer, in a polemic against the Ephrata leader pointed out its bases in Jewish and Christian thought, along with the ideas of Gichtel and of Beissel himself: "But for myself I can never be attached to him for the reason that I know that his teaching hitherto has been a compound of Moses, Christ, Gichtel, and Conrad Beissel."[38]

An early influence upon Beissel had been an academic of Heidelberg, a correspondent of Gichtel's and "strong suitor of the virgin Sophia." Julius F. Sachse, author of a lengthy early monograph on Ephrata, claimed to have found materials taken from Gottfried Arnold as the basis for Beissel's thought on anthropology and soteriology, with some lesser influence from Böhme.[39]

The traces of the influence of Böhme and Arnold are also clearly found among the Harmonists. Very early in the development of the Separatist movement in Württemberg, inquiring authorities documented that the works of these men were in the dissenters' possession, along with the Berleberg Bible with its Radical Pietist glosses. Georg Rapp testified in Iptingen in 1787 in response to a query about which books the Separatists used in their meetings (in the interrogator's paraphrase): "Nothing but the Bible, in addition to which each person had all kinds of mystical books. He has a portion of Böhme's writings. . ."[40] The Harmonist scholar Arndt rightly concluded that a "pastoral letter" from Rapp's hand in 1794 "reflects the strong influence of Jacob Böhme on Rapp's preaching;" the ungrammatical letter incorporated the distinctive Boehmist commentary on the Virgin and Christ's atonement, as well as the typical vocabulary of "tincture," "light," and "fire."[41]

The same dependency was preserved over the years by the Harmonist faithful. One of Rapp's successors, R. L. Baker, repeated this version of the creation in 1857:

> The first influence practiced on man by the serpent's head (or by the evil spirit) was to inflame his imagination in favor of an external helpmate, when he discovered the animals before him to be male and female. Gen. II, 19-20. Just at this juncture the first fall of man took place, by which Adam violated his own inward Sanctuary and his own female function by means of which he could have been (as Gen. I, 28. has it) fruitful and multiply without an external helpmate, after the order of a Hermaphrodite then, and after the order now, see Luke XX, 34-36.

Some Harmonists joined another German-American group in Bethel, Missouri; when many of its members moved to Oregon under Wilhelm Keil, the settlement there was called Aurora, doubtless inspired by the booktitle of Böhme. Keil had given his favorite daughter the same name.[42]

The same orientation is found in the Blooming Grove colony led by Dr. F. C. Haller, Rapp's early associate. A library of some 300 books has been preserved there; it contains a heavy concentration of Radical Pietist literature, with many works by Böhme, Arnold, and Gichtel. The only known book to have been published by the Blooming Grove Dunkers was a reprint of a universalist treatise by Christoph Schütz. (It was from the Radical Pietist writings of Schütz' that the Harmonist symbol, the Golden Rose, was derived.)[43]

These quotations and references from Ephrata, the Harmonists, and from Blooming Grove can stand for many others from the German-American communitarian societies whose histories have been sketched earlier. One possible exception to this dependence upon Böhme, Gichtel, and Arnold might be thought to be the Community of True Inspiration (Amana), based as it was on the belief by members that their leaders derived direct revelations from God. However, these leaders were also profoundly impacted by Radical Pietist ideas and their converts came from that milieu. Eberhard Ludwig Gruber, for example, was directly influenced by the chiliastic ideas of the Philadelphians in Germany (the Petersens and others), which led to his dismissal by the church authorities in Württemberg. The leading American scholar of the Amana Society, Jonathan G. Andelson, has convincingly demonstrated the Inspirationists' dependence upon Böhme, with particular reference to their attitude about marriage; he has documented specific references to Radical Pietist writers in the Inspired literature.[44]

The point is clear: the spiritual and theological foundations of these communities are found in the writings of mystical spiritualists and Jakob Böhme. From this base came the separatist stance that led to confrontations with the state and church. It was this that led them to their harsh criticisms of traditional church life into which they had been born. From this base they were encouraged to seek to follow in the footsteps of the "first and best Christians."

It is only by comprehending this foundation that their exaltation of celibacy and disparagement (if not complete rejection) of marriage and childbearing may be understood. The language of their religious discourses and especially of their hymns is clearly taken from the Boehmist and mystical vocabularies; to this day that language (with its arcane and seemingly erotic imagery) has usually been misunderstood or found so peculiar that it has been ignored.

Only to the degree that communitarian scholarship penetrates the abstruse depths of theosophy and mysticism will it be able to gain a working understanding of the motivations, practices, and goals of these early Radical Pietist communities of German-American origin.[45]

APPENDIX

Examples of Christian Communitarian Societies

Radical Reformation Communitarians
Hutterian Brethren (1528)
Polish Brethren (1569)
Society of Brothers (1920)
Koinonia Farm (1942)
Agape Community (1947)
Reba Place Fellowship (1957)
Plow Creek Fellowship (1971)
Fellowship of Hope (1971)
New Covenant Fellowship (1972)

Radical Pietist Communitarians
Bohemia Manor / Labadists (1683)
Philadelphian Society (1694)
Society of the Woman in the Wilderness (1694)
Renewed Moravian Church (1727)
Ephrata Community (1732)
Trevecka Family (1751)
Blooming Grove (1804)
Harmony Society (1805)
Separatists of Zoar (1817)
Community of True Inspiration / Amana (1843)
Bethel and Aurora (1844-1855)
Bishop Hill Colony (1846)

Radical Puritan Communitarians
Diggers (1649)
United Society of Believers / Shakers (1787)
Jerusalem (1788)
Brook Farm (1841)
Hopedale Community (1842)
Oneida Community (1848)
Cokelers (1850)

Radical Christian Communitarians
Doukhobors (1750)
Jesus Families (1927)
Catholic Worker (1933)

Holy Apostles Community of Aiyetoro (1947)
Zion's Order (1951)
Ecumenical Institute (1962)
Church of the Redeemer (1965)
Padanaram (1966)
Movement for a New Society (1971)
Sojourners / Post-American (1971)
New Creation Christian Community (1973)

NOTES

[1]An earlier version of this article was publ. in *Pietismus u. Neuzeit* 16 (1990): 112-131.—
Arthur Bestor, *Backwoods Utopias: The Sectarian and the Owenite Phase of Communitarian Socialism in America, 1663-1829*, 2nd ed. (Philadelphia, 1970), 277-285; Robert S. Fogarty, *Dictionary of American Communal and Utopian History* (Westport, Conn.,1980), 173-233. The study by the geographer Hermann Schempp, *Gemeinschaftssiedlungen auf relig. u. weltansch. Grundlage* (Tübingen, 1969), 300ff., counts communities between 1663 and 1874, with additional listings of 156 Hutterian colonies; by count, he found only 11 religious and socialist communities in Germany.

[2]Rosabeth Moss Kanter, *Commitment and Community: Communes and Utopias in Sociol. Perspective* (Cambridge, Mass., 1972); for a critique, see Jon Wagner, "Success in Intentional Communities: The Problem of Evaluation," *Communal Societies* 5 (1985): 89-100; a forthcoming book, ed. by Donald E. Pitzer, *America's Communal Utopias: The Developmental Process*, will argue that communal living is a generic social mechanism available to all religious and secular movements, which is sometimes adopted in a formative stage as a means of survival.

[3]Hans Schneider, "Der radikale Pietismus in der neueren Forschung," *Pietismus u. Neuzeit* 8 (1982): 15-42, and 9 (1983): 117-151, esp. 17-31.

[4]The growing lit. on Arnold is tracked in a spec. edition of the bibliogr. listings in each issue of *Pietismus u. Neuzeit*. His importance is only slowly being recognized outside of Germany. A recent article begins: "The name of Gottfried Arnold is hardly a household word in the English-speaking world."—Frank Roberts, "Gottfried Arnold on Historical Under-standing: An Early Pietist Approach," *Fides et Historia* 14 (Spring-Summer 1982): 50-59. The article is a summary of the author's diss., "Gottfried Arnold as a Historian of Christianity: A Reappraisal of the *Unparteiische Kirchen-u. Ketzerhistorie*" (Vanderbilt Univ., 1973). Gichtel is even less known; the most recent longer article on Pietism in a reference work—F. E. Stoeffler, "Pietism," *The Encyclopedia of Religion*, ed. Mircea Eliade (New York, 1987), 11: 324ff.—fails to mention him.

[5]A discussion of many of these points is found in Donald F. Durnbaugh, "Work and Hope: The Spirituality of the Radical Pietist Communitarians," *Church History* 39 (1970): 72-90. A longer treatment, although hampered by an inadequate definition of Radical Pietism, is Delburn Carpenter, *The Radical Pietists: Celibate Communal Societies Established in the U.S. before 1820* (New York, 1975). See also Victor Peter, "The German Pietists: Spiritual Mentors of the German Communal Settlements in America," *Communal Societies* 1 (1981): 55-66.

[6]There are two monographs on the Plockhoy colony, both containing his writings: Leland Harder and Marvin Harder, *Plockhoy from Zurik-See: The Study of a Dutch Reformer in*

Puritan England and Colonial Amercia (Newton, Kans., 1972) and Jean Seguy, *Utopie Cooperative et Oecumenisme: Pieter Cornelisz Plockhoy van Zurik-See, 1620-1700* (Paris, 1968). See also the important article by Irvin B. Horst, "Pieter Cornelis Plockhoy: An Apostle of the Collegiants," *Mennonite Quarterly Review* 23 (1949): 161-185. The best study of Bohemia Manor is still Bartlett B. James, *The Labadist Colony in Maryland* (Baltimore, 1899), *Johns Hopkins Univ. Studies in Hist. and Pol. Science*, 17, no. 6, repr. (New York, 1978); see also Ernest I. Green, "The Labadists of Colonial Maryland," *Communal Societies* 8 (1988): 104-121. On Labadie, see Trevor J. Saxby, *The Quest for the New Jerusalem: Jean de Labadie and the Labadists, 1610-1740* (Amsterdam, 1987).

[7]On Zimmermann, see the standard church histories of Württemberg; his writings are listed in Gottfried Mälzer, *Die Werke der württ. Pietisten des 17. u. 18. Jhs.* (Berlin/New York, 1972), 398-404; Martin Brecht, "Chiliasmus in Württemberg im 17. Jh.," in *Pietismus u. Neuzeit* 17 (1988): 36-79; Information also in K. K. Klein, "Magister Johannes Kelpius Transylvanus, der Heilige u. Dichter vom Wissahickon in Pennsylvanien," in *Festschrift seiner Hochwürden D. Dr. Friedrich Teutsch* (Hermannstadt, 1931), 57-77.

[8]The most recent extensive study of Kelp and his community is Willard M. Martin, "Johannes Kelpius and Johann Gottfried Seelig: Mystics and Hymnists on the Wissahickon," diss. (Pennsylvania State Univ., 1973); this replaces the earlier discussion of Kelp in Julius F. Sachse, *The German Pietists of Provincial Pennsylvania* (Philadelphia: author, 1895), repr. (New York, 1970). Sachse trans. and ed. Kelp's diary: *The Diarium of Magister Johannes Kelpius* (Lancaster, 1917). See also Elizabeth W. Fisher, " 'Prophecies and Revelations': German Cabbalists in Early Pennsylvania," *Pennsylvania Magazine of Hist. and Biogr.* 109 (1985): 199-233; Klaus Deppermann, "Pennsylvanien als Asyl des frühen dt. Pietisten," *Pietismus u. Neuzeit* 10 (1984): 190-212; Ernest L. Lashlee, "Johannes Kelpius and His Woman in the Wilderness," in *Glaube, Geist, Geschichte: Festschr. f. Ernst Benz*, eds. G. Mueller and W. Zeller (Leiden, 1967), 327-338; and Ernst Benz, *Die protestant. Thebais* (Wiesbaden, 1963).

[9]Nils Thune, *The Behmenists and the Philadelphians* (Uppsala, 1948) and Serge Hutin, *Les Disciples anglais de Jacob Böhme* (Paris: Dance, 1960).

[10]Oswald Seidensticker, "The Hermits of the Wissahickon," *Pennsylvania Magazine of Hist. and Biogr.* 11 (1887): 427-441; E. Gordon Alderfer, ed., *A Method of Prayer* (New York, 1951). For a more recent discussion of Kelp's writings, see Harold Jantz, "German-American Literature: Some Further Perspectives," in *America and the Germans: An Assessment of a Three-Hundred-Year History*, eds. Frank Trommler and Joseph McVeigh (Philadelphia, 1985), vol. I, 283-293.

[11]John Greenleaf Whittier, *The Pennsylvania Pilgrim and Other Poems* (Boston, 1872), 33f. "Behmen's Morning-Redness" refers to Böhme's major work, commonly referred to as *Aurora*.

[12]There is extensive reference to Köster in Sachse, *German Pietists* (1895), esp. 251-278. See also Alfred A. Vagts, *Deutsch-Amerik. Rückwanderung* (Heidelberg, 1960), 64, based on Johann Chr. Adelung, *Geschichte der menschl. Narrheit* (Leipzig, 1785), 5: 86ff.

[13]An unsympathetic biography is Walter C. Klein, *Johann Conrad Beissel, Mystic and Martinet* (Philadelphia, 1972). A more favorable portrayal is found in the more recent study of the Ephrata Community, E. Gordon Alderfer, *The Ephrata Commune: An Early American Counterculture* (Pittsburgh, 1985). See also Guy T. Hollyday and Christoph E. Schweitzer, "The Present Status of Conrad Beissel/Ephrata Research," *Monatshefte* 68 (1976): 171-178. Recent research indicates that the given name was "Georg Conrad" rather than the accustomed American usage of "Johann Conrad." Geneal. information on Beissel's parentage

and relations (although flawed by errors) is found in James D. Beissel, Sr., ed., *The Wedge: Beisel/ Beissel Internat. Genealogy* (Ephrata, 1990), esp. 251-283.

[14]The schism is described in the sourcebook, Donald F. Durnbaugh, ed., *The Brethren in Colonial America* (Elgin, Ill., 1967), 63-89.

[15]There is an extensive bibliogr. on Ephrata: for works up to 1943 consult Eugene E. Doll, "Sources for the Hist. of the Ephrata Cloisters," in *The Ephrata Cloisters: An Annotated Bibliogr.*, eds. Eugene E. Doll and Anneliese M. Funke (Philadelphia, 1944), 3-81; the most recent listing is Philip N. Dare, *American Communes to 1860: A Bibliogr.* (New York, 1990), 61-71. A useful early listing was: Emil Meynen, ed., *Bibliogr. on German Settlements in Colonial North America, Esp. the Pennsylvania Germans and Their Descendants* (Leipzig, 1937), 108ff., repr. with rev. title *Bibliogr. on the Colonial Germans of N. America* (Baltimore, 1982).—There is an extensive lit. on Ephrata's cultural accomplishments, all noted favorably by contemporary observers. More recent studies: Betty Jean Martin, "The Ephrata Cloister and Its Music, 1732-1785: The Cultural, Religious, and Bibliogr. Background," diss. (Univ. of Maryland, 1974); Russell P. Getz, "Music in the Ephrata Cloister," *Communal Societies* 2 (1982): 27-38; Frank M. Sommer, "German Language Books, Periodicals, & Manuscripts," in *Arts of the Pennsylvania Germans*, ed. Scott F. Swank and others (New York/London, 1983), 265-304; Frederick S. Weiser and Howell J. Heaney, eds., *The Pennsylvania German Fraktur of the Free Library of Pennsylvania* (Breinigville, Pa., 1976). See also the earlier monographs by John Joseph Stoudt, *Pennsylvania German Folk Art: An Interpretation* (Allentown, 1966) and Donald A. Shelley, *The Fraktur-Writings or Illuminated Manuscripts of the Pennsylvania Germans* (Allentown, 1958-1959), as well as their other writings on the subject.

[16]Thomas Mann was intrigued by Beissel's music theories and incorporated material on them in his *Doctor Faustus*, trans. H. T. Lowe-Porter (New York, 1948). The material was taken, almost verbatim, from Hans Theodore David, "Hymns and Music of the Pennsylvania Seventh-Day Baptists," *American-German Review* 9 (June 1943): 4ff. Mann commented that the memory of Beissel "haunts the whole novel"—*The Story of a Novel*, trans. Richard and Clara Winston (New York: 1961), 39f., 63f. The definitive study of the relationship is Theodor Karst, "Johann Conrad Beissel in Th. Manns Roman *Doktor Faustus*," *Jahrbuch der Dt. Schillergesellschaft* 12 (1968): 532-585; the most recent treatment is Christian Bunners, "The Birth of Freedom out of Bondage: Th. Mann and the German-American Poet-Composer Johann Conrad Beissel," *The Hymn* 36 (July 1985): 7-10.

[17]Sauer's version of the dispute is given in a pamphlet, publ. in English trans. in Samuel W. Pennypacker, "The Quarrel between Chr. Sower, the Germantown Printer, and Conrad Beissel, Founder and Vorsteher of the Cloister at Ephrata," *Pennsylvania Magazine of Hist. and Biogr.* 12 (1888): 76-96, repr. in *Pennsylvania in American Hist.* (Philadelphia: W. J. Campbell, 1910), 327-363. A bibliogr. of Sauer's imprints, containing the Ephrata material, is Felix Reichmann, ed., *Christopher Sower, Sr., 1694-1758* (Philadelphia, 1943); this has been supplanted by more complete listings included in Karl J. R. Arndt and Reimer C. Eck, eds., *The First Century of German Language Printing in the U.S.A.* (Göttingen, 1989).—Most Ephrata imprints are listed in Anneliese M. Funke, "Ephrata, The Printing Press of the Brotherhood, 1745-1794," in Doll and Funke, *Ephrata Cloisters* (1944), 83-128; they are included in Arndt and Eck, *First Century* (1990). Lamech and Agrippa (pseud.), *Chronicon Ephratense; A Hist. of the Community of Seventh Day Baptists at Ephrata, Lancaster County, Penn'a*, trans. J. Max Hark (Lancaster, 1889), repr. (New York, 1972). There is a considerable lit. on the Anabaptist martyrology; the most recent discussion is in John S. Oyer and Robert S. Kreider, *Mirror of the Martyrs* (Intercourse, Pa., 1990).

[18]On Miller, see the articles by Leo Schelbert, "From Reformed Preacher to Pietist Monk in Pennsylvania: The Spiritual Path of Joh. P. Müller," in *Germany and America: Essays on Problems of Internat. Relations and Immigration,* ed. Hans L. Trefousse (New York, 1980), 139-150, and "Die Stimme eines Einsamen in Zion: Ein unbekannter Brief von Bruder Jaebez aus Ephrata, Pa., aus dem Jahre 1743," *Zeitschr. f. Kirchengeschichte* 85 (1974): 78-86.

[19]The most complete study of Snow Hill is Charles W. Treher, *Snow Hill Cloister* (Allentown, 1968).

[20]The authoritative historian of the Harmonist movement was Karl J. R. Arndt; see his *George Rapp's Harmony Society, 1785-1847* (Philadelphia, 1965) and *George Rapp's Successors and Material Heirs* (Cranbury, N.J., 1971). He has also edited a series of lengthy source books on the Harmonists (1975-1987); these and other references are listed in Dare, *American Communes* (1990), 93-104. For the German beginnings, Arndt drew extensively on Julian Rauscher, "Des Separatisten G. Rapps Leben u. Treiben," *Theol. Studien aus Württemberg* 6 (1885): 253-313.

[21]Although Owen's own communal experiment there, New Harmony, failed, it succeeded in bringing many well-educated reformers to Indiana, whose influence in social and educational improvements was large; see Bestor, *Backwoods Utopias* (1970), 202-229. Interestingly, the famous theologian Paul Tillich (known as a religious socialist) chose to have his ashes buried in New Harmony; a memorial park is dedicated to him. The relationship is described in Rüdiger Reitz, *Paul Tillich u. New Harmony* (Stuttgart, 1970).

[22]The story of the dissolution of Economy is told in a self-serving book by one of the last trustees, John S. Duss, *The Harmonists: A Personal History* (Harrisburg, 1943); see the withering review by Karl J. R. Arndt—*Western Pennsylvania Hist. Magazine* 26 (Sept.-Dec. 1943): 109-116. A detailed description of the hist. site is found in Charles Morris Stotz, "Threshold of the Golden Kingdom: The Village of Economy and Its Restoration," in *Winterthur Portfolio 8*, ed. Ian M. G. Quimby (Charlottesville, 1973), 133-169.

[23]The standard account is still Joseph H. McMinn, *Blooming Grove . . ., A Hist. of the Congregation of German Dunkers Who Settled in Lycoming County, Pa., 1805. . .* (Williamsport, Pa. 1901); a more recent description is Donald F. Durnbaugh, "The Blooming Grove Colony," *Pennsylvania Folklife* 25 (Spring 1976): 18-23.

[24]For Keil's early life see Carl G. Koch, *Lebenserfahrungen* (Cleveland, 1871); a basic work on his communities is Robert J. Hendricks, *Bethel and Aurora: An Experiment in Communism as Practical Christianity with Some Account of Past and Present Ventures in Collective Living* (New York, 1933; repr. 1971); a good summary is A.J.F. Ziegelschmid, "Dr. Wilhelm Keil's Communal Enterprises: Bethel, Mo./Aurora, Or.," *American-German Review* 14 (Dec. 1947): 28ff.

[25]Karl J.R. Arndt, ed., *Economy on the Ohio, 1826-1834: The Harmony Society During the Period of Its Greatest Power and Influence and Its Messianic Crisis: George Rapp's Third Harmony: A Documentary Hist.* (Worcester, 1984). See also his articles: "The Genesis of Germantown, Louisiana: or the Mysterious Past of Louisiana's Mystic, Count de Leon," *Louisiana Hist. Quarterly* 24 (April 1941): 378-433, and "The Life and Mission of Count Leon," *American-German Review* 6 (June 1940): 5ff., 36f., (Aug. 1940): 15ff.

[26]See the booklets ed. by Adolf E. Schroeder, publ. on behalf of the Bethel community (c. 1990): *Bethel German Community, 1844-1883: "Viele Hände machen bald ein Ende; Many Hands Make Quick Work; Bethel German Colony, 1844-1879: Religious Beliefs and Practices;* and *The Musical Life of Bethel German Colony, 1844-1879.*

[27]There are two basic articles written or ed. by William G. Bek: "A German Communistic Society in Missouri," *Missouri Hist. Review* 3 (Oct. 1908): 52-74, and "From Bethel, Missouri,

to Aurora, Oregon: Letters of William Keil, 1855-1870," *Missouri Hist. Review* 48 (April 1953): 23-41, (Jan. 1954): 141-153. These letters were orig. publ. as "The Community at Bethel, Mo., and Its Offspring at Aurora, Or.," *German-American Annals* 7 (Sept. 1909): 257-276, 306-328, 8 (April 1910): 15-44, 76-81; see also John E. Simon, "William Keil and Communistic Colonies," *Oregon Hist. Quarterly* 36 (June 1935): 119-153; Deborah M. Olsen and Clark M. Will, "Musical Heritage of the Aurora Colony," *Oregon Hist. Quarterly* 79 (1978): 233ff.; Clark M. Will, *The Story of Old Aurora in Picture and Prose, 1856-1883* (Salem, Or.: author, 1972); a popularized but accurate account is Steward H. Holbrook, *Far Corner: A Personal View of the Pacific Northwest* (New York, 1852), 60-69.

[28]The newer books on Zoar are popular treatments: Catherine B. Dobbs, *Freedom's Will: The Society of Separatists of Zoar* (New York, 1947) and Hilda Dischinger Morhart, *The Zoar Story* (Dover, Oh., 1967); an academic study on its administration is David W. Meyers, "The Machine in the Garden: The Design and Organization of the Separatist Society of Zoar," MBA thesis (Ohio State Univ., 1980); the older histories remain useful: George B. Landis, "The Separatists of Zoar," *American Hist. Assoc., Annual Report, 1898* (Washington, 1899); E. O. Randall, *Hist. of the Zoar Society, From Its Commencement to Its Conclusion: A Sociol. Study in Communism*, 3rd ed. (Columbus, Oh., 1904), repr. (New York, ca. 1971); Edgar B. Nixon, "The Society of Separatists of Zoar," diss. (Ohio State Univ., 1933); further lit. in Dare, *American Communes* (1990), 197-198.

[29]From its inception the Inspirationist movement has been well documented. More recent studies are: Amana Society, *The Amana Colonies: Seven Villages in Iowa* (Amana, 1977); Lawrence L. Rettig, *Amana Today: A Hist. of the Amana Colonies from 1932 to the Present* (South Amana: author, 1975); Diane L. Barthel, *Amana: From Pietist Sect to American Community* (Lincoln, 1984); and Walter Grossmann, "The European Origins of the True Inspired of Amana," *Communal Societies* 4 (1984): 133-149; the anticipated monograph by Hans Schneider will provide useful information on the European beginnings of the Inspired. His article, "Inspirationsgemeinden" in *Theol. Realenzyklopädie*, 16 (1988): 203ff., has an excellent bibliogr.; Matthias Benad has publ. material on the Inspirationists in the early period as well, e.g. in *Toleranz als Gebot christlicher Obrigkeit: Das Büdinger Patent von 1712* (Hildesheim, 1983). Jonathan G. Andelson (Grinnel College) is preparing a lengthy study of the Inspirationists in Europe and America, building on his diss. (Univ. of Michigan, 1974): "Communalism and Change in the Amana Society, 1855-1932."

[30]These developments have been portrayed in Hillel Schwartz, *The French Prophets: The Hist. of a Millenarian Group in 18th-Century England* (Berkeley, 1980), and Clarke Garrett, *Spirit Possession and Popular Religion: From the Camisards to the Shakers* (Baltimore, 1987).

[31]More recent studies: Walter Grossmann, "Eberhard Ludwig Gruber über wahre u. falsche Inspiration," *Pietismus u. Neuzeit* 13 (1987): 47-67, and Donald F. Durnbaugh, "Eberhard Ludwig Gruber & Johann Adam Gruber: A Father and Son as Early Inspirationist Leaders," *Communal Societies* 4 (1984): 150-160; for bibliogr. on Amana see Dare, *American Communes* (1990), 19-27.

[32]Emanuel Hirsch, *Geschichte der neueren ev. Theologie* (Gütersloh, 1960) 2: 208f. See discussion on this point in Durnbaugh, *Work and Hope* (1970), 85ff.

[33]C. David Ensign, "Radical German Pietism (c.1675-c.1760)," diss., (Boston Univ., 1955).

[34]F. Ernest Stoeffler, *German Pietism During the 18th Century* (Leiden: E. J. Brill, 1973), 168-216.

[35]*Chronicon Ephratense* (1889), 286.

[36]See the discussion in Peter C. Erb, "Eschatology at Ephrata," in *The Coming Kingdom: Essays in American Millennialism*, eds. M. Darrol Bryant and Donald W. Dayton (Barryton, N. Y., 1983), 19-43; some of the same text is publ. in Erb's introduction to his *Johann Conrad Beissel and the Ephrata Community: Mystical and Historical Texts* (Lewistown, Me./Queenston, Ont., 1985), 16-20.

[37]Felix Reichmann and Eugene E. Doll, eds., *Ephrata As Seen by Contemporaries* (Allentown, Pa., 1953), 123; the passage is from a letter from "K." in Pennsylvania, publ. in the *Berlinsche Monatschrift* (1785) and republ. in *Der deutsche Pionier* 13 (1881-1882): 10-17.

[38]Reichmann and Doll, *Contemporaries* (1953), 26. The comment is from an extended polemic written by Sauer to justify his controversy with Beissel, publ. in English trans. by Samuel W. Pennypacker, *Pennsylvania in American Hist.* (Philadelphia, 1910), 326-363; *Chronicon Ephratense* (1889), 5.

[39]Julius F. Sachse, *The German Sectarians of Pennsylvania, 1742-1800: A Critical and Legendary Hist. of the Ephrata Cloister and the Dunkers* (Philadelphia: author, 1900).

[40]Karl J.R. Arndt, ed., *George Rapp's Separatists, 1800-1803: The German Prelude to Rapp's American Harmony Society: A Documentary Hist.* (Worcester, Mass., 1980), 106. (Later lists of Harmonist books in the U.S. featured the writings of Arnold, the Boehmist Jane Lead(e), the quietist mystic Madame de Guyon, and simliar authors); Karl J. R. Arndt, ed., *A Documentary Hist. of the Indiana Decade of the Harmony Society, 1814-1824: Vol.II, 1820-1824* (Indianapolis, 1978), 440f.

[41]Arndt, *Separatists* (1980), 242ff.

[42]Robert J. Hendricks, *Bethel and Aurora* (New York, 1933); John F. Simon, "William Keil and the Aurora Colony," *Oregon Hist. Quarterly* 36 (1935). "Dr." Keil had been a student of "mysticism, theosophy, alchemy, magnetism, botany, and his *Universaltinktur*"—A.J.F. Ziegelschmid, "Keil's Communal Enterprises: Bethel, Mo. and Aurora, Or.," *The American-German Review* 13 (Dec. 1947): 28ff.; Elizabeth Siber White, "The *Wiedergeburt* in the Religion of the Zoarites," MA thesis, (Western Michigan Univ., 1985).

[43]Durnbaugh, *Blooming Grove* (1976), 20f.; Arndt, *Separatists* (1980), 84.

[44]Jonathan G. Andelson, "The Gift to Be Simple: Celibacy and Religious Enthusiasm in the Community of True Inspiration," *Communal Societies* 5 (1985): 1-32, esp. 5-13. Older studies of the Inspired mention Böhme in the context of the mystical background of the movement, without documenting specific influence: William R. Perkins and Barthinius L. Wick, *Hist. of the Amana Society of Community of True Inspiration* (Iowa City, 1891), 4f.; Martha M. H. Shambaugh, *Amana That Was and Amana That Is*, (Iowa City, 1932), 295.

[45]Even a rather well-informed overview still overemphasizes the commercial motivations of the Pietist communities: Klaus J. Hansen, "Auf der Suche nach der Neuen Welt. Gütergemeinschaftsexperimente in Nordamerika," in *Allen gehöret Alles: Das Experiment Gütergemeinschaft vom 16. Jh. bis heute*, ed. Hans-Jürgen Görtz (München, 1984).

4 | From the Wetterau to Ebenezer and Amana: A Demographic Profile of the Inspirationists in America

Jonathan G. Andelson, *Grinnell College*

Among the more than five million Germans who immigrated to the United States in the 19th century was a small group of religious separatists called *Die Gemeinde der wahren Inspiration* (Community of True Inspiration). To escape persecution, approximately 1,500 True Inspirationists followed the call of their divinely-inspired leader and left their homes for settlements in the New World, initially at Ebenezer (near Buffalo) New York, and later at Amana, Iowa where descendants of these immigrants still live.

For several reasons the Inspirationist migration, although small, is of special interest from the perspective of German-American studies. Involving as it did a religious community, the migration was clearly motivated, carefully planned, and relatively well-defined. For these reasons it is also well-documented. However, unlike some other religious communities, the Inspirationists did not come from a single village or even a single region in Germany. Rather, the group was a conglomeration of individuals and families from half a dozen German provinces as well as Switzerland and Alsace. Although it lies beyond the scope of this paper, the process by which this diverse assembly was amalgamated into a coherent whole bears close examination. Finally, the Inspirationist story is of interest because of the strong German character which the Amana community retains some 150 years after the arrival of the first immigrants. German oral traditions, crafts, and even language survive to a great extent, and the religious beliefs and practices around which the immigration revolved persist nearly unchanged— except for the incorporation of English—in the churches of Amana. The Community stands as testimony to the durability of ethnic and religious identity in a foreign land.

Available accounts of the Inspirationist migration are virtually all in the form of anecdotal narratives. These can be found in the writings of members of the Community. In particular, there was Christian Metz, its principal leader for fifty years, whose diary (*Tagebuch*, 1875) is an important source; Gottlieb Scheuner, the group's historian, whose *Inspirations-Historie* (1891) contains an overview based on several primary sources; and there are the letters and diaries of several other individuals. Outside scholars of the Community, including Perkins and Wick (1891), Shambaugh (1932), and Lankes (1949), offer brief descriptions based almost entirely on Metz's and Scheuner's writings. All of these accounts treat the immigration as a brief if difficult and memorable episode in the Community's history which began with a reconnaissance trip which Metz and three companions made to New York in 1842 and ended three years later—after 700 Inspirationists had arrived safely in Ebenezer.

None of the available sources treat the immigration in broad demographic terms. In fact, nearly half of the 1,500 people who left Europe and came to the Inspirationist settlements in America came after 1850, including a large contingent of new members early in the 1880s. From a demographic point of view, the immigration lasted forty years, from 1843 to 1883.

This paper describes the Inspirationist migration to and settlement in America from a demographic perspective. It supplements earlier narrative accounts of this migration and offers a quantitative summary of the immigrants' place of origin, their age and marital status at the time of immigration, and the changing character of their population in America. The data are based on three sources: the Inspirationists' own records of membership; U.S. census records for 1856, 1860, 1870, and 1885; and death records for the State of Iowa. With respect to those immigrants who eventually died in Ebenezer or Amana the data are complete. Those who left the Community could often not be traced; they represent the main gap in the information. Based on census materials, missing data for this period amount to possibly 5% of the total. Lacking evidence that the people who left the In- spirationist communities were demographically atypical, it is assumed here that the margin of error this group introduces is less than 5%.

Historical Background to the Migration

The history of the Inspirationists reaches back well over a century before their immigration to America. In 1714, Eberhard Ludwig Gruber, a former pastor, and Johann Friedrich Rock, a pastor's son, having grown dissatisfied with the state church and been attracted to the teachings of Pietism, came under the influence of radical separatists carrying the message of the French prophets ("*Camisards*") about the ongoing possibility of divine inspiration (Schwartz 1980). The small group of like-minded women and men who gathered around Gruber and Rock at Himbach, in the Wetterau district of Hesse, constituted the beginnings of the Community. Nine of them, including Rock, began to experience inspiration and receive messages from God, while Gruber, never himself inspired, codified the group's creed in a series of writings.

Besides their basic teaching that certain individuals, whom they referred to as *Werkzeuge* (instruments) were divinely favored to receive and share messages from God, the Inspirationists advocated a simple, pious worship of God through Christ, dispensed with ordained clergy in favor of lay elders, performed the *Liebesmahl* (Love-Feast, or Holy Communion) but not baptism, and, of special significance for their future demographic character, held celibacy in greater esteem than the married state. Despite the persecutions visited upon them on account of these beliefs, and also their refusal to swear oaths or bear arms, Inspirationist congregations soon sprang up throughout the Wetterau, and Rock and the other "instruments" began to undertake journeys to proselytize in more distant regions. They attracted substantial followings in Baden, Alsace, Switzerland, and the Palatinate. By the 1730s as many as several thousand people may have been affiliated more or less closely with dozens of Inspirationist congregations. This was mostly due to Rock's efforts, since by 1720 all of the other instruments had lost their inspiration, and Gruber died in 1721. Rock remained a charismatic, energetic, and able leader until his own death in 1749. Thereafter, the principal elders carried on the work of faith in the scattered congregations, but gradually, in the absence of inspired leadership, the size, number, and spiritual intensity of the Inspirationist congregations declined.

Early in the 19th century Inspirationism appeared likely to disappear, when suddenly the congregations in the Wetterau were stirred by a reawakening of faith. Between 1817 and 1820, three new instruments appeared and began to revive the old congregations and attempt for a second time to spread the word of God. Once again, their success met with official persecution. And once again, all but one of the instruments fell away from that special and difficult calling. Christian Metz emerged as the major figure in 19th century Inspirationism, destined to lead the faithful to a new land and to establish there a more intense form of community life than they had known in Europe.

The foundation of Inspirationist communitarianism in America was actually laid in Europe as the result of persecution. When in the 1830s

Inspirationists in some areas were being forced to repudiate their beliefs or face expulsion from village or province, Metz urged them to gather in the relatively liberal Wetterau district of Hesse. There, the Community was able to lease space at five locations (Engelthal, the Ronneburg, Marienborn, Herrnhaag, and Arnsburg, which they renamed Armenburg) to accommodate the refugees. On these estates, the members not only worshipped together but often labored and ate in common, and paid their rent from a general coffer.

A few years later, however, the Community's hopes for continued official toleration began to fade. When on top of tension over the swearing of oaths and the education of their children the landlords raised their rents, the leading elders took heed of a prophetic dream Metz had had in 1826 that God would lead them "through great waters" to a new home "in the wilderness" (quoted in Shambaugh 1932:53). What once was obscure suddenly became clear: it was the Community's destiny to find a new home in America.

Immigration and Settlement in America

An advance party consisting of Metz and three leading elders arrived in the fall of 1842 with the mission of locating suitable land to purchase. Hearing of a likely spot in the western end of New York State, they set out by steamship to Albany and thence by canal boat to Buffalo. Five miles southeast of the city, they discovered a fertile, partially wooded, well-watered tract and, after overcoming several obstacles, acquired rights to 5,000 acres. Through inspiration the place was given the biblical name "Ebenezer," signifying "Hitherto the Lord hath helped us" (Scheuner 1987 [orig.1891]: 194).

Metz sent word that the members should prepare themselves to join him in America. Quite obviously, they could not do so in one large body. Not only did their arrival have to be paced so as not to overwhelm the resources of Ebenezer, a way also had to be found for the less affluent members to purchase passage. This was accomplished by having the members pool their money. The first members came in 1843, most by way of Bremen but some through Antwerp: 65 in April, 75 more in June, 43 in July, and 67 in October. The next year, a large group of 217 arrived in June and a second group (number not known) came in August. Another 100 members arrived the following August, and a small party of 18 came in October. By the end of 1845, about 700 Inspirationists had made the journey from Europe to America. The members who had been living at Engelthal, the Ronneburg, and the other estates were disproportionately represented among this number since their living situation had been the most precarious. By 1846, the congregations at the estates had virtually disappeared. Some of the members who chose not to emigrate drifted away from Inspirationism, but others remained in contact with the Community and came at a later date.

The settlement at Ebenezer was planned to take maximum advantage of the site's resources. Seneca or Big Buffalo Creek ran close to the northern boundary of the tract, and along it the colonists established three villages roughly a mile apart: Middle Ebenezer, near the western boundary and closest to Buffalo; Upper Ebenezer, near the eastern boundary; and (somewhat later) New Ebenezer. The southern boundary of the Community's land was defined in part by the north branch of Cazenovia Creek, and adjacent to it the settlers located a fourth village, Lower Ebenezer. The locations near water were essential for the various mills the Inspirationists erected: woolen mills in Middle and New Ebenezer, an oil mill in Middle, grist mills in Upper and Lower Ebenezer, and sawmills in Middle, Upper, and Lower Ebenezer. In three of the villages (Middle, Lower, and New Ebenezer), the colonists created races to channel water more reliably from the creeks to their mills (Lankes 1949:83ff). Somewhat later, the Inspirationists acquired more land in Canada and established two small settlements there, mostly for the extraction of timber.

In addition to these industrial developments, the Inspirationists utilized the land for a variety of agricultural purposes. They planted orchards in or near three villages (Middle, Upper, and Lower) and engaged in diversified farming on the 2,200 acres of land they had cleared—out of total holdings of roughly 8,000 acres by 1855 (Lankes 1949:50). A contemporary source (H.A.P. 1847:248) lists their field crops as wheat, oats, corn, barley, and hay; and garden vegetables including lettuce, cucumbers, cabbages, beans, peas, and corn, though the lists are only representative. Each village operated its own farm.

The members who did not work in one of the mills or on the farms were occupied with an assortment of tasks to provide for the Community's needs. Men worked as blacksmiths, tinsmiths, bakers, butchers, broom and basket makers, carpetmakers, shoemakers, coopers, masons, and carpenters, among other things. Women worked principally in the kitchens and the large kitchen gardens. The Community operated its own schools through the eighth grade, staffed by its own teachers. Other members served the group as doctors and dentists. The settlement as a whole, and even each village, was substantially self-sufficient, though the Community maintained stores where members could spend credit allowances on a limited range of items brought in from the outside.

Three developments with significance for the group's demographic character occurred during the Inspirationists' stay at Ebenezer. One of these was the formal adoption of a communal economic system, in which members of the Community collectively owned all the land, improvements thereon, and capital. They worked for the general good without compensation and in return received from the Community food, housing, most of their clothing, health care, day care and education for their children, the aforementioned spending allowance, and burial. Clearly, this arrangement made possible and sustained the Inspirationists' settlement pattern in America as well as their ability to send for and accommodate new members.

The second change was the appearance of a second inspired instrument. Actually, "reappearance" would be more accurate, for Barbara Heinemann Landmann had been a leader of the reawakening of 1817, but had lost her gift of inspiration in 1823 upon marrying. Now, over 25 years later, she was "again favored by the Lord," as the records state, and remained an instrument until her death in 1883. This, too, bears on the Community's demographic history, for it was upon Landmann's death that the Inspirationists virtually ceased accepting new members from Europe.

Third, the process of immigrating to America and establishing a communal order at Ebenezer appears to have generated an intense degree of spiritual zeal among the Inspirationists. One result of this, examined in more detail elsewhere (Andelson 1985), was a heightened conviction about the religious merits of celibacy. A substantial proportion of members of the Community who reached marriageable age in Ebenezer never married, and those who did marry tended to have small families. This had significant effects on the Community's population structure that were felt for the next fifty years.

The Inspirationists' stay at Ebenezer was relatively brief. By the early 1850s, it was becoming clear that their proximity to Buffalo, however desirable from an economic point of view, was bringing the members into too much contact with the "world." Also, the need for more land due to a growing population proved increasingly difficult and expensive to satisfy. Metz and the elders again decided that a move was necessary, and again they sent a delegation to search for a new home in the wilderness. Late in 1854, a party brought back favorable reports about a spot in eastern Iowa along the Iowa River which possessed the requisite qualities: water, timber, excellent farmland, and isolation. So desperate were the leaders to relocate the Community that they immediately sent another party to purchase the land. The following spring, the removal to Amana (a biblical name signifying "Remain True") began.

The Community's relocation followed the same pattern as had the earlier immigration. Land was purchased (in this case a much larger tract, ultimately 26,000 contiguous acres), advance parties were sent to begin building villages (which eventually numbered seven), and contingents of members were sent as places were readied. The move was again measured and well organized, and required ten years to complete. By the end of 1864, the Inspirationists had completely vacated and liquidated the Ebenezer holdings, and the population of Amana stood at 1,228.

The settlement pattern at Amana was dictated by both practical and religious considerations. The seven villages were laid out in a 2 x 5 mile rectangle on either side of the Iowa River. At the northwest corner of the rectangle lay West Amana; proceeding eastward, one encounters High Amana, Middle Amana, Amana (the administrative center of the Community), and East Amana, at the northeast corner. Opposite West Amana on the south side of the river was South Amana, and to its east (at the southeast corner of the rectangle) Homestead. The villages were positioned in such a way, it was said, that a man with a team of oxen could comfortably reach any parcel of the Community's property in less than half a day from one of the villages. The leaders also feared that large concentrations of people tended to foster immorality. Size is of course a relative matter, but Metz and the other elders would have thought a single village with all 1,200 members not only impractical but unwise.

The collective economic arrangement of Ebenezer was replicated at Amana. The Community obtained legal status under state law as a not-for-profit religious association called "the Amana Society." As in Ebenezer, the Inspirationists engaged in a mixed economy of agriculture and industry. They erected two woolen mills (Amana and Middle Amana), several flour mills, sawmills, a tannery, and a calico print factory. Again they excavated a long race to bring water to the mills. They raised crops and livestock on the better land and left the remainder in timber.

The Inspirationists' combination of industriousness and simple living proved favorable for material prosperity. By the time of Christian Metz's death in 1867, the Community was well on its way to having a stable economy, and its members a secure and comfortable existence. No doubt these were among the reasons that others still in Europe continued to contact the Society seeking admission. The ruling Council of Elders would evaluate applicants for membership on the basis of their sincerity, religious faith, and practical skills. In the fifteen years after Metz's death, the Council admitted nearly 450 more people from Europe into membership.

The Inspirationist migration essentially ended with Barbara Landmann's death in 1883. After that year, the Council admitted only a scant handful of new members, perhaps because the elders were uneasy about bringing into the Community people who had never witnessed the leadership of divine inspiration. In 1883, the population of the seven Amana villages stood at

1,774. Thereafter, with virtually no more in-migration, the gains from natural increase approximately balanced the losses from withdrawal until 1904, when the population was 1,773. Between 1905 and 1932, the year the Society abandoned communal economic organization, the population fell to 1,365. The remainder of this paper will deal with the demographics of the migration period only.

Three Cases

Before turning to the aggregate statistics, we will consider three families whose experiences convey a rough idea of the spatial and temporal boundaries of the Inspirationist migration. It is, unfortunately, easy to forget, when working with quantified information, that behind the numbers are real people.

In 1835, ten-year old Samuel Scheuner accompanied his parents, already members of an Inspirationist congregation in northern Switzerland, to Hesse, Germany, where they joined other persecuted Inspirationists at the former cloister of Engelthal northeast of Frankfurt. Eight years later, Samuel, his parents and six brothers and sisters emigrated from there to the U. S., to the small Inspirationist settlement at Ebenezer. There his father died, and in 1856 Samuel (then 31) and one of his brothers moved again, this time to the new Inspirationist colony of West Amana, where the following year his mother and other siblings joined them. Like all of his siblings, Samuel remained unmarried, accepting the group's belief that the celibate life was a higher calling. He died in 1861 at the age of 36, unusually early for an Inspirationist.

A quite different story is that of Sophia Foettinger from Strassburg, Alsace. Never married, she came alone to Ebenezer in 1855, at the age of 56, to be with her sister and brother-in-law, who had settled there five years before. It is unclear whether or not she was an Inspirationist in Europe, but like everyone who sought admission to the Community, she was required to declare her adherence to the group's teachings. Eventually, she and her sister's family moved to Amana, where she died in 1872.

Eight years after Sophia Foettinger's death, in 1880, Adolf and Johanna Kaempf and their three children were among a large influx of new immigrants to Amana from Saxony. In Saxony, the Kaempfs had been Methodists. Although the circumstances of their conversion to Inspirationism are unclear, like the other new Saxon members they became fully integrated members of the Community, Adolf being assigned the job of carpetmaker. Their two sons left Amana in the 1890s, while a daughter remained, married, and raised a family of her own. Johanna died in 1899, Adolf not until 1910 at the age of 87.

Place of Origin

The Inspirationists who eventually emigrated to America came from many parts of Germany as well as from Switzerland and France. The significant questions are: (1) how many Inspirationists came from each region? and (2) did members from different regions tend to come at different times during the forty-year migration?

A clear majority of the Inspirationists hailed from the provinces of central Germany. Though Hesse was where the Community originated, where Rock and Gruber lived, where the revival began, where Metz lived and Landmann settled, and where the estates leased in the 1830s were situated, surprisingly it ranked third, behind Saxony and Baden, as a source of members. Then came, in order, Switzerland, Prussia, Alsace, the Palatinate, Württemberg, and Bavaria. Smaller numbers of members came from France, Canada, and the U.S., though most of the North Americans were of German ancestry. The actual numbers and percentages are given in Table 1.

Table 1   **Number and Percentage of Inspirationists Emigrating to America, 1843 to 1883, by Region**

Region	Number	Percentage
Alsace	107	6.9
Baden	282	18.3
Bavaria	40	2.6
Hesse	205	13.3
Palatinate	78	5.1
Prussia	118	7.6
Saxony	467	30.3
Switzerland	149	9.7
Württemberg	69	4.5
Other	25	1.7
Total	**1540**	**100.0**

What hypothesis can be offered to account for the varied contributions of different regions to the Inspirationist migration? For one thing, the overwhelming majority of the immigrants came from areas marked by heterogeneity in religion. Following the Reformation, central Germany became a middle ground between the Catholic south and the Protestant north, a mosaic of pockets of different faiths, not only Protestant and

Figure 1   **Age and Marital Status by Year of Immigration for Inspirationists Born in Alsace**

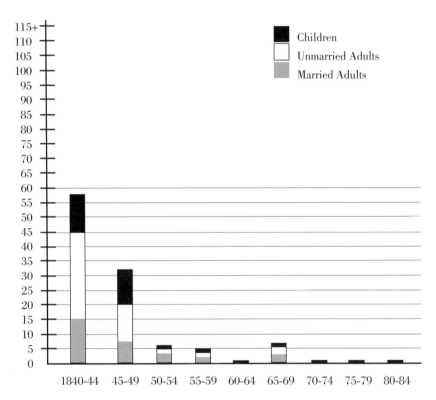

Catholic, but Anabaptist as well, and the Protestants divided among Lutherans, Calvinists, and others. Switzerland and Alsace likewise were divided. In contrast, few of the Inspirationists came from Bavaria; and although a modest number were Prussians, most of these came from the part of Prussia near Hesse rather than from the more solidly Protestant areas to the north or east near Bremen, Hamburg, or Berlin. One might possibly explain Inspirationism's appeal in these regions on the grounds that people here were more accustomed than elsewhere to experimenting with new faiths; or because in a religiously confusing environment it seemed to offer in the phenomenon of inspiration some tangible communion with God. This hypothesis, though, cannot explain the relatively small number of Inspirationists from Württemberg. In this particular case, two charismatic personalities seem to have met the principal needs for renewal of the faith from within the heart: Johann Georg Rapp, who led his Harmonists to America in 1804, and Johann Michael Hahn (1758-1819), the "father" of

Figure 2   Age and Marital Status by Year of Immigration for Inspirationists Born in Switzerland

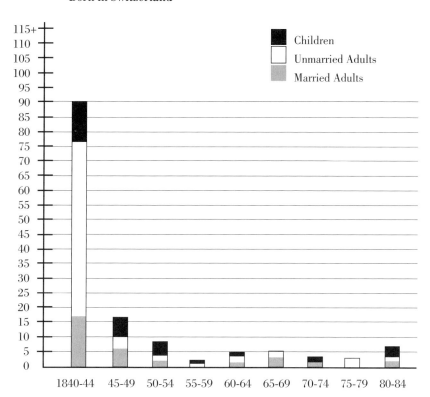

Swabian Pietism, whose followers organized the *Hahn'sche Gemeinschaft* in 1876.

When we correlate the Inspirationists' places of origin with their emigration dates, we find a tendency for people to come from different regions at different times, which raises additional questions. (In about 5% of cases, we know where an individual came from but not the precise date of emigration. The percentages reported below are based only on those cases in which the date is known). For example, 85% of the 107 Inspirationists who came from Alsace had emigrated by 1850, that is, during the initial settlement of Ebenezer; analogously, for Switzerland it is 76% (see Fig. 1 and 2). A lack of religious toleration in these areas is the probable cause. Most of the German provinces show a similar pattern, though less pronounced. From the Palatinate, 66% emigrated before 1850, from both Baden and Hesse, 63% (see Fig. 3 and 4), and from Prussia 61%.

Figure 3   Age and Marital Status by Year of Immigration for Inspirationists Born in Baden

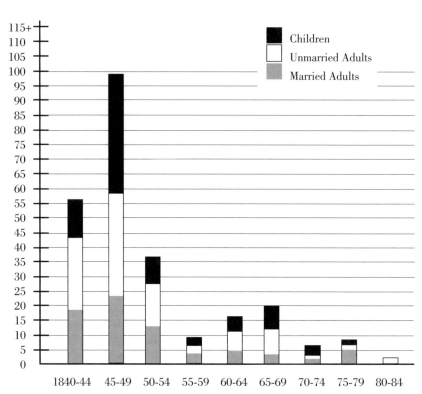

A major exception to the general pattern is seen in the case of Saxony. Emigration from Saxony was relatively high throughout the migration period, but it increased dramatically at the very end (see Fig. 5). In just three years (1880 to 1882), more people immigrated to the Community from Saxony than came from Alsace, Bavaria, the Palatinate, Prussia, Switzerland, or Württemberg during the entire Inspirationist migration. Even without this late surge, Saxony supplied more members to the Community than any other region. With it, nearly one-third of those who came from Europe to the Inspirationist settlements in America came from Saxony. The cumulative contributions of the several regions are shown in Fig. 6.

Saxony was not the geographical center of Inspirationism. None of the great leaders were Saxon by birth. Saxony does not figure prominently in the group's history. Why, then, did so many Inspirationists come from there? An economic hypothesis seems most promising at this point. Saxony was one of the most rapidly industrializing areas of Germany in the middle of the 19th

Figure 4   Age and Marital Status by Year of Immigration for Inspirationists Born in Hesse

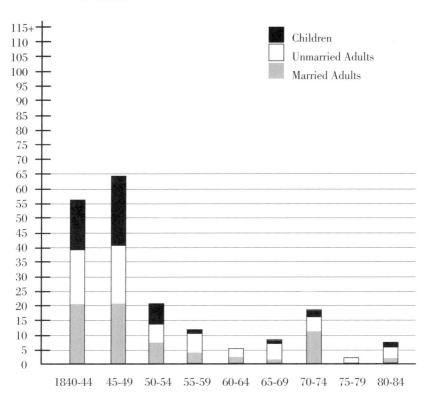

century. By 1870, it was a coal-producing region as well as a textile manufacturing center. And between 1850 and 1910, the population of Saxony more than doubled (Moore 1987:112). Such a combination can cause displacement, dispossession, and alienation in a significant segment of a population. Saxons might have been more likely than other Germans to seek relief from these conditions in a faraway community where moral values were "still strong" and industry had a human face.

Again, this hypothesis needs to be tested. What should be a promising source of information—records kept by the Inspirationists themselves—is of little help on the subject of the Saxon migration, and especially its late surge. The Community's official historian (Scheuner 1891) says little about it, and the record of elders' decisions (which often reported action on applications for admission) is strangely silent on this issue. Oral tradition in Amana today maintains that the leadership actively sought to recruit members in the late 1870s. Especially needed were agricultural laborers and semi-skilled

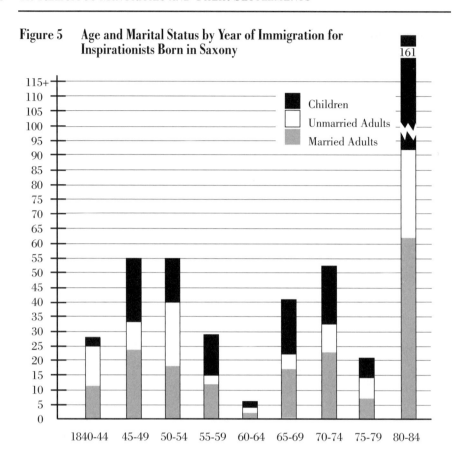

Figure 5   Age and Marital Status by Year of Immigration for Inspirationists Born in Saxony

workers for the Community's two woolen mills. This appears to be precisely what the immigrants from Saxony provided. It is not clear how much contact they had with one another in Saxony, nor is the source of their interest in Inspirationism apparent. They appear not to have come from Inspirationist congregations in Saxony, but all joined the Community when they arrived— rather than working, as some others did, in the capacity of hired hands.

To summarize, the great majority (nearly 84%) of the Inspirationist immigrants to America came from the provinces of central Germany, with an additional 7% from Alsace and not quite 10% from Switzerland. The 40-year period of immigration occurred in three phases: an initial period from 1843 to 1850, during which a few large parties comprising about half of the total of 1,540 emigrants arrived in Ebenezer; a long middle period from 1850 to 1879, when individuals and family groups totaling about 600 people immigrated to Ebenezer or Amana; and a final phase from 1880 to 1882 when 180 new members came to Amana. The immigrants tended to come

Figure 6   European Origins of Inspirationists in America in Selected Years, 1849-1884

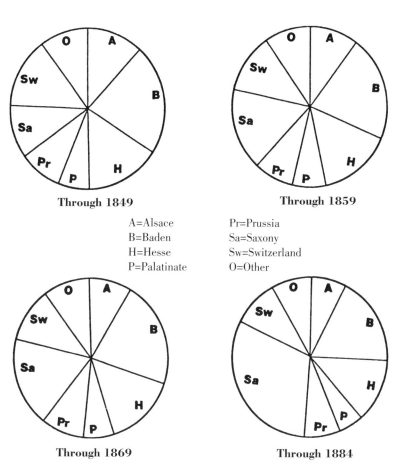

Through 1849

A=Alsace   Pr=Prussia
B=Baden   Sa=Saxony
H=Hesse   Sw=Switzerland
P=Palatinate   O=Other

Through 1859

Through 1869

Through 1884

from different regions at different times. Every region contributed to the first phase, but nearly all of the Alsatian and Swiss members emigrated at that time. Members arrived from each of the German provinces during the middle period, while Saxony completely dominated the final period. Saxony, Baden, and Hesse sent the most members, together providing over 60%.

Marital Status and Age

Figures 1 through 5 identify for five of the regions of origin the marital status of the Inspirationist immigrants and how many at the time of immigration were adults (17 and over) and children (under 17). Immigrants from the other regions fall within the limits set by these five.

Some striking differences can be seen in the marital status of the immigrants from the five regions. A very high proportion of the Swiss adult members arrived unmarried. This was especially so during the first wave of emigration, when the *single:married* ratio of Swiss adult immigrants was 3:1. During the same period, the Alsatians show a nearly 2:1 ratio, those from Hesse and Baden about 1:1, and the Saxons 1:2. The proportion of unmarried immigrants was somewhat lower for all regions for the remainder of the migration period, and in Saxony it fell to between one-third and one-quarter of the total.

Explanations for these regional differences in marital status have proven somewhat elusive. But at least it can be determined that the differences in marital status are not simply due to age differences. That is, it is not the case that a higher proportion of the Swiss immigrants was unmarried because they were on average younger than the Saxons. In fact, the opposite was true; the average unmarried Swiss immigrant was 31.05 years old and the average unmarried Alsatian 31.30, while the average unmarried Saxon immigrant was 29.20 years old. Alternatively, a higher proportion of unmarried Swiss might have chosen to join the Inspirationists and emigrate, or a higher proportion of the general Swiss population might have been unmarried.

Whatever the reason, the demographic consequences of the discrepancy are clear. The Swiss and Alsatian immigrants, being more likely to arrive unmarried and no more likely to marry after immigrating, had fewer children as a group than Inspirationists from other regions. This reinforced the trend noted above (Figure 6) for the proportion of Community members of Swiss and Alsatian descent to decline over the period of migration.

People of all ages left Europe for the Inspirationist communities in America. Overall, about 27% of the immigrants were under seventeen, and most of these came with parents or other relatives. Here, too, we find differences between the various regions of origin and changes over the migration period. Switzerland had the smallest proportion of children among its immigrants (21%), while Saxony had the largest (35%), with Alsace (26%), Hesse (28%) and Baden (32%) in between. The order seems to fit a pattern, and the numbers surely contributed to the aforementioned trend. Over the course of the migration period, the proportion of children immigrating to the Inspirationist communities fluctuated. Children comprised one quarter of the immigrants in the 1840s; the proportion rose to 30% in the 1850s, dropped to a low of 21% in the 1860s, again rose to 30% in the 1870s and then to 41% of the Saxon migration of the 1880s.

There were 83% among the Inspirationist immigrants age 17 or over; their average age was about 36. This did not vary significantly among the various regions of origin; the average adult Alsatian was 35.74 years old, and the average adult Saxon was 36.65 years old. A typical age spread is shown in Table 2 for a representative group of 120 Saxon immigrants.

Table 2   **Age Distribution of 120 Saxon Immigrants, 1843-1884**

Age Group	#	%
17 to 19	8	6.66
20 to 29	28	23.33
30 to 39	38	31.66
40 to 49	29	24.16
50 to 59	13	10.83
60 to 69	4	3.33
Total	**120**	**100.00**

There does not seem to be any statistically significant trend in the age of adult immigrants over the course of the Inspirationist migration.

Population Structure of Amana

Finally, what kind of population structure did the Inspirationist migration, combined with natural increase and out-migration, produce in the Community in America? We will focus on Amana since the immigration was only half complete during the time when the Inspirationists were in Ebenezer.

Fig. 7 shows the Amana population in 1860. The settlement had begun only five years earlier, and the majority of the Inspirationists were still in Ebenezer. The profile is typical of a pioneering community. Young men represent the bulk of the population, and there are very few children or elderly individuals. Fewer women than men were present, except in the 40-to-49 age group, and there is an unusually small number of women aged 35 to 39.

Ten years later, with the resettlement from Ebenezer complete, the population shows a more characteristic pyramidal structure (see Fig. 8). The sex ratio is more balanced, and there is a larger number of children comprising a broad population base. The major anomaly in the population of 1870 concerns the small number of teenagers. Calculating back, this implies a low birthrate in the 1850s. One reason for this is the small number of women in their late thirties, who normally would have had children in the 1850s. No explanation has emerged for the small size of this cohort. A second

Figure 7   Population Profile of Amana, 1860

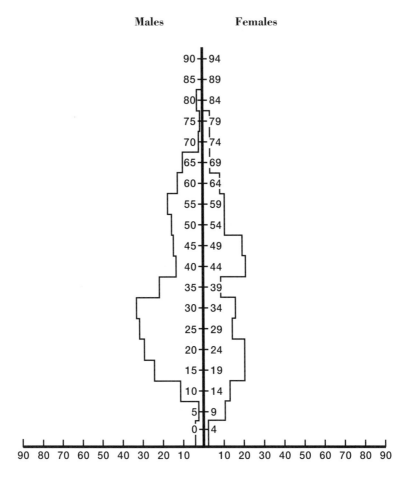

reason for the low birthrate of the 1850s goes back to the high proportion of celibate members in the first period of immigration. A remarkable 44.7% of the Inspirationists born in the 1820s and surviving to adulthood remained unmarried. Had they married, they would have borne children during the late 1840s and throughout the 1850s. This high rate of celibacy was, at least in part, the product of heightened religious enthusiasm associated with the migration and the introduction of a communal order (see Andelson 1985 for a detailed presentation of this argument). One can envision this cohort reaching their twenties and eventually producing the labor shortage discussed above.

Figure 8   Population Profile of Amana, 1870

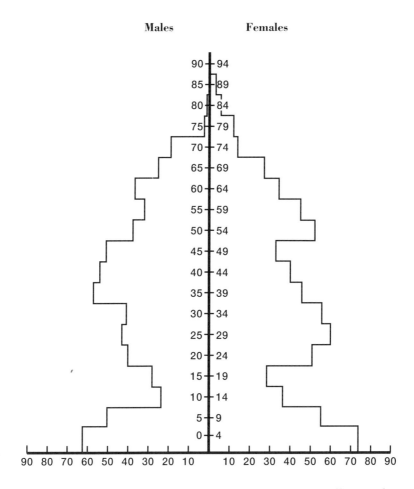

The profile for 1885 (Fig. 9) shows Amana's population following the third and final period of immigration. The Saxons have arrived with their relatively large families, modifying but not fundamentally altering the population's configuration. They contributed to an increase in the number of teenagers, but so did a higher birthrate during the 1860s for the population already in Amana. Also, the small birth cohort of the 1850s, which has now reached the age of 25 to 34, has not been erased, and their small number is in turn reflected in the small number of their children, seen in the constriction in the 0-to-4 age group. In general, Fig. 9 does not represent a stable population in Amana.

Figure 9   Population Profile of Amana, 1885

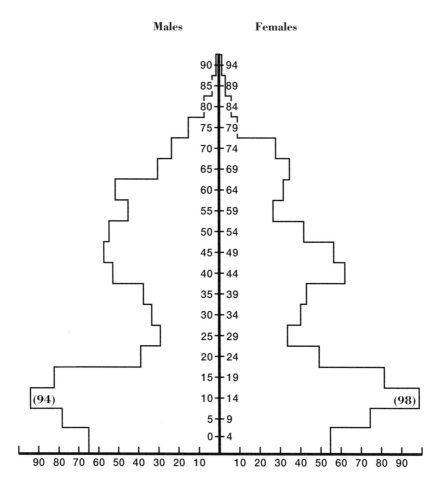

Conclusions

Religious doctrine shaped the Inspirationists' settlement pattern and
demographic composition directly and indirectly at many points. Indirectly, it
influenced the regions from which Inspirationism drew most of its members,
and it affected directly the manner in which the migration took place, the
communitarian and isolationist nature of the settlements at Ebenezer and
Amana, and the high proportion of celibacy, especially among those who
came of age in Ebenezer. The pattern of settlement and the demographic
composition of the community in turn had a series of effects. A low birth rate
in the 1850s created a labor shortage in the communal economy which led to

attempts to attract new members. The arrival of a large group from Saxony in the early 1880s satisfied the need, at least initially.

Although by 1885 the Inspirationist migration was essentially over, the population profile of Amana naturally continued to change. As the various age cohorts moved up the age scale, individuals and the system as a whole struggled to adjust to the fluctuations caused by unevenness in their numbers. After the turn of the century, out-migration became increasingly common among 20-to-40 year olds. The usual explanation for this is that more and more of Amana's young adults felt an irresistible pull from the world outside the Community. A glance at the 1885 population profile suggests another, fully compatible, explanation: that as the large group of teenagers of 1885 reached their mid-20s around the turn of the century, they found they outnumbered the meaningful work opportunities in the Community. In short, they were pushed out as well as pulled out. Over 400 left, probably too many, leaving the Community with an hour-glass-shaped population profile and a depleted labor force. Importing additional members from Europe was no longer considered an option, and in any case was probably no longer possible. Accumulating strains finally resulted in 1932 in a consensus to reorganize the Community from a communal theocracy into a profit-seeking joint-stock corporation completely separate from the church (Andelson 1981)—Amana's present configuration.

The Inspirationist migration is but a small chapter in the big story of the massive relocation of German-speaking people to the New World. However, the coherent and systematic nature of their migration and settlement, their way of life that was directly linked to the kind of community the True Inspirationists forged in Europe, and the religious beliefs they brought with them to America—all this deserves a permanent place in the annals of German-Americana. One cannot understand the pattern of the Inspirationists' migration without knowing something of their nature as a religious community, but neither can one fully understand the Community's history in Ebenezer and Amana without knowing something of the demographic aspects of their immigration.

BIBLIOGRAPHY

Andelson, Jonathan G., "The Double-Bind and Social Change in Communal Amana," *Human Relations* 34 (1981): 111-125; "The Gift To Be Single: Celibacy and Religious Enthusiasm in the Community of True Inspiration," *Communal Societies*, 5(1985), 1-32.
H.A.P., "German Ebenezer Society," *The Cultivator* 6(8), (Albany, N.Y., 1847): 248-249.
Lankes, Frank J., *The Ebenezer Community of True Inspiration* (Gardenville, N.Y., 1949: privately publ.).

Metz, Christian, *Tagebuch* (Amana, 1875).

Moore, R.I., Rand McNally *Atlas of World History* (Chicago, 1987).

Perkins, William Rufus and Barthinius L. Wick, *History of the Amana Society or Community of True Inspiration* (Iowa City, 1891), repr. 1975 by Arno Press, New York.

Scheuner, Gottlieb, *Inspirationis-Historie, oder Hist. Bericht von der neuen Erweckung, Sammlung u. Gründung der Wahren Inspirations Gemeinde. . . 1817-1867* (Amana, 1891); *Inspirations-Historie. . . 1817-1850,* partial trans. of Scheuner 1891 by Janet W. Zuber (Amana, 1987).

Schwartz, Hillel, *The French Prophets: The History of a Millenarian Group in 18th-Century England* (Berkeley, 1980).

Shambaugh, Bertha M.H., *Amana That Was and Amana That Is* (Iowa City, 1932).

III.
CHURCH AND COMMUNITY

5 | The North German Lutheran Church in Cincinnati: An "Osnabrück" Congregation (1838)

Wolfgang Grams, *Universität Oldenburg*

At the "Third Protestant Memorial Church," located at the southern edge of the University of Cincinnati campus, the records go back to 1838, the founding year of this congregation. They shed light on that time and the circumstances which led to the establishment of the North German Lutheran Church, the so-called "Plattdeutsche Kirche." These records also give information about the life of those German immigrants getting off the rafts and Ohio steamers in great numbers at the public landing.

At present, the experiences of these "Low German" ("Plattdeutsche") newcomers, and thus the history of their congregation, are being reconstructed at the Oldenburg Research Center for Lower Saxon Emigration to the USA.[1]

My research is less concerned with the *church* history of these early German congregations than with the social history and the course of life of its members. This in turn, however, is closely connected with the history of the congregation. The one is not possible without the other, but we are dealing with different points of view outlining the research questions and methods.

*

Die Deutschen Lutherischen haben diesen Sommer eine schöne Kirche gebaut, welche sie heissen die Norddeutsche Lutherische Kirche. Diese sind lauter Plattdeutsche und haben sich von den Hochdeutschen, welche mehrst kommen aus den südlichen Gegenden von Deutschland, getrennt.

The German Lutherans have built a beautiful church this summer which they call the North German Lutheran Church. All of them are Low Germans having separated

from the High Germans who are mostly from the southern German regions.
Johann Heinrich zur Oeveste, 31 Oct., 1839.[2]

Zur Oeveste was writing from Cincinnati back home to his parents and
brother. (The original site of the new congregation's church was at the corner
of Walnut and Buckeye [Chapel] Streets in the south of Cincinnati's German
district—"Over the Rhine".) Zur Oeveste's name is number 138 in the list of
charter members of that congregation. What he wrote about its founding to
his family on their farm in Rieste, a small village in the Kirchspiel of
Bramsche, near Osnabrück, is basically a story of separation affecting the
German congregation that had been there since 1822. The (German-kept)
Minutes tell how that separation was settled:

> After long negotiations and mutual claiming and bidding the following purchase
> agreement was arrived at: The committee-men of the South German congregation,
> after lengthy bidding and claiming, have offered the North-German Committee the
> sum of $2,800, provided the latter would altogether leave the church, and on
> condition that Authenheimer's bank would accept the notes as a first payment. The
> rest to be paid in the following installments:
>   1/3 after 3 months
>   1/3 after 6 months
>   the last 1/3 after 8 months
>   all of which at an interest rate of 6%.[3]

The contract includes a copy of the books for the new congregation as
well as the right to use the classroom for teaching the North Germans, at a
rent of $6.

With these agreements worked out, the South Germans and the Low
Germans went their separate ways. What had led up to this point? And what
is it that makes socio-historical migration research take an interest in this
separation?

This act of separation was preceded by ongoing arguments in the
"German Evangelical Lutheran and Reformed Church" that had been in
existence since 1814. (Prior to this, German prayer hours are first mentioned
in 1810 by the Methodist Rev. Behm.)[4]

The German congregation in Cincinnati tended to show dividing lines
from early on. By 1830 it consisted of approximately 60 to 80 immigrants, the
majority were Württembergers, and a considerable number were Swiss. From
1830 on, as more and more immigrants, mainly from Northern Germany,
swelled the congregation, typical Germanic particularism became aggravated.
At the end of the 1830s there were already about 600 members and their
families living "Over the Rhine." Feuding started between the "Low" and the
"South" or "Upper" Germans: people found the doors of the church locked,

sermons were interrupted by hecklers and protesters, people walked out of the service, members walked out of the board meetings, a job advertisement for a teacher was made anonymously and had to be dropped in an attempt at arbitration by the congregation—and there seemed to be no end to it. "Perhaps the good old pioneers enjoyed a fight. . . conditions developed, almost unbelievable."5 And a city chronicler summarizes apprehensively: "After all, there was almost violence."6

Quarrels—that was nothing new. As early as 1833, plans had been discussed to hold two services in succession, to employ two pastors, even to elect separate congregation councils and have separate budgets. Five years later the mutual question in this specific North-South conflict again came down to "whether those who have joined the others can still be regarded as members of this congregation?"7

Earlier this very question had led to a first break up when the Rev. Hauser, the theological spokesman of the disenchanted, left to start the United Protestant Church.

Now, in a similar constellation, the election of a new preacher led to renewed arguments. Party lines formed according to regional origin. The North Germans from Prussia, the Grand Duchy of Oldenburg and the Kingdom of Hanover, especially from the Osnabrück area, vs. the South Germans, who were mainly from Baden and Swabia. The preacher in question, a "compatriot" of the North Germans, the Rev. Dietrich Herrmann Heinrich Wilhelm Möllmann from Börstel Seminary near Osnabrück, was then elected by the newly formed congregation in 1837.

The reverend's father had been a preacher in the Kirchspiel of Menslage, where he tried to establish and spread rural reading societies in the late Enlightenment. He left an extensive library of theological and popular educational books.8 Some of these his son took along when he emigrated to America in October 1835, arriving in New York City on Christmas Day. This young intellectual was no less a victim of the conditions in Germany than those who had emigrated to Cincinnati before him. The latter had been driven away by poverty and starvation, by the pressures of a growing population, by an overpowering British competition for the home weaving and textile manufacture, by inheritance laws affecting the farms, by the decline of seasonal income (the so-called "Hollandgängerei"), by long-term military service, illegitimate children, and mounting debts. And some had been deported, either for crimes committed or for constituting socio-political risks. Möllmann was ordained in September of 1835, but only on condition that he would never preach in Germany. He was driven out of the country by a "clergy surplus", by "clergy unemployment".

At the election in the Cincinnati congregation, Rev. Möllmann was able to notch up 286 votes for a narrow victory. His opponent, the South German Rev. Steinmaier, who had received his theological training in Switzerland, got 231 votes. Tired of all the fighting, Steinmaier returned to Germany for a presumably less stressful life as a professor at the University of Bonn.

Möllmann's position was hampered by the North-South controversy up to the sell-out of the North Germans, which was then concluded very quickly. Three days later, on 20 Dec. 1838, a new committee was charged with finding a location for the Sunday service and everybody was called upon to look around "for a good place suitable for building a church."[9] By 23 Dec., the "assembly of the Möllmann congregation" expressed "general satisfaction" with the settlement negotiations, discharged the committee and decided to build:

> Resolved, that 10 men be appointed to inspect the proposed lots and report back in half an hour.

This entry in the Minutes is immediately followed by:

> Resolved, that the site on Walnut Street between 8th and 9th Streets be purchased. . .[10]

This quick resolve is flanked by a call for a founding committee to draw up a new constitution. All this is read aloud, approved, and as early as the following March the assembly is pleased about the laying of the corner-stone by Möllmann. Nine months later the church is consecrated, just about one year after the split. It was a tremendous financial risk and almost the end of the road for the congregation, as the minutes and the payments made by the members clearly show. Again and again appeals for donations are made, membership fees are raised, members are asked for loans, and, finally, IOUs are issued ($10 minimum, and at 6%) bringing $3,610 from the loyal faithful. But now the building fund was sound.

*

The new constitution of the Low Germans contains some elements that are a consequence of the motives leading to the split. Unfortunately, Para. 3 of the constitution is lost (missing page), but it must have addressed the language issue, as can be surmised on the basis of an amendment in the Minutes of 30 Dec. 1838:

> *So lange noch fünf Gemeindeglieder beim Gottesdienst die deutsche Sprache wünschen, soll kein Englisch in unserer Kirche gepredigt werden.*

As long as there are five members of our church wishing the service to be held in German, sermons in our church shall not be in English.[11]

Next to this long-range language maintenance regulation there are other paragraphs worth noting. For church council membership it was not considered sufficient to be 1) male; 2) living a Christian life, pious, modest, honest and peaceful; one had to be 3) able to speak *Low German*—and for seemingly good reasons:

As a consequence of the quarrels of 1838, nobody can be elected to the church council without a command of Low German.[12]

The new constitution with this language provision was accepted by the 361 members. Their regular annual contributions were projected to total $1,550; 14 members were allowed smaller amounts; 4 were recognized by the council as *bona fide* poor and hence exempt from monetary obligations; 38 failed to pay their quarterly assessment or turned elsewhere for their spiritual welfare. In the end there were 313 North German emigrants founding the "Low German" congregation in Cincinnati. On 23 Dec. 1838 these charter members signed to it that they "indeed think it necessary under the present circumstances. . . to join together in brotherly community."[13]

*

The *Sterberegister* (Register of Deaths) provides demographic aspects of the membership structure of the new congregation. In the beginning there are only a few entries; the researcher could easily know them all "personally". But for the years 1840 to 1847 there are already 432, with 268 of the deceased listed as children who died at a very early age.[14]

Four persons obviously moved to Cincinnati after having lived in other regions of the USA. But 159 persons seem to have come to Cincinnati directly from Germany. Although the place of origin of 77 persons can no longer be ascertained, it is likely that they came from Northern Germany. For 82 persons the exact place of origin is given: only one is a "South German" (from a Low German perspective only) from Hesse; only five are from eastern Prussian provinces, while 76 are from North-West Germany.

Looking at the birthplace entries, if mentioned in the church register, a more specific pattern of origin emerges: 64 of these North-West Germans are from the area around Osnabrück, in today's south-western Lower Saxony. Early in the 19th century, this area was subjected to change of political boundaries. In our context, the "area around Osnabrück" includes—after the secularization of the Prince-Bishopric State of Osnabrück (1803)—sections that became part of the Kingdom of Hanover and Westphalia, of the Grand

Duchy of Oldenburg, and of France. After Napoleon's demise in 1815 most
sections reverted back to the Kingdom of Hanover. The great majority of
these North Germans recorded in the church register emigrated in the 1830s
and thus had been Hanoverian subjects; the next larger group hailed from the
Grand Duchy of Oldenburg. Still, both were from the Osnabrück area, which
supplied about 80% of the membership of the North German Church at
Cincinnati. Even without exact proof of birthplace, at this time, for many
charter members of the congregation, the prevalence of the Osnabrück area is
more than just likely.[15] This is corroberated by Emil Klauprecht (1864) when
he, tongue-in-cheek, describes the separation of the Cincinnati congregation:
"Osnabrück and surroundings now left the congregation to found the North
German church."[16]

The information that can be extracted from the source materials of the
North German Church is significant for north-west German emigration to the
U. S. in the first half of the 19th century, both for patterns of migration and
acculturation. It reveals a strong denominational, regional—and often also
familial—cohesion. In the early days of the congregation the "Register of
Deaths, Marriages and Baptisms" often records siblings, uncles and
nephews, aunts and nieces. This sense of belonging together is documented
also in letters. For example, in 1853 the nephew of J. H. zur Oeveste (an
1834 emigrant) followed his uncle to Cincinnati. The uncle had written home
upon his arrival in Baltimore in 1834 that he had seen familiar faces from
neighboring villages on the usual route to Cincinnati:

> The first acquaintances I saw were Ludwig Aschendorf and Twiefels Menke, both
> from Vörden, later I met Friedrich Hussmann and Gertrud Greve from Stickdeich.[17]

Rieste, Vörden and Stickdeich are only about 5 km apart. And when zur
Oeveste was ready to marry in Cincinnati, the lady of his heart was Regina
Louise Geist from the village of Hassbergen, also near Osnabrück. Thus, the
founding history of the "Low Germans" reflects in many ways the pattern of
the well-known *chain migration*. This chemistry of cohesion proved to have
been important also for later mobility of immigrants within the USA. If
Cincinnati was the large gateway to points west, the "Low Germans" in the
Queen City also became a good-sized turn table to other places and
congregations. The connections with St. Johannes Church on the White
Creek in Bartholomew County, Indiana were particularly close.[18] Presumably
about half of its (male) charter members had first been members of the "Low
Germans" in Cincinnati. The person best known to us there is the often
mentioned J. H. zur Oeveste. But there are also the Burbrinks, Nordmanns,
Vorwalds, Auf der Heides, Trentmanns and other names from the North

German Church register. Gerhard Heinrich von dem Fange, for instance, who had been married in Cincinnati in 1841, visited his former congregation six years later, and for a very special reason: to collect for the new branch among the old "Low Germans" in Cincinnati. He did not come in vain. He was even given the communion-cup to take back to the pioneers at the White Creek.

The founding history of these congregations clearly shows a central networking role of the church for developing and shaping a sense of belonging for the ethno-linguistic community.

*

Since the North German congregation in Cincinnati is one of the early ones it is possible, by means of biographical data of its members, to study the patterns of migration and acculturation at precisely the time when German immigration was just beginning to accelerate to ever larger proportions.

The new congregation's valuing of unity and stability is certainly understandable given the immigrants' willing or unwilling participation in the incredibly dynamic growth of the city that was still a doubly new environment for them: foreign and urban.

In the early 19th century, Cincinnati's "Over the Rhine" was one of the most densely populated districts in the USA. The newcomers were living in very small, very confined flats which normally had neither a heating system nor sanitary facilities. The "Rhine," a stinking canal serving to connect the Ohio with the Great Lakes region, was part of an ambitious development concept. There was hardly anything *romantic* about life on the banks of this body of water. "Over the Rhine" was a place of social commotion and turnover. Regional historical estimates have up to 200 people arrive every day at the public landing, looking for relatives and friends, seeking accommodations and work, wanting to start a new existence, and looking around on the marriage market. Every day many also left the city after having worked there for some time, only to be replaced by continuous waves of new arrivals. In the decade from 1830 to 1840, Cincinnati's population grew from ca. 25,000 to 50,000. Approximately 14,000 of them were of German origin, and "The immigration from Northern Germany in particular was immense." In only ten years the number of houses climbed from 3,000 to almost 7,000. "As if by magic, new streets and districts were created."[19]

Taking into account the social and psychological narrowness of the villages the immigrants had left in the Northern German provinces in the early 19th century, Cincinnati must have been experienced as a Moloch: a mixture of fascinating modernity and threatening social and cultural facelessness and anonymity. This makes the newly founded congregations

Genealogy of Some German Evangelical Churches in Cincinnati, Ohio

Showing congregation splits, major name changes, church locations, and ministers serving the congregations.

Compiled from Cincinnati City Directories and various Church Records and Histories by:

Robert C. Rau
2452 Fleetwood Ave.
Cincinnati, Ohio 45211

12 Feb 1989

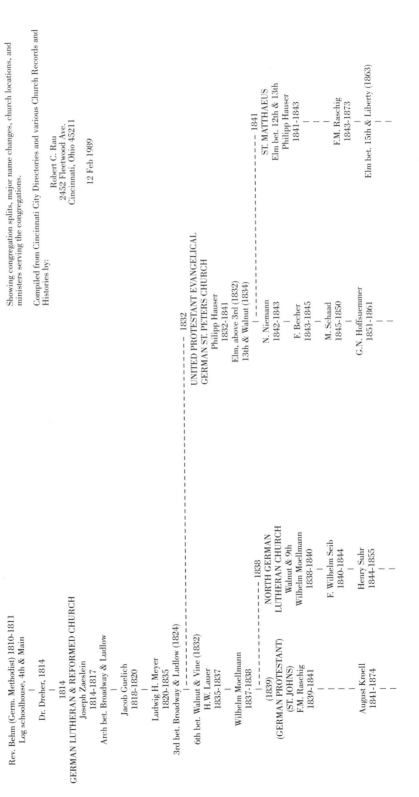

Rev. Behm (Germ. Methodist) 1810-1811
Log schoolhouse, 4th & Main

1814

Dr. Dreher, 1814

GERMAN LUTHERAN & REFORMED CHURCH
Joseph Zaeslein
1814-1817
Arch bet. Broadway & Ludlow

Jacob Guelich
1818-1820

Ludwig H. Meyer
1820-1835
3rd bet. Broadway & Ludlow (1824)

1832

6th bet. Walnut & Vine (1832)
H.W. Lauer
1835-1837

Wilhelm Moellmann
1837-1838

1838

(1839)
(GERMAN PROTESTANT)
(ST. JOHNS)
F.M. Raschig
1839-1841

August Kroell
1841-1874

UNITED PROTESTANT EVANGELICAL
GERMAN ST. PETERS CHURCH
Philipp Hauser
1832-1841
Elm, above 3rd (1832)
13th & Walnut (1834)

NORTH GERMAN
LUTHERAN CHURCH
Walnut & 9th
Wilhelm Moellmann
1838-1840

F. Wilhelm Seib
1840-1844

Henry Suhr
1844-1855

1841

ST. MATTHAEUS
Elm bet. 12th & 13th
Philipp Hauser
1841-1843

N. Niemann
1842-1843

F. Becher
1843-1845

M. Schaad
1845-1850

G.N. Hoffsuemmer
1851-1861

F.M. Raschig
1843-1873

Elm bet. 15th & Liberty (1863)

GERMAN EVANGELICAL ST. PAULS CHURCH — 1845
2nd, b Vine & Walnut

Casper H. Straeter 1845-1846
Robert Clemen 1846
Carl F. Goebel 1847-1851
15th & Race (1851)
Adolph Gerwig 1851-1856
Gustave Eisenlohr 1857-1879
Edward Voss 1879-1910
Andrew Nemenz 1910-1924
Paul C. Bekeshus 1924-1948

ST. PETER & ST. PAUL — 1948
Queen City & Ferguson
J. Peter Wagner 1948-1966
Donald J. Barthelmeh 1966-1983
Robert W. Bonham 1983-

Edward Speidel 1861-1867
H.W. Pohlmeyer 1867-1887
McMicken & Main (1875)
J.C. Kramer 1887-1893
Ewald Haun 1893-1910
Hans Haupt 1910-1933
J. Peter Wagner 1938-1948

INDEPENDENT GERMAN EVANGELICAL PROT. ST. PETERS CHURCH — 1888
Elm & Findlay Sts.
H.W. Pohlmeyer 1887-1901
Emil Schmidt 1890-1902
Emil Baum 1903-1906
F.W. Bertram 1907-1917
Disbanded 1918

Jacob Kaemmerer 1873-1881
Elm & Liberty (1877)
Jacob Pister 1881-1890

PHILIPPUS — 1890
McMicken & Ohio Ave
Jacob Pister 1890-1907
F.L. Dorn 1907-1922
Walter W. Bunge 1922-1923
Gerhard W. Grauer 1923-1941
William J. Witt 1941-1958
Clarence K. Gebhart 1959-1966
Stephen T. Szilagyi 1967-1972
W. Norman McFarlane 1973-1983
Gregory D. Smith 1983-
George T. Siddall Jr. Assoc. 1985-

Wm. B. Rally 1855-1856
Carl Heise 1856-1858
Carl Tuerck 1858-1882
J. Carl Scholz 1875-1884
Hugo G. Eisenlohr 1884-1931
12th & Elm, (1863)

(THIRD GERMAN PROTESTANT CHURCH) (1879)
Henry Haeffner 1882-1923
Carl L. Grauer 1923-1935
(THIRD PROTESTANT) (MEMORIAL CHURCH) (1927)
Ohio & Calhoun
Clifton (1928)
Wesley J. Runk 1935-1952
Herman J. Helfrich 1953-1982
Walter F. Crosby 1982-

(ST. JOHNS UNITARIAN) (1924)
Julius F. Krollfifer 1931-1955
320 Resor Clifton (1952)
Clarke D. Wells 1956-1966
David G. Sammons 1967-1977
Robert S. Lehman 1978-1979
Paul L'Herrou 1979-1987
Richard S. Hasty 1987-

even more important. In the course of life—for the majority of immigrants—each of the church steeples in the "Over the Rhine" quarters of the city helped mark the reassuring presence of a socio-psychological safety net before it was time for the enterprising to look for new horizons.

*

For good historical reasons, the German national anthem begins with the word *Einigkeit*—a reminder that *unity* has traditionally been more of a desideratum than a reality. Having been transplanted to the New World would not change the Cincinnati Germans' disposition in this regard. The original congregation's fall from unity had almost something inevitable about it. For the city chroniclers and pastorial records the cause was clearly a theological one: the incompatibility of a south German liberal and reformed tradition on the one hand and a north German, orthodox Lutheranism on the other. In the words of Rev. Eisenlohr's chronicle:

> I am convinced, that at the bottom of the difficulties there was really a difference between the orthodox and the liberal element, between outspoken Lutherans and the more liberal view of Zwingli.[20]

Whether this retrospective interpretation does indeed reflect the actual significance of theological debates for the everyday life of the early immigrants of 1838 must be questioned, especially since elsewhere the chronicles tell of largely irrational quarrels dating back to the founding of the first German congregation in the 1820s. Varied dynamics of continuous sneering remarks and daily fights, intrigues and hindrances ignored synodal teachings and what the German-language press later assumed to have been a German identity.

In our interpretation the primary fault line was not so much theological in character but rather ethno-linguistic, continuing the traditional North/South differences and mutual dislikes, and finding expression in the communication barriers brought about by the dialects involved. Peace and psychological stability could only be achieved through an amicable separation into a North and a South German church where the respective dialects could "flow from the soul"—or from the psyche.

*

A few years into the life of the North German congregation the tenets of separateness—for the sake of stability through unity—faced reality testing. One notices a cautious process of opening up, religiously, socially, and ethno-linguistically, at first towards the other German congregations. In the beginning it would have been unthinkable to find an entry in the minutes referring to Pastor Kröll from the "High German" mother congregation officiating among the "Low German" renegades.

Another signal of change toward more openness is the increasing number of non-members in the Register of Deaths. Only after a short nine years some 50% of the burials conducted were for such non-Low Germans or non-members.

And as to the seemingly ironclad constitutional exclusion from the church council for anyone not conversant in "Plattdeutsch," there are no references in the church books attesting to either applying or contesting this rule. Nor can it be said with certainty to which degree council business was conducted in Low German dialect(s).

*

The case of the founding of the "Plattdeutsche Kirche" is but one of a thousandfold-repeated but varied process, both within churches and secular associations formed by immigrants. It shows that it might first take an act of separation for a non-homogeneous group of newcomers in order to achieve social, cultural, religious and psychological stability while learning to feel at home in a foreign land and learning the ropes of acculturation and the virtue of tolerance.

NOTES

[1]The church registers from approx. 45 congregations in Cincinnati and south-eastern Indiana are being examined there, thanks to the cooperation of the Indiana Hist. Soc. and the Ohio State Library where the books are preserved on microfiche. (Our quotes from the records refer to these documents.) The data included in the church registers at the time are recorded also in Oldenburg in data bank. They provide raw data for an information data file on emigration as well as for community studies, cultural-hist. analyses and interpretations—integrated into qualitative methods and biographical source material.

[2]Copies of the letters are also at the Bartholomew Co. Hist. Soc., Columbus, Ind., the Indiana Hist. Soc., Indianapolis, and Oldenburg Univ. See also: Antonius Holtmann, ed., *"...ferner tuhe ich euch zu wissen..." Briefe des Johann Heinrich zu Oeveste aus Americka* (1834-1876), (Bremen, 1995), and the Holtmann paper in this volume.

[3]"Protokolle des Kirchenraths u. der Gemeindeversammlungen der Norddt. Luth. Kirche seit dem Trennungsakt vom 17. Dec. 1838 bis zum 1. Jan. 1840," in Church Registers of St. John's Unitarian Church, Cincinnati.

[4]Bob Rau, "History and Genealogy of German Ev. Churches in Cincinnati," unpubl. ms. (Cincinnati, 1989).

[5]Hugo A. Eisenlohr, "History of St. John's Unitarian Church Cincinnati 1934," 3, in Church Registers of St. John's German Protestant Church, Cincinnati, "History, Constitution, Minutes 1822-1943."

[6]Armin Tenner, ed., *Cincinnati sonst u.jetzt* (Cincinnati, 1878), 47.

[7]"Protokolle der Dt. Luth. u. Reform. Kirche, 27. April 1833," in Church Registers of St. John's German Unitarian Church, Cincinnati, "Minutes, Vol. 1."

[8]Karl-Heinz Zissow, "Ländliche Lesekultur im 18. u. 19. Jh. Das Kirchspiel Menslage u. seine Lesegesellschaften 1790-1840," in *Materialien zur Volkskultur nordwestl. Niedersachsen,* Vols. 12 & 13 (Cloppenburg, 1988).

[9]"Protokolle. . . 20. Dec. 1838" (See fn. 3).

[10]ibid., 23 Dec. 1838.

[11]ibid., 30 Dec. 1838.

[12]ibid., Constitution, Para. 10.

[13]ibid., 23 Dec. 1838, list of charter members.

[14]The premature death of so many children makes for the alarmingly low life expectancy average of approx. 17 years—20 for women, and only 15 for men.

[15]There is extensive biogr. material on two of the "Osnabrück people." Next to the set of the J. H. zur Oeveste letters (see fn. 2) written to the village of Rieste, there are the memoirs of Gottfried Martin Weber, born in 1803 in the Kirchspiel Engter—only about 10 km away from Rieste and likewise in the former Grand Duchy of Oldenburg. Weber appears as number 11 on the list of charter members. The rather clumsy, handwritten "Kurze (Lebens)beschreibung von Gottfried August Weber von Cincinnati, State Ohio, Nord-Amerika zum Geschenk an Wilhelm Rittman zu Barenaue, Colone Langefeld on the Langefeld farm bei Engter, Osnabrück" dates back to 1877. The ms. is available in Oldenburg where it is being prepared for publication.

[16]*Dt. Chronik in der Geschichte des Ohiothales u. seiner Hauptstadt Cincinnati ins Besondere,* 173.

[17]J. H. zur Oeveste, "Briefe," Baltimore, 19 May 1834 (see fn. 2).

[18]See A. Holtmann's article in this vol.

[19]Klauprecht, 170. Elsewhere Cincinnati's 1840 population is listed as 45,000.

[20]Eisenlohr, 4.

6 | An "Osnabrück" Congregation in Indiana: The "Deutsche evang.-luth. St. Johannes-Gemeinde am White Creek" (1840)

Antonius Holtmann, *Universität Oldenburg*

"The patriarchal authority of the pastor gave way to greater lay participation on the American model."[1]

This statement about the Missouri Synod in the 1920s implies that the patriarchal authority of the pastor, based on his spiritual position, more or less determined the decision making processes in previously submissive congregations. In this paper I will question this interpretation of assumedly perpetuated pastoral authority on the basis of the records at St. John's congregation at the White Creek in Indiana's Bartholomew County. To be sure, whether pastoral authority was also checked and challenged in other congregations—perhaps even on a more far-reaching scale—can only be ascertained through further congregational studies, that is, research into everyday history "from below."

On the basis of holdings at the Central Archives of the Missouri Synod's Indiana District at Fort Wayne, one gains the impression that the history of the Synod has largely been written "from above," by historians from within the hierarchy of the administration or from the teacher- and pastoral training programs. For example, in the "St. John on the White Creek" folder in the St. Louis archives, one finds only the by-laws from about 1853 and a commemorative volume of 1965, written by the congregation, in which its history is presented and pictured above all as a history of its *pastors*. The history of the *membership*, their discussions and decisions, all that is hidden in the minutes and the account books. In addition, clergy supremacy may have been deduced from the rigorous orthodoxy of the Missouri Synod and from the episcopal intentions of some of its founding fathers.

The "history from below" approach in our White Creek study proves that it was primarily the congregational assembly that decided not only questions of everyday operations, but also of church discipline, duties of the pastor and his support, as well as decisions against him or against the synod. Unaccounted for is the strength of personality of any given pastor. The minutes give few clues on that topic. Basic theological controversies of congregation vs. pastor or vs. synod are not specified.These assertions will be presented and substantiated from the viewpoint of the congregation, as recorded in their books.

The Records

In the title on the register book of 1840 the congregation called itself the "*Evangelisch-Lutherische St. Johannes Gemeinde am White-Creek*". The account book of 1846 bears this title: "*Vereinigte Evangelische-Lutherische und Reformierte Gemeinde an der Whitekreeik.*" Later, the "*Vereinigte. . . und Reformierte*" was crossed out, thus returning to "*Evangelisch-Lutherische Gemeinde.*" At the synodal conference of 1855 it was listed as "*St. Johannes Gemeinde am White Creek, Bartholomew C., Ia., Postamt Jonesville, Bartholomew Co., Ia.* [sic]²" Today the church building of 1862 still carries the inscription "*Deutsche evang.-luth. St. Johannes Gemeinde.*"

The register of 1848 records an Evangelical-Reformed/Lutheran marriage and one crossing the Lutheran/Methodist line; and in 1850 and 1852 there was a Methodist and a Reformed baptismal sponsor. From 1847 to 1850 three Lutheran/Reformed ("*unirte*") mixed marriages are recorded (of which two are marked "*jetzt lutherisch*", i.e., "*früher unirt*"), and one Lutheran/Methodist. From 1848 to 1850 there were also two couples listed as "*reformiert = eigentlich evangelisch.*" On Jan. 27, 1850, Pastor Carl Fricke recorded a conversion:

> *Bernhard Heinrich Adolph Burbring u. dessen Ehefrau, Marie Elise geb. Busch, waren bisher sogenannte Evangelische. Nach vorhergegangenem Unterricht erklärten sie: die Lehren der reformierten Kr. von Taufe, Abendmahl usw. seien falsch und irrig, die der luth. Kr. dagegen richtig, dem Worte Gottes gemäss; auch erkannten sie an, dass sie diesem Bekenntnisse u. dem darauf erfolgenden Abendmahlsgenusse zufolge, nun Glieder der lutherischen Kirche, also Lutheraner seien u. mit Gottes Hülfe bleiben wollten. Indem sie dieses bona fide erklärten, so reichte ich ihnen das Abendmahl.*[3]

Pastor Fricke (1847-1851) practiced the tolerance of a self- confident, orthodox Old-Lutheran. His congregation's rustic founders of 1840 had come mostly from the Osnabrück region and via the "*Norddeutsche Lutherische*

Kirche" ("Plattdeutsche Kirche") of Cincinnati. After they had bought their land in the forest along the White Creek, they kept attracting "Osnabrückers" for two decades—Lutherans, above all, plus a few Reformed from Tecklenburg. (In the Bishopric of Osnabrück there had been Catholic and Lutheran episcopal authority in succession ever since 1648.) These "Osnabrückers"—hired hands and farmers' sons and daughters without inheritance rights—took part in the canal and railroad boom in Ohio and Indiana, and in factories in Cincinnati, earning sufficient money to buy acreage in the wilderness (*"sich in den Busch einzuhacken,"* so J.H. zur Oeveste, Sept. 30, 1834; see fn. 22).

Without pastoral help, these farmers built their first log cabin church in 1842 and paid their "circuit riders" (Vajen and Isensee, Meissner and Boettcher). In February 1848 a new church was built, in part financed with funds treasurer Gerhard Heinrich von den Fange had collected from the first "American" church congregation of most of the settlers, the *"Norddeutsche Lutherische Kirche,"* also called *"Plattdeutsche Kirche"* or *"Osnabrücker"* founded in Cincinnati in 1838. This congregation also provided the communion service for their compatriots and numerous relatives in the wilderness.[4] Carl Fricke, also a former circuit rider, became the first resident pastor at White Creek. He resided in the old first church and in 1855 went to St. Paul's Lutheran Church in Indianapolis (Missouri Synod).[5]

In 1852 Rudolf Klinkenberg, from Stargard, became the second pastor of the congregation. "In Nürnberg. . . he had come under the influence of Pastor Wilhelm Löhe, and through Pastor Löhe. . . had been induced to join the seminary of the Lutheran church in the U.S." In 1846 the "Old-Lutheran," Wilhelm Löhe, had founded a theological seminary in Fort Wayne, which he brought into the Missouri Synod in 1847. There Klinkenberg studied further and then accepted his first call at White Creek.[6]

Löhe endorsed clergy supremacy, but the leaders of the Missouri Synod advocated a laity/clergy balance. At the time of the organization of the Missouri Synod in 1847 Löhe commented: "We fear, and certainly not without cause, that this strong emphasis on democratic, liberal and congregation-centered principles in your constitution will cause great harm, just as the power positioning of princes and secular authorities has done in our country." The break came in 1853, and in 1854 Löhe helped organize the Iowa Synod.[7] Around 1852 the congregation joined the "Old Lutheran" Missouri Synod; we do not know whether by the initiative of the lay members or Pastor Klinkenberg. But we do know how they dealt with the balance between clergy and laity supremacy within the Missouri Synod.

The Minutes

• *The congregation supported its pastor.* Up to 1864 the pastor's support came strictly from collections. The first salary was then set a $350 for the year. Raises came in 1865 to $400, in 1870 to $500 and in 1877 to $600 (the previous amount was "scarcely sufficient to meet the costs of supporting a family"). In 1903 the salary dropped back to $450, and $375 for the teacher. The congregation put the parsonage at the pastor's disposal, repaired and expanded it, erected stables for his horse and cow, and "fenzet" a "Kuh-Päster" (June 1875), and built a "Schmockhaus" and a bake house, and also a new parsonage in 1874. On July 30, 1864, under the heading *"über den Pastor seine Sistern"* it was decided *"das unsern Herr Pastor diesen Herbst eine Sistern gemacht werden soll, auch eine zimlich grosse so das wen Trockenheit eintrefe Er Sein Essen und trinkwasser dar aus haben könne."*[8] On December 19, 1857, it was decided that "the wood for Pastor's stove be cut in smaller pieces than usual." The marginal annotation, in large letters, reads: "canceled." The congregation allowed the pastor to preach in "Rockfort" two Sundays a year and gave him permission to serve the preacherless congregation at Waymansville on Sunday afternoons (1869). In April 1878 they allowed him an extra two weeks after his participation in the Synod's meetings at St. Louis "so that, God willing, he might overcome that irksome fever of his." In April 1905 "pastor requested permission to make a journey, and it was granted."

• *The congregation gave him assignments.* In October 1869 they "elected" the pastor to the "building committee." In April 1856 "it was decided that it should be entrusted to the pastor to make an effort and write to determine whether a school teacher could be obtained who could teach English" (the word for "entrusted" was struck and the stronger equivalent for "assigned" was substituted). The pastor should invite preachers for the mission fest (1893-1904) and, "together with the elders, admonish those who didn't send their children to school on a regular basis" (1901). He should also condemn the behavior of tardy payers, frequent absentees and obvious sinners, and he should deliver invitations to them to appear before the congregation. He should "pray the Lord's Prayer at the conclusion of the service" (1893) and "preach often in English" (1903). In 1905 the congregation decided "that small children should be subject to sermons."

• *The congregation obligated their pastor.* They resolved "that Lenten preaching should be held evenings when the moon was shining, otherwise in the afternoon" (1901); that the service should begin at 9:30 a.m. (1905); and that he should not confirm anyone before age 14, "as our pastor has already been practicing for 20 years" (1886). In 1897, though, "a significant majority" decided that children who had turned 13 before Christmas would be confirmed, and the pastor was "directed" to follow this new resolution strictly.

• *The congregation obligated the pastor even against his own will.* In 1878, congregation members in and around Jonesville were allowed to found their own congregation. But the territorial boundaries were contested: "Especially Pastor presents reasons why these boundaries were proper and necessary. The congregation, however, was not convinced and voted against it."[9] In 1890 it was resolved "that persons not belonging to the congregation (outsiders) could not be defined as non-Christian by Pastor and he should bury them if so requested, and with the same full honors that are accorded to members."[10]

A year later the pastor was directed not to wear his choir robe for the actual burial services. In March 1884, when he asked whether to give communion to a member who had not paid his full dues, they decided "not before the obligations had been met." In March 1873 he stood alone against the congregation; a member owed $80 and firewood:

> . . . he shows no interest in the maintenance of the church and the school. He does not mend his ways and doesn't care if the members and the congregations bear his share. . . Now a motion was made to excommunicate him. One side (Pastor) moved to formulate the resolution in such a manner that it would have to be approved at the next meeting. The congregation overruled him. . . Excommunication was unanimously decided by all of those present rising.[11]

• *Not the pastor but the congregation exercises control over church discipline and membership (Matt. 18, 15-18),* covering matters such as admission and dismissal, orthodoxy and the conduct of one's life, contributions to the church (money, materials, work), and for the services and the congregational assembly. The latter observes and admonishes, discusses, judges and decides, from the withdrawing of voting rights to dismissal and excommunication. It deals with impenitence, slander and adultery, with betrothal rights and compulsory Lutheran schooling, dues and church attendance, frivolous bankruptcy and drunkenness. Matt. 18, 15-18 prescribes the steps to be taken: admonishing sinners first by one person, then by two and finally three (usually including the pastor), followed by summons before the church council, and finally before the congregation as the decisive authority, all in order "to bring them back from the way to hell!" (March 1870). If they remain "stubborn, despising all Christian admonitions" (Aug. 1858), "impenitent in their obvious sins," then they have "thrown away the faith and their good conscience and have excluded themselves from the kingdom of God." Then the congregation decides to exclude Messrs. X and Y and "to have their excommunication publicly announced, which Pastor was ordered to do from the pulpit next Sunday" (May 1870). He did as told: "The banishment is declared, therefore both of them will be excluded from the assembly of the holy Christian Church. . . until they do their penance and turn again to God through true belief in Jesus Christ" (May 1870).[12]

• *The pastor's latitude was narrow, even if his personality might have enlarged it some.* He keeps the records, mediates and smoothes over, admonishes and consoles, baptizes and confirms, marries and buries, and gives communion. He is the spiritual advisor (*"Seelsorger"*). The minute books capture some of these activities:

In August 1857 the congregation accepts the offer of "our Herr Pastor" that he "ride around our congregation to collect from debtors." He offers instruction when the teacher position at school is vacant; he has his children ring the church bell; his daughter is to be a teaching assistant, and he himself at times an organist, paid by the congregation (1857, 1869, 1874, 1885). In May 1862 he pleads for a cross on top of the church tower, "with a lengthy dissertation. . . and indeed spoke for a good hour long. . . , so that no one could say for this or that reason that it appeared Roman Catholic. . . since the Catholic churches also have them. . . it is the same. . . the true symbol of the Christian church, so that anyone who could see it would be instinctively reminded of Christ and his death on the cross." With 39 vs. 8 votes the pastor's idea found acceptance. He makes out a release certificate (1865), admonishes "for one's soul and for its eternal salvation" to pay the full amount of dues (1888), and speaks about the "terrible sin of self-exclusion" (1897). In June of this year he holds a "serious discussion concerning our church service affairs, touching on issues like: 1) leaving the church before the service ends; 2) the church is empty in front; he admonishes them to sit in front where it is cool and comfortable; 3) parents not bringing their children to church more diligently."

In October 1904 the congregation decided that "it should be left up to Pastor to collect money for the building of the college in Fort-waine [sic]."

The congregation called its pastor, met with the opposition in his former congregation, but also resisted against a calling that was issued to its pastor. The pastor could not leave when he wanted to, even if he succeeded in obtaining a call by his own skill or through the assistance of other pastors. In Nov./Dec. 1886 Pastor Jüngel received a call from Zion's Church in Fort Wayne. The question was whether "the call came from God"? Pastors Schmidt from Indianapolis and Seymour thought so, but the congregation did not: "The application was rejected by a vote of 46 to 16." Pastor Jüngel stayed. Eight good reasons were sent to Fort Wayne, the last one pretty shrewdly telling the city folks that White Creek "has long since been known within Synod as the *fever hole.*" Pastor Jüngel has "survived the fever and has been healthy for many years." A new one, like the teachers, could not stand it for more than two or three years. "We could issue calls every year and end up with such a bad reputation that no decent pastor would accept; and those that come cheaper by the dozen are not what we are looking for."[13] Zion's renewed the call and with pastoral support by synodical dignitaries, St. John's congregation finally gave in: "If Pastor Jüngel believes it to be a divine call, we let him go in peace, although with heavy hearts." The question put to him this way made him feel that it was a "divine call."

The Constitution

What the laymen wrote in their minutes, partially in a clumsy German— but not entirely without irony and humor—was an expression of their "Constitution." It stems from the early 1850s with paragraph 14 (church discipline) modified in 1871. This constitution prefaces the minutes book (1880-1905). Its model was the *Gemeindeordnung für die deutsche ev.-luth. Gemeinde ungeänderter Augsburgischer Confession in St. Louis, Mo., 1843* that was published on March 5, 1850 in *Der Lutheraner*, the church paper of the Missouri Synod. It also reached the congregation in the form of a brochure.[14]

The constitution defined the foundations of orthodoxy: *The Old and New Testaments, Luther's Small Catechism* and the *Unaltered Augsburg Confession* upon which doctrine should be taught and examined, and any disagreement about doctrine should be resolved (para. 3). "The congregation in its entirety has the highest authority in the administration of the external and internal affairs of the church and the congregation. No regulation or decision for the congregation or for an individual member as such has any binding force, whether stemming from an individual or a body of the congregation, if it has not been transacted in the name of, and according to, general or special authority granted by the congregation." Whatever is decided in this way may at any time be referred to the congregation as the "supreme court." But even the congregation is limited in its authority when it comes to deciding anything "against God's Word and the symbols of the pure Ev. Luth. Church" (para. 6). Only the congregation in its entirety has "the right to call, elect and accept ministers, school teachers, elders and all other officials of the congregation"(para. 8). It obligated the elders to the administration of the congregation (para. 9) and the pastor to follow the fundamental doctrines and fulfill the spiritual needs of the congregation, and "to preach every time. . . only in the *German* language, . . . as long as three congregation members so desire." The congregation can release him when he is called, and they must release him if illness no longer allows him to fulfill his duties of office, "or if he persists in false doctrine or offensive conduct, or both, in spite of all admonitions (according to Matt. 18, 15-17), also by Synod, and has therefore already been excluded by Synod" (para. 11-16). The pastor consecrates the elders (para. 8), who in turn "have to provide for the support of the pastor and pay him his salary quarterly," and he can also call for meetings of the elders (para. 9). Members are obligated "to accept all that he is doing in his sacred office as pastor, and also accept personal admonitions with willingness and not to embitter the pastor in his office" (para. 12). However, "the congregation exercises church discipline within itself according to the instructions of our Lord Jesus Christ in Matt. 18, 15-17" (para. 14); this provision being inserted and established on Dec. 17, 1871, thereby stating the "supremacy of the local congregation."

The Missouri Synod

The Missouri Synod intended this local supremacy. Johann Gottfried Scheibel (5th deacon of St. Elizabeth Church and theologian at the Universität Breslau), in protest against the state-church union of the Reformed and Lutherans, had already made the claim in 1830 that "the congregation watches over the preservation of the doctrine, of the service and of the constitution."[15] This position was successful within the synod, in opposition to the clergy supremacy, and to the semi-episcopalian form of "government" of the Prussian pastor Johannes Grabau (Buffalo Synod, 1845) and of the preacher Martin Stephan (d. 1846),[16] the leader of the "more than 600 devout, well-organized Saxons"—known as the Stephanite emigration[17], among whom was also Carl Ferdinand Wilhelm Walther. This Saxon pastor, president of the Missouri Synod (1847-1850 and 1864-1878), and the Lower Saxon Friedrich Christian Dietrich Wyneken, president from 1850-1864, carried through the "laity/clergy balance. . . and the supremacy of the local congregation." They wanted the synod to be "an advisory body to which a congregation in need of advice might have recourse" (letter of Pres. Walther, 21 Aug. 1845).[18] The *Constitution of the German Evangelical Lutheran Synod of Missouri, Ohio and other States* (1854) had set forth this right and added that "synodical resolutions have binding force only when the individual congregation has voluntarily accepted them through a formal congregational resolution.—Should a congregation find a synodical resolution not in conformity with the Word of God, or unsuited for its circumstances, it has the right to disregard it, i.e., to reject it" (IV, 9)[19]

In August 1856 a "delegate" of the congregation went to the conference of the Middle District in Cincinnati for the second time, being reimbursed for half of the travel costs. In January 1857 "a few synodical resolutions or articles. . . will be extensively debated, so that their importance would be understandable to everyone." In August 1857 money was lacking to send a delegate. "A church collection will be made to raise funds for Pastor's journey to the synodical conference." And "the General President of Synod shall have $5 for this year." In October 1863 things were put in order. The congregation would pay "Pastor and also school teachers half of the travel costs to the synodical convention." Delegates did indeed stay home sometimes when funds were lacking (1861, 1865). Usually, they were sent with binding voting instructions and were urged to "vote their best convictions" (July 1880).

The congregation was also in opposition. In September 1872 they decided "to protest the election of Herr Schick as Rector. . . of our institutions." A letter, signed by the pastor and the elders in the name of the congregation, went to St. Louis:

> Herr Rector Schick has for years, through exaggerated complaining about the health situation in the college, insured its reputation, and one does not know whether he regrets his exaggerations. For years he had in mind to resign from office. . . We had wished that he would abide by his resignation. We wish this all the more after the board of control there did not grant his wish to have the office back again. . . We cannot think otherwise than that they must have had good reasons.

The secretary of the election committee, Theodor Brohm, replied, "one had well-founded reasons to believe that a sincere change of mind has occurred in Herr Schick," and he is "a capable teacher in the linguistic field." The congregation "declared itself satisfied and gave its approval to the election."

Another example: The congregation asked the synod for advice on whether a betrothal was as insoluble as marriage, and if the marriage ceremony had to follow soon. The pastor cited biblical evidence, and from "Luther and other teachers of the church," and above all from 1 Corinth. 7, 4-5, that it is so. But this did not settle the dispute between the engaged couple and their parents. "Pastor, thereupon, proposed that the congregation obtain an opinion on this sad case from Luth. theologians at St. Louis. . . to finally settle the matter" (8 June 1873). The opinions of Professors Schaller and Bäumer supported the pastor's instructions: "From the Bible passages of Gen. 29, 21; Matt. 1, 18-20; Deut. 22, 23-24 it follows undeniably that a legitimate betrothal has the same binding force as a consummated marriage (see Walther's *Pastoral Th[eses]*, p. 22,5)." "However, unity in the

congregation was not achieved; commotion and aversion increased instead."
With 16 vs. 12 votes "the theological opinion" was finally recognized "as the
resolution of the congregation," with several members abstaining. "Here the
meeting had to be concluded because it had already lasted very long, and
Pastor didn't feel well" (29 June 1873). The case did not appear again for
discussion.

In April 1872 dancing became an issue. Children of the congregation
were striking out on their own. Many of the older people saw "the world and
its temptations. . . penetrate into the congregation and spoil the youth. . .
After lengthy consultation it was unanimously agreed that the congregation
shall not tolerate that members give permission for their homes to be used for
dancing parties, nor that members permit any of their family to attend such
dances and participate therein. Disregard for this ruling shall have
disciplinary consequences".[20] *Der Lutheraner* was also the pulpit of the
synod. It had already warned against dancing on 9 Nov. 1853 (*"Was lehrt Dr.
Luther vom Tanzen?"*). On 15 Aug. 1874 another important article dealt with
the dancing issue (*"Tanzen hat seine Zeit, Pred. 3, 4"*), "Salomo did not know
the dancing practiced nowadays, hence didn't mean it, and evil comes under
God's rule as well." In Jan 1875 dancing was censured on the basis of the
Catechism ("We should fear and love God, so that we live in purity and
modesty in words and deeds"): "And indeed not only does shameful dancing
occur among us but also and not infrequently the defense of the same.
Phooey!" (p.5). After this, dancing was discussed no more in congregational
meetings. But, presumably, dancing continued.

On 26 Dec. 1875 the congregation decided "that all of its buildings
should be insured by the German Fire Insurance Society on White Creek."
On 1 Nov. 1869 *Der Lutheraner* had warned against "so-called mutual aid
societies" and against "life insurance (1870, No. 18), as well as insurance in
general which, "in the light of the divine Word. . . is despicable belly care,
mini-faith or un-faith, if you. . . mistrusting divine insurance are looking for,
and trusting in, human insurance."[21]

The congregation made use of its right of self-government and thus of its
right to disregard synodical admonitions and resolutions.

Johann Heinrich zur Oeveste (1801-1870), one of the founders of this
congregation on the White Creek in 1840, wrote in June 1870 to his brother
in Rieste, parish of Bramsche in Prussia (Kingdom of Hannover until 1866):
"Almost everyone here subscribes to two papers, me, I have the *Welt-Boten*, a
political paper on a Christian basis, and *Der Lutheraner*. Both are read in
Germany too."[22] In 1854 *Der Lutheraner* hailed the *Welt-Boten* with "cordial
pleasure" (No. 9), but in 1860 it saw in it a "henchman and prophet of a
fanatical Chiliasm" which led "naive Christians along a dangerously wrong

path" (No. 9). In 1873 (No. 8) *Der Lutheraner* called the *Welt-Boten* an "organ of the crudest religious mixtures and the crassest superstitions" with its "religiously indifferent wishy-washy articles." This was followed by the demand that "a Christian who takes his religion seriously. . . not keep this miserable, dangerous paper for another hour." We don't know whether or not zur Oeveste consequently canceled his subscription; the 1860 editorial attack had not disturbed him.

In general, at the White Creek in Indiana, things were not "eaten" as hot as they were "cooked" in St. Louis.

On the other hand, they did pay heed to matters of orthodoxy within the Missouri Synod. When a member (Jan. 1882) desired "a release from the congregation in order to join that of Pastor Frese of the Ohio Synod, the congregation decided to postpone the matter, . . . because in recent times the Ohio Synod has been deviating from the truth on a certain point." Two months later the member renewed his request, joined by another person, "because they had a closer and better road to that church." The congregation remained unsympathetic, "because the Ohio Synod has deviated from the true Christian concept of God's grace and thereby distanced itself from us and the entire Synodal Conference. As a consequence, it has taken a hostile stance toward us. . . denying in slanderous fashion our true teaching of God's Word and falsely accusing us of gross errors."[23] Since that congregation "with their pastor belong to the Ohio Synod. . . it is concluded that we cannot refer a member of our congregation to them."

Summary

The minutes books give no indication of a patriarchal authority of the pastor, nor of a laity/clergy balance professed by the Missouri Synod and prescribed in the constitution. To date we find no evidence that would belittle the laity supremacy exercised by the farmers in relation to their called, paid and supported "academics" (pastors and teachers). These White Creek pioneers came from the traditions of patriarchal but enlightened political and religious authorities of the Catholic/Lutheran prince-bishopric of Osnabrück (since 1802/1815 Kingdom of Hannover).[24] As dependent farm workers and leaseholders they had been exposed to officially exercised enlightenment through sermons, schools, and the combined church/civil administration, while at the same time growing up in socio-economic subordination and Lutheran piety that was not blurred by the top-down ordered "Union" with the Reformed Church in 1817.[25] Neither the claims and promises of enlightenment nor the reality of their situation offered promising perspectives: the dependence of the leaseholders (*Colonen*) on their landlords remained until the 1840s; and the burdens of the dependent farm workers (*Heuerleute*) in the service of the leaseholders kept getting worse. They were hurt by the reallocation of landholdings, by the rapid decline of the home weaving industry caused by Britain's competitive advantage with her mechanized cotton factories, by a 50% decline of summer work in Holland (so-called *Hollandgängerei*) around 1835, and finally by a rapid population increase. The prospect for making a living was spelled A m e r i k a.[26]

What had been impossible for the Osnabrück men and women back in Germany became possible at the White Creek: land ownership and independence (including the right to marry, which had been withheld back home until one had his own homestead).

Religious and politico-religious motives had led to the "1839 immigration of more than 600 devout, well-organized Saxons."[27] The emigrants from the Osnabrück area had economic motives and were not "well organized," but they were brought together in Cincinnati through the initiative of their fellow countryman, Pastor Möllmann, of the "North German Lutheran Church" (also *"Osnabrücker Kirche"* or *"Plattdeutsche Kirche"*).

I presume that membership in the Missouri Synod was not a problem; they had about a decade of success taming the wilderness at the White Creek and seven years of religious practice without their own pastor. They weighted the "laity/clergy balance" self- confidently to their own advantage, and the difficult living conditions gave the old Lutheran piety a good chance. During their Cincinnati period, some of them had been affiliated with the *Deutsche Lutherische und Reformierte Kirche*, but in 1838 most of them joined the *Norddeutsche Lutherische Kirche*. At White Creek they began as Lutherans, expanded into a united Lutheran and Reformed congregation in 1846, only by the end of the decade to be good old Lutherans again with traditional denominational steadfastness, but also with a degree of indulgent tolerance.And they remained what they had become in Cincinnati and at White Creek: a congregation largely in charge of its own affairs. The Missouri Synod's rejection of the notion of a state church and episcopal administration was in accord with the experiences of the White Creek farmers.

Thus most of them remained Lutherans, despite the founding of a very active Methodist congregation nearby in 1846.[29] "There were several of our Germans here who said that they were really converted to God" (zur Oeveste letter, 28 May, 1847). The multitude of religious sects was a new experience for the Germans. But most of them agreed with what zur Oeveste had read in his "textbook"—the Bible—and what he wrote home for his family's peace of mind: "But I say, continue in the ways in which you've been brought up and can trust."[30]

On this basis the people who had gone through the economic crisis around 1840, through homesickness and illness, had achieved self-confidence. Again the letter writer zur Oeveste:

> Everybody here makes a better living than in Germany. I didn't believe it either the first years when I was roaming around the country before I got married. Now I can write you truthfully that the dear Lord is with me in America. I and my wife are happy and satisfied. My two children give me a friendly smile when I come and go. And nobody can command me around.[31]

During the 1890s and at the beginning of the 20th century the retreat of the laity, an individualization and secularization of church discipline, and a worldly independence of the congregation members is indicated. In 1896 "the congregation decided that it would be permissible to found a singing society," and in April 1901—for the first time—there was a discussion of a *"Frauen Comite"* which should collect money for painting the church. In July 1892 an engaged couple separated, by mutual agreement. They were not subjected to church discipline, but one of the fathers maintained that "Pastor was hostile toward him." The congregation decided to reject this as slander and to strike him from membership "as one who had separated himself from the congregation." The rules were increasingly applied without biblical supplement (Matt. 18, 17: Heathen and Publican) and without reprimand from the church, whether it had to do with "drunkenness" (June 1889), with a "bankruptcy situation" (April 1897) or with delinquent obligations (Jan. 1895; Oct. 1896). "Because stubbornness and wickedness. . . are hard to prove," settling such matters was also "left to one's own conscience" (Sept. 1889). And when in one case "weakness in knowledge, belief and love" was seen as the cause of that member's problems, the position was that "we will still patiently support him as a weak brother. (Jan. 1889). A father "must live with his own conscience" if he doesn't send his children to school regularly (Nov. 1900). In July 1904 they continued "to have Pastor collect money for the college construction in Fort Wayne." In August 1905 they had "the benches, doors, windows and everything made in wood painted and grained," although "there is not enough money in the treasury." Above all, the task of the first brotherly admonition (Matt. 18,15) was more and more transferred to the pastor.

From this "retreat" of the laity the "patriarchal authority of the pastor" could have developed, which around 1920 "gave way to greater lay participation on the American model."[32]

Notes

[1]Kathleen Neils Conzen, "Germans," in: Stephan Thernstrom, ed., *Harvard Encyclopedia of American Ethnic Groups* (Cambridge, 1980), 405-425, here 419.

[2]*Verhandlungen der ersten Sitzungen des mittl. Districts der Ev.-Luth. Synode von Missouri, Ohio u. anderen Staaten im Jahre 1855* (St. Louis, 1855), 6f.

[3]"Bernhard Heinrich Adolph Burbing and his wife, Maria Elise, nee Busch, until now have been so-called *Evangelicals*. After prior instruction they declared: the teachings of Baptism, Holy Communion, etc., of the Reformed Church are wrong and mistaken, but on the other hand the teachings of the Luth. Church are correct, according to the Word of God; they also realized that, in consequence of this confession and the following Holy Communion, they are now members of the Luth. Church; thus they are Lutherans, and with the help of God will remain so." Since they declared this *bona fide*, "I gave them Holy Communion. Pastor C. Fricke." "Kirchenbuch," 19.—The records, account books and minutes are on microfilm at Indiana State Library, also at Family History Centers (Genealogical Libraries) of the LDS (Mormon) Church, Film No. 1510414, and at the "Forschungsstelle Niedersächs. Auswanderer in den USA" at Universität Oldenburg.

[4]"Kirchen-Rechnungsbuch," 9 (see fn. 28).

[5]*Our God, our Help in Ages Past. . . 1840-1965, Commemorating The 125th Anniv. of St. John's Luth. Church, White Creek, Ind.* (1965), 6.

[6]Otto Hanser, *Irrfahrten u. Heimfahrten* (Buffalo, 1910), 101.

[7]Carl S. Meyer, ed., *Moving Frontiers. Readings in the Hist. of the Luth. Church—Missouri Synod* (Saint Louis, 1986), 122.

[8]". . . that a cistern should be built for Pastor this fall, a rather large one, so that when a dry spell comes he may have potable water."

[9]"*Sonderlich vom Pastor werden die Gründe vorgelegt, warum diese Grenzlinie eine guthe u. nötige Ordnung wäre. Die Gemeinde konnte sich doch nicht von der Nützlichkeit derselben überzeugen u. stimmte in der Mehrzahl dagegen.*"

[10]". . . *beschloss die Gemeinde das Personen die nicht zur Gemeinde gehören (Fremde sind) u. doch der Pastor nicht sagen kann das sie kein Christ sind sollen von dem Pastor beerdigt werden wenn es verlangt wird, aber sie sollen mit dieselben Cerimonien verehrt werden als ein Gemeinde Glied.*"

[11]". . . *an der Erhaltung von Kirche u. Schule läge ihm gar nichts. Er verharre in Ungerechtigkeit gegen die anderen Mitglieder der Gemeinde, weil er die immer für sich bezahlen lasse. . . Nun wurde der Antrag gestellt ihn auszuschliessen. Von einer Seite (dem Pastor) wurde darauf angetragen, diesen Beschluss so zu fassen, dass er in nächster Versammlung erst bestätigt werden möchte. Die Gemeinde ging aber darauf nicht ein. . . So wurde denn sein Ausschluss einstimmig durch Aufstehen aller Anwesenden beschlossen.*"

[12]See *Thesen f.d. Lehrverhandlungen der Missouri-Synode u. der Synodalconferenz bis zum Jahre 1893* (St. Louis, 1894), 54ff.

[13]"*So können wir alle Jahre berufen u. werden schliesslich so verrufen, dass wir keinen ordentlichen Pastor mehr bekommen; u. mit solchen, die immer u. überall zu haben sind ist uns auch nicht gedient.*"

[14]Meyer, 167-170.

[15]Ibid., 76.

[16]Ibid., 131ff., 164.

[17]Conzen, 419.

[18]Meyer, 122, 143, 166.

[19]Ibid., 149-161. Orig. German version in *Der Lutheraner* (21 June, 1853), 145-151.

[20]"*. . .die Welt mit ihrer Lust. . . in die Gemeinde eindringen u. die Jugend verderben. . . Nach längerer Berathung einstimmig beschlossen, dass die Gemeinde es von keinem ihrer Mitglieder dulden will, seine Wohung dem jungen Volk zum Tanzen zu überlassen, oder den Seinen zu erlauben, solche Tänze zu besuchen u. mitzumachen. Wer muthwillig dawieder thut, soll in Kirchenzucht genommen werden.*"

[21]"*. . . im Lichte des göttlichen Wortes. . . schändliche Bauchsorge, Kleinglaube, oder Unglaube, wenn Du. . . der göttlichen Assekuranz misstrauest, u. indem Du menschliche Assekuranz suchst u. ihr vertraust.*"

[22]"*. . . hier hält fast jeder 2 Zeitungen ich halte den Welt Boten eine Politische Zeitung nach christl. Grundsätzen u. den Lutraner beide werden auch in Deutschland gelesen.*"—Copies of these letters are at Bartholomew County Hist. Society., Columbus, Ind., at Indiana Hist. Society, Indianapolis, and "Forschungsstelle Niedersächs. Auswanderer in den USA" at Univ. Oldenburg. See also: A. Holtmann, ed., "*...ferner tuhe ich euch zu wissen...*" *Briefe des Johann Heinrich zur Oeveste aus Amerika* (Bremen, 1995).

[23]"*. . . da sich die Ohio Synode wegen der reinen Lehre von der Gnadenwahl von uns u. der ganzen Synodal-Konferenz losgesagt u. eine ander Lehre angenommen hat u. in Folge davon uns feindlich gegenüber steht u. uns in. . . verleumderischer Weise die wahre Lehre des göttl. Wortes abspricht, dagegen aber gräuliche Irrthümer unterschiebt.*"

[24]From 1768 to 1783 the British administration in Osnabrück was headed by Justus Möser (1720-1794). Through his popular contributions in the *Wöchentliche Osnabrückische Anzeigen* (from 1766), which he had started, he promoted modernization of administration and commerce, crafts and agriculture.

[25]Karl-Heinz Ziessow, "Orthodoxe Camera obscura oder aufklärerische Vivisektion? Das Kirchspiel im Urteil Osnabrücker Pastoren um 1800," in *Jahrbuch f. Volkskunde* (1988), 7-31.

[26]Walter D. Kamphoefner, *The Westfalians: From Germany to Missouri* (Princeto, 1987).—These problems were seen by Thomas Hodgskin, *Travels in the North of Germany* (1820), vol. I, (New York, 1969), 312.

[27]Conzen, 419.

[28]Dietrich Hermann Heinrich Wilhelm Möllmann (1804-1840), from the "Stift Börstel, Fürstenthum Osnabrück, Kgr. Hannover," was ordained as pastor in 1835 in Osnabrück on condition that he emigrate to the U.S. In 1837 he was elected preacher of the "*Deutsche Luth.-Ref. Gemeinde an der 6. Strasse zu Cincinnati.*" He was a co-founder of the "*Norddt. Luth. Gemeinde, der Kirche an der Walnut Str.*" See the article by Wolfgang Grams in this volume. Quotes are from the church books of the Norddt. Luth. Kirche ("Begrabene von 1840"), vol. 1, 357, on microfilm at Hamilton Co. (Cincinnati) Public Library and the "Forschungsstelle Niedersächs. Auswanderer in den USA" at Universität Oldenburg.

[29]*Hist. of White Creek United Meth. Church 1846-1984* (White Creek United Meth. Church, 6730 W 930 S, Columbus, IN 47201).

[30]2. Tim. 3,14: *Du aber bleibe in dem, was du gelernt hast u. dir vertraut ist, sintemal du weisst, von wem du gelernt hast.*

[31]"*. . . ein ieder macht sein Leben hier besser wie in Deutsland dieses glaubte ich die ersten Jahre auch nicht wie ich mich noch ledig hier in diesem Lande herum trieb ietzt kan ich euch mit wahrheit Schreiben das der Liebe Gott mit mir ist in Amerika ich lebe Glücklich u. zufrieden mit meiner Frau meine beiden Kinder Lachen mir Freundlich entgegen, wen ich ein u. aus gehe mir hat niemand zu befehlen.*"

[32]Conzen, 419.

7 | Help from Vienna: Father Joseph Kundek and the German-Catholic Settlement in Dubois County, Indiana

Heiko Muehr, Angela Sasse, *OSB*, Mary Kenneth Scheessele, *OSB*, and Rev. John Schipp, *Indiana German Heritage Society*

In September 1836, Simon Bruté de Rémur, Bishop of Vincennes, Indiana, reported to the Vienna office of the Leopoldine Society, an Austrian mission society, that he had safely arrived at his home in Vincennes after a dangerous transatlantic crossing. He had "sailed from France on the first of June with nineteen missionaries, among whom were ten clerics." After the arduous overland trip of 800 miles, Bishop Bruté immediately began to send the missionary priests into the field:

> Among those who were appointed are two that speak German; namely the Reverends
> Mueller and Schaeffer. The first mentioned is stationed at Fort Wayne and the
> second in Chicago on Lake Michigan. Father Neyron is stationed nearer to us,
> namely at New Albany, where there are also Germans whose language he
> understands fairly well and in which he will probably perfect himself.[1]

Previously, there was only one veteran German-speaking priest working in the diocese, Father Joseph Ferneding, who had been ordained by Benedict J. Flaget, Bishop of Bardstown, Kentucky, in 1833. Father Ferneding first ministered to German Catholics in the vicinity of Louisville, but after his transfer to the Diocese of Vincennes, he concentrated his endeavors in southeastern Indiana.

The shortage of German-speaking priests that plagued the Diocese of Vincennes, where Catholics from Germany, Switzerland and Alsace would by mid-century form the majority of the faithful, was keenly felt in many

American Catholic sees. As the numbers of German-speaking immigrants increased in the 1830s, many American Catholic bishops were eagerly looking for priests that were able to minister to the immigrants' needs in their native language.[2]

In his on-going correspondence Bishop Bruté therefore highlighted the desperate need for priests who were able to converse in German. Thus in 1837 he was elated to hear that a German-speaking priest had volunteered to work in his diocese. In a letter to the Archbishop of Vienna, on October 10, 1837, the prelate wrote:

> With yearning I await the arrival in the near future of a new priest, Fr. Joseph Kundek from Croatia, whose coming has been announced both by Your Princely Grace as well as by himself. It would be most tragic if he changed his mind, for just now I need most of all such missionaries who are familiar with the German language.[3]

I

Joseph Kundek was born in 1810 in Ivanich, Croatia. He attended the Gymnasium at Zagreb on a church scholarship. Kundek was a good student who showed a special facility for learning foreign languages. He studied for the priesthood in Zagreb and as a seminarian was active in the "Illyrian movement" that worked for the creation of a Croatian literary language.[4] Kundek himself published poetry in Latin and in one of the Croatian dialects. In 1833 he was ordained and served for the next three years as assistant pastor and pastor in small Croatian villages. In 1836 Father Kundek approached an Austrian mission society, the *Leopoldinen-Stiftung im Kaiserthume Oesterreich*, which in America was known as the Leopoldine Society, with the intention of volunteering for the North American mission field. To prepare him for his role as a missionary priest, Kundek received English-language training at a mission center run by the society in Vienna. The mission society also contributed his travel expenses for journeying to Vincennes, Indiana.

The Leopoldine Society had been founded in 1828 when Friedrich Rese, a Hanoverian priest and Vicar General of the Diocese of Cincinnati, convinced members of the Austrian episcopate and the Habsburg imperial family to create a society that would shore up the fledgling missionary efforts of the American Catholic church.

Within a few years the society evolved into a giant support network for needy American Catholic prelates and their impoverished dioceses. Thousands of faithful from across the Habsburg empire contributed to the society, gave alms, took part in local chapter meetings, and prayed regularly for the American missions. The society published annual reports, the *Berichte der Leopoldinen-Stiftung im Kaiserthume Oesterreich*, that informed the public about its ongoing missionary endeavors.[5]

In order to win support for his idea of an Austrian missionary society, Friedrich Rese translated and edited reports about Ohio that had been published in the yearbooks of the French Propagation of the Faith Society.[6] His *Abriss der Geschichte des Bisthums Cincinnati* described mainly missionary activities among Native American groups in the Michigan Territory, which was at that time part of the Diocese of Cincinnati. Romantic notions associated with proselytizing among the unchurched "savages" helped to fill Austrians with missionary zeal.[7]

In his *Abriss* Rese had only briefly mentioned the plight of the scattered unchurched Catholic immigrants in the Ohio Valley, who later became the main focus of the Leopoldine Society's work. American bishops, who were desperately looking for funds to provide churches for the poverty-stricken stream of new arrivals, constantly reminded the Austrian mission society of their needs for money and German-language priests.

Bishop Bruté was one of the preferred beneficiaries of Austrian funds. The bishop's trip to Vienna in April 1836, interviews with members of the imperial family, the Austrian statesman Prince Clemens von Metternich, and officers of the Leopoldine Society, had helped to forge a close relationship between the Diocese of Vincennes and the *Leopoldinen-Stiftung*. The frontier bishop from Indiana impressed his powerful Austrian patrons, and his report on the condition of the American Catholic Church was reprinted in the Leopoldine Society publication *Berichte der Leopoldinen-Stiftung*. Bruté stressed repeatedly that the Diocese of Vincennes "is as important in its location as it is in its extent, since it is nearly one third as large as France."[8]

Brute's diocese, which included the entire State of Indiana and the eastern third of the State of Illinois, was constantly on the brink of financial collapse. Scattered communities of impoverished immigrants, who made up the bulk of the Catholic population, were unable to support the clergy and did not contribute sufficient funds to create even the barrest minimum of church infrastructure. In a letter written to the Vienna office of the Leopoldine Society in September 1836, Bruté thanked the Archbishop of Vienna for the financial help that he had received, but also pointed out to his Austrian patrons "that their rich contributions for the Diocese of Vincennes, for which I thank God, will by no means suffice." The bishop believed "that this Church cannot be made self-sustaining in this new country where people are still continually coming and going and are, therefore, very poor."[9]

II

When Father Kundek arrived at Vincennes in September 1838, he was assigned to the southwestern part of the diocese. After Bishop Bruté was satisfied regarding the qualifications of the new arrival, he appointed Father Kundek to be pastor to the German immigrant congregation at Jasper, the seat of Dubois County, some forty miles from Vincennes. Father Maurice de St. Palais accompanied the young priest as the Bishop's representative and installed him as pastor of St. Joseph Parish in Jasper on September 28, 1838.

Jasper had been settled about 1820 at the site of a Patoka River ford by Scotch-Irish families, who had come to Dubois County from the Upland South. In 1834, on the occasion of the first recorded visit by a Catholic priest, only two or three Catholic families were living in the little settlement. The Catholic community grew rapidly after the arrival in 1836 of the first sizable group of German immigrants, 12 families from Baden. By Easter 1838 the Jasper area's German population had grown to 50 families, and by December 1839 it consisted of 90 families.

Kundek biographer Dunstan McAndrews wrote:

> The young priest was a sound realist: first, he made the best of what he had; secondly, he reached out for more . . . To have some means of subsistence, Father Joseph Kundek acquired farm property and hired somebody to work it. From the proceeds of this farm he made his living, since it was clear to him, that at least for some time he could not expect but scant support from his parishioners, not even funds for the most necessary parish developments.[10]

Being the only German-speaking priest in southwestern Indiana, Father Kundek ministered to German-speaking Catholics in an area roughly bounded by the East Fork of the White River and the Ohio River, 30 miles to the south of Jasper, and St. Mary-on-the-Knobs, near New Albany, and Evansville, 60 miles to the west. Shortly after his arrival in Jasper, Father Kundek returned to Vincennes to minister to the Germans there, and then continued to Piquet's Settlement in southern Illinois, a colony of Alsatians. From there a 15-hour ride brought him to Evansville. Later he continued on to Boonville, and finally reached Jasper again. Shortly afterwards he made journeys to New Albany and to the White River, to minister to Catholics working on Indiana's canal project. The culmination of his travels, however, was a 700-miles trip that took him as far north as Chicago and Lake Michigan. The constant trips exhausted Kundek:

> My mission, which I traverse on horseback, is about as large as the territory encompassing Vienna, Preßburg, Schottwein, St. Pölten, and Linz. A second priest familiar with the German language would be very welcome to me.[11]

His incessant labors undermined his health. During the winter of 1843/44 Father Kundek went to New Orleans, for a much-needed rest. Upon arrival there he found that German Catholic immigrants in Lafayette (now a part of New Orleans) were meeting in a rented hall without the services of a German-language priest. At the request of the bishop of New Orleans, Kundek stepped in to rectify the situation. During his six-month stay in New Orleans, while convalescing, Kundek organized the building of a church—the first German Catholic one in New Orleans—and ministered to the spiritual needs of the parish.

Father Kundek also had a keen interest in civic affairs. He supervised the construction of a courthouse at Jasper and was elected to the Dubois County Board of School Examiners for the years 1853 to 1857.[12] However, he declined an offer of election to the Indiana House of Representatives:

> I must confess that the Americans have a rather high esteem for me, probably more than I deserve; they want to elect me representative for Dubois County, where I am presently at, and send me to Indianapolis. As far as I can tell they consider everybody a citizen, independent of any spiritual office. I can excuse them if they can not recognize the characteristic qualities of a Catholic priest, and I thank them for their trust and good will; for I am a missionary, not a senator, legislator, or anything of that sort.[13]

III

In 1839 Father Kundek wrote to the Leopoldine Society: "I am about to found a new town and parish 12 miles south of Jasper. The place is only 18 miles from the Ohio River."[14] Five days earlier the 360 acre site had been purchased from the government with funds provided by the Leopoldine Society. On January 8, 1840 the site was surveyed and the 276-lot town was laid out. Father Kundek named the town Ferdinand, after Ferdinand I, Emperor of Austria and patron of the Leopoldine Society.

"The region is healthful, the soil fertile. . . In the middle of the town there is a Catholic church; in the neighborhood of the town there are about fourty farmers." These and other claims about the town appeared weekly from early January through April 23, 1840 in advertisements in the *Wahrheits-Freund,* an influential German-Catholic newspaper published in Cincinnati. The first sale of lots was scheduled for April 22, 1840. Though none were sold that day, 84 lots were sold by May 15, 1840. "Founded April 22, 1840," however, is what Father Kundek inscribed on the title page of the parish books.

About 30 families set out from Pittsburg, Marietta, Cincinnati and Louisville by flatboat and followed the Ohio River to Troy, Indiana. Two scouts that they sent out reported that at the town's site they had found nothing but a clapboard nailed to a large oak with the name "Ferdinand" roughly burnt into the wood. Several families then continued on to Evansville, but the majority traveled the Troy-Jasper road to the designated location and settled there or in the vicinity.

Father Kundek continued to promote the town in letters to the *Wahrheits-Freund* and *Catholic Telegraph,* in his reports to the Leopoldinen-Stiftung, and in lectures in Louisville, Covington, Cincinnati and Pittsburg. The original twenty families of German origin, and nearly all subsequent German Catholic settlers, promoted further settlement in letters to relatives and friends in the United States and Europe. Frequently, within a few years of an immigrant's arrival in the Ferdinand area, relatives and friends followed. So many Germans came in response to the efforts of Father Kundek and the early settlers that Matthäus Hassfurther, one of the German Catholic pioneer settlers, wrote in January 1842 that "the Germans are coming like snowflakes."[15]

Father Kundek had not been in Indiana very long before he realized the value of establishing Catholic colonies. In a letter to Vienna he gives reasons why colonies of Catholic Germans were desirable, even necessary. He wrote:

> I established a new mission. . . My purpose in this was to give the German Catholics greater stability. . . The land in the vicinity is so good that in general few Catholics are better situated. . . As for the market, anything can be sold here. Many a German Catholic is agreeably surprised he can travel four, five, or even ten miles in a wooded region settled by Catholic families and discuss matters pertaining to religion without contradiction. Here a German is truly respected. . .[16]

Father Kundek's colonization scheme for the area between Troy, Perry County, and Jasper, Dubois County, gradually became reality. The establishment of Ferdinand in 1840 was followed by the founding of Celestine in eastern Dubois County in 1843. In 1847 Father Kundek established the community of Fulda, with its parish of St. Boniface, in Spencer County, about halfway between Troy and Ferdinand.

As McAndrews states:

> Probably no work performed in Indiana by Father Joseph Kundek left a more lasting impression than the stimulus he gave to Catholic colonization. To this day the traces of this work are to be seen in sections of the State of Indiana where the Germans settled. Anyone traveling through Dubois county and nearby regions will find large numbers of German-speaking farmers, who still retain customs brought by their ancestors from the Fatherland and carefully fostered by Father Kundek.[17]

IV

Father Kundek was deeply concerned that there be German-speaking priests for the rapidly growing parishes he had founded in southwestern Indiana. He wanted a religious order to take over, because only the presence of such an order would guarantee *"gute und ewige Priester"* (perpetual priests). In 1841 and again in 1848, Father Kundek unsuccessfully sought help from the Redemptorists in Philadelphia.

In 1851, Kundek, who had been appointed to the office of Vicar General, made a trip to Europe to recruit German-language priests for the Diocese of Vincennes. This trip became one of Kundek's major accomplishments: He was able to bring back to Indiana sixteen missionaries and also managed to persuade the Benedictines from the Swiss Abbey of Einsiedeln to send two emissaries to southwestern Indiana to survey the conditions there. The Swiss Benedictines established a priory at St. Meinrad that eventually became St. Meinrad Archabbey.

Father Kundek's incessant work in his parishes continued for 19 years until the time of the final breakdown of his health in March 1857. He remained an invalid until he died in Jasper on December 4, 1857.

Kundek's vision of a homogeneous and church-centered community with a strong moral order and revered traditions manifested itself in a rich religious life that endured for many decades. Eventually, twentieth century pressures brought various degrees of cultural change. The umbrella of common faith and ethnicity, however, has not been abandoned in Dubois County's Catholic parts. Rural isolation encouraged the retention of Old World customs and of German-American dialects, which are still spoken today by many.

NOTES

[1]Simon Bruté de Rémur, Bishop of Vincennes, to Eduard Vincent Milde, Archbishop of Vienna, Sept. 6, 1836, Correspondence Files, Leopoldine Society Records, Archdiocesan Archives, Vienna, Austria. These records have been microfilmed and are also available at the Archives of the Univ. of Notre Dame, Notre Dame, Ind.

Simon Bruté was born in Rennes, France, the son of an overseer of the royal domains in Brittany. He entered the Sulpician Seminary in Paris, and upon ordination in 1808 joined the Society of Saint-Sulpice. In 1810 Bishop-elect Benedict J. Flaget of Bardstown, Ky., recruited him for the American missions. Bruté then taught philosophy at St. Mary's Seminary in Baltimore, Md., and Mount St. Mary's College in Emmitsburg, Md. After three years as president of St. Mary's College in Baltimore, Bruté returned to Emmitsburg in 1818, where he remained until 1834. Then he was named bishop of the new Diocese of Vincennes, a frontier mission, where he ministered to a scattered flock of about 25,000 Catholics. Starting out with only one other priest at his disposal, Bruté, despite incredible hardships, still managed to hold the Diocese of Vincennes together. Bishop Bruté never recovered from the effects of a hard winter trip from Indiana to the Third Provincial Council of Baltimore in 1837. He died in Vincennes, Ind., on June 26, 1839.

    Mary Salesia Godecker's *Simon Bruté de Rémur: First Bishop of Vincennes* (St. Meinrad, Ind., 1931) is the standard English-language biography. Charles Lémarie's *Monseigneur Bruté de Rémur: Premier Évêque de Vincennes aux États Unies (1834-1839)* (Paris, 1974) brought to light previously unused French manuscripts.

    2Jean F. Vogler underlines the importance of the recruitment efforts for German-language priests when he writes, that "perhaps, though, the most important use of *Leopoldinen-Stiftung* funds was the assistance given to missionaries both in travel money and support after arrival in the U.S." See Jean F. Vogler, "The Leopoldine Society and the Mission Church in Indiana" (M.A. thesis, Univ. of Innsbruck, 1969), 18.

    3Simon Bruté de Rémur to Eduard Vincent Milde, Oct. 10, 1837, Correspondence Files, Leopoldine Soc. Records.

    4Norbert Krapf is currently editing Kundek letters for his forthcoming book, *Finding the Grain: Pioneer German Letters and Journals from Dubois County, Indiana* (Indianapolis, 1995/96). The most recent biography of Kundek is Dunstan McAndrews, *Father Joseph Kundek, 1810-1857: A Missionary Priest of the Diocese of Vincennes* (St. Meinrad, Ind., 1954). Kundek's papers include a large body of materials pertaining to his dealings in land. See Joseph Kundek, Records and Papers, Diocesan Priests, St. Meinrad Archabbey Archives, St. Meinrad, Ind. Albert Kleber wrote three valuable community and parish histories that cover aspects of Kundek's life: *St. Joseph Church, Jasper, Indiana* (St. Meinrad, 1937); *Ferdinand, 1840-1940: A Bit of Cultural History* (St. Meinrad, 1940); *St. Pius Catholic Church* (Troy, 1947). Kleber also authored the comprehensive *History of St. Meinrad Archabbey, 1854-1954* (St. Meinrad, 1954).

    5The best treatment of the Leopoldine Society is Gertrude Kummer, *Die Leopoldinen-Stiftung (1829-1914): Der älteste österreichische Missionsverein* (Vienna, 1966).

    6This society, known in German Catholic circles as the "Lyoner Verein," had already provided large sums to American Catholic institutions. It was organized in Lyon, France, on May 3, 1822, at a meeting called to raise funds for the Louisiana missions. The Society for the Propagation of the Faith was originally under the control of a council of French laymen. In 1922 it became an organ of the papacy charged with the collection and distribution of money to support Catholic missions throughout the world.

    7Friedrich Rese, *Abriss der Geschichte des Bisthums Cincinnati in Nord-Amerika: Nach den französischen Berichten der Jahrbücher der Gesellschaft zur Weiterverbreitung des Glaubens* (Vienna, 1829).

    8Bruté to Milde, Sept. 6, 1836.

    9*Ibid.*

    10McAndrews, 12.

    11Joseph Kundek to Eduard Vincent Milde, Aug. 5, 1840, Correspondence Files, Leopoldine Soc. Records.

    12George R. Wilson, *History of Dubois County from Its Primitive Days to 1910* (Jasper, Ind., 1910), 197ff.

    13Joseph Kundek to Eduard Vincent Milde, in *Berichte der Leopoldinen-Stiftung im Kaiserthume Oesterreich* 14 (1841):67f. Kundek always considered himself a missionary priest and signed all his letters thus, mostly with the Latin form "missionarius."

    14Joseph Kundek to Edward Vincent Milde, Dec. 10, 1839, Correspondence Files, Leopoldine Soc. Records.

[15]Matthäus Hassfurther to Nikolaus Gerhard, Jan. 6, 1842, Nicholas Gerhard Collection, St. Meinrad Archabbey Archives. This collection (1826-1852) includes a traveling journeyman's book, various family documents, and a large number of family letters.

[16]Joseph Kundek to Eduard Vincent Milde, in *Berichte der Leopoldinen-Stiftung im Kaiserthume Oesterreich* 18 (1845):40.

[17]McAndrews, 17f.

APPENDIX

Dubois County, Indiana (1850)
Map highlights Father Kundek's missionary and colonizing areas

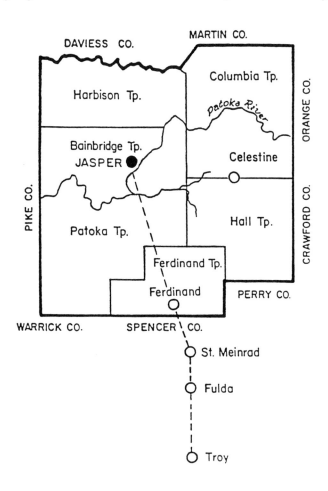

8 | Cultural Change in Milwaukee's German Evangelical Lutheran Congregations of the Missouri Synod, 1850-1930

Bettina Goldberg, *Freie Universität Berlin*

This report on cultural change in Milwaukee's German Lutheran congregations of the Missouri Synod focuses on the most evident appearance of that cultural change: the shift from German to English. It is connected with my research on the assimilation process of German immigrants in Milwaukee between 1850 and 1930. Language transition is obviously a central feature of that process. Especially for German immigrants, who were divided along economic, political, and religious lines, ethnic identity has basically to be defined in cultural terms. The vernacular, however, was the most prominent cultural bond and thus of crucial importance for the very existence of the ethnic group.[1] My research focuses on language transfer in Milwaukee's schools, churches, and societies, and I discuss the gradual displacement of German as both indicator and catalyst of the assimilation process.

The German Evangelical Lutheran Synod of Missouri, Ohio, and Other States was founded in Chicago in 1847. Its charter members were Old Lutheran immigrants, mainly from Saxony, who had not been willing to accept the merger of the Lutheran and Reformed churches in the German States and thus had been faced with persecution there. During the second half of the 19th century, due to heavy immigration, especially from the Protestant northern and eastern parts of Germany, the Missouri Synod gained much in size. Expanding from the Midwest to both coasts, it developed into the largest Lutheran immigrant denomination while retaining an almost exclusively German-American constituency. It became well known not only for its staunch conservatism in doctrinal matters but also for its distinctly

German style. Both these characteristics were to be perpetuated by a self-contained system of German Lutheran parochial schools and pastoral as well as teacher training institutions.[2]

By the turn of the century, the Synod's reputation as "one of the strongest bulwarks of. . . *Deutschtum*" was so marked that the German-American liberal, Karl Knortz, though a strong opponent of fundamentalist Lutheranism, emphasized the Synod's merits for the maintenance of German language and culture while, at the same time, Ernest Bruncken criticized it for being "one of the most important means of preventing rapid Americanization of the German. . . element."[3]

The Missouri Synod has retained its fundamentalist-literalist theological outlook well into our present times. Today it is one of the most conservative Lutheran denominations in the U.S. It has been transformed, however, into an English-speaking, American church body. It cast off the German language and most other German assets which once had been held to be prerequisites for doctrinal purity.[4]

This cultural and particularly linguistic assimilation of the Missouri Synod has often been interpreted as a result of the anti-German hysteria in the U.S. during World War I. According to Alan Graebner, whose argumentation can be considered typical, "the Missouri Synod had not changed greatly from the mid-nineteenth century" by the eve of the War. Although the "time to move quickly to English had come," he argues, "there was little in the Synod's heritage which promised a graceful and speedy acceptance of the inevitable. In 1914 the most informed prediction would have been of a debilitating, embittering struggle which would continue for decades." The heavy attack on everything German during World War I, Graebner concludes, "was precisely what was needed. Drastic intensification of the linguistic problem helped solve it. . . Instead of lasting a generation or more, the worst of the language battle was over within a decade after the war."[5]

For those who share the widely accepted assumption that the pre-war Missouri Synod was a rather monolithic German-speaking religious denomination, this interpretation seems quite plausible. But is the assumption valid? I submit that the German Lutheran congregations affiliated with the Missouri Synod during the pre-war period, though united in religious doctrine, showed a remarkable degree of variation with respect to language. While for many of the rural congregations World War I may indeed have constituted a decisive cultural and linguistic turning point, in the case of the Missouri Synod's urban congregations this was rather unlikely.[6]

In Milwaukee the German immigrants found themselves in a position of strength from the very beginning; therefore they faced less pressure to assimilate than their compatriots in other urban centers.[7] This favorable condition notwithstanding, Milwaukee's Missouri Synod congregations did not possess, as Graebner argues, "a sufficient reservoir of German culture to continue Old World ways into the second and. . . third generation."[8] Quite to the contrary, even in Milwaukee the English language soon began to threaten the initial dominance of German. Since it was in the "nurseries" of the congregations, i.e. in their schools,[9] that the English language gained ground first, and since the shift to English in other spheres of church life was partly due to the effects of parochial education, a discussion of the development within the Lutheran schools will be at the center of this paper.

It will be demonstrated that although German as medium and subject of instruction was given up in most of the schools during the First World War or shortly thereafter, the war had functioned only as a catalyst, not as a cause for abandoning German. The crisis of German-language instruction had already made itself felt before the turn of the century. It was neither caused by attacks from the outside, nor was it brought about by a clergy eager to enforce the Americanization of the schools and parishes. It resulted, rather, from social and mental changes that had been taking place within the German-American community for several decades.

I will first briefly characterize Milwaukee's Missouri Synod congregations and schools, then focus on the use of German in these schools, describing a process of displacement that led to the marginalization of this once dominant language. And finally, I will discuss the causes of language transition in the schools and its effects on other parts of congregational life.

The sources that have been evaluated include congregational records, school board proceedings, local German-American newspapers, synodical reports and statistics, as well as educational pamphlets and journals that were published by the Missouri Synod during the 19th and early 20th centuries.[10]

I

During the second half of the 19th century, Milwaukee developed from a relatively small city of 20,000 into an urban center with approximately 300,000 inhabitants by 1900. This population growth was mainly due to European, particularly German immigration. In 1850, German immigrants constituted more than a third of the city's population, while the Irish, the second largest group, only made up 14%. In 1900, 19% of Milwaukee's inhabitants were German-born, and if their American-born children are added, almost 50% of the population were of German descent by that time.[11]

The German predominance had its impact on the city's churches. Milwaukee was a center of both German-American Catholicism and Lutheranism. From the outset, the Roman Catholic Church constituted the largest single religious body; it drew its members mainly from the Irish-, German-, and later on also from the Polish-American community. On the Protestant side, there existed a variety of different groups and churches; none of which, however, reached the numerical strength of the Lutheran denominations which, since the 1860s, ranked second in size.[12]

Though there were a few Scandinavian and, after 1889, also English Lutheran churches, during the 19th and early 20th centuries, Milwaukee's Lutheranism bore a distinctly German-American imprint. German immigrants and their descendants founded the overwhelming majority of the congregations, and most of these became affiliated with either the Missouri or the Wisconsin Synod. These two synods—although both ethnically homogeneous and confessionally conservative church bodies—had to overcome a whole series of doctrinal differences, until in 1872 they eventually formed the Synodical Conference which turned out to be a rather solid basis for cooperation.[13]

Milwaukee's first Old Lutheran immigrants came from Pomerania and Silesia in 1839. In 1841, they organized St. Paul's congregation. Since they had emigrated under the leadership of Pastor Johann Grabau, meanwhile head of the Buffalo Synod, they voted to join that Synod. Only a few years later, however, the hierarchical structure and authoritarian spirit of the Buffalo Synod caused a split within the congregation. After consultations with the Saxon Lutheran immigrants in Missouri, who were known for their outspoken congregationalism, the dissenting members founded Milwaukee's German Evangelical Lutheran Trinity Church, which in 1847 belonged to the 12 original charter congregations of the Missouri Synod.[14]

Trinity Church in downtown Milwaukee initially served the whole city. In the early 1850s mission work was begun on Milwaukee's South Side. Religious services and a parochial school were started in a rented building in 1853, and only shortly thereafter Trinity Church peacefully released some of its members. They formed the nucleus of a second congregation, St. Stephen, formally organized in 1854. This pattern was to prevail in the following decades when, in order to keep pace with Milwaukee's population growth and area expansion, the founding of more congregations became necessary.[15]

In 1917, 16—or slightly over 40%—of Milwaukee's German Lutheran congregations were affiliated with the Missouri Synod. Half of those had been founded in the last two decades of the 19th century, i.e. either during or shortly after the third wave of German immigration. More than two thirds of the congregations were located on Milwaukee's Northwest Side, where inhabitants of German descent made up 60-80% of the population.[16]

Almost all congregations maintained schools. It was a condition for membership in the Missouri Synod from the beginning that each congregation provide a Christian education for the children of its members. In rural areas many churches lacked funds to offer more than part-time instruction in catechism and biblical history, but in Milwaukee, as well as in other urban centers, the congregations of the Missouri Synod were quite successful in establishing full-time elementary schools which were meant to be an alternative to the secular public school system.[17]

German-American Lutheran clergymen, in contrast to their Catholic competitors, did not question the right of the public schools to exist, nor did they fight for a share of the public school fund which, they feared, would involve the same kind of state interference they had suffered in Germany. They insisted on the principle, however, that Lutheran children be educated in Lutheran schools, where they received proper religious instruction and where the secular subjects were taught from a Lutheran perspective as well.[18]

Milwaukee's Lutheran school system reached its peak by the end of the 19th century when more than 3,000 children attended the parochial schools of the Missouri Synod and about 2,500 those of the Wisconsin Synod. After the turn of the century, enrollment began to decline and one congregation after another felt the need to also open a Sunday school in order to provide religious instruction for the growing number of Lutheran public school children. The establishment of Sunday schools did not mean, however, the end of the day school system. Although some congregations had to consolidate their schools, at least until 1930, none was forced to close down its school totally.[19]

German Lutheran immigrants founded parochial schools not only for religious reasons but also for retaining their language and culture. Ethnic and religious needs were linked in the conviction that the German language and true Lutheranism were inseparably bound together and that the loss of the one would necessarily result in the loss of the other and thus threaten the very existence of the church. Thus the coming generations had to grow up with the language and culture of their German home country if they were not to become alienated from the Lutheran church and faith.[20] Despite this conviction, the school became, as we shall see, the first public sphere in parochial life where the English language gained ground.

II

Milwaukee's first parochial schools of the Missouri Synod, founded in the 1840s and 1850s, started out as all-German institutions. By 1870, at the latest, they were forced to introduce English-language instruction. Gradually, German was displaced both as medium of instruction and as subject.

At Trinity School, which opened in 1847, English-language instruction was introduced during the 1860s. By 1869 English reading, writing, and grammar had become an integral part of the curriculum. Except for these language lessons, however, all instruction was still given in German. Twenty years later the situation had drastically changed. In 1889, 15 hrs. or almost half of the weekly classes were taught in English. The curriculum did not only contain lessons in English reading, writing, grammar, and penmanship, but beyond that, English had also replaced German as the medium of instruction in arithmetic, geography, American history, the sciences, and drawing.[21]

The development within the other parochial schools had been similar. With the exception of "world history," which was mainly a synonym for German history up to the time of the Reformation, all secular subjects were taught in English. While in 1889 in most of the schools most students spoke both German and English, at Immanuel School English already prevailed as the students' vernacular.[22]

Despite these changes, however, by 1890 instruction in German still played a prominent role within Milwaukee's Lutheran parochial schools of the Missouri Synod. This was not due to German language lessons—which took up no more time than their English counterpart; it was due to religious instruction which comprised almost a third of the school week and was entirely given in German.[23]

German lessons and German religious instruction did, of course, continue after the turn of the century, but their character changed. What once had been instruction in the vernacular turned into foreign-language instruction. As early as 1901, the synodical *School Journal* warned the congregations that if they were not going to introduce English religious instruction into their parochial schools, they would risk losing their young people for whom English rather than German was becoming the mother tongue. Every congregation, it was argued, would sooner or later be confronted with the language transition; therefore every congregation should be prepared for that situation. And even in instances where all religious services were still being held in German, at least a bilingual approach to religious instruction should be adopted.[24]

In 1911 a revised curriculum for the parochial schools was presented by the Milwaukee Teachers' Conference, of the Missouri Synod. The curriculum did not provide for English as the medium of instruction for the religious subjects.[25] This, however, no longer reflected the situation in the schools. It is true, there were only few parochial schools which officially introduced religious instruction in English before America's entry into the First World War. But even in the majority of the schools where German was abandoned either during or shortly after the war years, English had already become very important for the teaching of religious subjects. The development at Bethany School can be considered as typical. There a bilingual approach had been adopted around 1910. It soon became obvious that the children's knowledge of German was so limited that English had to be employed to teach catechism and biblical history. Thus, in 1918, when the medium of instruction was officially changed to English, this did not make much of a difference. For quite a number of years religious instruction had been German only in name.[26]

III

The shift from German to English in Milwaukee's Lutheran parochial schools of the Missouri Synod took place in three stages: 1) the transition to bilingual education; 2) the gradual displacement of the German language; and 3) its final abandonment.

In Milwaukee, the first step toward bilingual schooling took place in the late 1860s. As in other cities, it was brought about by pressure from the parents. German Lutherans wanted to retain the language and culture of their home country, but at the same time they recognized that a knowledge of English was a prerequisite for their children's social and economic mobility in the New World. Since the public schools had started to offer an optional German lesson daily in addition to their otherwise English-language curriculum, many Lutherans were attracted to these schools despite repeated warnings from the clergy. Thus, by introducing English-language instruction, the German Lutheran parochial schools tried to keep up with their public competitors.[27]

The displacement of German during the following decades has often been interpreted as a result of the Bennett School Law of 1889. This law placed parochial and other private schools under the control of the state and prescribed English as the sole language of instruction for elementary subjects. The immigrant churches attacked the law vehemently.[28] Though it cannot be denied that the law had an influence on the political climate and that especially in some rural areas it played an important part in raising the standards of parochial education, its role has been overestimated.[29] The law was on the books less than a single year and, unlike its counterpart in Illinois, it was never enforced.[30]

Furthermore, at least in Milwaukee, it did not take the prescriptions of a state law to ensure that English rather than German become the medium of instruction for secular subjects in the Lutheran parochial schools. A change to that effect had already been recommended by the Northwestern Teachers' Conference of the Missouri Synod at its meeting in Milwaukee in 1877. *"Die englische Sprache ist die Sprache des Heimathlandes unserer Kinder,"* German-born Johann Wegner, teacher at Trinity School, pointed out at that conference, *"dieselben haben späterhin auch an ihren Mitbürgern englischer Zunge kirchliche Missionsaufgaben, und neben ihren Berufspflichten auch Bürgerpflichten zu erfüllen. . . In Erwägung dieser Umstände,"* Wegner continued, *"erscheint es ungenügend, wenn man die englische Sprache in unseren Schulen nur als Unterrichtsfach treiben wollte."* Instead he recommended all subjects be taught in English with the exception of religious instruction and German language lessons. This plan was unanimously adopted by the Teachers' Conference and put into practice by the schools.[31]

Once again, the conference proceedings reveal, it was competition with the public school system that had brought about the change. If the parochial school teacher does not offer his students at least the same advantages that are said to be offered in the public grade schools, it was argued, many parents will feel justified in sending their children to the public schools and, as a result, these children will become alienated from our parochial life.[32]

By the time the Bennett Law was enacted, Milwaukee's Lutheran parochial schools of the Missouri Synod had already made far-reaching adjustments toward the public school curriculum. They had even introduced many of the textbooks that were used by their public competitors. English had been widely adopted as the medium of instruction and, except for the religious subjects, the German language did not take up more time in the Lutheran schools than it did in the city's secular schools.[33] This was what the parents wanted. They were ready to see German lessons reduced; they were not willing to accept an education for their children that did not meet the standards of the public school system.

After the turn of the century, German-language instruction was not felt to be crucial any longer by Milwaukee's German-American Lutherans. Immigration from Germany was declining, and by 1910, the majority of parishioners were either born in the U.S. or had already been living there for 20 years and more.[34] Many still subscribed to German-language newspapers or were members of German-speaking societies, and most attended religious services held in German, but they did so for reasons of habit and tradition. They were not monolingual any longer and, therefore, did not depend on their children's knowledge of German to communicate with them. On the contrary, numerous complaints of clergymen, educators, and journalists suggest that English rather than German was the language spoken in most homes most of the time.[35]

This caused difficulties for the schools, and teachers found themselves in a dilemma. They were supposed to give their students a keen understanding of the Lutheran faith and church, and they were expected to do so in German. German still was the language of most religious services but no longer their students' vernacular. Thus it had to be taught as a foreign language. New, bilingual teaching methods were introduced. But even those could not restore what had been vanishing for some time: the sense of a genuine need and vital necessity for German-language instruction.

The marginalization of German within the school environment did, of course, affect other parochial activities as well. At first, it made itself felt within the so-called *Christenlehre*, a German catechism study, obligatory for all young congregation members up to the age of eighteen, which was held every Sunday afternoon. On the eve of World War I, due to dwindling attendance at the *Christenlehre* and a growing number of Lutheran public school children, most congregations had established bilingual or all-English Sunday schools which can be regarded as a suitable means to compensate for the lack of regular English services on Sunday mornings. Furthermore, at least some of the congregations had already started English confirmation classes in addition to those conducted in German.[36]

With the adults, the transition to English proceeded at a slower pace. It was not until the 1930s that this process found its completion.[37] This should not disguise the fact that English had already made inroads after the turn of the century. As early as 1902 when St. Stephen congregation celebrated the consecration of its new church and when, just for this occasion, an additional English service was held in the evening; this attracted so many people that the church was crowded beyond standing capacity and hundreds could not be let in.[38] Nine years later, in 1911, Milwaukee already had three German Lutheran churches of the Missouri Synod that offered English evening services on a regular basis.[39] By that time, even those congregations which had not yet started English services were well aware of the fact that the language transition was going to come soon and that it was imperative for the continuing existence of the church. The revised constitution of Immanuel congregation, adopted in 1913, still prescribed the use of German for services and voters' meetings. But in contrast to earlier constitutions, the prescription was no longer immutable. *"Diese Bestimmung bleibt so lange in*

Kraft," the addendum explains, *"als die Gemeinde vermittelst der deutschen Sprache ihrer Missionspflicht ihren Gliedern gegenüber nachkommen kann."*[40]

Thus, we may conclude that within Milwaukee's German-American Lutheran community the use of German was on the decline long before, and independently of, World War I. As I have demonstrated in a different paper, this was similarly true for Milwaukee's German-American Catholic community.[41] Both German Lutheran congregations and German Catholic parishes underwent a process of change that eventually transformed them into English-speaking, American institutions. This process was accelerated by the experience of the First World War, but it was rooted in, and carried forward by, the changing aspirations of Americans of German descent who formed the church membership.

NOTES

[1]See Kathleen Neils Conzen, "The Paradox of German-American Assimilation," *Yearbook of German-American Studies* I (1982), 153-60, and "German-Americans and the Invention of Ethnicity," in *America and the Germans. An Assessment of a Three-Hundred Year History*, eds. Frank Trommler/Joseph McVeigh (Philadelphia, 1985), vol. I, 131-47; David Gerber, "Language Maintenance, Ethnic Group Formation, and Public Schools: Changing Patterns of German Concern, Buffalo, 1837-1874," *Journal of American Ethnic Hist.* 4:1 (Fall, 1984), 31-61.

[2]See Wilhelm Ivan, *Die altluth. Auswanderung um die Mitte des 19. Jhs.*, 2 vols. (Ludwigsburg, 1943): Ralph Dornfeld Owen, "The Old Lutherans Come," *Concordia Hist. Inst. Quarterly* 20:1 (April, 1947), 3-56; Walter O. Forster, *Zion on the Mississippi: The Settlement of the Saxon Lutherans in Missouri, 1839-1841* (St. Louis, 1953); Walter A. Baepler, *A Century of Grace. A Hist. of the Missouri Synod 1847-1947* (St. Louis, 1947); *100 Years of Christian Education*, ed. Arthur C. Repp (River Forest, IL, 1947).

[3]Karl Knortz, *Das Deutschthum der Ver. Staaten* (Hamburg, 1898), 69; Ernest Bruncken, "How Germans Become Americans," *Wisconsin Hist. Soc. Proceedings* (Madison, 1898), 108f. By stating that the English language had gained only very little influence within the Missouri Synod at the close of the 19th century, historian Frederick C. Luebke gave a similar, though less emotional characterization almost 70 years later: "The Immigrant Condition as a Factor Contributing to the Conservatism of The Luth. Church-Missouri Synod," *Concordia Hist. Inst. Quarterly* 38:1 (April, 1965), 23.

[4]See Luebke, "Immigrant Condition," 27.

[5]Alan N. Graebner, "The Acculturation of an Immigrant Luth. Church: The Luth. Church-Missouri Synod, 1917-1929," diss. (Columbia Univ., 1965), 13, 103f.; for a similar argumentation, see, e.g., L. G. Bickel, "The Period of Integration 1914-1947. From World War I to the Present," in *100 Years*, 196-198; Frederick Nohl, "The Luth. Church-Missouri Synod Reacts to U.S. Anti-Germanism During World War I," *Concordia Hist. Inst. Quarterly* 35:2 (July, 1962), 52 and 59; LaVern J. Rippley, *The German-Americans* (Boston, 1976), 99.

[6]Many of the articles and monographs that focus on the assimilation process of the Missouri Synod suffer from one or the other of the following shortcomings: 1. they attach too much importance to official synodical statements; 2. they overemphasize the language of

religious services as indicator for the state of the assimilation process while neglecting other aspects of church life (e.g., schools and societies); 3. they investigate the synod at large or, at best, one of their state districts and do not differentiate between urban and rural surroundings.

[7]See Kathleen Neils Conzen, *Immigrant Milwaukee 1836-1860. Accommodation and Community in a Frontier City* (Cambridge, MA, 1976); Bayrd Still, *Milwaukee. The History of a City* (Madison, 1965).

[8]Graebner, "Acculturation," 13f.

[9]The metaphor "nursery" (*Pflanzstätte*) is often used in Synodical publications to emphasize the fundamental significance of parochial education for the future of the churches; see, e.g., *Kirchenordnung der Ev.-Luth. Bethanien-Gemeinde zu Milwaukee, Wis./Constitution of Bethany Ev.-Luth. Congregation of Milwaukee, Wis.* (n.p., n.d.), §4.

[10]Research was done in the following institutions and archives: Milwaukee County Hist. Soc.; Milwaukee Pub. Lib.; Legislative Ref. Lib. of Milwaukee; Milwaukee Area Research Center at the Univ. of Wisconsin-Milwaukee; State Hist. Soc. of Wisconsin, Madison; Concordia College, Mequon, Wis. (Archives of Concordia College, formerly Milwaukee, and of the South Wisconsin District of The Luth. Church-Missouri Synod); Concordia Hist. Institute, St. Louis; Wisconsin Luth. Seminary Lib. and Archives (WELS), Mequon, Wis. (Archives of the Wis. Ev.-Luth. Synod).

[11]Polish immigrants constituted 6% and Irish immigrants less than 1% of Milwaukee's population in 1900; see *12th U.S. Census on Population*, Pt. 1 (Washington, 1901), 800-803, 876, 884, and 900; Still, *Milwaukee*, 570f., 574f.; Gwen Schultz, "Evolution of the Areal Patterns of German and Polish Settlement in Milwaukee," *Erdkunde. Archiv f. Wissenschaftl. Geographie* (Bonn), X (1956), 138.

[12]Conzen, *Immigrant Milwaukee*, 159 and 275; Still, *Milwaukee*, 419f., 472; for a more detailed account of the Roman Cath. Church in Milwaukee, see Johann Haug, *Geschichte der Kathol. Kirche in Wisconsin* (Milwaukee, 1899), 241-304; Coleman Barry, *The Cath. Church and German Americans* (Milwaukee, 1953).

[13]See *Memoirs of Milwaukee County*, ed. Jerome A. Watrous (Madison, 1909), vol.I, 348ff.; Roy A. Suelflow, *Walking with Wise Men. A Hist. of the South Wis. District of The Luth. Church-Missouri Synod* (Milwaukee, 1967); Carl S. Meyer, "Intersynodical Unity Fostered Through Co-operation in Education (1859-1874)," *Concordia Hist. Inst. Quarterly* 29:2 (Summer, 1956), 50-66; David Schmiel, "State Synods and Geographic Parishes: The Abortive Movement of the 1870's," ibid., 38:4 (Jan., 1966), 191ff.; for a hist. of the Wis. Synod, see John Philipp Koehler, *The History of the Wis. Synod* (St. Cloud, Minn., 1970).

[14]See Friedrich Lochner, *Geschichte der Ev.-Luth. Dreieinigkeits-Gemeinde U.A.C. zu Milwaukee, Wis. Im Auftrag der Gemeinde zur Feier ihres 50-jähr. Jubiläums den 17. Okt. 1897* (Milwaukee, 1897), 2-11; Ronald Tabbert, "Milwaukee's Trinity Designated a 'Landmark'," *Concordia Hist. Inst. Quarterly* 41:4 (Nov., 1968), 154; Suelflow, *Walking*, 18-43; for a critical discussion of Missouri Synod's congregationalism in theory and practice, see Alan Graebner, "Thinking About the Laity in The Luth. Church-Missouri Synod," *Concordia Hist. Inst. Quarterly* 45:2 (May, 1972), 125-39.

[15]See B. Sievers, *Kurzgefasste Geschichte der Ev.-Luth. St. Stephanus-Gemeinde zu Milwaukee, Wis., zur Feier ihres 50jähr. Jubiläums 1854-1904* (Milwaukee, 1904), 7; for the organization of further congregations, see, e.g., Otto Hattstädt, *Kurzgefasste Geschichte der Ev.-Luth. Immanuelsgemeinde zu Milwaukee, Wis. Zur Erinnerung an ihr 50-jähr. Jubiläum. 1866-1916* (Milwaukee, n.d.); *1884-1909. 25-jähr. Jubiläum der Ev.-Luth. St. Martini-Gemeinde zu Milwaukee, Wis.* (Milwaukee, 1909).

[16]These figures were computed from congregational records, Milwaukee directories, and an ethnically mixed sample of 1090 Milwaukee households (based on the ms. schedules of the *U.S. Census on Population* for 1910).

[17]See *Moving Frontiers. Readings in the Hist. of the Luth. Church-Missouri Synod*, ed. Carl S. Meyer (St. Louis, 1964), 150; Walter F. Wolbrecht, "The Period of Expansion 1864-1894. From the Opening of the Addison Teachers' Seminary to the Founding of the Seward Teachers' Seminary," in *100 Years*, 74ff., 79; Christ. Koerner, *The Bennett Law and the German Protestant Parochial Schools of Wis.* (Milwaukee, 1890), 11 and 23.

[18]See, e.g., H.F. Sprengeler, *Schulpredigt gehalten am Ersten Sonntag nach Epiphanias in der Ev.-Luth. Dreieinigkeits-Kirche zu Milwaukee, Wis.* (Milwaukee, 1897), 10-12; Koerner, *Bennett Law;* for the school policy of the Cath. Church, see Jay P. Dolan, *The American Cath. Experience. A Hist. from Colonial Times to the Present* (Garden City, N.Y., 1985), 262-93; Timothy George Walch, "Cath. Education in Chicago and Milwaukee, 1840-1880," diss. (Northwestern Univ., 1975).

[19]See, e.g., "Milwaukee, Wis.," *Ev.-Luth. Schulblatt* 33 (1898), 29; "Schulnachrichten," *Ev.-Luth. Gemeinde-Blatt* (Wis. Synod) 58 (1923), 262; Heinrich Sprengeler, *Geschichte der Ev.-Luth. Dreieinigkeits-Gemeinde U. A. C. zu Milwaukee, Wis. vom Jahre 1897 bis zum Jahre 1922. Zum 75. Jubiläum der Gemeinde* (Milwaukee, 1922), 7 and 17; Ev.-Luth. Bethanien-Gemeinde, *Jahrbuch* III (1912), 4-6; for the Synod's position on Sunday schools, see also John F. Stach, "The Period of Assimilation 1894-1914. From the Opening of the Seward Teachers' Seminary to World War I," in *100 Years*, 163.

[20]See, e.g., G. A. Witte, "Bemerkungen über den Gebrauch zweier Sprachen in unsern Schulen," *Ev.-Luth. Schulblatt* 3 (1867/68), 149ff.; "Wie wahren wir den dt. Charakter unserer ev.-luth. Gemeindeschulen?" ibid., 24 (1889), 292; see also Arthur C. Repp, "The Luth. Church in America a Century Ago," *Concordia Hist. Inst. Quarterly* 20:3 (Oct., 1947), 155.

[21]See *Goldene Jubelfeier abgehalten in der Ev.-Luth. Dreieinigkitskirche am Sonntag, den 5. Jan. 1919, zur Erinnerung an die Einweihung der Dreieinigkeitsschule am Sonntag, den 3. Jan. 1869* (Milwaukee, 1919), 7; Koerner, *Bennett Law*, 23; "Lehrplan f. d. Gemeindeschulen der ev.-luth. Missouri-Synode zu Milwaukee, Wis. (Von der Milwaukee Lehrer-Konferenz)," *Ev.-Luth. Schulblatt* 25 (1890), 97ff.

[22]See "Lehrplan" 1890; "Ueber die luth. Gemeindeschulen Milwaukee's," *Ev.-Luth. Schulblatt* 30 (1895), 119-20; Koerner, *Bennett Law*, 23; for Milwaukee's parochial schools of the Wisconsin Synod, which had undergone a similar process, see "Statistik der Gemeindeschulen der Synode von Wisconsin im Synodaljahr 1891-92," *Schul-Zeitung* [Wis. Synod] 18 (1893), 12.

[23]See "Lehrplan" 1890.

[24]"Engl. Religionsunterricht in unseren Gemeindeschulen," *Ev.- Luth. Schulblatt* 36 (1901), 161-70; for a more detailed account of the method of bilingual religious instruction, see "Sollte in unsern Schulen Religionsunterricht in engl. Sprache erteilt werden; und wenn, wie sollte er erteilt werden?" ibid., 46 (1911), 133-39.

[25]See "Revid. Lehrplan f. d. Gemeindeschulen der Ev.-Luth. Missourisynode zu Milwaukee, Wis. (Von der Milwaukee-Lehrerkonferenz)," *Ev.-Luth. Schulblatt* 46 (1911), 193-224.

[26]See "Eine wichtige Frage," *Bethanien. Gemeindeblatt der Ev.-Luth. Bethanien-Gemeinde* 1:5,6 (Mai/Juni, 1918), 1f.; Ev.-Luth. Bethanien-Gemeinde, *Jahrbuch* 8 (1917), 11, and 9 (1918), 8; for a similar development in other parochial schools, see, e.g., Sprengeler, *Geschichte*, 25; W. F. Laesch, *History of the Ev. Luth. Zion Congregation at Milwaukee, Wis.*,

Commemorating Its 50th Anniv. . . . 1883-1933 (n.p., n.d.), 49; *Bethlehem Kirchenbote* 2:9,10 (Sept./Okt., 1919), 4.

[27]See "Die Wichtigkeit der engl. Sprache als Unterrichtsgegenstand in unseren Gemeindeschulen," *Ev.-Luth. Schulblatt* 1 (1865/66), 207; "Ueber den Gebrauch zweier Sprachen in unsern Schulen," ibid., 3 (1867/68), 230; for German language instruction in Milwaukee's public schools and its effect on parochial schools, see Milwaukee Board of School Commissioners, *Annual Report* (1876/77), 87; Bettina Goldberg, "Die Achtundvierziger u. das Schulwesen in Amerika: Zur Theorie u. Praxis ihrer Reformbestrebungen," *Amerikastudien/ American Studies* 32:4 (1987), 490, esp. fn. 38.

[28]See, e.g., Koerner, *Bennett Law*, which also includes the text of the law; for more recent accounts of the issue, see Roger E. Wyman, "Wisconsin Ethnic Groups and the Election of 1890," *Wisconsin Magazine of Hist.* 51 (1968), 269-93; Robert James Ulrich, *The Bennett Law of 1889. Education and Politics in Wisconsin* (New York, 1980).

[29]See, e.g., Stach, "Period of Assimilation," 137-141; Heinz Kloss, "Die deutsch-amerikanische Schule," *Jahrbuch f. Amerikastudien* 7 (1962), 154, 173, and "German-American Language Maintenance Efforts," in *Language Loyalty in the U.S. The Maintenance and Perpetuation of Non-English Mother Tongues by American Ethnic and Religious Groups,* ed. Joshua Fishman (London, 1966), 236.

[30]See "Der Schulsuperintendent der städt. Freischulen von Milwaukee," *Schul-Zeitung* 14 (1889), 92f.; "Im Staate Illinois," ibid., 137; "Folgen des Schulzwangsgesetzes im Staate Illinois," ibid., 15 (1890), 30; "Die Wahl am 4. Nov.," ibid, 139.

[31]"Die 'Nordwestl. Lehrerconferenz'," *Ev.-Luth. Schulblatt* 12 (1877), 271, 275ff. ("The English language is the language of the home country of our children; later on, our children have to do mission work also among their English-speaking fellow Americans, and, besides their professional obligations, they have to fulfill their responsibilities as citizens. . . In view of these circumstances it does not seem to be sufficient to teach English only as a subject in our schools"). Johann Wegner, born in Altona, Germany, emigrated with his parents to Illinois when he was five years old. He graduated from the synodical teachers' seminary in Fort Wayne in 1864. From 1867 until his retirement in 1911, he taught at Milwaukee's Luth. Trinity School (Lochner, *Geschichte*, 74; *Goldene Jubelfeier*, 7f.).

[32]"Nordwestl. Lehrerconferenz," 275. *"Die Befürchtung, durch ausgedehnten engl. Unterricht 'americanisire' man die Kinder,"* it was added, *"ist dabei eine unbegründete. Nicht der engl. Unterricht, sondern der Einfluss falsch- u. ungläubiger Lehrer u. Mitschüler erzeugt die gefürchteten Uebel"* (ibid., 275f.).

[33]cf. fn. 22. After the turn of the century, this tendency of the Luth. schools to adjust their secular curriculum to that of the city's public schools became even more marked. To counteract a decline in enrollment, Luth. schools were anxious to become accredited by the city's Board of School Commissioners, i.e. to get official recognition of their diplomas and thus of their equivalency with the public schools. See, e.g., *100th Ann. 1847-1947. Trinity Luth. Church Milwaukee, Wis.* (n.p., n.d.), 21; Hattstädt, *Kurzgefasste Geschichte;* "Revid. Lehrplan" 1910.

[34]Computed from an ethnically mixed sample of 1090 Milwaukee households, based on the ms. schedules of the U.S. Census on Population for 1910.

[35]See, e.g., Knortz, *Deutschthum,* 67f.; "Die Deutschen u. die dt. Sprache," *Germania u. Abendpost* (Milwaukee), 13 June 1900; "Engl. Religionsunterricht in unseren Gemeinde-schulen," *Evang.-Luth. Schulblatt* 36 (1901), 163; "English in Our Parochial Schools," ibid., 43 (1908), 313; Louis Zobel, "Die Erhaltung der dt. Sprache," ibid., 49 (1914), 97-104.

36See, e.g., *Kirchen-Ordnung der Gemeinde der Dt. Ev.-Luth. Immanuels-Kirche Ungeänderter Augsburg. Confession zu Milwaukee, Wis. Rev. 1884* (Milwaukee, 1884), §11; Ev.-Luth. Ebenezer Gemeinde, Jahrbuch X (1914), 16; *1888-1938. Golden Jubilee. Bethlehem Ev.-Luth. Church* (Milwaukee, 1938), 6 and 10; *25th Anniv. of the Sunday School. Trinity Ev.-Luth. Church* (n.p., n.d. [1939]), 5.

37See, e.g., *90th Anniversary, 1847-1937, Trinity Ev.-Luth. Church Milwaukee, Wis.* (n.p., n.d.), 7; *Bethany 1893-1983* (n.p., n.d.), 3; *A Brief Hist. of Luther Memorial Chapel on Its 25th Anniversary* (n.p., n.d. [1941]); see also Graebner, "Acculturation," 160f.

38Sievers, *Kurzgefasste Geschichte*, 28.

39See Martin W. Strasen, *Golden Jubilee 1894-1944. Ebenezer Luth. Church. Milwaukee, Wis.* (n.p., n.d.); Ev.-Luth. Ebenezer Gemeinde, *Jahrbuch* X (1914), 15f.; *1888-1938. Golden Jubilee. Bethlehem*, 6; *Ev.-Luth. Bethlehems-Kirche* 1:3 (Sept., 1911); Ev.-Luth. Bethanien-Gemeinde, *Jahrbuch* II (1911).

40*Revid. Kirchenordnung der Dt. Ev.-Luth. Immanuels-Gemeinde zu Milwaukee, Wis. 1913* (Milwaukee, 1913), §4 ("This directive remains effective as long as the congregation is able to meet its missionary responsibilities in the service of its members by means of the German language"); cf. *Kirchen-Ordnung der Gemeinde der Dt. Ev.-Luth. Immanuels-Kirche Ungeänderter Augsburg. Confession zu Milwaukee, Wis., 1869* (Milwaukee, 1869), §9 and 20; *Revidirt 1884*, §9.

41See Bettina Goldberg, "The German Language in Milwaukee's Grade Schools, 1850-1920: The Case of the Cath. Schools," John F. Kennedy-Institut f. Nordamerikastudien. Freie Univ. Berlin, *Working Paper* No. 17/1989.

9 | Amsterdam, Montana: In America, not of It? A Fractured History of Ethnic Continuity

Rob Kroes, *University of Amsterdam*

Dutch emigration to America has a history of over three centuries. The immigrants came by tens of thousands and in a number of separate waves. They first arrived early in the 17th century, settling in what was then known as the New Netherlands. They have left a lasting imprint on the evolving American society. One of the oldest denominations in the United States, the Reformed Church in America, is an offshoot of the Reformed Church of the Dutch Republic. A second influx, a great wave compared to prior immigrations, began to pick up in the late 1840s. It would bring a large number of the so-called Seceders (an orthodox break-away from the official Reformed Church) to America, along with their religious leaders. It led to the founding of a second variety of Dutch Reformed life in America: the Christian Reformed Church (CRC), with its center in the area of initial settlement, Grand Rapids, Mich.

This denomination in particular received an additional, strong infusion of members from a third wave of Dutch immigration around the turn of the century. In the Netherlands, under the charismatic leadership of Abraham Kuyper, a new religious awakening had occurred, very much an emancipation movement of the socially low. Many immigrants, freshly under the impact of this movement, came to reinforce the CRC ranks in America. Their trek across the continent, and their subsequent settlement on what was then the frontier, in the Dakotas, Nebraska, Montana, Washington and California, also brought the expansion of the CRC into what was only then a truly nationwide denomination. One such area of settlement, the Western Gallatin Valley, with a history of well-nigh a century of Dutch-American ethnic life, will concern us in this article.

The names on the mailboxes along the road do not leave one in doubt. Here, in a far-away valley in the American West, live people of Dutch origin. We see the names of Flikkema, Alberda, Sinnema, Weidenaar. In a few cases one is briefly misled by an Anglicized spelling. But there are always helpful residents to confirm one's hunches that, yes indeed, Cole used to be Kool, and Fisher Visser. In his frontyard one resident has proudly planted the little roadsign of Amsterdam that had until recently, soiled and tilting, indicated a stop on the nearby railroad spur. The spur having fallen into disuse, its tracks have been removed. Yet, clearly, the need for a marker has remained. There is no denying it: We are in Amsterdam, Montana. Here, in close mutual proximity, live a group of people who clearly value the preservation of a history which ties them all to the Netherlands. They have married mostly within their own group; they are not just neighbors, they have also become relatives. They have an uncanny sense, reminiscent almost of preliterate, tribal societies, of the kinship networks that tie them together. They are aware of their own separate identity; in conversations with them, one is struck by the fact that they refer to outsiders as "Americans," as if they had not been Americans themselves for a long time. The great majority of them have joined a church which spans the entire continent, but whose members are almost exclusively of Dutch descent. They live scattered across the fertile hilly area in the western part of the Gallatin Valley. There is no clear center of settlement remotely similar to Dutch villages or small towns. Yet, to someone who would be hovering over the area on a Sunday morning, the community would become clearly visible. It is like a spider's web in the early morning light of an autumn day. Like so many dewdrops, an army of cars converging on the church would show the structure of the social web, its center, its connecting points, its reach. At an elevation of some 1,500 meters above sea level, the Gallatin Valley lies surrounded by mountains. The natural scenery is dramatic, and so is its history. This is Lewis and Clark country. Three rivers, which rise in the nearby mountains, and which these early explorers named after Madison, Gallatin and Jefferson, here meet to form the mighty Missouri. Long ago the valley was the bed of a lake that has long since vanished. The soil is fertile and drains well. Its central part is relatively flat. Toward its edges, in broad undulating movement, it rises into an attractive hilly landscape. All around there is always a view of the mountains, nearby, if one looks East or South, as a firm demarcation of the valley, more distant towards the West, in a blue haze, deceptively low, gathering mass only at dusk when their jagged line dents the evening sky. The memory of early explorers like Bridger and Bozeman still lives on in the local geography, in the name of the Bridger Mountains that rise towards the

North-East, or of the town of Bozeman, the main urban center in the valley, seat of the county government and home to Montana State University. Although settlement goes back to the 1860s, the valley was really opened up for settlement by the construction of a railway line in the 1880s.

About the year 1890, Henry Altenbrand from New York, the son of a German immigrant and president of the *New York and Brooklyn Maltino Company,* had picked the Gallatin Valley with a view to growing malting barley there. Until that time the only barley, fit for malting, had come from Canada. But Altenbrand had his mind set on changing that. In 1888 he had been the main driving force in raising the tariff on malting barley from 10% to 30%. It gave him the protection he needed to start the cultivation of high-grade malting barley in the United States. From Germany he ordered 2,000 bushel of the famous Saale barley, which he then had planted in a number of selected areas. As it turned out, only the crop that had grown on irrigated land in the Gallatin Valley, was deemed satisfactory. It had in fact shown an improvement compared to the original seed material.

Then Altenbrand proceeded in a grand manner. Jointly with a number of East-Coast brewing and railroad interests, in 1889, he set up the *West Gallatin Irrigation Company.* Its first task consisted of the construction of an irrigation network that would take water from upstream the Gallatin River across the hilly land in the Southwestern part of the valley. The result of that first effort is still there. A pier of stones, stretching into the river like a bent arm, leads the water to the headgate of the irrigation system. From there it flows, following the natural contour of the land, through the main ditch and a number of laterals, covering a large area. In a short period of time, two systems were built, with different inlets on the river: the *Highline Canal* and the *Lowline Canal.* Eventually, the two systems would have a total combined length of over a hundred miles. There were a number of teething problems in the early years. At times the loose banks of the ditch would wash out, blocking the flow. Sometimes they would break, undermined by gophers. And worst, in some summers, they would fall dry too early in the growing season.

All this effort, of course, served the purpose of growing malting barley. As appears from the county records in Bozeman, the irrigation company, in 1892 and 1893, acquired large tracts of land from the Northern Pacific Railroad. Brought under irrigation the land produced well, so well in fact, that the first crops of barley caused a sensation in Europe. In 1893, the Imperial Ministry of Agriculture in Berlin, Germany, even despatched a staff of experts to the Gallatin Valley to report on the conditions there.

In 1890, Henry Altenbrand had also, jointly with a number of brewers from the East, founded the *Manhattan Malting Company.* On the railway line, immediately to the North of the irrigation area, they built a malting house for the processing of at least part of the harvest. The remainder was shipped East by train to be sold there or exported. Manhattan, the little railway town that grew around the malting operation, was like the malting company itself an expression of this link: Manhattan was whence the barley came, Manhattan was where it went.

The report to the Imperial Ministry of Agriculture made mention of a number of ten families of "Hollanders" that as early as 1891 had settled on land of the *West Gallatin Irrigation Company*. These families had all emigrated to America earlier. They were mostly all of Friesian origin. They had come to the older settlement areas in Michigan and Iowa. There, they must have heard about the new possibilities in Montana from a man who was to play an important role in the recruitment of Dutch settlers: the Rev. A. Wormser. Of Dutch origin himself, he was active in the West working for the Board of Domestic Missions of the Presbyterian Church in America. He was rather well connected among the Dutch immigrant population in Michigan and Iowa. It is hard to reconstruct how his link to Altenbrand was established, but in 1891, as an agent for the *West Gallatin Irrigation Company*, it was his task to recruit Dutch farmers, in America as well as in the Netherlands.

His timing could not have been better. The numbers of emigrants, leaving the Netherlands for America in search of work or of land, had gone up again. Emigration was predominantly from the rural areas where jobs in agriculture had diminished due to the mechanization and modernization of farming, and where no alternative employment opportunities in industry had come. In addition to this reservoir of poor and landless emigrants, there was a smaller, but socially important, contingent of sons of well-to-do farmers. They left the Netherlands, pushed not so much by the lack of work as by the lack of land and farming prospects there.

The emigration lists in the National Archives in Groningen do make us realize that there were rather marked differences among the emigrants in terms of their available cash resources. Pieter Alberda and Pieter Van Dijken, both from Bedum, are registered as "well-to-do", the others, among whom Jacob Kimm from Bierum, and Harmannus Klugkist from Bedum, as "less-well-off". None of those who got ready to move to Manhattan, was registered as "needy". Yet the difference does not tell us much. For one thing, we know that amongst their number, in the early years, there were no laborers or farmhands. They all came from the relatively small upper stratum of landholding rural families. Also, in many cases, there were intricate links of intermarriage. Pieter Alberda's wife, for instance, was a Klugkist, and if, at the National Archives in Groningen, one leafs through the pages of the genealogy of the old, elite Wigboldus family, one comes upon a number of names that also occur among the first group of Groningen emigrants to Montana. Thus, for instance, two of the three Van Dijken brothers who migrated to Montana in the 1890s, were married to a Wigboldus. As the emigration lists also tell us, the Montana group, when they left the country, were not homogeneous in religious terms either. Some were members of the established Dutch Reformed Church, others, like Alberda or Kimm, appear as Christian Reformed, in other words as members of more orthodox break-away churches. Yet, for all practical purposes, they acted as a cohesive group following their arrival in the Gallatin Valley.

When, for instance, the Dutch immigrants did have to move outside their own small circle, as they had to in the case of formal transactions such as the acquisition of a homestead or of citizenship, they selected the official witnesses from among their own people. Over and over again, in the official records we come upon the same Dutch names, in varying combinations. There are only a few exceptions, as in the case of Arien Doornbos who was among the later arrivals and was the last to acquire a homestead at what was then the far western corner of the Dutch settlement area. His only Dutch neighbor, John Weidenaar, and two of his American neighbors appear as witnesses on his naturalization and homestead documents.

Most of them, shortly after their arrival in the Gallatin Valley, filed their homestead applications, accompanied—as required by law—by their applications for citizenship. It is amusing, after so "many years, to go over these documents. At the time of his naturalization, after the statutory five years of residence had lapsed, the new citizen had to declare under oath "that he will support the Constitution of the United States of America, and that he doth absolutely and entirely renounce and abjure all allegiance and fidelity to every foreign Prince, Potentate State or Sovereignty whatever, and particularly to" (then follows a dotted line on which we see written:) "Wilhelmina Queen of the Netherlands." That is how it went, in case after case—Our Kingdom for a Homestead.

In addition, some also proceeded to buy land from the irrigation company. It can serve as a further corrective to the rough-and-ready categorizing of the emigration lists. Jacob Kimm, for instance, although registered as "less-well-off", never bothered to apply for a homestead but bought land directly from the irrigation company. Pieter Van Dijken did likewise. Pieter Alberda and Lambertus Van Dijken did both: they took out a homestead and bought company land in an adjacent section. In all cases this must have been some form of installment purchase, since, according to the records at the County Court House in Bozeman, all company land, bought by the settlers, was only registered in the name of the Dutch owners after some five, or six years.

As the ledgers of the *Manhattan Malting Company* show, the agrarian production rapidly took off. In November and December there are entries for the barley crops of P. Alberda, J. Balda, J. Braaksma, W. Broekema, A. Brouwer, J.P. Van Dijken, L. Van Dijken, P.P. Van Dijken, J.R. Kimm, W. Koning, J. TeSelle, J. Weidenaar. Payments ranged from $400 for TeSelle to $85 forWeidenaar. Kimm, Brouwer and Alberda were in the same range with incomes of about $370. According to a letter from Pieter Van Dijken, son of one of the early settlers, who at the time worked for Kimm, Kimm's crop had been 35 bushels of oats per acre in 1894. From the same time we have a report, perhaps overly roseate, from a D.J. Walvoord, teacher at the little country school in the hills near the old cemetery. Crop returns, as he mentions them for October 1894, are an approximate 45 bushels of barley per acre.

Walvoord had come from the Dutch community in Cedar Grove, Wisconsin. His report, dated 12 October 1894, appeared the following year in the *Sheboygan Herald* in Wisconsin. It is a clear case of that general repertoire of advocacy writing which must have made Dutch immigrants in the older settlement areas in the East and Midwest aware of possibilities further West. As he put it:

> I was met at Manhattan by Reverend Wormser and Reverend Van den Hoek of Chicago, who was here on his second trip, and who since his first visit has been an enthusiastic admirer of Montana climate, fertility of soil, and beautiful scenery. I may state right here, that fertile as our own good state of Wisconsin is, I never saw such fields of grain and other produce. In every direction could be seen fields of golden and heavy grain still in the shock. Everybody I met was abundant in praise of irrigation, by which a large crop is secured year after year. . . . One of the farms we visited was the one belonging to Jan TeSelle, who was formerly of Cedar Grove, and lately of Sioux County, Iowa. They had threshed 3500 bushels of grain, from 120 acres, part of which had been plowed for the first time last spring, and not a foot of which had been under cultivation for more than two years.

He also mentioned his visit to the farm of Reverend Derk E. Deuninck, a friend and colleague of Van den Hoek. Deuninck had just recently acquired a homestead himself, south of the TeSelle place, and had bought additional land from the irrigation company. Walvoord concluded by saying: "I have decided to spend the winter here, and have been engaged to teach a district school, soon to be opened in the settlement." It was a personal note which could only enhance the appeal of his report.

Going over the documents pertaining to the acquisition of land, as well as the case files concerning homestead land, one is able to reconstruct the early settlement history. A total of 26 Dutch immigrants filed for a homestead and acquired one. Doornbos was the last. In 1912 he received title to his land. If one looks at the settlement pattern across the map, it forms a relatively continuous band following the irrigation network of the *Highline* and *Lowline* canals, stretching from the hills area in the south towards Manhattan where the land begins to level off. Dutch homestead land is concentrated at both the southern and northern ends of this band of settlement. The area in between was mostly farm land bought directly from the irrigation company or from earlier, non-Dutch homesteaders. Today it is hard to imagine how—despite the poor connections of the early years—two cores of settlements could have formed, one in the hills, the other around Churchill and Amsterdam. The small world that Pieter Van Dijken described in 1894 in a letter to the Netherlands was in fact the beginning of the community in the hills. His daily world really ended at the somewhat more northerly farm of Jacob Kimm on Godfrey Creek just south of Churchill. It took him over an hour to get there. He got home only for the weekends. Religious meetings, mostly Bible reading, were held initially at his uncle Pieter's place. At the insistence of Rev. Wormser a Presbyterian congregation was formed, which later on would meet in a nearby school. The congregation bore the name of *Second Holland Presbyterian Church.*

The more northerly group at first oriented itself more toward nearby Manhattan. H.J. Bos, for instance, had his homestead in the area in addition to a blacksmith shop in town. Others found work there for longer or shorter periods. The *First Holland Presbyterian Church* also was in Manhattan. The first pastor to serve both groups was the pastor-farmer Derk Deuninck. Somewhat later his friend and colleague Van den Hoek would join him, an emeritus from Chicago, and like Deuninck quick to apply for a homestead, slightly to the east of the southern core of settlement.

Thus, the early Dutch immigrants found themselves organized within a church of essentially Anglo-Saxon origin. It may have been as good a solution as any. Doctrinally and organizationally, English Presbyterianism is close to the Dutch-Reformed church. Also, their early ministers, Wormser, Deuninck, Van den Hoek, were all Dutch-born, and thoroughly familiar with Dutch churchly traditions and teachings. Yet, as we shall see shortly, this arrangement would only be transitional.

In yet different ways did the separation into two spheres of organized social life appear, as it was imposed by the geographical dispersal of the settlers. Given the poor connections, schools could not be too far from their pupils' homes. Parents were free to petition the county government to organize their neighborhood into a separate school district. It was not long before a number of little one-room schools were set up, scattered across the entire area of settlement of the Dutch. And among the members of the different school boards, once again we come across their names. In the more southerly District 52, the so-called *Little Holland District* in the hills, we meet the Weidenaars, the Braaksmas, Broekema, Veltkamp, Alberda, Balda, and of those that had come later, like Cornelius Lucas, Sam Dijk, and G. Van der Ark. The composition of the school boards was solidly Dutch. The teachers too were all Dutch. District 34, at the northern tip of Godfrey Canyon, near present-day Churchill, shows the names of those that had settled there, like Lambertus Van Dijken (who had bought land nearby) and his son Pieter, Jacob Kimm, and one non-Dutch resident, Amos Walrath. More northerly again, there was the Heeb School, named after a farmer in the area, in District 30. There Henry TeSelle and somewhat later Garret Te Hennepe (a man from the province of Gelderland in the Netherlands who had gotten there via Wisconsin) together with non-Dutch residents formed the School Board. At the far north, in District 3 in Manhattan, not surprisingly the role of the non-Dutch is predominant, but even so we come upon the name of J.H. Bos representing the Dutch contingent there. Finally, toward the western edge of the Dutch settlement, at the behest of Arien Doornbos, two school districts were formed, of which District 8 in particular showed a gradually increasing Dutch character of its School Board. It was a reflection of the increasing westward expansion of Dutch settlement. This local variety of the "Westward trek", which had gathered momentum during World War I, at a time when agricultural prices were high and rainfall relatively precipitous,[1] in fact meant that people had moved beyond the irrigated area to take up "dry farming" on land that they, for the most part, had leased.

Some ten years earlier a clear need for a consolidation of the community around one center of religious life had made itself felt. As Pieter Van Dijken, the one who wrote the early letter of 1894, remembered it some sixty years later,[2] religious life in the community had begun to stagnate, especially in its more isolated branch in the hills. But also among those who lived not far from Manhattan there was dissatisfaction. At the time, services in the Presbyterian church there were only held in English by a pastor from Bozeman. A missionary from the Classis Orange City, Iowa, of the *Christian Reformed Church* visited the area during the summer of 1902 and held services in both the Hills School in the South and the Heeb School in the North.

He was a moving force behind the drive toward consolidation. In 1903 a group of nineteen families and five single men, from North and South, jointly decided to found a ChristianReformed congregation. The first consistory, in its membership, reflected the consolidation of the community. The first elders were J.H. Bos, A. Elings and W. Broekema, the first deacons E. Bos and J. Braaksma. North and South were equally represented among them. One of their first constitutive acts concerned the erection of a church. They decided to locate it on Churchill (or Church Hill, as the contemporary spelling more appropriately had it), in the center of the settlement, halfway North and South. It was to be a clear beacon, in more than one sense. As a guiding light it was to turn the dispersed settlers inward upon themselves, inspiring a sense of their own vital center, their common tradition. At the same time it would also be a demarcation, setting them apart from their American environment. The congregation would see a rapid increase in its numbers, due to the influx of new settlers in the years up to World War I. In 1904 it counted a total of 40 families, in 1908 a total of 50, and in 1913 of 90 families.

This first act of consolidation would be followed by others. It was not long before it was decided to set up a separate, denominational school system parallel to the established system of public education. Financially that was a daring step indeed. Like other Americans the Dutch settlers would have to continue to support public schools in addition to shouldering the full burden of their own schools. One gets a sense of the symbolic dimensions of this organizational withdrawal from the established forms of American society, if one reminds oneself of the fact that already in their various school districts, the Dutch were in relative control of public education. Yet, as they saw it, that was not enough. They felt insufficiently free to bring up their children in their own Christian way of life. Again, as with the church, their first school was built right at the center of the settlement, on Church Hill. But distance affects schools differently than it does church-going. With only one Christian school, consolidation could have only a limited effect in the area of education. However, when in 1909, on financial grounds, the county government decided to discontinue the public school in the hills, parents there decided to set up a Christian School as well. They kept it going until 1920, when after a number of years of drought and low prices, they were forced temporarily to close the school door.

In 1904 we see the adoption of this strategy of separate, denominational schools. On May 12th the first general meeting took place of the "Vereeniging ter oprichting en instandhouding van Christelijk Onderwijs, op Gereformeerden Grondslag" ("Association for the Founding and Maintenance of Christian Education on a Reformed Basis"). A great many members, from all across the Dutch settlement, had joined the association. The basis and object of the association was formulated thus: "The basis of the Association is God's Word according to the three formulas of Unity;" "The object of the Association is the founding and maintenance of Christian schools of a Reformed nature in our area, to the extent that there are members." Thus people took up a Dutch tradition of religious life that went back as far as the

Synod of Dordrecht of 1618-19. (Then Calvinism in the Netherlands received its characteristic Dutch imprint for the consolidation of Dutch community life in a distant and alien America.)

One cannot fail to notice that in this process of consolidation around church and school little emphasis was being put on the preservation of the Dutch language. In the General Meeting of Members of April 1909, for instance, it was decided that only the first year of grade school would be taught in Dutch. "In the other grades Dutch will be taught for half a day every week. Bible classes too will be in Dutch. All other subjects will be taught in English." What remained of a Dutch education left much to be desired, as recorded by the school board in 1910: The schoolmistress in her Dutch classes mixed "English and Dutch too much." In 1914 it was considered whether Bible classes should henceforth be taught in English. And in 1919 it was decided to translate the Statutes of the Association into English. In 1924, finally, in an amended version of the Statutes, it was agreed to "abolish Dutch in the first grade." Gradually, step by step, the next generation was being linguistically disinherited. The Dutch language clearly was not considered crucial to the heritage that people did indeed wish to preserve.

Thus, in the early 20th century, a consolidation of the community had occurred around the institutions of church and school. But we must not overstate the point. Not everyone involved in the movement went along in every single respect. There were those that joined the new church congregation but never sent their children to the Christian school. Others, after a shorter or longer period, stopped supporting Christian education. Still others stood aloof altogether from the consolidation of the Dutch community. They had begun to mingle with their American fellow citizens and continued doing so. They most likely lived in or near Manhattan, like the Fabriek family, or the Presbyterian minister Van den Hoek and his son who was to become a banker in Manhattan, or Chris Buitenhof who was to collect a fortune as an apiculturist. When we speak of consolidation, therefore, it is only in a relative sense. Never did the process include all Dutch settlers. There was always a grey zone where the community blended into the American environment. We would do well to conceive of consolidation as a strategy of ethnic survival, with its advocates and activists vying for cultural hegemony within their ethnic community with those who put a lesser emphasis on ethnic cohesion.

The twenties and thirties were a high point in this battle of rival affinities. They were times of hardship and depression in agricultural life; yet, characteristically, the tensions were expressed in language that centrally concerned the sense of identity of this Dutch-Calvinist group. In a collection of letters, sent to relatives and friends in the Netherlands, J.R. Kimm and his wife Willemina Omta, one of the established and central families of the community, we find telling references to the cultural clash within the settlement.

During the 1920s religious revival movements had been active in the immediate vicinity of the settlement. Their appeal had not gone unheeded among the Dutch. One influence was the revivalist preacher Linus (or Lyness) who made some early conversions among people who were on the fringe of the Dutch community. But there were more cases where an outside call found a willing response within the community and where it led to the formation of small church groups, composed jointly of Dutch and American believers. Precisely this response within the Dutch community to siren voices outside can help us understand why religious conflict was most acute within the community, resulting in a long drawn-out and high-pitched debate about the proper definitions of their own pure faith. It was not a matter of a united front of the Dutch confronting the outside world. A rift began to open up ever more clearly, cutting right through the community. Elsewhere in America, among the Dutch-Americans, a schism had already occurred, beginning right at the center of Christian-Reformed life: Grand Rapids. There, in 1924, the Reverend Hoeksema and a number of like-minded followers had been expelled from the Christian Reformed Church on account of their deviant doctrinal teachings. The news had reached Montana and other places of Christian Reformed life through various channels, through reports and polemical writings in the Journals of the Christian Reformed Church, the *Wachter* and the *Banners,* through personal channels such as letters, and through the formal meetings of the regional church Classis where consistory members from Churchill were delegated.

In 1926 Kimm mentions the unrest in his letters.

In the area of church and school there is much commotion, among the Hollanders in the United States. Church teachings are being preached in a way as if man has it in his power to do much through good works. Well, we know better than that. On our own we can do nothing but through God's grace. There are already 11 congregations that have left the Chr. Ref. church, partly expelled, and in other places congregations are being organized, separate from the Chr. Ref. church, which for the time being have the name of the *protesting* church. Well, the protesters are much purer in their teaching and preaching than the Chr. Reformed. Recently we had Rev. Bultema from Muskegon here. That is another fine speaker, but of course he was not allowed to speak in the church, so it had to be in a school house. He has preached six times, 3 times English and 3 times Dutch. Always a large audience, for a sparsely populated country. Always the school brimming over with people. You may have read about Bultema; and also about Danhof, Hoeksema, and others. Would it all were to God' s honor and our salvation.

People like Hoeksema, Danhof and Bultema were uncompromising in their
return to a number of old doctrinal tenets of Dutch Calvinism, especially in
such areas as the doctrine of predestination and God's covenant with His
Chosen People. God's sovereign grace, as these theologians saw it, was not
open to arrangement with such as hoped to win His kind-heartedness through
good works.

Kimm's wife Wilhelmina too goes into the religious dispute in a letter of
December, 1930.

> There is turmoil here in every area, church and school. Many people leave church
> who have come to different views. There are alien preachers here, and there they
> come to see the light, they say. They find the preaching more appealing. There is a
> whole awakening going on. They can tell what the Lord has done to their souls. They
> do not believe in child baptism any more, nor in many other things. That is why they
> can no longer go to church here. The millennium is all they can talk about. They
> have themselves baptised again in the river. It is a strange world nowadays. But I
> think it is good for all of us. People talk much more about God's Word than before.

The social position of the Kimms gave them a certain distance in their
observations of the commotion and change going on in their community. The
economic depression was no personal emergency for them. They were never
alarmist about signs of decay or slippage, in the outside world or in their own
midst. The turmoil in the church they observed with relative equanimity.
They knew where they stood themselves and that sufficed. In 1932, in perfect
detachment, Kimm overlooks the increase in religious diversity. He is even
capable of discovering elements of unity in diversity.

> There is a lot going on here among the Hollanders. Marvel, marvel! Near us we have
> the Reformed church. A mile west of us (in Amsterdam) the free evangelical
> association. In Manhattan town, another evangelical variety, and then the
> presbyterian church also controlled by Hollanders. Two brothers-in-law of Henry
> Kimm's wife (his own daughter-in-law) do services there as elders, not reading, but
> leading.

It is a very astute observation. Whatever diversity might have occurred, it
did not diminish the fact that on either side of every fissure there were
"Hollanders," friends, relatives, in-laws. Manifold ties kept people together
who had each gone their own separate ways in religious matters.

Undoubtedly, then, it is not so much church and faith that have cemented
the Dutch community in the Gallatin Valley, but rather what one should call
ethnic consciousness. The latter is able to transcend religious divisions and
draws a wider, more encompassing circle around a group of people, defining
their characteristic sense of identity. Yet it is by no means a very rigid

boundary. It gives no exhaustive definition of their identity. At best their sense of ethnicity, of Dutchness, is no more than a rather vague sentiment that affects their behavior only in certain areas, in their choice of friends, or of marriage partners. And sometimes not even there. There is always a wide, grey zone where an ethnic community tends to blur into its environment. But if we move inwards from the margin toward the center, ethnicity becomes more of a guiding force, leaving its imprint on an increasing number of institutions of an unmistakably ethnic character. If we look at it that way, we have another vantage point from which to consider the role of the church in the Dutch community.

All my spokesmen who were convinced of the role of the church in the preservation of their community do have a point, but in a rather complex way. Yes, if we look at their past, we see a history of conflict and fissure. It does not seem to help us fathom the continuity of their communal life. Yet my spokesmen have given a crucial clue. Their views give us an insight in what to them formed the overarching dimension of their society: religion. Their social order based itself on their conviction to be a Covenanted People, secure in their anticipation of God's special Grace. Ethnicity to them only counts in this light. As partners to the Covenant, they are aware of their perennial links to a distant country where their fathers had first seen the light. Thus, they are in a line of Dutch descent in a very special, Providential sense, connecting them to the Synod of Dordt, to the Secession and to Kuyperianism—high points in a history of Dutch Calvinist orthodoxy—rather than to such accidental places on the map as Friesland, or Groningen, or Zeeland. Their line of descent links them securely to an old promise of collective salvation. At the same time it places them in a tradition that is forever intent on deviation and false prophets. They brought with them an age-old virtuosity, defending and defining the "true church." They saw signs, they spoke a language, which could divide them against themselves, yet could also set them apart, collectively, as a group, from any environment that stood in a different tradition. And since their emigration their environment was no longer Dutch, but American. Their constant alertness could take on the "ethnic" appearance of a defense of their heritage against Americanization. If they felt it was necessary, for a clear and unambiguous demarcation from the environment, to draw the line right through their own community, that is what they did. But, remarkably, the over-all effect was for the parties on either side of the dividing line to carry on their fight, not unlike soccer teams after the kick-off. There was a unity of discourse, a continued interaction, a frenetic involvement in a fight whose rules and nuances were only known to them. Thus, in this rather intricate way, one can argue that indeed, in spite of schisms and fights, religion has been a factor of their continued communal existence.

Interestingly, the traditional language of religious debate, which had fostered many a church schism in the Netherlands, served to give expression to their endeavour to protect their Dutch heritage against American encroachments. Religion served as a border-protecting device. Most potently, the debate about God's grace being general, extending to all of creation, or particular, including solely His Chosen People, served to draw a hard line in the defense and definition of a Dutch American identity in the midst of an overbearing American environment. Precisely on that issue the Christian Reformed community broke up in 1939, with the hardliners withdrawing upon an uncompromising position of special grace. They were in the world, but not of it. They were in America, but not of it. Pulling up the bridges behind them, they withdrew within an ethnic bastion, narrowly defined, leaving the doubters in their midst to fend for themselves.

Looking at the lines that were drawn and that set up contending parties within the community vying for control of the definition of their identity, an outside observer may feel tempted to see it as a mere epiphenomenon. He may set out on a reductionist quest for real interests underlying the surface conflict. Yet, in whatever way we try to do this, no clear underlying lines of fissure can be seen. It is not a matter of hidden class conflict: we find rich and poor, tenant and farmer, on both sides of the dividing line. Nor is it a matter of periphery versus centre: again, we find a mixture of both on either side of the line.

Therefore, we should take the language of their conflict as a meaningful expression of the conflict as the contenders saw it. We should try to look at it through their eyes. That, however, would only take us back to our initial question: can religion have been the ingredient of this community's continued cohesion, if, at the same time, it was an element of fissure? There is, it seems, a dialectical answer to this quandary.

Early sociologists and anthropologists have already reminded us of the integrating function of conflict. Therefore, rather than trying to reduce the religious conflict to its assumed "real" causes, we are well advised to look at it in terms of its functions. Thus, one main actor in the conflict, the Reverend Bernard Kok, who came to the area in 1938 as a missionary fire-brand minister of the Protestant Reformed Church to work toward a schism, pounding away on the theme of God's particular grace, used one tactical device that clearly worked to integrate rather than to divide the Dutch community. Trying to expose the local CRC establishment as half-hearted backsliders, who had neglected the cause of Christian education, he actually shamed the entire community into a renewed effort to support and expand the

Christian school. Both religious camps that he left in his wake actually worked harmoniously together toward that goal. An element of integration was as much a result of his efforts as the church split that he had effected.

But in a much more general sense, it appears, the raging conflict over fine points of religious doctrine has served to draw the entire community more closely together. Spending their mental energies on a religious conflict of which all participants could see the implications and ramifications, they were kept from dividing along more secular lines precisely at a time of economic hardship. Their common quest was precisely to find sense and significance in their trials and tribulations in language that they understood, looking at temporal events in the light of God's plans. Whatever the outcome, they were acting out a highly stylized and linguistically articulate conflict of which they, and they alone, exactly knew the rules. As if they were playing a folkloristic game from their homeland they were turning their backs upon an environment that had no inkling of what they got so worked up about. Both contending parties were busy fighting over a religious tradition which left them revitalized as a community, in America, but not (quite) of it.

In conclusion, let us highlight some of the aspects which make our case of the Dutch settlement in Montana especially interesting in the context of the history of the American West.

Firstly, much of the history of the West is still written in a main-stream Anglo-Saxon mould. The history of the Dutch settlement in the Gallatin Valley may remind us of the ethnic dimension to the settling of the West and make us aware that ethnic enclaves are not just a feature of the urbanized immigrant East, changing the ethnic make-up of the nation there while the West managed to keep its pristine "American" character.

Secondly, much of the rhetoric of the frontier is still cast in terms of rugged individualism, of settlers individually breaking the land, powerfully sustained by the availability of free land. The history of the Dutch settlement may teach us that behind the success of this particular community, as of many others, was a combination of homestead history and large-scale capitalist development ventures. The latter provided the means for investment in land development without which many settlement ventures were to end in dismal failure.

Lastly, and most importantly, the history of this one settlement may teach us much about the way a vague and general concept like ethnic cohesion has in fact been expressed in meaningful language and significant social strife. It makes us aware of the intricate relationship between religion and ethnicity, as well as of the complex dialectics between conflicts and schisms on the one hand and cultural and social continuity on the other.

A Note on Sources

This article is based on the research for my book *Nederlandse Pioniers in het Amerikaanse Westen* (Amsterdam, 1989); the title of the English language edition is *The Persistence of Ethnicity: Dutch Calvinist Pioneers in Amsterdam, Montana* (Champaign, IL, 1992). My sources were many and varied: Archives in the Netherlands and the United States, pertaining to emigration records, church and school board records, court records, land acquisition records; collections of letters; interviews; diaries; published material such as religious periodicals and immigrant memoirs.

Notes

[1]For figures concerning annual precipitation and wheat prices, for the period from 1892 to 1935, see Meinte Schuurmans, "The Church and Assimilation in an Isolated Nationality Group: A Study of the Role of the Christian Reformed Church in the Dutch Community near Manhattan, Montana," M.A. thesis (Michigan State College of Agriculture and Applied Sciences, 1941), 88.

[2]He wrote down this memoir on the occasion of the 50th anniversary of the Christian Reformed Church in Churchill. It would be printed in *The High Country* (3/31/1976).

IV.
SECULAR SETTLEMENTS: CONCEPTS AND REALITIES

10 | New Germany in North America: Origins, Processes, and Responses, 1815–1860

Stefan von Senger und Etterlin, *Freie Universität Berlin*

W hen the young German poet Ludwig Boerne, in his Paris exile in the year 1832, was asked to join an acquaintance of his in emigrating to the United States, he jokingly replied:

> I would be rather inclined to do that, if I were not afraid that, as soon as there were 40,000 of us on the Ohio and there would then be formed the new state, 39,999 of those good German souls would pass a resolution to send for one of their beloved young princes in Germany to be their Head of State.[1]

With this response, Boerne touched upon problems inherent in the idea of forming a German state, a "New Germany," on America's frontier. Why would Boerne immediately associate the notion of emigrating to America's West with the idea of creating a German state there? And was he right in assuming that Germans would cling together and prefer being ruled by a monarch rather than becoming members of the American republic? What was so ludicrous about the whole idea?

This paper explores two main theses: First, the idea of forming a New Germany in North America was a projection of the dreams of a united, strong, prosperous, and culturally dominant Germany, dreams which could not be fulfilled in Europe at the time. Second, in so doing, the schemers almost entirely disregarded the wishes of the overwhelming majority of the emigrants and misjudged completely the reality of the North American continent.

1. ORIGIN AND CHARACTER OF THE IDEA OF A NEW GERMANY

The idea of a New Germany was born in the late 1810s out of a mixture of statesmanly paternalism and romantic adventurism. The first wave of mass emigration from the devastated southwestern German states to North America in 1816-1817 had not only put into question the existing state of affairs in the petty German kingdoms, but had also aroused the patriotic spirit of some observers. Among them was the young administrative accountant Friedrich List and the representative of the Netherlands at the Bundestag in Frankfurt, Hans Christoph Baron von Gagern.

Friedrich List

Friedrich List was charged by the Württemberg government to report on the reasons for and conditions of the unheard-of mass emigration.[2] The young man's observations led him to conceive of the role emigrants could play in advancing the German national economy. As he later admitted, in the mid-1820s, he was convinced that the Germans in North America could keep their language and customs and could become both producers of raw-materials for the home-country as well as consumers of manufactured goods from Germany. List even planned to found a German settlers colony on his own in Michigan Territory.[3] However, once living in the U.S., he quickly lost interest in the project. Nevertheless, he integrated the idea of emigrant colonies in his theory of world trade. The possession of settlement colonies to him was a natural outflow of the superiority of the "Germanic race." The settlers were to spread material civilization and political culture over the globe. By 1846—while England concentrated on Africa and Asia—List thought Central- and South America (including Texas) to be natural prey for the Germans.[4]

Trade and Emigration

List exemplified the curious combination of liberal political thought with a pre-imperialist expansionism, which came to be a hallmark of the liberal-national movement in the 1830s and 1840s. The economic profits, made by the different trades connected with the emigration process, were felt most strongly in the places of embarkment such as Bremen and Hamburg. The Hanse towns welcomed the opportunity for passenger traffic on their ships sailing across the Atlantic—it cheapened the back-freight consisting of tobacco, tar, or cotton.[5] Hanseatic trade companies also established branches in the American seaports and slowly developed a network of associates in inland towns. Quite naturally, they contributed to greater sales of German products.[6] Some were so enthusiastic about the prospects of trade in the wake of mass emigration that they proposed the German Customs Union should negotiate protective agreements with the U.S. Government. German settlements were to be given special considerations for importing German goods.[7] Others demanded the installment of warehouses in connection with the creation of special emigration consuls sent by the German states to all major American cities.[8] Nothing came of those plans.

As mass emigration set in again after 1830, a wave of pamphlets, articles, and other public announcements began to espouse the idea of organizing emigration along national lines. Liberals interested in the social effects of emigration demanded individual freedom of movement and called for national remedies. In that sense, they contributed to a slow but certain advancement towards safer and healthier travel conditions, legal guarantees, etc. On the other hand, they thought emigration to be a huge loss of manpower and capital. Consequently, Germans abroad had to be organized in ways useful to themselves *and* to the fatherland. At least their "Germandom" should not be lost for the nation.

Hans Christoph Baron von Gagern

Possibly no one did more to arouse the public's attention to the necessity of so doing than Hans Christoph von Gagern. In the late 1810s he wrote several memoranda to the German Bundestag asking for unified action. He also sent his cousin, Moritz von Fürstenwärther, on a mission to the U.S. to garner more reliable data on the conditions of emigrating and settling. Gagern surely was a patriot and convinced that the Germans could fare better in the New World if they stuck together. In fact, one of his instructions to Fürstenwärther was to be on the lookout for areas particularly suited for German group settlements.[9] As a life-time member of the Upper Chamber of the Grand Duchy of Hesse-Darmstadt, Gagern continued to raise the issue of emigration and the necessity to organize it nationally well into the late 1840s. At the same time he became the *spiritus rector* of many emigration associations. But Gagern was never a proponent of a completely separate German community in North America. Rather, he wished the German settlers in America to become a colony of Germany in the ancient Greek way. They were to be seen as autonomous spin-offs of the mother country, bringing German culture to the prairies and generally raising America's conscience of, and friendship with, Germany.[10] The concept of such an informal kind of colony received wide support by many of the writers on emigration. Germans were to penetrate the western part of the U.S. and thus to achieve at least regional predominance. In the literature of the day there was a strong undercurrent espousing the idea of the Germans' cultural superiority; it would thrive even if the Germans were to Americanize in more superficial matters. On the other hand, there was also an element of conscious departure from a repressive political system. The New Germany in America was to fulfill the republican ideals of many liberals.

Romanticism and the Agitation for a New Germany

Romantic notions of a "German fatherland" extending "as far as the German tongue is spoken"[11] or being "of a higher kind"[12] made many contemporaries watch the flow of emigrants in the optimistic belief that these people would serve the expansion of the German nation. In 1847 the liberal professor Robert Mohl thought the German people would never fulfill their mission if they didn't do their share spreading "European morals and nationality over the other continents." Germandom was equally worthy of expansion as were the other *Culturvölker*.[13]

The notion of "colony" in the early 1800s vascillated between what was sometimes called the "old" versus the "new system" of colonization. The old system was exemplified by the former British, Spanish or French colonial possessions. These were politically dependent entities settled primarily by subjects from the mother country. Trade was rigidly controlled. This system broke apart with the American Revolution. The new system of colonization was much more informal. Trade relations were based on the idea of a more or less free exchange. The new system relieved the former colonial powers from administrative and financial burdens and still offered hefty profits while providing territory for overpopulation at home.

Thus agitation for a German settler colony in North America commenced at a time when dependent colonies were going out of style. In addition, it was clear that neither the *Deutsche Bund* nor any of its member states had any inclination or the power to acquire colonial property. Agitation for a German colony, therefore, usually set limited goals. Only in rare cases did authors fantasize about possible new empires. In 1830 or 1840, Germany's might consisted of human bodies seeking their luck elsewhere. If there was to be a larger role for Germany in the world, these emigrants somehow had to become carriers of Germandom. Thus the notion of *colony*, by and large, took on the meaning of *settler colony*.

Generally, the discussion on purpose and nature of such colonies would fall into three categories:

(1) the idea of a "focal point," which would serve as a magnet to further immigration, eventually leading to the Germanization of a whole region or state;

(2) the plan to form a separate community (state), but as a member of the U.S.;

(3) the intention to create a German republic entirely independent from the U.S. and to provide a maximum of interchange with Germany.[14]

Ludwig Gall, Karl Follen and Gottfried Duden

In 1819, Gagern's activities spurred Ludwig Gall, a young administrator from Trier, to plan an emigration society of his own. But since the Prussian government was unwilling to charter it, Gall left for Bern and in 1819 led about 240 emigrants to Indiana. He then traveled throughout the Pennsylvania and Ohio German settlements and formulated a plan to create a "Deutschheim," a German city, which was to become the nucleus of further German penetration.[15]

The political refugee Karl Follen, who had been the leader of the radical Giessen-based fraternity "The Blacks" in the early 1820s, wrote a secret pamphlet elaborating his idea of a "free abode [Freystätte] for oppressed Germans and a source of income" in the form of a German university in the northeastern U.S. Drawing many Germans to settle nearby, the university, Follen hoped, would develop into "a state which would be represented in Congress. . . (and) which would be a model for the mother country."[16] When he arrived in America, however, he soon gave up the plan and himself became a professor at Harvard College instead.

The most well-known German traveler to America espousing the idea of a New Germany was Gottfried Duden. In 1824 he arrived in Missouri and experimented with a farm. It was to be his model for a successful settlement of his countrymen. Upon his return to Germany, he published a flamboyant report. Duden soon became subject to criticism, for he had given too romantic an image of life on the frontier. But at first his talk of a "rejuvenated Germania" west of the Mississippi, of a *Pflanzerstadt* that could become the magnet of German culture in North America, fell on fertile ground. As a result, at least five large emigration societies formed and actually sent members to Missouri (and onwards): associations from Berlin, Mühlhausen/Thuringia, Frankfurt, Solingen, and Giessen.

Preferred Areas of Settlement

Beginning in the early 1830s, there were writers who delineated in some detail where Germans would find the best opportunities for group settlements and forming a state of their own. For some, this state was to be part of the U.S.; others recommended areas in the far West. In 1829, Jonas Gudehus thought the western territories in North America to be better suited. If asked by a well-managed emigration society, some leaders theorized, the American government would surely grant them a large piece of land.[17] Karl von Sparre believed the German nation should not forego colonies and sea-trade—nay, it should "give the world an example of what German strength and endurance" were able to achieve. The emigrants should be led to Texas, "form German colonies there and receive ordinances by the German cabinets."[18] Traugott Bromme, usually quite sober an observer of American realities, had drafted a plan for a German settler colony in Michigan as early as 1834.[19] In 1847 he still reminded his fellow countrymen how easy it would be to unify the four million [sic] Germans in North America and establish a "new Germany" with them.[20] Another widely read author of emigration handbooks, Ernst Ludwig Brauns, asked whether "the German nation should never cease to see in her tribal folks abroad the apes and donkeys of all nations." He wondered whether a guided emigration might not create a new Germany in the trans-Mississippi area. There, he felt, where as yet no other "European nations or Anglo-Americans trying to impress their spirit unto all other nationalities settling next to them."[21] For him, the southwestern Pacific coast of California was to be the blossoming *Neudeutschland*.[22] In 1846, the editors of one of the two major emigration journals, the *Allgemeine Auswanderungs-Zeitung* printed in Rudolstadt, were convinced that not even the Nativist movement in America could prevent the Germans from "Germanizing" the West and sending likable representatives to Congress.[23]

Comments during the 1848-1849 Revolution

During the revolutionary year of 1848, the rhetoric regarding Germany's chances of acquiring colonies gained unprecedented fervor. The *Nürnberger Kurier* supported the idea of an exclusively German state in North America's West because it alone could become a receptacle for Germany's growing and dangerous proletariat which in turn would serve the fatherland's export interests and would spread the "Germanic element."[24] Even composer Richard Wagner enthusiastically exclaimed: "Now let us sail across the sea and found a Young Germany there!" The colony should be better than the English or Spanish ones. "We want to do it the *German* way, in a gorgeous way: from sunrise to sunset, the sun should behold a beautiful, free Germany. . ."[25]

Emigration Societies

The year 1848 also marked a mushrooming of new emigration societies. The earliest ones had been founded as a side-effect of the 1830 revolution. Generally speaking, there were two types of societies: (1) societies which were set up by emigrants themselves in order to provide mutual assistance. These were usually disbanded once the members had reached their destination (mutual emigration societies); (2) societies which were founded by people not intending to emigrate, but wishing to spread useful knowledge and to help individuals or groups actually emigrating. They were usually guided by altruistic or speculative motives or both (support societies). In the 1830s the mutual emigration societies were more numerous than the support societies; in the 1840s the proportion was reversed.

In both categories the borderline between associations formed for pragmatic reasons and associations formed for patriotic ones was quite blurred. There was a slight tendency among the Germany-based "support societies" to favor patriotic motives more than the settler-run "mutuals" would. The most high-aimed society of the second kind was the "National Association for Emigration and Colonization," founded in May 1847 by Dr. Heinrich Künzel, a teacher, and by Herr Lauteschläger, the chairman of the Hessian Geographical Society. It was supposed to unify the activities of at least two dozen other emigration support societies throughout Germany. It formed branches in many states. Künzel realized the spuriousness of forming dependent colonies and therefore supported the opinion of most of the other emigration authors who favored informal German settler colonies. F. A. Neumann, the president of the Silesian branch in Breslau, wrote:

> What the German needs is space—a new and larger field for his activities, and America offers just that in unlimited quantity. . . He [the German] is welcome because there is space enough for everybody; the native is not jealous of him, since he knows that a population increase will raise and improve the strength and life of the whole as well as of the individuals.[26]

The Midwest, Texas, Alta California and Oregon Country would offer the space the Germans needed. The "Central Emigration Association" in Cologne and Düsseldorf promised to pay particular attention to the "concentration of emigration into certain states of America so that completely German colonies would form there, and that land be acquired in America's interior in order to resell it to the emigrants."[27] This last sentence points to the method by which these associations were meant to work: as long as one could not obtain government subsidies, private investors were supposed to provide the necessary capital. The associations then intended to send emissaries to North America to locate *and* acquire suitable land.[28] Subsequently this land was to be advertised in Germany. Emigrants could then buy options on the land or, once arrived, pay the full price. For the settlers this system had the advantage of not wasting time and money in searching for land. The associations, on the other hand, could realize profits from the resale of land and concentrate settlers according to the liberal-national lore.[29]

So much for the theory. In reality, few German support societies did purchase land; but most did their utmost in interesting emigrants for certain regions in order to at least achieve the Germanizing settlement pattern they had emphasized in their bylaws and brochures. The Hessian branch of the "National Association for Emigration and Settlement" devised a full-fledged plan for a settler colony,[30] sent emissaries and helped transport a few hundred emigrants to America—who apparently dispersed upon arrival. The Württemberg branch commissioned drafts of two settlement plans: one was done by the branch's founder and president, Johannes von Werner, who also held a high position in the Treasury Department of the kingdom, the other was done by the American consul in Stuttgart, Carl Ludwig Fleischmann. The latter's plan was naturally free of any patriotic sentiments and stressed the profit motive.[31] The Baden branch of the "National Association" effected the resettlement of 944 persons.[32] The nuances of all these plans are unimportant. Noteworthy, however, is that there was a broad movement for the organization of emigration along patriotic lines. It was basically made up of middle-class intellectuals, writers, journalists, hobby travelers, mid-level bureaucrats, teachers, and members of the professional class. Most of them shared a great belief in the ability of organizations to funnel emigrants into venues that could be useful for the fatherland. They also agreed that the various governments should take up the issue and lend their support.

Cabinet Governments

Calling on the state was a typical phenomenon of the liberal-national movement. But the cabinets in the 39 sovereign states and city-states of the German Federation—with few exceptions—did not regard the organization of settler colonies as within their duty, let alone power. However, agitation going on outside governments did not pass unnoticed. When H. Chr. von Gagern in 1840, once again, called for some action in the Hessian Upper Chamber, he prompted Minister of State du Thil to give a full explanation of the cabinet's emigration policy. In the next session, du Thil declared that Germany lacked men of independent means and broad horizons who would position themselves at the helm of colonization societies, as was the case in Great Britain. In Germany, the time had come for the governments to take the place of private entrepreneurs and help organize emigration. After all, emigration was the preferred way to relieve the state from dangerous overpopulation pressures. The inauguration of American President Tyler had now given rise to the hope that an immigration agreement could be reached with the U.S. government. If the Assembly committed funds, du Thil was willing to begin negotiations with Washington.[33] This was an unusual departure from previous policies. Apparently, Hesse-Darmstadt did try to negotiate with the Tyler administration, but to no avail.[34]

Several prominent politicians in other state assemblies also championed the cause of emigrants. Among them was Karl Theodor Welcker of the Grand Duchy of Baden, co-editor of the famous *Brockhaus Encyclopedia*, who in 1842 lamented that the Germans in North America lacked the unity required for a profitable interchange with the fatherland. He, therefore, demanded the founding of German settler colonies in northern Brazil.[35] In 1846 another deputy in the Lower Chamber of the Duchy of Nassau said the time had come when one had to take the patriotic dream of a German colony and a German fleet out of the hands of poets. Treaties with overseas powers should be enacted, and emigration consulates set up by the German Federation.[36]

None of these demands amounted to anything. But in a way, that didn't matter for the agitators. Since government support was lacking, the schemers continued to pursue the most far-flung dreams of future success. They were never really in danger of having to prove the feasibility of their plans. The situation changed with the advent of the Revolution, or so it seemed.

The National Assembly of 1848-1849

The freedom to emigrate was codified in Sec. VI, Art. I, Para. 136 of the newly drafted Imperial Constitution of March 1849.[37] However, there were few delegates asking the envisioned central government to do more. Men like Professor Johann Ludwig Tellkampf, Carl Theodor Gevekoth, and Dr. August Ziegert pleaded for an emigrant's right to keep German citizenship and argued for close relations of the mother country with "Germandom" abroad. No one was more direct in his demands for a German colony than the high school superintendent Friedrich Schulz from Weilburg. He advocated sending an expert commission to North America to acquire the healthiest regions there. Surely, the Imperial Government would face no difficulties "to get from the United States large sections of land under conditions more favorable than the individual could." Schulz actually preferred German colonization in eastern Europe along the Danube. But as long as there was no Greater Germany in sight, he recommended emigration to the great rivers of North America:

> On the shores of the great ocean, a powerful and gorgeous New Germany can arise which will strengthen considerably our natural friendship with the United States. But if we do not hurry, we might come too late, even in America, at least for large-scale settlements, which could exercise an independent influence.[38]

Curiously, the assembly applauded enthusiastically, but without practical consequences. The only measure remotely connected with the colonial plans was a subsidized tour around the world for German writer Friedrich Gerstäcker who had promised the Imperial Government to report on the conditions and prospects of German settler communities abroad. In 1849 Gerstäcker actually went to South America, then only briefly to California before returning via the South Pacific.[39] An explanation for the general acceptance of recommendations such as Schulz's may lie in the fact that they expressed the newly-kindled spirit of pride in the yet to be re-born German nation.

And there was speculation about Germany's rightful place in the world. It comes as no surprise, then, that high hopes were connected with the attempted deployment of an Imperial fleet whose first purpose would have been to break the Danish blockade of the Baltic Sea.[40] Some thought the fleet could also be an instrument to protect German settlements and trade interests abroad.[41]

The Plan for a Prussian California

It is an irony of history that the same Danish fleet that was to be fought in 1848 played a prominent and positive part in the most far-flung colonial plan to be espoused by German politicians in the first half of the 19th century. This was the plan to acquire Alta California from Mexico. The story began in 1837, when Prussia's chargé d'affaires in Mexico, Friedrich Baron von Gerolt, was asked by President Anastasio Bustamente whether the Berlin government would like to purchase this northern-most province. The Mexicans had just gone through the trauma of the Texan revolution, a direct consequence of the influx of American settlers. They could expect the same to happen with California. Did it not make sense, then, to anticipate the seemingly inevitable and try to make a profit from the abandoned land, turning it into a foreign buffer state on Mexico's northern border, thereby checking the expansion of the hated Yankees? Gerolt reported back to Berlin several times, mentioning in glowing terms the prospect of steering German emigration to this part of the New World.[42] At that time, however, Prussia did not harbor overseas intentions, especially in view of the fact that she did not have a fleet.[43]

A few years later, the idea again crept up in the correspondence of U.S. Senator William Hogan from New York to his friend, the Prussian consul in London, Bernhard Hebeler.[44] Hogan also talked to the Prussian minister in Washington, Friedrich von Rönne, who had just visited the American West, impressed by the number of German settlers there. He felt that they could surely be brought together. Enthusiastically he joined the scheme and started private talks with the Mexican minister in Washington, Juan Nepomuceno Almonte. Rönne then sent private messages to his counterpart in London, Carl Josias Bunsen,[45] who himself was a close friend of the new king, Friedrich Wilhelm IV. Bunsen, for his part, had just meditated the growing social tensions in Britain and the ensuing necessity of finding a safety valve for coping with the disaffected proletariat. He saw Britain's advantages with the possibility of sending large groups of people to settler colonies of her own, in Australia and New Zealand. Rönne's recommendation came thus at the right time and was, after all, not so unusual.

Bunsen wrote to the king, describing the advantages a Prussian California would offer for Germany's trade and social stability.[46] He also vented Rönne's idea to employ the Danish fleet for securing colonial possessions at the Pacific cost. Denmark was to become a full-fledged member of the German Customs Union and, in turn, would offer use of her gunboats. The actual price for California was never mentioned, but Rönne later remembered the figure of $6,000,000.[47] Friedrich Wilhelm in 1842-43 was not an adventurous soul. His advisors were also skeptical about the project's viability. Most likely it was the then elderly Alexander von Humboldt, a regular guest at the royal couple's intimate dinners, whom the king consulted. Humboldt, the only person at the court with first-hand knowledge of California, may have told him the story of his friendship with Thomas Jefferson. The venerable former president had written to him in 1813 that the beginning revolts in the Spanish colonies harbingered a day when the entire American hemisphere would be free from European influence: "America constitutes a hemisphere unto itself. It must have its separate system of interests, which must not be subordinated to those of Europe."[48]

Given Prussia's maritime deficiency, it is probable—although no direct proof exists—that Humboldt reminded the king of Jefferson's vision. California really was off limits!

2. National Group Settlements in Practice

Germans emigrated to America as individuals, families, village communities, mutual support societies, religious sects, utopian societies, and as patriotic or "national" groups. All groups have some motives in common. Traveling in company provided a sense of security and social support. Whether the migrants' motives were economic, religious, utopian, pragmatic, or national in nature—or a combination of any of these—the idea of arriving and finding one's way in a foreign country in the company of folks from the same area, the same religion, and the same nationality was reassuring.

General Characteristics

Those groups driven primarily by a patriotic mission differ from the rest only because of the motives of their leaders. It is difficult to ascertain how far participants in patriotic group emigration really shared their leaders' optimism concerning the creation of a New Germany. The two most prominent patriotic emigration societies, the Giessen Society and the Texas Association, received letters and other written statements suggesting that many members were particularly impressed by their society's patriotic goals.[49] Between 1820 and 1860 some 10,000 persons emigrated as members of such societies. Thousands more would have participated, had there had been no limits and had they gotten good news from the settlements. In general, this was not the case.

Throughout the period under discussion, the colonization projects underwent changes, largely also in conjunction with the development of German and American affairs:

(1) Beginning with the early 1830s, a succession of politically motivated emigration groups left for America. Their leaders strove to maintain the groups' national identity while welcoming political freedom within the U.S.

(2) By the mid-1830s, a wave of German-American settlement projects illustrated ethnic self-assertion.

(3) During the 1840s, German-American settlement projects primarily served the interests of land speculators. Germany was a convenient field of recruitment; and references to the settlements' ethnic homogeneity were little more than a public relations routine. (The colonization project of the Texas Association is in a category of its own.)

(4) After the arrival of the Forty-Eighters, few new colonization projects were undertaken. And if so, they were inspired by primarily socialist ideals.

Small Emigration Societies

Patriotic group emigration had a peculiar start with Ludwig Gall's "Bern Society." Their original plan called for joining the 1804-founded Swiss settler colony of New-Vevay in Indiana. But they dispersed on arrival. Gall himself was appalled by the Americanization of the founding generation.[50] In 1819 his friend Friedrich Ernst from Hanover, who at first had shared Gall's plan for a German colony, led a group of about 300 emigrants to his favorite spot, **Vandalia**, Illinois.[51] But also this society disbanded rather quickly. A year later, Ernst died from "tropical fever."[52]

In the early 1830s, Arkansas attracted a few groups for its cheap public land and its remoteness offering sought-after seclusion. A group from Mühlhausen in Thuringia, led by Christoph von Dachröden, J. A. Etzler, H. Hupfeld and J. A. Röbling (the father of the Brooklyn Bridge builder), intended to establish a settlement there, inspired by humanistic principles. But most of the few dozen participants ended up in Pennsylvania. Some went on to Missouri and founded **Sachsenburg**. Due perhaps to the impact of Gottfried Duden's travel account, a "Berlin Society" settled in the same area a few years later, founding **Washington**. Other groups to settle in Arkansas came from Bremen[53] and Dürkheim, both in 1832.[54]

Renewed supression of political movements and civil liberties after the 1832 Fest of the university fraternities at Hambach Castle led many a patriot to emigrate. There was a general hush in the press about plans to found a new and better Germany abroad.[55] Individuals from around Stuttgart called for the creation of German colonies in North America. The owner of a silk-hat plant, named Schworetzky, believed America was the place "where we will find everything we now miss."[56] Persons directly involved with the abortive attempt to set off a revolution in Frankfurt in April 1833 formed the "Frankfurt Society" and emigrated to the trans-Mississippian West. Some stayed in the vicinity of Duden's farm in Missouri, but the majority moved to **Belleville, Ill.**, among them Gustav Körner, Theodor Hilgard, and Ferdinand Jakob Lindheimer.[57] Frustrated by the autocratic Prussian regime, Friedrich Steines, a teacher from Solingen, left in February 1834 leading a group of 153 people. Most of these Solingers also settled in Missouri.[58]

The Giessen Emigration Society

The largest and best known of the patriotic emigration societies of the early 1830s was the Giessen-Society, headed by Pastor Friedrich Münch and Paul Follenius, a lawyer a younger brother of the well-known Karl Follen.

Having been members of the outlawed Black Fraternity in the late 1810s, they suffered from the lack of civil liberties in Germany. The combined effects of reading Duden, experiencing frustration over more restrictions imposed after the Hambach Fest, and seeing friends and other groups depart, resulted in their forming an emigration society with the explicit aim of "forming a German state" in North America. This state was to be a member of the U.S. "but with its own form of government [*Staatsform*] which would ensure the continued existence of German customs and the German language. . ."[59] It was hoped the community would become a "German model republic."[60]

Münch and Follenius prepared the colony in minute detail. Individuals from all over Germany and even Prague and Vienna were interested in joining.[61] But only 500 persons were selected and divided into two groups, one sailing to Baltimore, and the other to New Orleans. The plan was to reconvene in St. Louis (Arkansas had been envisioned but discarded because of negative reports). Both parties suffered from severe mishaps and lost members due either to quarrels or sickness. Once they arrived, the followers of Münch and Follenius became so dispirited that no one thought any longer of the glorious new republic. They dispersed, some with Münch to Warren County, Missouri, where the former pastor managed to eke out a living under hard conditions, but later became a successful winegrower and State Senator. Follenius remained in St. Louis where he died of yellow fever.

German-American Settlement Societies

It comes as no surprise that the first wave of German intellectuals arriving in America as a result of this kind of organized emigration did have an effect on German-American community life.[62] Most Germans intended to become "good citizens" but keep their ethnic identity. As an outgrowth of ethnically-driven activities in the established German communities on the East Coast, plans were made to establish German settlements in the midsection of the country. German-American settlement associations were either motivated by the prospect of speculative gains on the sale of company land, or they believed that some form of separation of the German element from the Anglo-American mainstream was desirable. That German life styles and German mores would go under if they faced massive competition by the "Yankees" was a truism for most German-American leaders at the time. A separation that would still allow Germans to be members of the republic and exert influence on the politics affecting them seemed the best solution.

The Germania Society of New York

The earliest genuinely "German-American" settlement plan came about in 1835 when the first signs of a nativist movement in New York led to a new cohesion among the German community.[63] The "Germania Society" was formed with the aim of "further uniting the Germans living in the U.S., in order to maintain and foster among them a strong German character, good German mores and German education."[64] There was an element of missionary spirit: Since there were quite a few recent exiles in the wake of the Hambach Fest, the hope to affect things back home was still alive.[65] It seemed that the best way to guarantee cohesion and create a democratic model for the fatherland was to form a settler colony. Texas, Oregon or Wisconsin were discussed as possible sites. Apparently, a memorial petitioning for a land grant was sent to Congress; however, no copy has survived.[66] In any case, the Germania-Society disbanded rather soon over internal conflicts and a lack of enthusiasm.

A few years later, another "Germania Society" was formed in New York—sometimes mistaken with that of 1835. But the two do not seem to have been connected. The new Germania, with an eye on the new Republic of Texas, actually corresponded with Texan President Mirabeau Buonaparte Lamar, asking for both a land grant and a large tract of land to be set aside for future German immigration.[67] We have no record of an answer, but if there was one it must have been encouraging enough for the Society to dispatch a first group of about 130 colonists from New York. When they arrived in Galveston, a bout of yellow fever was ravaging the city of Houston. Many, therefore, returned to the U.S., including their leader, Dr. Schuessler; some settled on their own in the vicinity of Houston.[68]

The German Settlement Society of Philadelphia

In 1836, the largest and most successful patriotic German-American settlement association in the U.S. was founded in Philadelphia by the editor of the *Neue und Alte Welt*, Dr. Johann Georg Wesselhöft. Many well-established German-American businessmen, journalists, lawyers and other professionals joined. Their aim was:

> to form a German settlement in a suitable part of the U.S., possibly Pennsylvania, where a large number of Germans would have the opportunity to exercise and apply their industry and know-how in a way profitable and agreeable to them.[69]

The Society's president, Wilhelm Schmoele, was even more explicit when he said the ultimate goal was to unify the Germans in North America "and thereby found a new German fatherland. . ." Then "a great German nation could thrive in the land of freedom."[70] Because the Society succeeded in attracting investors, the members rejected a proposal to ask Congress for a land grant.[71] Instead, the associates sent delegates to the West who acquired about 11,000 acres on the Gasconade River, not far north from Gottfried Duden's former farm.[72] The first settlers arrived in the new town of **Hermann** during the winter of 1837-38. As usual, the beginnings were modest, and the bank crisis of 1837 did contribute to a temporary decline of interest in the settlement. Not long afterwards the settlers felt they would rather manage their own affairs than be guided by the association in distant Philadelphia. They formed their own board of management, leading to the Society's demise in 1839. At that time Hermann already sported 90 houses and 450 settlers. It continued to grow until 1860, reaching its peak with 1,500 inhabitants. Compared to other western municipalities, this growth was more than modest for a town that enjoyed a healthy balance of productivity and cultural amenities.

Settlements in Southern States

During the 1840s, more settler colonies were founded by German-Americans, mostly in the southern frontier states. In 1842, the "Deutscher Bundes-, Cultur-, und Gewerbeverein" established the town of **Hermannsburg, Va.** on a 15,000 acre area.[73] The "Tennessee Colonization Company" was a joint venture of American, Belgian, and German-American entrepreneurs who, in 1844, acquired 180,000 acres in Morgan County, Tenn. and advertised the land, particularly in Saxony. A first group of emigrants from the Saxon *Erzgebirge* arrived in 1845 to found the town of **Wartburg**. Within three years, some 500 German immigrants had moved there.[74] In 1848, a group of 60 wealthy German-Americans from South Carolina formed the "German Settlement Society of Charleston" and bought 20,000 acres in the Blue Ridge Mountains' Occonee County. A decade later the town of **Walhalla** had attracted about 1,500 German settlers, but it remained the only German community of any size in the Carolinas.[75]

Socialist Settlements

Socialist associations also tried to establish German settlements, but these were not inspired by primarily national or patriotic aims. Some German intellectuals in New York got together in the early 1840s to form the association of *"Die deutschen Freiheitsfreunde"* and to advocate a settlement in the West based on "liberty and equality." The colony was to be based "on the principles we fought for in Germany. . ., the practicability of which we seek to prove in a small state."[76] Apparently no activities beyond this declaration of intent followed. The Turners of Cincinnati were more successful. Under the leadership of Forty-Eighter Wilhelm Pfaender from Heilbronn, they formed the "Settlement Association of the Socialist Turnerbund" in 1856. Shortly afterwards they acquired the township of *New Ulm* in Brown County, Minn., which had just been founded by the "German Land Association of Chicago."[77] It was more a matter of convenient recruitment than ethnic exclusiveness which in its early years made New Ulm a German town. The idea to found a German state, "great and important as it might be"—as the Turners said—was not behind the founding of New Ulm. The Turners wanted to restrict themselves to "practicable enterprises."[78]

Association for the Protection of German Immigrants to Texas

Finally, the activities of the Mainz "Association for the Protection of German Immigrants to Texas" must be mentioned. Through the initiative of Carl Count von Castell, some two dozen aristocrats founded this society in 1842 with the express purpose of (1) providing a new home abroad for the poor masses in Germany, (2) creating a profitable trade between the settler colonies and the fatherland, and (3) protecting those emigrants who settle in the Association's colonies.[79] Two delegates, Count Joseph von Boos-Waldeck and Prince Viktor von Leiningen, were sent to Texas to look for land and negotiate with the Texan government for a large grant. Except for the purchase of a small farm in the Republic's settled Northeast (Nassau Farm), they came back empty-handed. In early 1844, a French owner of a land contract in Texas, Alexandre Bourgeois d'Orvanne, approached the Association about selling them his land titles if they provided settlers. After an agreement was reached, Prince Carl von Solms-Braunfels was sent to Texas in June 1844 together with Bourgeois to prepare the arrival of the first emigrants. Because the Association had advertised widely, hundreds of Germans were eager to go. Since each one had to come up with at least $300, they were not exactly from the poorer rungs of society.

Meanwhile, the Bourgeois-Ducos grant had expired. This forced the Association to find a quick remedy, which was offered to them by the new Texan consul in Bremen, Henry Fisher, also a land grant holder. Situated in Northwest Texas, it was far away from any settled areas and thus seemed to offer the desired seclusion from Anglo-Texans. But the Association completely underestimated the difficulties in merely getting there, let alone creating a thriving community and profitable trade. So when the first few hundred settlers arrived in December 1844, Solms led them only to a way station between the coast and the proposed settlement area where they first founded the town of **New Braunfels**. Solms left in May 1845, somewhat disgruntled with the ingratitude of settlers who had expected to be fed, housed and equipped by the Association and therefore seemed to lack the initiative for life on the frontier.

Solms successor, Hans Ottfried von Meusebach (later "John O. Meusebach"), didn't fare much better with the settlers, since he stopped most payments and services in order to relieve the Association's debt. Failing credit, bad weather, and the coming of the war with Mexico contributed to a catastrophe when about 3,000 new immigrants arrived in late 1845. Meusebach was no more able than Solms to transport them into the interior, nor was it possible to feed and house them properly on the shoreline at Indianola. Diseases ravished the tent city and about half of the future settlers died. During the following summer, Meusebach and some of the survivors and former arrivals at least succeeded in founding the town of *Fredericksburg* close to the Fisher-Miller land grant. The Association's popularity in Germany sank immediately, leaving little hope that it could continue directing thousands to Texas. Although the Duke of Nassau immediately sent about $100,000 to Texas when he heard of the disaster, the money came too late to save the settlers and it was not enough to continue the colonization plan in grand style.

After the Mexican-American War, however, the Association again managed to recruit several hundred new settlers annually until activities were terminated in 1852. All in all, during the Association's existence a total of 10,000 Germans disembarked in Galveston, though not all of them under its tutelage. In addition to New Braunfels and Fredericksburg, the Association founded the towns of *Leiningen, Castell, Bettina* and *Schoenburg*. The counties of Comal and Gillespie became heavily Germanized.

Texan Independence and British Diplomacy

Despite obvious failures, the Texas Association's activities had greater results than those of any other emigration society. Its appearance on the Texan scene had an importance beyond the dreams of a New Germany. For a short time it seemed the Association might become a tool of British (and to a lesser degree, French) world politics. Britain was eager to keep Texas independent from the U.S., since she wanted to check both American expansion to the West and the proliferation of slavery. Moral recriminations, economic self-interest, and *Realpolitik* combined to favor Texan independence which, after the rejection of the annexation treaty of 1844 by the U.S. Senate seemed to be ensured, if Mexico would also agree to recognize Texas' sovereignty. The Texans' inclination toward annexation could be suffused if there were fewer people of Anglo-American stock. Therefore, the influx of German settlers was welcomed by the British government. The Texas Association was aware of this and, using their close family ties to the British royal family, Solms-Braunfels as well as Prince Karl von Leiningen tried to elicit British support for their settlement project. When the danger of war with Mexico became more acute, Count Castell hoped the Association's immigrant ships would be placed under neutral British protection.[80] Both in the German and the Texan press, there were rumors at the time that England was pulling strings for European immigration.[81]

At least during the early stages of the undertaking, association members placed hope on Texan independence. A Galveston newspaper of Feb. 23, 1845 expressed why: "Only as an independent state can Germandom achieve predominant power in Texas."[82] In fact, Prince Solms once tried to have the British government help with the importation of 10,000 German settler-soldiers. His idea, however, was passed over with silence in London.[83] The most Lord Aberdeen did to comply with a (possible) request from Prince Albert was to have Undersecretary of State Henry Addington write to Consul William Kennedy in Galveston asking him to do what he could to assist Prince Carl.[84] Kennedy personally liked Solms and wished him luck. Not much else could be done. Still, the British chargé d' affairs in Galveston, Charles Elliot, speculated that Mexico could be won over to recognizing Texas if assured of future immigration from England, Germany, and France—rather than from the U.S.[85]

Negotiations with the Texan Government

The Texan Government generally welcomed the Association's settlement project, since every new immigrant meant more human capital. German settlers were known to improve their land in a systematic and lasting way. President Sam Houston and his successor, Anson Jones, personally expressed their welcome to any new immigration and to the Texas Association in particular.[86] On the other hand, Texan statesmen had no doubt that the immigrants would have to become Texans. A separate German commonwealth or even political entity in their midst was inconceivable, a condition that didn't always seem so clear to the Association. Count Boos-Waldeck and Prince Leiningen in 1842 had tried to come up with an agreement for preferential treatment in trade matters, but without success.[87] Prince Solms himself set two major tasks in negotiating with the Texan government: (1) to repeal the usual stipulation in acts granting land that alternating sections had to be reserved for the state; (2) to do everything he could to foster the Texan determination to stay independent. In his view, both measures would best ensure the special status and cohesion of a German settler colony. In fact, Solms derided the prospect of annexation when he besought his "lobbyist" with the Texan Congress, Henry Fisher, to

> tell the Congressmen and anyone else you like, that I have defrayed considerable sums for this country, that I will spend even more, that I am going to build a corduroy road [double wooden rails] from the upper country I, [. . .?] to the Bay— who else has done so much for this country as the Association—but only for the free Texas; for the territory of the U.S. not one cent.[88]

But Solms' fervor for an independent Texas was seldom shared by his colleagues. The incorporation of the Association's settlement faced a rocky road in Congress. According to Meusebach, some Congressmen even held serious suspicions against "an association led by princes and noblemen."[89] After Texas had joined the Union, the former Texan consul at The Hague, Colonel William Henry Daingerfield, who had always been favorably disposed to the Association, began lobbying both the U.S. Congress and the Texan State Assembly for favorable treatment of the Association's claims. And he was able to report back to Count Castell that Congress would handle the claims "in a most liberal manner."[90] Soon the town of New Braunfels was incorporated and made the county seat of Comal County, which gave the community a certain degree of autonomy. The Germans were allowed to run their own schools, publish local ordinances in German and vote their own judge and sheriff into office. By 1848, the Texan Government had appointed a "Commissioner for the German Colonies" who was to regulate open claims, finally giving 320 acres of land to single immigrants and 640 acres to married immigrants.[91]

3. American Responses to National Group Settlements

When the German emigration societies appeared on the American scene, the U.S. Government had already established a policy toward group settlements ethnically different from Anglo-American stock. Briefly, this policy was to leave open to anyone the purchase and sale of private land, no matter how large; but when asked for favorable treatment with regard to setting aside public land or receiving favorable credit conditions, the answer would be negative.

American Statesmen

Public sentiment toward immigration has always been ambiguous in the United States. Thomas Jefferson's rhetorical question in his inauguration address, "Shall oppressed humanity find no asylum on this globe?" stressed traditional American openness and generosity. On the other hand, even Jefferson himself had harbored serious doubts about the "expediency of inviting them by extraordinary encouragements"—and so did many Americans.[92] There was fear that immigrants might one day outnumber the old stock and endanger the political system.[93] When Börne joked about the Ohio Germans yearning for monarchy, he corroborated this traditional American fear. Both Washington and Jefferson expressed strong criticism of the Germans' tendency to cling together in closed settlements. In 1817, the year of the first mass emigration to America after the Napoleonic wars, Jefferson specifically referred to the Germans when he wrote that immigrants should be prevented from forming compact masses, "wherein, as in our German settlements, they preserve for a long time their own languages, habits and principles of government."[94]

In 1817 Moritz von Fürstenwärther was told by Secretary of State John Quincy Adams that "principle and conviction or national pride" would make Americans "greatly disinterested in foreign immigration," and the expectation would prevail that "the population of the United States would grow sufficiently without it."[95] Immigrant groups, "if they chose to become citizens," had to expect "equal rights with those of the natives of the country"[96] and, as Adams added in a letter to Fürstenwärther:

> They must cast off the European skin, never to resume it. They must look forward to their posterity rather than backward to their ancestors; they must be sure that whatever their own feelings may be, those of their children will cling to the prejudices of this country."[97]

Congress and Land Grants: Some Precedents

Congress dealt with foreign immigrant groups only when faced with a petition. Usually the legislators' opinion reflected the attitude of the administrations' highest officials. When in 1804 George Rapp petitioned Congress for a land grant "of about 30,000 Acres. . . in the Western Country," the Representatives were divided.[98] During the debate of the bill in January 1806,[99] Rep. Gideon Olin (Vt.) had qualms about handing out preferential credits to foreigners, and Rep. William Ely (Mass.) warned, "such a body of one sect, of one language, will wish to seclude itself from the rest of the Union." On the other hand, Rep. John Smilie (Pa.) found no objection in the fact that the petitioners were foreigners: half of Pennsylvania was settled by foreigners. And Rep. James Holland (N.C.) stated that a settlement similar to the one proposed by Rapp, namely that of the Moravians in his state, turned out to be of much benefit. The final vote was 47:46 against the Rappites' petition.

The close vote shows that an actual policy towards requests by organized immigrant groups had not yet been formulated. During the next decade, some petitions were granted,[100] others rejected.[101] In 1818, three Irish-American immigration societies tried for a land grant on extended credit in Illinois Territory.[102] Their attempt exhibited an unprecedented, sophisticated lobbying effort. The Irish societies even dress-rehearsed the Congressional committee hearing, practicing answers to anticipated criticism.[103] But in the end, Congress rejected their petition. Marcus Lee Hansen called this decision the most far-reaching one in American immigration history. Foreign emigration organizations now knew what to expect from the American government with its newly established policy of non-preferential treatment.[104] When a Swiss group in 1820 desired to settle 3,000 to 4,000 families in Florida "on terms more favorable than the general law would permit," the House Committee for Public Lands drew up a report fully explaining the principle:

> The establishment of a community of foreigners within our country, secluded by their habits, manners, and language from an intimate association with the great body of our citizens, cannot be an event so desirable as to justify a departure from the general law. An unrestrained intercourse with the body of the American yeomanry affords to the emigrant the best, and probably the only means of acquiring an accurate knowledge of our laws and institutions. . ."[105]

A similar position was taken by the leading newspaper of the day, the *Niles' Weekly Register*, when a delegation from Rhenish-Bavaria in 1832 inquired about a land grant for their emigration society:

> We should give all such as these a hearty welcome, but the idea of settling in a large and compact body cannot be approved. . . Most reflecting persons, we think, have regarded it as unfortunate, that in certain parts of the United States, the German,

Irish or French population (so called, though the large majority may be *natives*) are so located as seemingly to have different *interests*, or at least different views of the public good—remaining as *separated* classes of the people, and so liable to particular influences which, perhaps, are sometimes prejudicial to the "general welfare. . ."[106]

The only exception from the rule of non-preferential treatment made in the following years was in favor of a group of 250 exiles from the Polish revolution.[107] In this instance, the Public Lands Committee wished to "manifest a proper regard for the sufferings of the unfortunate. . . and thereby exhibit to the civilized world a glowing contrast between the arbitrary rulers and the chivalry of the free people."[108] The Poles received a township in Michigan Territory, but no one ever moved there. In fact, the grant aroused a good deal of anger among the American pioneers who had cultivated and claimed the area before. In 1842 Congress withdrew its grant.

Except for the petition from the Rhenish-Bavarian delegation, and possibly the memorial of the "Germania Society" of New York, Congress never dealt with groups interested in founding a German *state*. The whole idea, it seems, had never been discovered by politicians or, if so, had not been taken seriously. Only twice did any of the American consuls in Germany report on the activities of patriotic emigration societies. In 1832 Ernest Schwendler, U.S. consul in Frankfurt, aired his view about the New Germany plans which had come to the attention of even the *Niles' Weekly Register:*[109]

The high sounding project to form a New Germany in the U.S., noticed in American prints—has indeed been planned last year by a small association of enthusiasts without any practical knowledge of the U.S.—

Their pious wishes and chimerical expectations were almost the only foundation of their plan and from what I learned by the managers, it appeared that they had neither the idea nor sufficient capital to purchase lands beyond the immediate wants of their small society consisting of abt. 50 families, but that they presumed most confidently that numerous similar associations would soon join them and that the nucleus which they intended to form in the Territory of Arkansas would rapidly, and like a snow lavine encrease to a complete State of the Union. . . [110]

One year later, Schwendler once more reported on a New Germany project, possibly that of the Giessen Society, and labeled it "preposterous."[111]

The American public was, of course, aware of the ever growing influx of Germans. In fact, the dominance of foreign immigrants in some areas of the larger cities gave rise to a Nativist movement. Rarely, though, did the Anglo-American public take notice of plans for a separate German state. Often there were vague notions that foreigners might scheme to overthrow the American form of government.[112] In 1841, George Flower, a correspondent with Thomas Jefferson, depicted the intention to seclude oneself from the American society as one of the main faults of German immigrants.[113] Carl Ludwig Fleischmann, an informed American citizen of some public standing in Germany, admonished Germans in his 1852 emigration handbook that Americans would regard the idea of "transplanting German nationality or even the founding of a New Germany" with great suspicion.[114] By 1856, however, the editors of the *North American Review* realized that the Germans' "ablest journals and. . . experienced men" had given up the idea of establishing a German republic within the U.S.[115]

The closest the American government and public ever came to discussing the effects of German group immigration was when supposed British claims on Texas served as a catalyst for a furiously annexationist campaign. American newspapers ran articles on how Britain had attempted to make Texas a colony by infusing capital and supporting European immigration.[116] In turn, President Andrew Jackson wrote an influential letter to Rep. Aaron V. Brown, claiming that the British could secretly lead 20,000 to 30,000 armed settlers into Texas.[117] At the height of the anti-British campaign of 1844, even Senator Henry Clay, otherwise known as an anti-annexationist, aired a clear warning:

> If any European nation entertains any ambitious designs upon Texas such as that of colonizing her. . . I should consider it as the imperative duty of the United States to oppose such designs by. . . determined resistance, to the extent, if necessary, of appealing to arms."[118]

The warning was specifically addressed to Britain and France and in this sense would have applied to any real support the British might have given the Texas Association. As far as can be seen, such a relationship was suspected only once in an anonymous open letter to John Q. Adams in a Texas newspaper. Adams, the fiercest among the anti-annexationists, was told:

> [a]lready contractors are in Europe for the purpose of bringing not their tens or hundreds but their thousands to this country; and we are well assured that so soon as things shall be measurably quiet here, that from England, France, Germany, and Belgium, thousands upon thousands will flock to the country. . . the day is not distant when a nation of Europeans, by the mere spirit of emigration, will be established on the continent of North America.[119]

While not mentioning the "contractors" by name, the hint to Bourgeois or Fisher is obvious. When annexation had come, James Hamilton, former Texan chargé d'affaires in London and Paris, wrote to John Calhoun that only the large land contracts for foreigners—among them "the Empresarios of the Prince"—had made him an annexationist, too. As a consequence of large-scale European immigration, slavery in Texas would have been abolished within five years.[120] Clearly, the fear of this type of foreign immigration into Texas served as a major argument in the annexation debate.

4. CONCLUSION

Leo Schelbert has called emigrants the "agents of empire." Paradoxically, the idea of concentrating German emigrants in North America was based on the *absence* of an empire. In some sense, however, these patriotic group settlements were expected to become the nucleus of an informal overseas "empire," an empire more of the mind than of matter. On the other side of the ocean, American immigration politics dealt with national group settlements in a way that would on the one hand foster the inclination to expand farther west (empire building), and on the other limit the influence of any non-Anglo-American ethnic group. During the final years of the Texas Republic, the German-state idea briefly, but never seriously, did come into play in British imperial politics.

In the end, German plans resulted in the actual founding of about a dozen towns, but a German state did not come into existence—at least not formally. The German strip, which by 1860 had developed from Wisconsin down to western Texas, was the result of mostly other factors in settlement patterns, such as chain migration or the availability of cheap land. At the time, even observers in Germany criticized the plans for lack of foresight, practical skill, and insolence. Later on, participants themselves clearly saw some of the inherent weaknesses they had not considered earlier. Too often, the projects were laid out in too minute a detail; too much effort and time was spent on bureaucratic niceties. Participants were led to expect all remedies to issue from the associations. Also, the patriotic fervor of the settlers had been grossly overestimated. In the absence of shared and strong sentiments like religious beliefs, the groups regularly broke apart. Open space and unforeseen opportunities, but also the traditional cleavages among the Germans themselves operated against group cohesion. Upon arrival in America, often a spirit of individualism set in. Finally, most of the German emigrants were guided by a homesteader psychology. Their aim was not to revel in grand schemes but to find a good piece of land on which to build a new home. Inasmuch as they sought a new life, their home had become America.

NOTES

[1]Ludwig Börne, *Gesammelte Schriften* 13: *Briefe aus Paris, 1832-1833*, 5. Theil (Paris, 1834), 32-33.

[2]The report is printed in parts in Günter Moltmann, ed. (with Ingrid Schoberl), *Aufbruch nach Amerika: Friedrich List u. die Auswanderung aus Baden u. Württemberg 1816-17. Dokumentation einer sozialen Bewegung* (Tübingen, 1979), 120ff.

[3]Draft letter to Martin Van Buren (Oct. 21, 1930), in Friedrich List, *Schriften, Reden, Briefe*, vol. 2: *Grundlinien einer polit. Oekonomie u. andere Beiträge aus der amerikan. Zeit, 1825-1832*, ed. by William Notz (Berlin, 1931), 303.

[4]Friedrich List, *Ueber den Wert u. die Bedingungen einer Allianz zwischen Grossbritannien u. Deutschland* (1846, repr. Leipzig, 1920), 25.

[5]Rolf Engelsing, *Bremen als Auswanderungshafen, 1683-1880* (Bremen, 1961), 49-85.

[6]Friedrich Prüser, "Bremer Kaufleute als Wegbereiter Deutschlands in Uebersee," *Koloniale Rundschau* 32:2 (July 1942): 75; cf. Walter Struve, *Die Republik Texas, Bremen u. das Hildesheimische: Ein Beitrag zur Geschichte von Auswanderung, Handel u. gesellschaftl. Wandel im 19. Jh. Mit den Briefen eines dt. Kaufmanns u. Landwirts in Texas, 1844-1845* (Hildesheim, 1983), 11.

[7]Eduard Süskind, *Die Auswanderung u. das dt. Vaterland: Ein Wort an das dt. Volk* (Ulm, 1845), 14.

[8]Carl August Spiegelthal, *Die Organisation des Auswanderungswesens u. ihr Einfluss auf die dt. Handelsverhältnisse...* (Leipzig, 1851), 24, 27f.

[9]No. 14, "Instructionen für den Freyherrn Moritz v. Fürstenwärther (zum Behuf seiner Reise u. Sendung nach Amerika), Abgereist von Frankfurt a.M., den 17. Juni 1817," in Fürstenwärther, *Der Deutsche in Nordamerika* (Stuttgart, 1818), 6.

[10]Speech Gagern's in the Upper Chamber of the Grand Duchy of Hesse-Darmstadt (Feb. 8, 1847), in *Der dt. Auswanderer* 8 (1847), 117.

[11]Ernst Moritz Arndt, cit. in Hagen Schulze, *Der Weg zum Nationalstaat: Die dt. Nationalbewegung vom 18. Jh. bis zur Reichsgründung* (München, 1985), 69.

[12]W. Frank, *Deutschland in Amerika: Das einzig rechte Ziel aller dt. Auswanderer* (Kassel, 1839), IV.

[13]Robert Mohl, "Ueber Auswanderung" [article of 1847], *Der dt. Auswanderer* 3 (Jan. 19, 1850): 41.

[14]Wilhelm Weber, "Die Zeitungen in den Ver. Staaten mit bes. Berücksichtigung der in dt. Sprache erscheinenden Blätter;" *Das Westland* 1:2 (1837): 200ff.; cf. "Gelegentliche Gedanken über die neueren dt. Emigrations-Projecte," *Janus* 2:1 (1846): 700f.

[15]L. Gall, *Meine Auswanderung nach den Ver. Staaten von Nordamerika im Frühjahr 1819 u. meine Rückkehr nach der Heimath im Winter 1820*, 2 vols. (Trier, 1822), I, 375f.

[16]The pamphlet exists as a copy in the Documents of the Central Enquiry Commission of Mainz as part of the "*Untersuchungssachen gegen den Gymnasialdirektor L. Snell zu Wetzlar (1819-20),*" Zentrales Staatsarchiv Dienststelle Merseburg [ZSTAM]. Ministerium d. Innern, Rep. 77, Tit. 25,O. Litt. S. 14, sheet 184ff.

[17]Jonas H. Gudehus, *Meine Auswanderung nach Amerika im Jahre 1822 u. meine Rückkehr in die Heimat 1825...* (Hildesheim, 1829), 1:4ff.

[18]Karl von Sparre, *Die Auswanderungen u. Ansiedlungen der Deutschen als Nationalsache, insonderheit Preussens Betheiligung an der Auswanderungsfrage* (Giessen, 1847), 26.

[19]Traugott Bromme, *Plan einer in Nord-Amerika zu gründenden dt. Kolonie* (Baltimore, 1834), 13.

²⁰Bromme, "Der Nationalverein f. Auswanderung u. Colonisation," *Der dt. Auswanderer* 9 (1847): 136.

²¹Ernst Ludwig Brauns, cit. by Hildegard Meyer, *Nordamerika im Urteile des dt. Schrifttums bis zur Mitte des 19. Jhs. Eine Untersuchung über Kürnbergers "Amerika-Müden." Mit einer Bibliogr.* (Hamburg, 1929), 37.

²²E.L. Brauns, *Neudeutschland in Westamerika oder welches ist die zur Ansiedlung für auswandernde Deutsche geeignete Weltgegend?.* . . (Lemgo, 1847), 77f.

²³"Die dt. Auswanderung u. das dt. Vaterland," *Allg. Auswanderungs-Zeitung* 5 (Oct. 27, 1846): 37.

²⁴*Nürnberger Kourier* (April 1848), repr. in *Allg. Auswanderungs-Zeitung* 18 (May 1, 1848): 278; *Der dt. Auswanderer* 21 (May 20, 1848): 322f.

²⁵Richard Wagner, "Speech before the Patriotic Society of Dresden," *Dresdner Anzeiger* (June 14, 1848), repr. in Karl Friedrich Glasenapp, *Das Leben Richard Wagners*, 5th ed. (Leipzig, 1910), vol. 2, 532.

²⁶*Der dt. Auswanderer* 28 (July 8, 1848): 435f.

²⁷Gov. Eichmann of the Prussian Rhine Province to Ministry of the Interior, Coblenz (July 18, 1848), Landeshauptarchiv Koblenz [LHA]: Best. 403, no. 7184, sheet 290.

²⁸Report of the "National Assoc. for Emigration and Colonization," *Der dt. Auswanderer* 2 (Jan. 8, 1948): 22; cf. Bylaws of the "Central Emigration Assoc. at Leipzig," *Der dt. Auswanderer* (Aug. 19, 1848): 534.

²⁹Bylaws of the Central Assoc. for German Overseas Settlement, *Der dt. Auswanderer* 47 (Nov. 18, 1848): 740.

³⁰"Plan einer geregelten dt. Auswanderung u. Ansiedlung in den Ver. Staaten Nordamerika's mit bes. Berücksichtigung unbemittelter Auswanderer," *Der dt. Auswanderer* 42ff. (Oct. 14, 1848): 662ff.

³¹Johannes von Werner, *Plan einer dt. Auswanderung u. Ansiedlung in den Ver. Staaten Nordamerika's mit bes. Berücksichtigung unbemittelter Auswanderer* (Reutlingen, 1848); Carl Ludwig Fleischmann, *Plan für dt. Auswanderung u. Ansiedelung (bzw. einer Reihe von Ansiedelungen) in den Ver. Staaten von Nordamerika. . .* (Stuttgart, 1849).

³²Th. Mandel, "Die Tätigkeit der Auswanderungsorganisationen um die Mitte des 19. Jhs. unter bes. Berücksichtigung von Südwestdeutschland," diss. (Frankfurt/M, 1922), 90f., 93f.

³³Memorandum of Minister of State du Thil, Darmstadt (Feb. 17, 1842), copy in ZSAM, Ministerium d. Innern, Rep. 77, Tit. 226, no. 73, vol. 1.

³⁴Georg Smolka, "Auswanderung u. auslandsdt. Kulturpolitik im vormärzlichen Preussen," *Jahrbuch des Reichsverbandes f.d. kathol. Auslandsdeutschen* (1933-34), 133.

³⁵"Verhandlungen der Ständekammer des Grossherzogtums Baden im Jahre 1841-42," Protokolle der 2. Kammer, 3. Protokollheft, 143ff., cit. by Hans Fenske, "Imperialistische Tendenzen in Deutschland vor 1866: Auswanderung, überseeische Bestrebungen, Weltmachtträume," *Histor. Jahrbuch* 97-98 (1978), 353.

³⁶*Verhandlungen der Landes-Deputierten-Versammlung des Herzogtums Nassau von dem Jahre 1846* (Wiesbaden, n.d.), [sess. of May 4, 1846] 266-273.

³⁷*Dokumente der Dt. Politik u. Geschichte von 1848 bis zur Gegenwart*, vol. 1: *Die Reichsgründung u. das Zeitalter Bismarcks, 1848-1890*, ed. by Johannes Hohlfeld (Berlin, 1951), 63f.

³⁸*Stenogr. Bericht über die Verhandlungen der dt. constituirenden Nationalversammlung zu Frankfurt a.M.*, ed. by Franz Wigard (Frankfurt/M, 1849), 8: 5721.

³⁹Pertinent documents in Bundesarchiv Aussenstelle Frankfurt/M [BAFfm], DB 58-181; cf. Günter Moltmann, "Ueberseeische Siedlungen u. weltpolit. Spekulationen: Friedrich

Gerstäcker u. die Frankfurter Zentralgewalt 1849," in *Russland, Deutschland, Amerika*, ed. by G. Moltmann, A. Fischer, and K. Schwabe (Wiesbaden, 1979), 56-72.

[40]Public agitation for a fleet had been widespread for quite some time. The Augsburger *Allg. Zeitung* had many articles on the necessity of a German fleet, e.g., no. 335, suppl. (Nov. 30, 1840): 266f.; no. 74, suppl. (March 15, 1841): 587f.; no. 197 (July 16, 1843): 1537; cf. Max Bär, *Die dt. Flotte von 1848-52, nach den Akten der Staatsarchive zu Berlin u. Hannover* (Leipzig, 1898); G. Moltmann, *Atlantische Blockpolitik im 19. Jh.: Die Ver. Staaten u. der dt. Liberalismus während der Revolution von 1848-49* (Düsseldorf, 1973).

[41]Ernst Dieffenbach, "Dt. Auswanderung u. Colonien," Memorandum to the Nat. Assembly at Frankfurt (May 1848), in *Der dt. Auswanderer* 23 (June 3,1848): 355.

[42]Gerolt to Ministry of Exterior Affairs [AA], Mexico (Oct. 1, 1837), Library of Congress [LoC]: Preussen, AA, Abt. III, Rep. 1. Auswanderungen ausser Europa, no. 2.

[43]Minister of State von Werther to King Friedrich Wilhelm III. (June 8, 1838), ZStAM: Geheimes Zivilkabinett, 2.2.1., no. 13356, sheet 1ff.

[44]Copies of the correspondence in Carl Josias Bunsen's despatch no. 55 to AA, London (Aug. 16, 1842), ZStAM: Min. d. ausw. Angel., 2.4.1., Abt. I, no. 5272.

[45]Rönne to Bunsen, private, New York (Nov. 14, 1842; Dec. 12, 1842), LoC: Preussen, AA, Centralbüro, Abt. II. D., Acta betr. das Project der Acquisition von Californien, 1843, Nr. 5. The ZStAM does not have the originals any longer (probably lost during WW II).

[46]See fn. 42.

[47]Rönne to Imperial Ministry of the Exterior, New York (Dec. 6, 1848), BAFfm: DB 53-85, vol. 1.

[48]Jefferson to Humboldt, (Dec. 6, 1813), LoC: *Thomas Jefferson Papers*, reel 47, series 1, *General Correspondence*.

[49]*Briefe von Deutschen aus Nord Amerika: mit bes. Beziehung auf die Giessner Auswanderungs-Gesellschaft vom Jahre 1834* (Altenburg, 1836). In a sample of ca. 100 letters from "emigrants of the educated class" to the Texas Association, one tenth mention the patriotic mission. See Bundesarchiv Koblenz [BA]: Microfilm no. EC 1485 N, doc. no. CA 4b3, no. 13.

[50]Gustav Körner, *Das dt. Element in den Ver. Staaten, 1818-1848* (Cincinnati, 1880), 229f.

[51]F. Ernst, *Bemerkungen auf einer Reise durch das Innere der Ver. Staaten von Nord-Amerika im Jahre 1819. . .* (Hildesheim, 1820).

[52]"Die Nachkommen von Ferdinand Ernst u. seiner Begleiter," *Deutsch-Amerikan. Geschichtsblätter* 3 (1903): 9ff.

[53]Traugott Bromme, *Rathgeber* (1846), 67, 171.

[54]Sigrid Faltin, *Die Auswanderung aus der Pfalz nach Nordamerika im 19. Jh. . . .* (Frankfurt/M, 1987), 123f.

[55]Reprint of a despatch from the *Stuttgart Gazette* (Sept. 2, 1832), in *Niles' Weekly Register* 43 (Nov. 3, 1832): 148.

[56]Cit. by Gerhard P. Bassler, "Auswanderungsfreiheit u. Auswanderungsfürsorge in Württemberg, 1815-1875: Zur Geschichte der südwestdt. Massenauswanderung nach Nordamerika," *Zeitschr. f. Württembergische Landesgeschichte* 33 (1974): 125.

[57]For the Belleville Germans see Gustav Körner's *Memoirs;* Cf. G. Engelmann, "Die dt. Niederlassung in Illinois, fünf Meilen östl. von Belleville," *Das Westland* 1 (1837) 3: 298ff.

[58]William G. Bek, "The Followers of Duden," *Missouri Hist. Review* 14 (Oct. 1919) 1: 30f.

[59]Cit. by A. Eickhoff, ed., *In der neuen Heimath: Geschichtl. Mitteilungen über die dt. Einwanderer in allen Theilen der Union* (New York, 1884), 337f.

[60]Friedrich Münch, *Gesammelte Schriften* (St. Louis, 1902), 99.

[61]The story is told with a healthy dose of sarcasm by Münch himself in "Die Giessener Auswanderungsgesellschaft," *Der dt. Auswanderer* 35 (1847), 545ff.

[62]See, e.g., Karl J. Arndt, "German as the Official Language of the U.S. of America?" *Monatshefte* 68 (Summer, 1976), 129-151.

[63]Heinz Kloss, *Um die Einigung des Deutschamerikanertums* (Berlin, 1937), 190.

[64]C.F. Huch, "Die Gesellschaft Germania," *Mitteilungen des dt. Pionier-Vereins von Philadelphia* 9 (1908), 22ff.

[65]G.Körner, *Das dt. Element* (1880), 108.

[66]Franz Löher's claim in his *Geschichte u. Zustände der Deutschen in Amerika* (Cinicinnati, 1847), 282f., has been reprinted uncritically by later authors.

[67]Theodor Frontin to M. B. Lamar, New York (Feb. 22, 1839), Texas State Archives: M. B. Lamar Papers, no. 1082; in *The Papers of M.B. Lamar*, ed. by Charles A. Gulick jr. (Austin, 1921), 460.

[68]Gustav Dresel, "Tagebuch von G. D. über seinen Aufenthalt in Texas 1837-1841," *Deutsch-Amerikan. Geschichtsblätter* 20- 21 (1920-21), 433.

[69]Heinz Kloss, *Um die Einigung der Deutschamerikaner*, 192.

[70]*Alte u. Neue Welt* (Sept. 3, 1836), cit. by A. Falbisaner, "Hermann, eine Hochburg des Deutschthums," *Deutsch-Amerikan. Geschichtsblätter* 1(1901).

[71]John A. Hawgood, *The Tragedy of German America: The Germans in the U.S. of America during the 19th Century—and after* (New York, 1940), 116.

[72]Still the best book on the Society is William G. Bek's *The German Settlement Society of Philadelphia and Its Colony, Hermann, Missouri* (Philadelphia, 1907); cf. "Die dt. Kolonie Hermann," *Der dt. Auswanderer* 38ff. (1847): 593ff.

[73]G. Körner, *Das dt. Element* (1880), 72.

[74]Op. cit., 357; cf. J.G. Häcker, *Bericht aus u. über Amerika* (Leipzig, 1849), 47-54; "Berichte über die dt. Ansiedlung Wartburg in Ost-Tennessee," *Germania*, 2 (1848): 102-109.

[75]J.A. Wagener, "Die Deutschen in Süd-Carolina," *Der Dt. Pionier* 3 (1871-72), 234.

[76]Traugott Bromme, *Rathgeber für Auswanderungslustige—Wohin sollen wir auswandern. . .?* (Stuttgart, 1846), 174.

[77]A. Berghold, "Geschichte von New Ulm, Minnesota," *Der Dt. Pionier* 4 & 5 (1872) and 4-12 (1877); "Dokumentarische Geschichte des Turnerbundes u. der turnerischen Bestrebungen in den Ver. Staaten," ed. by Heinrich Metzner, *Jahrbücher der Deutsch-Amerikan. Turnerei* 1 (1890), 255f.

[78]*Amerikan. Turnerbund: Verfassungsentwurf des Ansiedlungsvereins des sozialist. Turnerbundes* (New Ulm, May 24-25, 1858).

[79]"Statuten des Vereins," *Gesammelte Aktenstücke des Vereins zum Schutze dt. Einwanderer nach Texas* (Mainz, Fürstl. Rentenkammer Schloss Braunfels, 1845), 3f.

[80]Castell to Solms, Mainz (Aug. 5. 1844), BA:EC 1493 N, CA 4c2, no. 2.

[81]"Der Verein zum Schutze dt. Einwanderer in Texas in Bezug auf die Sclavenfrage," *Frankfurter Journal* 196 (July 17, 1844). *The Galveston Journal* (Sept. 30, 1844) reported: "A new Republic is about to be established on our Western border." Cit. by William Kennedy, private letter no. 8 to Richard Pakenham, Galveston (Sept. 30, 1844), Public Record Office London [PRO]: F. O. 701. no. 29.

[82]"Die Deutschen in Texas," Correspondence from Galveston, anon. (Feb. 23, 1845), LoC: *Braunfels'sches Archiv*, Ca 4b3, No. 1.

[83]Solms to William Kennedy, on board the Texan Revenue Cutter "Alert," Galveston Bay (Dec. 3, 1844), Ephraim D. Adams, ed., "British Correspondence Concerning Texas," *Southwestern Hist. Quarterly [SWHQ]* 19 (1915/16): 305f.

84Addington to Kennedy, separate, Foreign Office (May 20, 1844), PRO:F.O.701, no. 29.

85Charles Elliot to Perry Doyle, private, Galveston (June 21, 1843). E.D. Adams, ed., "British Correspondence. . .", *SWHQ* 17 (1913-14): 72; cf. Doyle to Foreign Office, despatch no. 17, (n.p., June 24, 1843), British Library: Aberdeen Papers, MS 43184, vol. 146.

86See President Houston's veto-message against a bill repealing his right to extend land grants, in *Texas State Library, Republic of Texas, Department of State*, vol. 40, no. 299, cit. by Rudolph R. Biesele, *History of the German Settlements in Texas, 1831-1861* (Austin, 1939), 70; cf. Castell to Prince Leiningen, Mainz (Jan. 23, 1843), Fürstl. Leiningen'sches Archiv Amorbach: *Akten des Texas-Vereins* I, no. 8; Jones to Smith, Galveston (March 9, 1842), in George P. Garrison, ed., "Diplomatic Correspondence of the Republic of Texas," *Ann. Rep. of the Am. Hist. Ass. for the Year 1908* (Washington, D.C.: GPO, 1911), vol. II (2), part III (1908), 949-50, 963.

87See the report of the *Generalversammlung* in Biebrich (June 18, 1843), BA:EC 1483 N.CA 4b1. No. 3.

88Solms to Fisher (Dec. 28, 1844). LoC: *Braunfels'sches Archiv*, CA 4c2, no. 3.

89Report Meusebach to Association, New Braunfels (Nov. 10, 1845), BA:EC 1485, CA 4b3, no. 6.

90General report of the Association's board of management for the year 1846. BA:EC 1483 N.CA 4b1, no. 3.

91Dagmar Auspurg-Hackert, "Dt. Auswanderung nach Texas im 19. Jh.," diss., (Univ. Bochum, 1984), 74.

92*The Complete Jefferson: Containing His Major Writings, Publ. and Unpubl., Except His Letters*, assembl. & arrang. by Saul K. Padover (New York, 1943), 625.

93Ibid., 393.

94Jefferson to George Flower (Sept. 12, 1817), cit. by K. A. Arndt, "German as the Official Language of the U.S. . . .? *Monatshefte* 68 (Summer 1976), 146.

95M. v. Fürstenwärther, *Der Deutsche in Nordamerika* (1818), 28f.

96M.J. Kohler, "An Important European Mission to Investigate American Immigration Conditions and John Quincy Adams' Relations thereto, 1817-1818," *Deutsch-Amerikan. Geschichtsblätter* 17 (1917), 413.

97Adams to Fürstenwärther, Washington (June 14, 1819), Bundesarchiv Aussenstelle Frankfurt: Nachlass H.C. v. Gagern, FN 7, II-14, printed in *Niles' Weekly Register* 17, whole ser. (April 19, 1820), 157-58.

98Karl J. Arndt, *Rapp's Harmony Society* (Philadelphia, 1965), 83-90.

99*Annals of Congress* (9th Congress-1st Sess.), 463-478.

100*American State Papers* (12th Congress-1st Sess.), no. 190 and 256 [Dec. 5, 1811]; cf. (15th Congress-1st Sess.), 566, 711.

101"House Report" (H.rp.), 242 (28th Congress-1st Sess.), *U.S. Serial Set*, no. 445, vol. 1; *American State Papers* (9th Congress-2nd Sess.), no. 13, 288 [Dec. 8, 1806].

102*Annals of Congress* (15th Congress-1st Sess.), 202, 1013, 1053f.; cf. *Niles' Weekly Register* 14, whole ser. (May 30, 1818), 232f.

103Even Fürstenwärther cited the briefing paper—it must have been leaked to the *General Advertiser* (March 4, 1818), see *Der Deutsche in Amerika* (1818), 107ff.

104Marcus Lee Hansen, *Die Einwanderer in der Geschichte Amerikas* (Stuttgart, 1948), 132.

105*American State Papers* (16th Congress-1st Sess.), no. 312: 437 [March 3, 1820].

106*Niles' Weekly Register*" 43, whole ser. (Nov. 24, 1832), 196. 107 *American State Papers* (24th Congress-1st Sess.), no. 1490, 587 [March 25, 1836].

[107]*American State Papers* (24th Congress-1st Sess.), no. 1490, 587 [March 3, 1836].

[108]Ibid., (23rd Congress-1st Sess.), no. 1237, 145 [April 29, 1834].

[109]See fn. 56.

[110]Schwendler to Sec. of State Edward Livingston, Frankfurt (March 31, 1833), National Archives: Rec. of the Dept. of State, Consular Despatches from Frankfurt, M 161, reel T1.

[111]Schwendler, ibid.

[112]H.rp. 1040 (25th Congress-2nd Sess.), *U.S. Serial Set* no. 336, vol. 4, 91.

[113]G. Flower, *The Errors of Immigrants. . .* (London, 1841), 47.

[114]C.L. Fleischmann, *Wegweiser u. Rathgeber nach u. in den Ver. Staaten von Nordamerika* (Stuttgart, 1852), 7-8.

[115]"German Emigration to America," *North American Review* 82 (1856): 267. The editors claim this to be the first discussion on German emigration in an English-language paper.

[116]Kennedy to Aberdeen, private, Galveston (Sept. 6, 1843), F.O. Slave Trade, vol. 479, cit. by Adams, ed., "British Diplomatic Correspondence Concerning Texas," *SWHQ* 17 (1913-14): 205; cf. Justin H. Smith, *The Annexation of Texas* (1911; corr. ed. New York, 1941), 97, 163, 205.

[117]Jackson to Brown, Hermitage, Tenn. (Feb. 12, 1843) ["as sent to Martin Van Buren by Francis Preston Blair"], Washington (March 18, 1843), LoC: Martin Van Buren Papers.

[118]H. Clay in the *National Intelligencer* (April 27, 1844), cit. in Ambrose Dudley Mann's letter to James Calhoun, Bremen (Oct. 31, 1844), in Franklin J. Jameson, ed., "Calhoun's Correspondence," *Am. Hist. Ass. Rep.* (1899), 982.

[119]William Murphy to Sec. of State, despatch no. 11, confid. (encl.), Galveston (Nov. 9, 1843). Nat. Archives: Rec. of the Dept. of State. Consular Corr. from Galveston, T-728, reel 2.

[120]Hamilton to Calhoun, New Orleans (Feb. 18, 1845), in Jameson, ed., *Calhoun's Correspondence*, 1026f.

11 | Frontier Socialism: The Founding of New Ulm, Minnesota, by German Workers and Freethinkers[1]

Jörg Nagler, *German Historical Institute, Washington, D.C.*

In a recent Methodist description of New Ulm, it was alleged that this town was "founded by a group of German beer drinkers" whose "religion was found in athletics."[2] As usual, a bit of truth lies hidden beneath the surface of these kinds of disparaging commentaries: Beer drinking and athletics (mental as well as physical) were indeed a distinct part of the cultural and political expression of everyday life in New Ulm.

This article focuses on the process of the founding of this frontier settlement—its ideology, background, and ideals that formed a web of contributing factors for the decision to establish this Turner town—and on its initial experimental phase from 1854 until 1859. The scholarship and historiography on New Ulm has seldom explored the broader social and economic context of the 1850s as a contributing factor for its founding.[3] But this context is significant for better understanding the particular ideology of the Forty-eighters, which was influenced to a great degree by artisans, craftsmen, journeymen, and laborers. These groups were much more dependent on labor market developments and economic crises than their fellow compatriots from the intelligentsia.[4]

Since the individual steps of the founding process have been described elsewhere, I will concentrate on what I perceive to be the underlying essentials of this founding process and its broader significance and implications for politicized groups of German immigrants in mid-19th century America. The endeavor to create an ideal social microcosm sheltered from interference by the dominant society, or from the forces of exploitation, was not a new phenomenon in ante-bellum society—for Americans as well for immigrant groups. In the decade before the founding of New Ulm, more than forty cooperative communities were established in the U.S., which attracted intellectuals as well as workers and artisans influenced mainly by the French utopian Charles Fourier.[5] The generic term "utopian" has been applied to the many movements that created settlements in the U.S., the justification for such a common grouping being that, in one way or another, they all sought to realize an ideal of perfection in communal living. Individual perfection was often sought through the experience of cooperative living.

As we can learn from Thomas More's *Utopia*, the depiction of an "ideal society" always hints at deficiencies of the contemporary society, in our case the U.S. in the 1850s. Accordingly, the concept of this "ideal town" provides a good opportunity for students of ethnicity to explore such issues as acculturation and assimilation.

New Ulm is the famous singular example of the actual founding of a frontier community coupled with the attempt to implement the theory of Turnerism.[6] The political concept for this town derived from the revolutionary heritage and experience of the 1848 Revolution, hence from the cultural baggage of the German Forty-eighters immigrant group; at the same time, it also reflects their specific American experience. In ante-bellum America, the westward movement of workers was considered by some a panacea or, in Horace Greeley's words, a safety valve—through which the problems of surplus labor, poverty, and possibly increasing social tensions in the eastern cities might be solved. Although few workingmen actually left the eastern cities, the theoretical assumption maintained that the migration might increase the level of wages and prevent the accumulation of immigrant workers in the cities. In addition to these considerations, the propagation of "free land" was closely connected to a "free labor" ideology, which later was supported by the nascent Republican Party.[7]

The specific reasons for the founding of New Ulm afford us substantial information about the Forty-eighter mind set and perception of American society in the mid-1850s. The New World, which possessed for many of these refugees an almost mythical quality, meant the embodiment of democracy, the absence of a ruling class, the realization of the revolutionary goals of *liberté* and *égalité, Freiheit* and *Gleichheit*, liberty and equality. However, after the first years in exile, which many considered only temporary in the beginning, such romantic and euphoric notions of the "ideal republic" were superseded by a more realistic assessment of America, often combined with harsh social criticism.

The Forty-eighters criticized social evils such as corruption, slavery, and class tensions—for them a reflection of the hitherto unresolved problem of capital/labor relationships. Their experience of these ills coincided with the appearance of a strong nativism, personified by the Know-Nothings with their considerable political influence. Furthermore, the temperance crusade, which was inherently connected to nativism, amplified the critical assessment often through negative personal experiences in their "adopted fatherland." But these factors alone cannot explain their initial eagerness to establish a new community, free from the nuisances of nativism and temperance laws. It was primarily the negative economic situation, the crises of 1854/55, that was the actual transmission belt which set the town-founding process in motion.

Since many Turners were artisans, either masters or journeymen, urban centers attracted them, especially those communities with a significant German population. On the other hand, in these rapidly-growing industrial centers, the transformation process from the traditional skilled crafts into the new industrial era of unskilled labor was fast, for some too fast, and caused social dislocation. Fears of unemployment, amplified by the economic crises of the 1850s, made migration to the West plausible as a cure for economic hardship. It was thus no accident that the decision to found a settlement on the frontier coincided with this crisis that laid off a considerable number of journeymen.[8]

Carl Wittke links the failing of communitarian experiments to the specific situation of the 1850s: "The America of the 1850s, with cheap land and relatively good wages, was not a favorable atmosphere in which to nourish radical plans for a new social and economic system."[9] However, Wittke's statement is misleading and points in the wrong direction: While there was indeed a relative increase in wages for journeymen and laborers in this decade, real income actually declined in the wake of the considerably and disproportionately higher costs of housing and food.[10] One can therefore almost reverse Wittke and argue that the economic situation of the 1850s instigated communitarian experiments, which were at the same time jeopardized by this negative economic development.

New Ulm is the only community founded with an ideological concept mainly influenced by and derived from the socialist Turner movement, which Carl Wittke called one of "the most important results of the German immigration in the 19th century."[11] Let me briefly summarize its history. Founded in the wake of Napoleon's occupation of the German states, the Turner societies quickly became a vehicle for the expression of strong patriotism combined with an urge to create a free and united Germany. In order to achieve these goals, Turner societies were organized along paramilitary lines and were intended to raise the physical and mental skills of their members. Always centers of liberalism, the Turner societies were soon declared subversive and were forced to go underground in the two decades before the 1848/49 Revolution.[12] In the social upheavals of 1848/49, they played a major role in organizing the revolutionary troops, and the Turners were the most active barricade fighters in the streets of Berlin, Dresden, and other centers of revolutionary activities. Once transplanted into the New World because of the forced emigration of thousands of Forty-eighters, the Turner societies again became the nuclei of political radicalism in German-American communities.[13] Deeply rooted in their European experience, the members of the Turner societies, the majority of them skilled and unskilled artisans, and journeymen, were nonetheless able to transfer their social-egalitarian ideas into American society and thus became ardent abolitionists, later affiliated with Radical Republicanism.

In 1850 the various Turner societies met in Philadelphia. They discussed the formation of a national association not only to increase the communication between the individual societies but to foster political influence. This was clearly the first step toward active involvement in the pressing American political realities of the 1850s, and it signaled a process of acculturation. The fight against nativism, slavery, and temperance became the new specific American agenda of the Turners—besides fighting for the more encompassing ideals of general welfare, social justice, and education for all. The *Sozialistischer Turnerbund,* as the national organization was called after 1850, declared itself in support of the Free Soil Party, and when the Republican Party was founded in 1854, it enthusiastically propounded an anti-slavery stance. Of course, the Turners always remained aware of that party's strong nativist component embodied in the Know-Nothings.[14]

Two names stand out in the process of the founding of New Ulm: Ferdinand Beinhorn[15] and Wilhelm Pfaender.[16]—both representing different backgrounds and motivations for the founding of the town. Beinhorn, born in Braunschweig, had emigrated in 1852 and arrived in New York the same year. Probably due to the pressing social and economic conditions he faced, he immediately envisaged the founding of a German colony on the frontier. After moving to Chicago, and obviously having been influenced by more experienced and realistic compatriots, he came down to a more moderate plan: a model frontier settlement in the West based on the equal distribution of land—without the interference of land speculators—and the possibility of erecting decent homes for German workers. In 1853 he became the founder of the Chicago Land Verein, a land association that was designed to enable paying members to join this cooperative venture and to avoid the hardships of Chicago, to escape the uncertainties of the labor market, which were especially pronounced in the prevailing economic crisis, and to move west. Only one year later, and after advertising for members in the *Illinois Staatszeitung*, the association with Beinhorn as its president could boast of about 800 paying members, each of whom contributed a $3 membership fee and a $5 assessment. The overwhelming majority of the members were workers, class conscious enough to exclude clergymen and lawyers (*Pfaffen* and *Advokaten*) from membership.[17] Chicago's Turner Hall became the venue for the Land Verein meetings and simultaneously demonstrated the association's affiliation with the Turner movement.

After several attempts to find the ideal location for their town in territories recently opened for settlement, a site was discovered at the Minnesota frontier, approximately 70 miles southwest of Minneapolis at the confluence of the Cottonwood and Minnesota Rivers. The latter was navigable and thus met one precondition formulated by Beinhorn. The other prerequisite for the survival of a new autonomous settlement, according to the planning committee of the Chicago Land Verein, was the accessibility of ample timber to build houses and to have sufficient wood for stoves during the grim Minnesota winters. The site promised both, and the prairie soil west of the future settlement was also suitable for farming.

But what about the relations between the newly-arrived German pioneers and their Indian neighbors, the Sioux Indians? The Sioux claimed that the land chosen by the German settlers of the Chicago Land Verein belonged to their reservation.[18] Unfortunately, confrontations between the settlers and the Indians were almost unavoidable, since the boundaries of the reservation were not clearly defined. When winter set in, the Sioux moved to another area, but when they returned in the spring of 1855, they restated their claim that the New Ulm area belonged to their reservation. Upon the German settlers' refusal to accept the Sioux's claim, they started killing the settlers' cattle. Only the appearance of the army prevented a further escalation, and the Sioux had to withdraw.[19] After that intermezzo, which foreshadowed the Sioux Uprising in 1862 with its tragic consequences for New Ulm,[20] Beinhorn arrived in May 1855 with about 24 settlers, including a few women and children. At this time, one of these settlers, Jacob Haeberle, obviously of Swabian origin, named the settlement New Ulm in memory of his German home town.[21]

In accordance with the Pre-emption Act of 1841, the settlers now claimed a certain territory for their settlement before it was offered publicly for sale. Aware of the fact that once a federal land office was established in the region, they would have to pay fees of $1.25 an acre, the Beinhorn group realized that they needed to raise more money if they were to implement their plans of a settlement not too restricted in scope. The attempt to finance the

desired acreage was partly successful through assessment of an additional
$30 membership fee by the Chicago Land Verein. But that was still not
enough to pay for all the acreage the colony needed, since Beinhorn
envisioned an autonomous township supplied by surrounding and collectively
owned farmland.[22]

At this juncture, the history of New Ulm might have ended because of
financial strains. In the spring of 1856, however, help arrived in the person of
Wilhelm Pfaender, who had learned about the German colony in St. Paul
during his search for a Turner settlement. Pfaender, son of a poor, unskilled
artisan, was born in Heilbronn, Württemberg, in 1826, where he became a
shopkeeper apprentice. Very soon he was exposed to the philosophy of the
Turners and became one of the founders of the Heilbronn Turner society.
Although his active political involvement in the first expressions of the
upcoming revolutionary events, which finally led to the violent eruptions of
1848/49, was not really noteworthy, his decision to emigrate was mainly
influenced by political dissatisfaction with the oppressive climate in
Germany, especially the persecution of the Turners. In London, through his
brother, he met Marx and Engels. In 1848 he took refuge in the U.S., where
he finally settled in Cincinnati with its thriving German-American
community (German-born or of German parentage) that constituted well over
40% of the total city population. There he found employment in a German-
American-owned factory that manufactured safes.[23]

Almost simultaneously, one of the most celebrated heroes of the German
Revolution, Friedrich Hecker, arrived in the Queen City, greeted by an
enthusiastic demonstration on his behalf. This inspired the founding of the
first Turner society in the U.S. Pfaender became a charter member, prepared
to transplant experiences and principles of his German Turner years to
Cincinnati. When the *Turnhalle* was erected in 1850, Pfaender delivered the
inaugural speech, showing that he had become one of the most prominent
members of the Turner society. The Turnhalle very quickly became
Cincinnati's hub for political and cultural activity not only for the German-
American community.[24] Pfaender's concept of a German cooperative
settlement demonstrated to what degree his American experience had shaped
his ideas. He formulated his design of a Turner town in a letter of March
1855 to *Die Turnzeitung*, the mouthpiece of the newly founded national
organization of the Turners, and called it "Practical Turnerism." In that letter,
he stated that true reform in America could obviously only be pursued in an
environment chosen by those people who would strive for it. Nativistic
hostility against Germans, and especially the Turners, because of their
allegedly deviant social behavior—including public political agitation, beer
drinking, and their exotic outfits—often fomented suspicion and even

aggressive acts by the native-born. The combination of these factors made a
sheltered habitat for Turners desirable and pertinent.[25]

Pfaender appealed especially to workingmen, but he also directed the
attention of others to the "prejudices and arrogance of American Nativists
which becomes more and more crass from day to day." In his letter,
addressed mainly to workers and Turners, Pfaender called "for the
establishment of a settlement which would give us the opportunity to enjoy
undisturbedly the rights guaranteed to us by the U.S. Constitution and to
become happy and blessed after our own fashion."[26] Pfaender's concepts were
on a more moderate scale and more realistic than the contemporary
discussions on the founding of worker's colonies, such as Wilhelm Weitling's
"Communia" in Iowa, a strictly communistic settlement.[27] Pfaender's ideas
were certainly far from the notion of establishing a German state within the
U.S. Pfaender envisioned a rather small settlement where the physical and
mental aspects of Turnerism could be "practiced." In comparison to
Beinhorn's concept, however, Pfaender was much more radical and ambitious
in his philosophical approach, since he tried to establish a socialist
settlement, albeit one where private property was to be tolerated. When the
Turners of Cincinnati endorsed a committee to organize a shareholding
company to secure funding for the settlement, Pfaender, together with his
compatriot, the Forty-eighter Jacob Nix, introduced his plan to the national
Turner convention in Buffalo in September 1855.[28] The Turner organizations
of the West were especially supportive of his plans, and it was agreed that the
Turnverein in Cincinnati should take charge of the project.

Pfaender became the president of the Turner Colonization Society of
Cincinnati, and he drafted the charter, which was accepted at a special
convention in January 1856, when the society was renamed Settlement
Society of the Socialist Turnerbund. The following quote from the charter
defines the actual purpose of the founding process:

> The current state of affairs of our societal conditions is such that every thinking
> human being should be obliged to consider means through which the material,
> social, and political independence of a great body of the people could be secured
> more firmly and permanently than has previously been the case. Despite the often
> praised gigantic progress, many workers are unable to find suitable employment and
> a secure livelihood. For years, food has become disproportionately expensive, and
> crises like those of the years 1854 and 1855, as well as the corruption appearing
> ever more openly and shamelessly in all branches of the public administration,
> permit no hope for improvement. Recently added to these bleak prospects for the
> future have been the intense animosity of a great part of native Americans against
> the immigrant citizens, as well as the exertions of the temperance people. . . and the
> attempts to revive the Puritanical Sunday laws. And so it is about time to think of
> looking for a new home where one can remain aloof from such nuisances and where

we can invest our time into higher interests. The Settlement Association of the
Socialist Turner Society owes its founding to the accepted necessity of bringing men
of these opinions and aspirations together in one organization in order to implement
the described plans. It is the organization's purpose to offer its members, aside from
the basis of a secure existence, the benefits of a comprehensive, splendid youth
education, and in general to concern itself with the promotion of trade and industry,
the arts and the sciences, and at the same time to foster good German fellowship and
the right spirit (*Geselligkeit und biederen Sinn*).[29]

Pfaender's design for an egalitarian settlement at the frontier was also
important enough to have good model potential for other German-Americans
with similar ideological leanings. The initial step toward the founding of the
model settlement proved to be successful. Within a few months after
publishing the call for membership, the Settlement Society of the Socialist
Turnerbund achieved financial soundness through a membership fee paid by
some 1,300 men.

Meanwhile, financial troubles strained the Chicago Land Verein, since it
could not pay the land-office fees for all the acreage that Beinhorn had
envisioned for the colony. Since Pfaender was well equipped financially and
Neu Ulm appealed to him as the ideal location for the Turner settlement, he
proposed to Beinhorn a merger of the Chicago Land Verein and the Settlement Society of the Socialist Turnerbund. At that time the lots of the Chicago
Land Verein had not yet been distributed to its members. This provided a
chance to restructure the settlement according to the notion of the Turners.
The merger of the two settlement groups resulted in the creation of the
German Land Association of Minnesota, with Pfaender as president. When it
was incorporated less than a year later, the shares valued at $50 made for a
total capital of $100,000.[30] Pfaender bought the holdings of the Chicago
group, totaling 4,836 acres, for about $6,000, with the agreement that the
Settlement Society of the Socialist Turnerbund would arrange the building of
cooperative enterprises such as a mill, a warehouse, and a school, and would
buy additional land to attract a greater number of settlers.[31] Beinhorn and
Pfaender declared that their goal was "to procure a home for every German
laborer—popish priests and lawyers excluded—in some healthy and
productive district, located on some navigable river."[32]

After the merging of the two groups, the Turners brought up the subject
of the settlement's name again, and more than a dozen were proposed,
including Nibelungen, Thusnelda, Hutten, and Sparta. However, after long
discussions, the old name of New Ulm was eventually accepted for the
incorporated town.

But the most important step had to be taken now: the implementation of
Pfaender's and his compatriots' dream of establishing a "German settlement

with avoidance of speculation, and with educational opportunities for the children of liberals and freethinkers." Since the Turners had achieved their merger with the Chicago group before the latter defined a settlement layout, they instantaneously started to change the ways of land distribution according to their own ideas. The assignment of lots, divided between property within town, limited to a maximum of six lots per person, and four acres of "garden land" outside the town—comparable to the "truck gardening" concept—was arranged through a lottery system.[33] For those who pursued agriculture, more land could be purchased from the association, which became the center of planning and designing the town's socialist future. A long, detailed article in the *Neu Ulm Pionier* entitled "Cornerstone" (*Grundbaustein*) discussed the form of the association in historical perspective, showing that much time was dedicated to the theoretical and philosophical question of cooperative enterprises. It was argued that socialization was the only thinkable way of a future egalitarian socialist society, although it should not abolish "private property and individuality."[34]

The stockholders had empowered the German Land Association to undertake the necessary steps to develop the community and to guarantee the provision of technical equipment such as a saw mill, which was essential for erecting the first buildings, and the supply of goods.[35]

The planned design of the future city reflected the negative experiences of its planners in American cities. They wanted to avoid high population density with its negative effects such as in Chicago, which Beinhorn had once called "a miserable slough," so poor in sanitation that "hundreds succumbed to Cholera," and they envisaged a "handsomely landscaped boulevard" and "distinguished parks."[36]

New Ulm's population steadily increased and, after the Turners took over, a constant stream of new settlers arrived, mostly from Cincinnati. In 1857 the total population amounted to 440, among them three doctors.[37] As always in such experimental communities, there was a shortage of women. In its first issue, the *Neu Ulm Pionier* dedicated a paragraph to this vital problem:

> There is a great shortage of ladies. Approximately one hundred girls would be very much welcomed next spring and the warmest reception will be accorded them in town and country. We direct attention to the Pittsburgh Ladies' Committee, which intends to supply the West with well-behaved housewives and also intends to inform chaste candidates of that opportunity. We will not fail to recommend ourselves most gracefully.[38]

The rapid population growth, however, also had a negative impact on the economic situation in Neu Ulm. Supply and transportation of goods became a problem, since the closest source for both hardware and software articles was

over 70 miles away. Consequently, prices for these scarce articles rose
dramatically. In addition, an adequate supply of housing became a pressing
problem for the nascent community. Some settlers had to live in sod-weed
houses, others in primitive dugout shelters. Since these pioneers were mostly
of urban backgrounds, the hardships of frontier life with few affordable
luxuries had its effect on the general mood in the experimental settlement.
Like their intellectual Forty-eighter counterparts, the Latin farmers, the toil
of cultivating the land was something to which they could not easily adapt.
Voices were heard articulating frustration with the settlement's progress,
arguing that a "settlement of poor people could not thrive unless families
with means also settled and provided opportunities for others."[39]

The association, as the umbrella organization for the Chicago Land
Association and the Settlement Society of the Socialist Turnerbund, had to
reassure itself of the socialist loyalty of its members. This indicates that there
was obviously some dissent about the common social goals of the settlement.
In one of the many meetings of this sort, a resolution was adopted that reads,
in part:

> The whole settlement is social, because not only the respective branch of the
> Socialist Turner Association opted for socialism but also the present members of the
> Chicago Land Association (according to its origin) unanimously voted for a socialism
> not only in principle but in practice as well. Although socialism was unclearly
> defined by the Turner Association around 1850, it is nevertheless a recognizable
> progress for the German element.[40]

Very soon, however, members of the association realized that despite
their initial efforts and idealism, the success of the cooperative experiment
was in danger because of the declining financial condition. Once the land
had been purchased, there were no funds left for further projected enterprises
such as a warehouse, a quarry, a cemetery, and the acquisition of agricultural
equipment. In addition to the scarcity of capital, there were other factors
contributing to the disastrous financial situation: the Panic of 1857 and the
subsequent economic depression had its impact on Neu Ulm, as did the two
consecutive bad harvests in 1857 and 1858. Pfaender and his Turner
compatriots had to face reality. There was agreement that the concept of
cooperatives was about to fail, at least in financial terms. An extra convention
of the shareholders, to be held in May 1858 in Neu Ulm, was called to reveal
the situation and to discuss a possible solution.[41]

In particular, the first cooperative enterprise, the sawmill, was heavily in
debt and had not been able to compete with another privately owned sawmill.
Furthermore, the communal newspaper, the *Neu Ulm Pionier,* with its first
publication in January 1858, was already in financial trouble (it was later

sold to its editor). Its motto, "Independent in everything, neutral in nothing"—the dialectic expression for liberalism—reflects the founders' spirit. They visualized a paper that would be "independent of party cliques, advocating radical progress, disseminating knowledge regarding conditions in the territory, and serving as intermediary for members of an *Ansiedlungsverein* and the *Turnverein* of New Ulm,"[42] or "the organ for the propagation of radical fundamental principles."[43] It is a vital source of information concerning the self-perception of the Turners' communitarian ideas.[44] Interestingly, the editor understood Neu Ulm as a sort of model town after which other communities might be founded by German settlers. Showing awareness of other simultaneous experimental communities, like Étienne Cabet's Icarian utopian settlement in Nauvoo, Ill., the articles that concerned the philosophy of New Ulm reflect a strong sentiment against pure—thus impractical—utopianism, communism, and "state socialism." They favored a "practical socialism," which is defined by the needs and the will of the community. It also advocated the motto of the newly founded Republican Party: "Free soil, free men, free labor and a free press."[45] The paper also reflected the strong development of German-American cultural life in the young town. Several *Vereine* (societies, clubs) were founded immediately before and after the town's incorporation in 1857. Naturally, the Turner society, with its impressive hall genuinely built by voluntary work on Sundays, was first, followed by a *Gesangsverein, Arbeiterverein, Schulverein,* etc., building a microcosm of German America. The first locally produced beer, a substantial part of *Geselligkeit* or *Gemütlichkeit,* was celebrated in March 1858, and the commentator in the *Neu Ulm Pionier* looked forward to the first locally-grown wine, "Since Bacchus is a god, while Gambrinus is only a king."[46] The Methodist assessment of the Turner colony was not that inaccurate after all. In quite a different way from the temperance point of view, however, the favorable attitude toward drinking in Neu Ulm was not without some tragic consequences. The town developed into a center for the trade of liquor that was often used to acquire goods from the Indians. But this trade increased the animosity among Indians toward the Germans, since, once sober, they realized that they had been deceived.[47]

At the end of 1858, the declining financial situation alarmed the shareholders. They were increasingly afraid of losing their assets. The Cincinnati Turnverein demanded an investigation into the management of the association. It was stated that the original capital of $100,000 had been reduced to $7,400, and that debts were still constantly mounting. In the spring of 1859, after long discussions on the future of Neu Ulm, the German Land Association had to be dissolved because of its financial problems.

Sharing this demise were the communitarian enterprises that had formed the core of the experimental dimension of this frontier town.

One of the last acts of the association was in true accordance with one of the visions of Pfaender and his Turner compatriots concerning the development of Neu Ulm, namely to guarantee "Educational opportunities for the children of liberals and freethinkers." In order to implement this goal, a permanent school fund of more than $4,000 was created through the sale of some of the remaining land, and a resolution was adopted, which stated that a teacher should be paid from the interest accruing from this capital. Keeping in line with the secular, antireligious orientation of the Turners, no Bibles were to be found in the school library, and religious instruction was not to be part of the curriculum.[48]

By 1859 the socialist experiment in New Ulm, with its more than 800 inhabitants, was abandoned. But, even though the particularly socialist nature of the settlement could not prevail, New Ulm survived as a German settlement with a richly blossoming cultural life and economic importance. Today it is a town with more than 13,000 inhabitants and is still predominantly German in character.

NOTES

[1]The title of my paper has been inspired, in part, by the Socialist Turner Assoc., which had called for the foundation of a colony of "workers and freethinkers," cited in Hannes Neumann, *Die dt. Turnbewegung in der Revolution 1848/49 u. in der amerikan. Emigration* (Stuttgart, 1968), 135.

[2]Cit. by Hildegard Binder Johnson, "The Germans," in *They Chose Minnesota: A Survey of the State's Ethnic Groups*, ed. June Drenning Holmquist (St. Paul, 1981), 181, n. 41.

[3]The literature on Neu (later New) Ulm is rather extensive: Noel Iverson, *Germania, U.S.A.: Social Change in New Ulm, Minnesota* (Minneapolis, 1966); Hildegard Binder Johnson, "The Founding of New Ulm, Minnesota," *American-German Review* 12 (1946): 8ff.; Elroy Ubl, *A Chronology of New Ulm, Minnesota, 1853-1899* (New Ulm, 1978); Alice F. Tyler, "William Pfaender and the Founding of New Ulm," *Minnesota History* 30 (1949): 24-35; and LaVern J. Rippley, "Status vs. Ethnicity: The Turners and Bohemians of New Ulm," in *The German Forty-eighters in the U.S.*, ed. Charlotte L. Brancaforte (New York, 1989), 257-278.

[4]For ideological differences and commonalties between rank-and-file Forty-eighters and their intellectual counterparts see the superb study of Bruce Levine, *The Spirit of 1848: German Immigrants, Labor Conflict, and the Coming of Civil War* (Urbana and Chicago, 1992).

[5]Philip S. Foner, *History of the Labor Movement in the U.S.* (New York, 1982), vol. 1, 174ff.

[6]New Ulm invites comparison esp. with the almost simultaneously founded frontier settlement by German peasants in Minnesota, where the Cath. church played a significant role in the community life and was the actual guarantor of traditional family values transplanted from the Old World. See Kathleen N. Conzen, "Peasant Pioneers: Generational Succession Among the German Farmers in Frontier Minnesota," in *The Countryside in the Age of*

Capitalist Transformation, Essays in the Social History of Rural-America, ed. Steven Hahn and Jonathan Prude (Chapel Hill, 1985), 259-292; idem., "German Americans and Ethnic Political Culture: Stearns County, Minnesota, 1855-1915" (Working Paper No. 16, John F. Kennedy Institut f. Nordamerikastudien, Berlin, 1989).

[7]Eric Foner, *Free Soil, Free Labor, Free Men: The Ideology of the Republican Party before the Civil War* (New York, 1970), 26f.; P. Foner, *History of the Labor Movement*, vol. I, 188; James L. Huston, *The Panic of 1857 and the Coming of the Civil War* (Baton Rouge, 1987), 102. On the safety-valve thesis see Henry M. Littlefield, "Has the Safety Valve Come Back to Life?" *Agricultural History* 37 (1964): 47ff.

[8]R. Commons et al., *History of Labour in the U.S.*, 4 vols. (New York, repr. 1966), vol. I, 613.

[9]Carl Wittke, *Refugees of Revolution, The German Forty-Eighters in America* (Philadelphia, 1952), 174.

[10]See Steven J. Ross, *Workers on the Edge: Work, Leisure and Politics in Industrializing Cincinnati, 1788-1890* (New York, 1985), 143.

[11]Wittke, *Refugees of Revolution*, 147.

[12]See Karl Obermann, "Die polit. Rolle der Turnvereine in der demokrat. Bewegung am Vorabend der Revolution von 1848," *Theorie u. Praxis der Körperkultur* 12 (1963): 795-805.

[13]On Jacobin republicanism see Eric Hobsbawm, *The Age of Revolution, 1789-1848* (New York, 1962), 249.

[14]Easily accessible lit. on the Turners: Neumann, *Die deutsche Turnbewegung in der Revolution 1848/49* (see fn. 1); Horst Ueberhorst, *Turner unterm Sternenbanner: Der Kampf der deutsch-amerikan. Turner f. Einheit, Freiheit u. soziale Gerechtigkeit* (Munich, 1978); Augustus J. Prahl, "The Turner," in *The Forty-eighters: Political Refugees of the German Revolution of 1848*, ed. Adolph E. Zucker (New York, 1950), 79-110; Wittke, *Refugees of Revolution*, chap. 11; Rolf Wagner, "Turner Societies and the Socialist Tradition," in *German Workers' Culture in the U.S., 1850-1920*, ed. Hartmut Keil (Washington, 1988), 221-239.

[15]For biogr. information on Beinhorn see Tyler, "William Pfaender and the Founding of New Ulm," 28f.

[16]For biogr. information on Pfaender see Tyler, *op. cit.*; Zucker, *The Forty-eighters*, 326. Pfaender was an active supporter of the Republican Party on whose ticket he was elected to the Minnesota State Legislature in 1859. In 1860 he was a Lincoln elector. On his career as a Civil War officer see Kevin J. Weddle, "Ethnic Discrimination in Minnesota Volunteer Regiments during the Civil War," *Civil War History* 35 (1989): 249, 254.

[17]Tyler, "William Pfaender and the Founding of New Ulm," 28f.; Johnson, "The Germans," 164f.

[18]Only recently did Gary Clayton Anderson explore this subject. Cf. his excellent study, *Kinsmen of Another Kind, Dakota-White Relations in the Upper Mississippi Valley, 1650-1862* (Lincoln, 1984), esp. 240ff., 259, 266f. Although written from a more intellectual perspective, several articles in the *Neu Ulm Pionier* might have reflected the assessment of the German settlers toward their Indian neighbors. The prevailing (lamented) picture is that of a vanishing race destined to withdraw due to the pressures of civilization. See, e.g., *Neu Ulm Pionier*, 1 Jan. 1858, 2.

[19]Anderson, *Kinsmen of Another Kind*, 240; Alexander Berghold, *The Indians' Revenge; or, Days of Horror, Some Appalling Events in the Hist. of the Sioux* (San Francisco, 1891), 26-36. Fr. Berghold had been sent from Austria to work among the Minnesota Germans. He settled in New Ulm. On Berghold see LaVern Rippley, "Alexander Berghold, Pioneer Priest and Prairie Poet," *The Report, A Journal of German American History* 37 (1978), 43-56.

[20]On the Sioux Uprising, during which Neu Ulm suffered great losses of men and houses, see Anderson, *Kinsmen of Another Kind*, 260-278; Kenneth Carley, *The Sioux Uprising of 1862*, rev. ed. (St. Paul, Minn., 1976), 32ff. ; Don Heinrich Tolzmann, ed., *The Sioux Uprising in Minnesota, 1862: Jacob Nix's Eyewitness History. German/English Edition* (Indianapolis, 1994). The German original was privately printed to commemorate the 25th anniversary of the battle of New Ulm with the author in command.

[21]Tyler, "William Pfaender and the Founding of New Ulm," 30.

[22]Ibid.

[23]On Cincinnati see Bruce C. Levine, "In the Spirit of 1848: German Americans and the Fight over Slavery's Expansion," diss. (Univ. of Rochester, 1980), 210-256; Ueberhorst, *Turner unterm Sternenbanner*, 51.

[24]See Leonard Koester, ed., "Early Cincinnati and the Turners: From Mrs. Karl Tafel's Autobiography," *Bulletin of the Hist. and Phil. Soc. of Ohio* 6 (1948): 18ff.; Johnson, "The Germans," 162; idem., "The Founding of New Ulm," 10; Alice Reynolds, "Friedrich Hecker," *American German Review* 12 (1946): 4; Ross, *Workers on the Edge*, 174.

[25]Indeed, Turners were so abominated that in order to evade being mistreated they had "frequently. . . to take to the side streets," cit. in Ross, *Workers on the Edge*, 173.

[26]Tyler, "William Pfaender and the Founding of New Ulm," 26f.

[27]This settlement still deserves a more thorough investigation. So far see Carl Wittke, *The Utopian Communist: A Biography of Wilhelm Weitling, 19th-Century Reformer* (Baton Rouge, 1950), chap. 13; George Schulz-Behrend, "Communia, Iowa. A 19th Century German-American Utopia," *Iowa Journal of Hist. and Politics* 48 (1950): 27-54. On Weitling's American experience see Hans Arthur Marsiske, "Wilhelm Weitling u. die amerikan. Sozialreformer, 1847-1856," *Internationale wissenschaftl. Korrespondenz zur Geschichte der dt. Arbeiterbewegung* (IWK) 25, H. 1 (March 1989): 110.

[28]Ueberhorst, *Turner unterm Sternenbanner*, 52; Johnson, "The Germans," 181, n. 37.

[29]*Neu Ulm Pionier*, 20 May 1858, 3. Emphasis in the original. My trans.

[30]Johnson, "The Germans," 165; Iverson, *Germania, U.S.A.*, 61.

[31]For the text of the contract see *Neu Ulm Pionier*, 18 Feb. 1858, 3.

[32]Iverson, *Germania, U.S.A.*, 60.

[33]*Neu Ulm Pionier*, 18 Feb. 1858, 3.

[34]Ibid., 21 Jan. 1858, 3.

[35]Iverson, *Germania, U.S.A.*, 61.

[36]See Evan Jones, *The Minnesota: Forgotten River* (New York, 1962), 153f., 159.

[37]Ubl, *Chronology of New Ulm*, 6.

[38]*Neu Ulm Pionier*, 1 Jan. 1858, 3.

[39]Iverson, *Germania, U.S.A.*, 65.

[40]*Neu Ulm Pionier*, 8 April 1858, 3.

[41]See *Verhandlungen der Convention des Ansiedlungsvereins des Socialist. Turnerbundes von Nord-Amerika* (New Ulm, 1858).

[42]See Karl J. R. Arndt and May E. Olson, *German-American Newspapers and Periodicals, 1732-1955* (Heidelberg, 1965), 225.

[43]Ubl, *Chronology of New Ulm*, 5; Johnson, "The Founding of New Ulm," 11.

[44]On the *Neu Ulm Pionier* see Henry D. Dyck, "The Neu Ulm Pionier," *American-German Review* 18 (1952): 18, 35.

[45]See Carl Wittke, *The German-Language Press in America* (Lexington, Ky., 1957), 112. Although the *Neu Ulm Pionier* was supporting the Republican Party and claimed that Neu Ulm was a Republican town, the election for the state legislature in Oct. 1859 reflected a

different picture: There were 121 votes for the Republican Party and 72 for the Democrats, *Neu Ulm Pionier,* 15 Oct. 1859, 1.

[46]*Neu Ulm Pionier,* 18 March 1858, 2.

[47]Anderson, *Kinsmen of Another Kind,* 242f.

[48]Johnson, "The Founding of New Ulm," 12.

12 | German Socialists in a Utopian Workers' Community: The Llano Cooperative Colony

Hartmut Keil, *German Historical Institute, Washington, D.C.*

Conventional wisdom has it that secular utopian communities were phenomena confined to, and typical of, the 19th century. While they were founded apart and often in isolation from, sometimes even in opposition to, American society, they were a response to ideological, social and economic problems confronting society at large. According to an overly optimistic, evolutionary view of history, such communities were thought to correspond to specific stages in the process of social organization, and therefore had to become quickly outmoded when the American social order was fundamentally affected by modernization.[1] Thus early socialist communities building on concepts developed by Robert Owen, Charles Fourier, Étienne Cabet and Wilhelm Weitling were believed to be the first efforts, certainly serious and ambitious, although largely inadequate to come to terms with industrialization.[2] Labor and reform advocates after the Civil War relinquished utopian dreams of building separate communities, preferring instead, like the Knights of Labor, to launch cooperative experiments within the emerging labor movement in the hope of eventually converting the whole industrial order.[3] The arrival of Marxian "scientific" socialism, however, seemed to signal the demise of socialist communal experiments. Thus leaders of the German Social Democracy, in conformity with the General Council of the International Workingmen's Association, in 1873 warned immigrant workers from Saxony against participating in the prospective colony "Saxonia" to be founded in upper Michigan.[4] However, even workers sympathetic to socialism were not easily convinced of the futility of such endeavors. Until the end of the 19th century, announcements in the American and ethnic labor press advertised colonies that tried to implement ideas taken from Laurence Gronlund's version of socialism, *The Cooperative Commonwealth,* or from Edward Bellamy's widely popular utopian novel, *Looking Backward.* Practically all historians of the American labor and socialist movements agree, however, that this stage of utopian socialism finally came to an end with the split in the Social Democracy of America. As Seymour Bassett put it in 1952: "When the Debs-Berger minority withdrew from its temporary union with the Brotherhood of the Cooperative Commonwealth in 1898, the Marxian labor movement turned its back forever on secular utopianism."[5]

At a time when historians are taking a fresh look at the transitions that took place within American society from the 19th to the 20th century, discovering in the process important continuities,[6] we should not accept at face value this neat categorization that claims to close the whole book on the history of radical communitarianism. It seems to me, rather, that it was but a chapter in a story that ended, if it did, only in the 1930s. This essay will consider the example of the Llano Co-operative Colony, a radical workers' community. Originally founded by former socialist vice-presidential candidate Job Harriman in Antelope Valley, Cal. on the eve of World War I in 1914, it was transferred to Louisiana in 1917 and liquidated after 1936. One scholar has referred to this colony as "the most successful American attempt at secular communitarianism."[7] I will not attempt to give an account of the colony's history,[8] but will try instead to take up significant aspects of its economic, social and ideological orientation, concentrating on the period after it had been relocated in Louisiana. This essay will be guided by the following two observations:

1. The significance of Llano Co-operative Colony can better be gauged if it is studied not as an isolated community but in the context of both the history of American radicalism and broader societal developments. That is, many of its seemingly internal problems—and there was in fact an abundance of organizational, economic and personal antagonism within the colony—can be understood as direct results of the precarious position of American radicalism as well as of political and social developments outside the colony in the 1920s.

2. NewLlano can serve as an example for the increasing irrelevance of ethnic boundaries within the radical wing of the American working class in the early 20th century. Ideologically motivated attempts by workers' organizations to overcome ethnic divisions in the late 19th century finally came to fruition after the turn of the century, ironically first of all because of significant demographic changes. Thus ethnic radical traditions became submerged in multi-ethnic institutions and group life. If we want to evaluate the impact of the German socialist

heritage on American radical and working-class traditions, it is from the study of inter-ethnic institutions like the Llano Co-operative Colony that we must uncover it.

The Place of Llano Co-operative Colony in the Radical Network

The colony's spokesmen were well aware of the rich American communitarian tradition. They justified their own effort by placing it in this radical historical context—thereby also defusing prospective charges of subversion that a hostile society had raised against radical institutions and individuals during and after World War I. It is therefore no coincidence that Ernest S. Wooster, for some years the colony's manager, wrote a book in 1924, *Communities of the Past and Present* (produced and publ. by the colony's press), in which he recounted the histories of more than 46 colonies from the 18th century on. Wooster referred to well-known religious communities—Ephrata, the Harmonists, Zoar, the Shakers, Amana—as well as to early and late 19th-century secular experiments—Owenites, Fourierists, Icarians, communities based upon Gronlund's and Bellamy's ideas, Topolobampo, Rochdale, Ruskin, Orbiston, Eureka. These predecessors were believed to have contributed important experiences upon which NewLlano could build. In addition the colony's paper published reports on contemporary communitarian movements. Thus the *American Co-operator* and its successor, the *Llano Colonist*, kept their readers informed of developments in other co-operative organizations and colonies. News on the Pacific Co-operative League and the Universal Co-operative Brotherhood were regularly included in the *American Co-operator* as long as the paper was the official organ of those organizations as well.[9] Later accounts in the *Llano Colonist* give the impression of a lively exchange of visitors between extant colonies. The paper repeatedly carried reports of visits paid by members to other communities. Manager George T. Pickett on one of his frequent public relations campaigns visited a colony of the Shakers in 1924. Members conveyed their impressions of Lakeland and of Fairhope Colony, outsiders contributed articles on Eureka and the Doukhobours in British Columbia. Communitarian movements in Europe, and especially in the Soviet Union, were closely followed as well. Members of other communities, like Adolph Schillinger of the Herrenhuter Bruder Gemeinde, in turn visited NewLlano.[10]

In even more important ways the community's self-identity emerged from the radical working-class tradition that had shown signs of healthy growth in the late 19th century and in the years before World War I, only to be curtailed by the campaign of suppression of radicals following in the war's footsteps. A significant impetus toward the founding of Llano Co-operative Colony was, therefore, radicals' disappointment with the slow progress and lack of success of established forms of economic and political organization, i.e. of the trade unions and the socialist parties.

The colony's founder, Job Harriman, may serve as the most prominent example of this reorientation that resulted in a turn to communitarian organization. Vice-presidential candidate on the socialist ticket with Eugene V. Debs in 1900, Harriman afterwards engaged in urban politics. When his campaign for mayor of Los Angeles in 1910 failed, he became increasingly disillusioned with the political process and turned to the colony experiment instead, using a quasi-Marxian argument as justification for its foundation. Since he was convinced that economic changes had to precede political organization, he proceeded to create an exemplary environment of equality. A pragmatic as well as an idealistic element is evident in this approach. In the face of the impossibility of overall societal changes, Harriman hoped to demonstrate in a practical way, if only on a miniature scale, the viability of harmonious human relationships as envisaged by socialist theory. His initial utopianism was mellowed by an increasing pragmatism, as the colony's development did not follow the high idealistic expectations. Members had shown signs of selfishness und irresponsibility in their daily relations and activities.[11] Increasingly, practical considerations were foremost in the minds of new members, too, since they often simply sought refuge from the persecution aimed at socialists, trade unionists—esp. the radical Industrial Workers of the World—and pacifists. Some sought refuge also from the economic depression after the end of the war. The Llano Co-operative Colony thus became a haven for radicals to physically and emotionally survive the era of patriotic Americanism and economic crisis.

Both the idealistic motivation stemming from radical working-class goals and the practical need of offering radicals economic and psychic protection may be summed up by two quotes taken from the *Llano Colonist* of 1928. Ole Synoground, responsible for the colony's daily operations, then described Llano Colony as "a place and opportunity where we could make a practical demonstration in working out the ideal of a co-operative Commonwealth that will benefit all mankind."[12] An equally revealing characterization was contained in the caption of an article that decried the "irresponsibility of society" toward individuals by failing to provide for work and welfare. The article contrasted this attitude with the colony's efforts. The caption read: "A Safety Valve for Society."[13]

Although geographically far removed from America's industrial and urban centers, Llano Co-operative Colony succeeded in becoming well integrated into the radical network of the 1920s. Various means were employed to contribute to this result. George T. Pickett, who eventually ousted Job Harriman from control of the colony as general manager, devised an elaborate public relations campaign through a stream of endless letters and dozens of trips soliciting membership and outside financial contributions. The colony's paper reflected this sustained effort by continuing to advertise conditions of membership as well as by printing forms used for recording the surrender of private funds and individual inheritances to the colony. The pamphlet, *The Gateway to Freedom,* first published during the colony's California years, explained the colony's goals, its location, organization and membership conditions, industrial and agricultural production, the division of work, daily requirements of the members, leisure and cultural activities. The guide was periodically revised and later published under a different name intended to reflect changed conditions and improvements.[14] Shorter leaflets were distributed as well. These were always careful to point out the necessity of individual effort and personal sacrifice, and they warned prospective members of false expectations, painting what looked like a realistic picture of the colony's appearance.[15] Editors of the *Llano Colonist* saw it as one of their major tasks to report in minute detail exceptional events happening in the colony as well as the daily tedious chores that had to be done. For years a diary was published in the paper's columns, mostly written by George T. Pickett himself under a pen name, which seemingly recorded all noteworthy activities. Outside publications and visiting journalists were also tapped to convey the message of a dedicated colony family successfully struggling against all odds. Thus Kate Richards O'Hare published a series of favorable articles on NewLlano in her and her husband's journal, *American Vanguard,* a widely circulated radical paper which was moved to the colony in 1923. (They left the following year after Harriman's ouster and went to Mena, Ark.). The *Llano Colonist* carried the series in its own pages as well.[16] Besides covering the colony's activities, this paper also maintained a high journalistic standard, keeping its readership well informed on developments in Europe and America of interest in radical circles. Intellectuals in urban centers thus remained in touch with the Louisiana backwoods colony, sometimes made so curious by what they read about it that they undertook the arduous travel south in order to see for themselves what the colony looked like.[17] Thus the colony's hotel was frequented by guests whose visit often was the first step to eventually joining the colony, or who at least carried their impressions back to their friends and readership.[18]

NewLlano was therefore well publicized by its leadership, especially in radical intellectual circles, through its own promotional literature, its book, pamphlet and newspaper press as well as by sympathetic friends and journalists. This continuing media attention provided a fertile ground for membership recruitment.

Recruitment and Membership

Despite the obvious attraction that the Llano Co-operative Colony had for radical intellectual circles, the social and political context in which it was founded and developed had significant bearings on its membership. The backgrounds of persons that were attracted to the colony kept changing during the course of the colony's existence. In the early (California) phase from 1914 to 1917, the majority were socialists.[19] The colony's transfer to Louisiana not only decimated the membership decisively, it dropped from more than 900 members to about 300 in 1918. Of the third remaining, not all had indeed participated in the migration. This also changed the ideological composition from a relatively homogeneous one to include diverse and even disparate positions. The California years had been the halcyon period, coinciding with relative prosperity. The recession of 1920-21, and even more so the depression of the 1930s, stimulated membership applications for primarily economic reasons while the survival of the colony itself was at stake during most of the Louisiana period. Thus the colony was no longer united by an inclusive ideology, but instead, under George T. Pickett's leadership, reverted to general, vague humane principles and to pacifism. In California efforts had been made to pass an elaborate constitution taking into account any eventualities arising from leadership arrogance and membership grievances. However, the constitution was discarded as impractical even before the colony's removal to Louisiana. A Declaration of Principles was adopted instead, emphasizing the rights of the community over the individual and the individual's obligations to the community as well as to fellow members. The duty of the community was phrased in one non-committal sentence: ". . .to administer justice, to eliminate greed and selfishness, to educate all, and to aid anyone in time of age or misfortune."[20] These lofty goals were to be achieved by equality of opportunity, of income, and of ownership of productive property.[21]

Thus, it is indeed difficult to draw a membership profile. Typically, members had tried various paths toward communal living before applying to NewLlano. Some members had lived in colonies in the past or just before coming to NewLlano. Individual members had participated in Topolobampo at the end of the 19th century; they had come from, or went to, Equality, the Nevada Colony, the Colorado Co-operative Community, Fairhope Colony (Ala.), Lakeland (Fla.), the Koreshan Unity, Estero (Fla.), and the Delta Co-operative Farm in Rochdale (Miss.). Some members moved on to other colonies when becoming dissatisfied with conditions at Leesville, and some even founded new colonies, like the group dissenting from Pickett who left for Mena, Ark. in 1924. Thus persons with varied experiences applied to join the colony, often with no readily apparent ideological position. Many members had been, and continued to be, members of the Socialist Party; others were vegetarians or pacifists. This list could be extended almost indefinitely; no ideological test had to be passed to be accepted into the Llano Cooperative Colony. Rather the vague umbrella of the Declaration of Principles allowed for a growing heterogeneity. By 1932, one group of members, Unit No. 4, located three miles south of NewLlano, and called itself a Co-operative Christian (!) community. And before the presidential election of 1936, a substantial minority of the colony's adult population voted for Huey Long rather than Norman Thomas as second choice behind Franklin D. Roosevelt.[22]

The most obvious demographic characteristic was the drifting and shifting composition of the membership. The transfer to Louisiana had left the colony with a third of the previous membership. Numbers kept dwindling because of the extreme hardships that had to be faced initially. By the winter of 1918 only 12 men were still capable of doing the necessary arduous physical work. In the autumn of the following year only 15 families were in residence, but by the winter of 1921 the numbers had risen to 165 persons. With growing consolidation and prosperity, many of the old colonists—who probably had had no choice but to leave in order to make a living elsewhere—returned so that by 1923 membership numbers began to stabilize. The Great Depression precipitated a large influx of newcomers who now sought security against unemployment, hunger, and homelessness. Estimates of the total number of persons associated with the Llano Cooperative Colony in the course of its existence run as high as 10,000. Given this enormous membership turnover, the hard core of members who stayed over longer time periods was especially important for the colony's stability, leadership and direction.

Gender and age compositions yield some insight into the motivation of people to join the colony. Of the colony's population of 188 in 1927, there were 37 women and 86 men, the latter constituting 70% of its adult members, while 65 children made up 35% of the total population.[24] For the age composition we have to draw from statistics referring to the year 1935. They also reveal a higher percentage of men than women. Significantly, whereas the young generation of up to 19-year olds, and even the 20 to 44 age cohort, were underrepresented in NewLlano when comparing it to both the rural and the national population averages, the age group above 44 was heavily overrepresented, the percentage being twice as high (44.3) as the rural and national percentages (21.6 resp. 21.9).[25] Thus more single men than women joined the colony, and this happened relatively late in their life cycles, indicating a desire for economic and social security. Not unusual among the colony's members was the widower left with small children. Although the desire of older persons, especially males, to find security was an important motivation to join the colony, the sizable representation of kids and youngsters contradicts the interpretation that NewLlano was just another old people's home.

Ethnicity

The colony's ideological underpinnings of a general humanitarianism and undiscriminating communitarianism precluded emphasizing ethnic differences and traditions among the members.[26] It is therefore difficult to unravel the NewLlano members' ethnic and class compositions, especially since membership numbers fluctuated widely, depending on the colony's fortunes as well as on economic developments in the outside world. Statistics for 1926 indicate that there was a substantial proportion of first and second generation ethnics among the colony's membership. Of the adult population at that time, 22 members were of German, 11 of Scandinavian descent. There were also three Dutch, four English, one Russian, five French, "four Jews", and 73 Americans. Thus of 123 adult members 40.6% were of foreign birth or background, and Germans contributed the largest share with 44% (or 17.9% of all members). Professor Lasserre, the French visitor who had compiled the statistics, observed that "Europeans, particularly those from the north, are the better element of the Colony, because they adapt themselves more easily to the conditions of community life than the others and show their tenacity and attachment to the group," and he singled out the Germans and Scandinavians as holding "positions of confidence and responsibility."[27]

A look at some of the persons charged with important duties in the colony corroborates this observation. Thus Ole Synoground, a Scandinavian, was in charge of agricultural and industrial operations, and Carl Henry Gleeser, former editor of a socialist paper who joined the colony in 1921, made the *Llano Colonist* one of the outstanding English-language radical publications in the U.S. in the 1920s. The biographies of three other German-Americans illustrate the varied radical and intellectual backgrounds from which members came as well as the specific contributions they made to the colony.

Karl Besse joined the colony with his family in 1923 at the age of 45 only after having explored various alternatives to a fulfilling life. Born in Lower

Bavaria in 1878, a son to an official in the Bavarian Government, Besse received a proper high school education before he was apprenticed to become a brewer. As a journeyman he traveled through several European countries, learning foreign languages on the way, until he decided to migrate to the U.S. in 1904. He returned to Bavaria once more in order to enroll in the Weihenstephan Brewers Academy, where he received his diploma as brewmaster. Back in America he worked in several breweries in the East and Midwest until he became acquainted with socialist Charles Steinmetz, the renowned scientist at the General Electric Company. Besse, who had been active in the labor movement while still in Germany, now assisted in establishing a co-operative store at Schenectady. Becoming also interested in co-operative production, he decided to move to the Ruskin experiment in integral co-operation in Florida and, somewhat later, to Lakeland, Fla., where he bought a farm near that colony. Besse first visited NewLlano in 1920 and kept up correspondence with its leaders before finally selling his farm in 1923 and moving to Leesville where he soon was made a member of the Board of Directors. A carpenter by trade, he also contributed skills to the colony's logging operations, the ice and electric plants, and the colony garden.[28]

Louis Roedemeister's political consciousness was closely linked to his parents' experience who had emigrated from Germany after the failed revolution of 1848/49. When his father was thrown out of his job, which he had held for a long time ("his services were no longer required because he was too old"), young Roedemeister, "indignant" and "furious", joined the Knights of Labor in the late 1870s, later the union of his trade, i.e. the Harness Makers Union, and in 1902 the Socialist party. Roedemeister worked in many cities and participated in strikes and "other labor troubles." In addition, he did organizational work for the Socialist party in Ohio from 1905 until the outbreak of World War I. Having read about Job Harriman's newly founded Llano Co-operative Colony in California in the *Appeal to Reason*, he applied for membership and joined the colony in November 1915 at age 57—perhaps because his wife had died two years before and his children were already married. He was absent during the time of the colony's removal to Louisiana but rejoined it, bringing with him "cash and negotiable paper" worth $1,200 which he donated to the colony's treasury. In NewLlano he was a jack-of-all-trades besides contributing his specific skills: "Whenever he has no shoes to mend, nor to rejuvenate worn-out harness, or make new harness, he goes to any department that is short-handed, and helps there. I have seen him in the saw-mill, in the brick yard, in the garden, digging, dragging, lifting, hammering, carrying water, or wood, in short doing anything and everything imaginable."[29]

The author of these sympathetic observations, Theodor F. Cuno, could look back upon a long life of active participation in the European and American labor movements. Born in the Prussian province of Westphalia in 1846, he was apprenticed at Berlin and continued his education to become a mechanical engineer, first at the Borsig Co. in Berlin, then in various other European cities including Vienna. Early contact with the emerging German labor movement led to his joining the International Workingmen's Association for which he organized sections in Milan and in other northern Italian cities. Cuno came to the U.S. in the 1870s, and he settled in New York City where he became involved immediately in the city's heterogeneous labor movement. A Marxian socialist, Cuno also joined the Knights of Labor and served as this organization's Grand Statistician in the early 1880s, before conflict between the Order's leadership and New York City's District Assembly No. 49 led to his removal from that office. In the mid-1880s Cuno turned to the American Federation of Labor and to the German-American labor movement. For 30 years he was a reporter for the *New Yorker Volks-Zeitung,* the leading German-language socialist daily, for which he reported on the Haymarket Trial from Chicago in 1886. He wrote for other labor publications as well. According to Cuno's own statement, he himself "opened correspondence" with the Llano Co-operative Colony's management.[30] This happened in 1919, when the colony was desperately short of money. Cuno bought shares for himself and his wife and granted the colony a loan amounting to the substantial total of $6,000 that saved the colony.[31] He later lent the colony another $9,000 that was never repaid.[32] Cuno and his wife joined the colony the same year, he being 73 years old; they both died in NewLlano, his wife in 1925, and Cuno in 1934.[33] Cuno contributed his enormous knowledge and experience as a journalist to the colony's paper, writing (and lecturing) on a broad range of topics including "Darwin's theory of evolution, biochemistry, Greek mythology, morals and religion, European art, the crudity of American life, great literary masterpieces, psychoanalysis and Freud, Neanderthal man, the role of chromosomes and genes in heredity, sex education, the loyalty of dogs, Brook Farm. . . and other communal experiments, and women."[34] Despite the colony's geographical remoteness, he thus helped keep NewLlano's members informed of, and the colony tied into, the intellectual currents of the time.[35]

Goals and Achievements

What was the meaning of the decision of these men and other people to make a radical break in their lives and join Llano Co-operative Colony? Was it a sign of resignation, withdrawal, and despair? These questions raise the basic issue as to which perspective should be applied when we look at the members' activities and the colony's accomplishments and failures. The common standard has been to adopt an outsider's approach, viewing a colony's lifetime as the measure of success or failure. A useful alternative, however, would be to ask how and by which criteria members themselves evaluated its performance. Certainly the colony's leadership advertised it as offering a "New Deal" to people dissatisfied with the existing social order—several years before the term was also appropriated for the incoming Roosevelt administration in Washington.[36]

One criterion, both for insiders and outsiders, was economic success. Evidence is overwhelming that on this count the colony did not meet some of its most basic obligations. Apparently it never turned its agricultural and industrial productions into profitable operations, although it sometimes seemed on the verge of doing so. The colony's general manager, George T. Pickett, on all such occasions ambitiously sought additions to the colony, e.g., by buying land in Texas and by opening a branch in New Mexico. But poorly planned and administered, this overextended the colony's means and left it with new debts. Throughout its lifetime, NewLlano remained subsidized by outside contributions, by applicants making their down payments, and by members who relinquished their personal savings and who were unable to secure the funds they had given as loans to the colony, if they chose to leave again. As a result, members suffered economic hardship and a standard of living well below normal middle-class expectations in America's urban centers.

But members themselves often did not apply such a view. They were no worse off than their neighbors on the surrounding farms and in the area's villages and towns. More important, they had been prepared, and they had made a conscious choice in favor of the pioneering conditions they encountered in NewLlano. The colony's publications kept pointing out the need for people willing to do hard work, warning that "it is not an easy life that we are leading. It requires strength of character and a firm determination to conquer adversity. . . those unwilling [to work] will not be happy in the colony."[37]

Work and gender roles were arranged in a way that both specialization and discrimination were reduced to a functional minimum. Men and women could express preferences as to which kind of work they wanted to be engaged in but had to be flexible enough to also put up with other chores that needed to be done. Hence the variety of tasks for Besse and Roedemeister mentioned above. Reality did not always stand the test enunciated in writing that members "enjoy equal rights and participate equally in all products or profits."[38] However, women held authoritative roles in the hotel, the dining room, kitchen, laundry, bakery, and the cannery management. Perhaps more important, they were considered as social and economic equals by the men and were treated in this manner, including the housewives.

The colony's proudest accomplishment was the so-called "Kid Colony," which included a kindergarten, a grammar school, and an academy. Following Montessori's and Dewey's methods of "learning by doing," children were taught in class half a day, were engaged in constructive play as divised by Pickett, but also had to work in the kid garden in work gangs for several hours—a requirement that gave rise to charges of exploitation. Ironically, the education the young people received in the colony proved to be the single most valid asset they took with them when they became attracted to the outside world for its greater diversity and the higher wages it offered. Thus the colony suffered the loss of the very people that it had equipped with valued skills.

Probably the most important source of satisfaction was the richness of social relationships and cultural activities the colony offered. The library, with some 4,000 volumes by the early 1930s, was one of the more substantial ones in the northwest and west of Louisiana. Study classes for adults and lectures by both colony members and visitors offered continuing education on a variety of subjects. The colony's lay theater troupe staged productions and the orchestra gave concerts on an irregular basis. Picnics and special commemorative events like May Day were occasions for elaborate and extended celebrations following the tradition of labor festivities that had emerged from ethnic and indigenous sources since the 1870s. Colony neighbors, and especially young people from the surrounding countryside, were also attracted by these events that helped enrich their socially and culturally often barren lives in the absence of supportive institutions. Thus the colony's weekly dance parties on Saturday nights always drew a large crowd of members and outsiders, and it became famous in the Leesville area. These social and cultural communal activities were the most highly valued experiences that were badly missed when members left the colony. They were also fondly remembered later.[39] Members thus evaluated the colony's success less by material criteria than by the social and cultural rewards it offered them.

Conclusion

The secular communitarian tradition has received only a limited amount of attention by historians of the modern American labor movement. This is especially true with respect to workers' colonies, which have largely been neglected. Since members of such colonies were often radicals as well as immigrants, they were seen as even farther removed from the American mainstream than communitarian religious groups. A critical secular alternative had few adherents indeed and attracted little interest so long as the prospects of American economic growth seemed unlimited. However, historians studying the post-World War I period can look at the NewLlano communitarian experiment as a sensitive seismograph that recorded the grumblings and discontent from below—even before the seemingly prosperous 1920s came to an abrupt end—and at a time when voices of labor protest were subdued by aggressive demands for political conformity and by adaptation to mass consumerism as the ultimate indicators of true Americanism.

NOTES

[1]For general discussions of utopian thought, cf. Martin Buber, *Paths in Utopia* (New York, 1986); J.O. Hertzler, *The History of Utopian Thought* (New York, 1923); Karl Mannheim, *Ideology and Utopia* (San Diego, 1985); Arnhelm Neusüss, ed. , *Utopie: Begriff u. Phänomen des Utopischen* (Neuwied, 1968); Ruth Levitas, *The Concept of Utopia* (Syracuse, 1990); Krishan Kumar, *Utopianism* (Minneapolis, 1991); Richard Sage, *Polit. Utopien der Neuzeit* (Darmstadt, 1991); Barbara Goodman, *Social Science and Utopia: 19th-Century Models of Social Harmony* (Hassocks, 1978); for lit. dealing with the U.S. cf. Robert S. Fogarty, *Dictionary of American Communal and Utopian History* (Westport, Conn., 1980); Ivan Doig, ed., *Utopian America: Dreams and Realities* (Rochelle Park, N.J., 1976); Michael Fellman, *The Unbounded Frame: Freedom and Community in 19th-Century American Utopianism* (Westport, Conn., 1973); William Alfred Hinds, *American Communities and Co-operative Colonies* (Philadelphia, 1975); Robert V. Hine, *California's Utopian Colonies* (Berkeley, 1983); Charles Pierce LeWarne, *Utopias on Puget Sound, 1885-1915* (Seattle, 1975); Ernest G. Fischer, *Marxists and Utopias in Texas* (Burnet, Tex., 1980); John Egerton, *Visions of Utopia: Nashoba, Rigby, Ruskin, and the "New Communities" in Tennessee's Past* (Knoxville, 1977).

[2]Cf. T.D. Seymour Bassett, "The Secular Utopian Socialists," ch. 5, in Donald Drew Egbert and Stow Persons, eds., *Socialism and American Life*, vol. 1 (Princeton, 1952), 153-211, and the accompanying bibl. in vol. 2. More recent works on these four socialists and the communities modeled after their thought include Sidney Pollard and John Salt, eds., *Robert Owen, Prophet of the Poor* (London, 1971); J.F.C. Harrison, *Robert Owen and the Owenites in Britain and America* (London, 1969); Oakley C. Johnson, ed., *Robert Owen in the U.S.* (New York, 1970); Carol A. Colmerton, *Women in Utopia: The Ideology of Gender in the American Owenite Communities* (Bloomington, Ind., 1990); Gregory Claeys, *Machinery, Money, and the Millennium: From Moral Economy to Socialism, 1815-1860* (Princeton, 1987); Jonathan Beecher and Richard Bienvenu, eds., *The Utopian Vision of Charles Fourier* (Columbia, Mo., 1983); Charles Beecher, *Charles Fourier: The Visionary and His World* (Berkeley, 1986); Carl Guarneri, *The Utopian Alternative: Fourierism in 19th-Century America* (Ithaca, 1991); Albert Shaw, *Icaria, a Chapter in the History of Communism* (Philadelphia, 1972); Sylvester A. Piotrowski, *Étienne Cabet and the Voyage en Icarie: A Study in the Hist. of Social Thought*

(Westport, Conn., 1975); William M. Snyder and Robert P. Sutton, eds., *Immigration of the Icarians to Illinois: Proceedings of the Icarian Weekend in Nauvoo* (Illinois, 1987); Carl F. Wittke, *The Utopian Communist: A Biogr. of Wilhelm Weitling, 19th-Century Reformer* (Baton Rouge, 1950); Jörg Haefelin, *Wilhelm Weitling: Biogr. u. Theorie* (Bern, N. Y., 1986); Martin Huttner, *Wilhelm Weitling als Frühsozialist* (Frankfurt/M., 1985); Hans-Arthur Marsiske, *Eine Republik der Arbeiter ist möglich: der Beitrag Wilhelm Weitlings zur Arbeiterbewegung in den Ver. Staaten von Amerika, 1846-1856* (Hamburg, 1990).

[3]For the relationship between the American labor movement and utopian thought cf. Gerald N. Grob, *Workers and Utopia: A Study of Ideological Conflict in the American Labor Movement, 1865-1900* (Evanston, 1961); Norman J. Ware, *The Labor Movement in the U.S., 1860-1895* (New York, 1929); Leon Fink, *Workingmen's Democracy: The Knights of Labor and American Politics* (Urbana, 1983).

[4]Address of the General Council, Internat. Workingmen's Ass., 24 April 1873, IWA Papers, State Hist. Soc. of Wisconsin, Madison.

[5]D. Seymour Bassett, "Secular Utopian Socialists," 208; cf. Friedrich A. Sorge, *Friedrich A. Sorge's Labor Movement in the U.S.* (New York, 1987); Morris Hillquit, *Hist. of Socialism in the U.S.* (New York, 1971); Albert Fried, comp., *Socialism in America: From the Shakers to the Third International* (Garden City, N.Y., 1970).

[6]E.g. Warren Susman, *Culture as History: The Transformation of American Society in the 20th Century* (New York, 1984); Margaret Weir, Ann Shola Orloff, and Theda Skocpol, eds., *The Politics of Social Policy in the U.S.* (Princeton, 1988); Morton Keller, *Affairs of State: Public Life in Late 19th-Century America* (Cambridge, Mass., 1977); Robert H. Wiebe, *The Search for Order, 1877-1920* (Westport, Conn., 1980).

[7]Paul K. Conkin, *Two Paths to Utopia: The Hutterites and the Llano Colony* (Lincoln, 1964), viii;

[8]Works dealing with the Llano Co-operative Colony: Ernest S. Wooster, *Communities of the Past and Present* (NewLlano, La., 1924); Paul K. Conkin, *Two Paths to Utopia;* Alexander James McDonald, *The Llano Co-operative Colony and What It Taught* (San Antonio, 1950); Sid Young, *The Crisis in Llano Colony* (Los Angeles, 1936); Bob (Robert Carlton) Brown, *Can We Co-operate?* (Pleasant Plains, Staten Island, N.Y., 1940); Dolores Hayden, *Seven American Utopias: The Architecture of Communitarian Socialism, 1790-1975* (Cambridge, Mass., 1976); Paul Kagan, *New World Utopias: A Photogr. Hist. of the Search for Community* (New York, 1975); Fred Hanover, "Llano Cooperative Colony: An American Rural Community Experiment," MA thesis (Tulane Univ., 1936); Archie Roy Clifton, "A Study of Llano del Rio Community in the Light of Earlier Experiments in Practical Socialism," MA thesis (Univ. of Southern California, 1918); James N. Davison, "The Llano Movement: Experiment in the Extension of Self," MA thesis (McNeese State College, 1970); cf. also Kate Richards O'Hare, *Selected Writings and Speeches,* ed. Philip S. Foner and Sally M. Miller (Baton Rouge, 1982).

[9]This relationship began with vol. XIX, no. 22, Feb. 1922. Since only this one issue of the paper before June 1925 has been preserved, I was unable to establish how long this relationship lasted.

[10]"A Visitor's Story," *Llano Colonist,* 7 Aug. 1926; Theodor F. Cuno, "On a Visit to the Single-Taxers, At Fairhope Colony in Alabama", *Llano Colonist,* 19 June 1926. R.M. Springer, *Llano Colonist,* 1 and 8 May 1926.

[11]Job Harriman, "Introduction," in Wooster, *Communities of the Past,* iii-v.

[12]*Llano Colonist,* 12 May 1928.

[13]Ibid., 28 Jan. 1928.

[14]*Detailed Information about the Llano Co-operative Colony* (NewLlano, La., July 1932).

[15]"Look! Before You Leap!"—from an undated flyer: "Don't join this movement unless you are ready to serve the cause unselfishly and to your limit in every way. . . Too many people come here to grind an ax of their own. . . Look into yourself and see if you are really ready to cooperate with others on this world scheme and if you are ready to lay aside petty inconsequential notions in order to support the big idea. . . Don't assume we have entered in at the pearly gates or are even on concrete sidewalks, and paved roads. We still walk on boards, thru mud, and have very few modern conveniences, but we can with our own hands and our own labor overcome all these lacking conveniences, provided we are willing to do the work, and growling about it won't do the job."

[16]E.g. "Llano Co-operative Colony's Unique Success," *Llano Colonist*, 15 Aug. 1925; "A friendly Outside View of Llano Colony," *Llano Colonist*, 2 Jan. 1926; "Kuzbasing in Dixie," *American Vanguard*, 1923, repr. in *Llano Colonist*, 1 May -12 June 1926.

[17]Thus the journalist Robert Carlton Brown traveled to Leesville from New York in 1934 and stayed in the colony for several months to learn first-hand what life in NewLlano was like. He publ. a book about his experiences; cf. Bob Brown, *Can We Co-operate?* (Pleasant Plains, Staten Island, N.Y., 1940).

[18]An extant page from the Llano Hotel Register of 1931 gives an indication where these visitors came from. For the period 10 June to 20 July, it recorded visitors from Cal., Fla., Ind., Ky., Md., N.Y., N.C., Ok., Pa., Tex., Wash. For this copy and copies of a host of other documents, I am deeply indebted to Martha Palmer, Vernon Parish Historian, who has generously shared her research and sources on the colony's history with me.

[19]However, a more than summary statement cannot be made for lack of more specific sources; cf., however, Davison, "Llano Movement,"30.

[20]*Detailed Information*, 2.

[21]Ibid., 5-6, 9; cf. also *Gateway to Freedom* (Leesville, La., n. d.), 8-9.

[22]Hanover, "Llano Cooperative Colony," 185; Conkin, *Two Paths to Utopia*, 121.

[23]Estimate by Oliver Milton Thomason, assoc. ed. of *Llano Colonist*, reported by Hanover, "Llano Cooperative Colony," 85.

[24]*Llano Colonist*, 22 Jan. 1927.

[25]Persons through the age of 19 constituted 35.3% of the members against 49.4% of the farm population and 40.6% of the nation's population. Percentages for the 20-to-44 year olds were: NewLlano 20.3%, farm population 30%, national average 38%; Hanover, "Llano Cooperative Colony," 174.

[26]However, the colony shared the South's racism. It followed the larger society's policy of strict segregation even with respect to Asians, explicitly stating that "[N]o Negroes or Asiatics are admitted to the Colony" (*Gateway to Freedom*, 34).

[27]*Llano Colonist*, 22 Jan. 1927.

[28]Theo. F. Cuno, "We of NewLlano: Sketches from Co-operative Life," *Llano Colonist*, 17 April 1926.

[29]Theo. F. Cuno, "We of NewLlano: Sketches Drawn from Co-operative Life," *Llano Colonist*, 9 Jan. 1926.

[30]"Colony Diary," *Llano Colonist*, 28 May 1927.

[31]Conkin, *Two Paths to Utopia*, 116, writes that the membership fees plus loan amounted to $6,000. According to McDonald, *Llano Co-operative Colony*, 25, however, the loan of $6,000 was made in addition to $1,700 Cuno paid as membership fees for himself and his wife.

[32]McDonald, *Llano Co-operative Colony*, 25.

[33]For a short biogr. of Cuno see Conkin, *Two Paths to Utopia*, 165-66; also Cuno's autobiogr. information in "Colony Diary," *Llano Colonist*, 11 June and 2 July 1927; 18 Feb., 9

June, 15 and 22 Dec. 1928; his autobiogr. in Cuno papers, Institute of Marxism and Leninism, Moscow.

[34]Conkin, *Two Paths to Utopia*, 166.

[35]Conkin, 164, characterizes him as "the sage of Llano. . . the philosopher of cooperation, the wisest of colonists, a man of broad experience and of an unbelievably diverse number of interests."

[36]"A New Deal All Around," *Llano Colonist*, 15 May 1926.

[37]Cuno in *Llano Colonist*, 8 Aug. 1925; cf. also the statement in the *Llano Colonist* that "all must work or render some service unless incapacitated," 6 June 1925.

[38]Ernest S. Wooster, "They Shared Equally: The Story of a Significant Experiment in Cooperative Living and Collective Production," *Sunset Magazine*, July 1924, 22.

[39]As Hanover puts it: "Colonists. . . speak fondly and even touchingly of the rich social life they are privileged to share and regard it as one of the colony's major attractions. It was their fond recollections of the community's social life which brought back many who had left the colony because of dissatisfaction" (*"Llano Cooperative Colony,"* 156); cf. Davison, 86f., 100.

V.
CONTINUITIES AND DISCONTINUITIES OF REGIONAL AFFINITIES

13 | Mid-19th Century Emigration from Hesse-Darmstadt to Trenton, New Jersey

Peter Winkel, *Trenton State College*

In the summer of 1848 Georg Johannes Kleinkauf was summoned by the Hesse-Darmstadt grand ducal draft board to register for the draft, to undergo a physical examination and, if *tauglich*, participate in the annual lottery. He, however, did not appear. Instead, the clerk wrote in the draft register that Kleinkauf had left for "Amerika." The twenty-year old had in fact departed several months earlier. The register also reveals his occupation and his parents' names. Kleinkauf continued to work as *Schmied* in Mercer County, where he was employed as an engineer by the state asylum until his death in 1894. Kleinkauf was one of 18 men and six single women born in Bechtheim (a small village west of Worms) who left Rheinhessen between 1848 and 1856 to settle in Trenton, Mercer County, New Jersey. At least 38 persons from this village of about 900 took up residence in Trenton during this period. This high number suggests an active communications network through letters from immigrants to villagers praising opportunities in Trenton. It also reflects a sense of security and confidence among immigrants who attempted to begin a new life in America among friends and relatives.[1]

During this eight-year span, some 20 to 25 men were annually called up by the draft board. Each year about six men failed to appear. They had emigrated! They represented about 25% of the male population born 20 years earlier. Close to a third of these young men came to Trenton. The existing records do not indicate if the men had received permission to emigrate—the word *heimlich* appears neither in the annual draft registers nor in any official document. It may therefore be assumed that these Bechtheimers followed the standard emigration procedures established by the grand ducal government, a long and cumbersome process. It was applicable to individuals as well as groups. The government normally insisted on an orderly process to prevent young men from avoiding the draft and to assure that all debts had been paid. Occasionally, exceptions were made.

This paper examines the reasons for emigration and settling in Trenton. It focuses on 85 men whose arrival, occupation, residence and/or mobility within the community is documented by civil, church, census, and property records. Most of these men and their families lived in Hessian clusters or neighborhoods within four wards, and they enjoyed material success reflected by their purchases of property and their assets as stated in the 1870 Census.

Between 1848 and 1860 more than 140,000 inhabitants of the Grand Duchy of Hesse-Darmstadt emigrated to the U.S.[2] These years represent a pivotal period of change both for America and the German states. This includes both New Jersey and Hesse-Darmstadt, where the advent of industrialization left a distinct but contrasting economic impact on the citizens. In Hesse it eliminated cottage industries and forced thousands of women and men to seek employment in other states or to emigrate to North America or other foreign countries. Industrialization did not develop in Hesse during the middle of the 19th century.[3] New Jersey, by contrast, witnessed the emergence of new industries in the northeastern counties and Mercer County, accompanied by the construction of railroads. This attracted thousands of immigrants despite two American recessions during this time.

Most German emigrants were responding to economic uncertainties, social injustice and a feeling of impending catastrophe. This was not just felt by those wishing to leave but also by those who stayed at home. By the 1840s, emigration fever had spread to every area of Hesse-Darmstadt. The increasing number of emigrants demonstrated a breakdown of established social and economic patterns, which spilled over into every phase of life. The economic threat was all-pervasive, and emigration was the only real alternative for the hopelessly poor and hungry. The movement drew from all counties and the approximately 1,200 villages and towns of Hesse-Darmstadt, but most heavily from the eastern regions. The transport of hundreds of emigrants from different parts of Hesse to the Rhine River ports could not go unnoticed by those through whose villages the emigrants traveled. This spread the suspicion that something had to be rotten in the state, forcing them to leave their *Heimat*.

This emigration, which increased dramatically in 1852 and climaxed in 1854, was the continuation of a movement of discontent well under way by 1848. The social injustice and material hardships generating dissatisfaction and unrest had steadily grown to major proportions. Poverty, unemployment, hunger, and taxation were the main motivators.

A correlation between economic crisis and emigration existed between 1848 and 1860. The early 1850s witnessed rainy summers and severe winters that caused short harvests and inflation, propelling emigration to its highest peak. The heaviest rainfall between 1848 and 1860 occurred during the summer of 1854, the second heaviest in 1852. December 1853 and February 1854 were the coldest and third coldest months in that decade.[4] These two years produced the highest number of departures not only from Hesse but other areas of Germany as well. This points to the direct relationship between weather and emigration in the 1850s.

Close to 10,000 Hessians emigrated to New Jersey between 1848 and 1870. But why did almost 900 Hesse-Darmstadters settle in Trenton? And more specifically, why did 38 Bechtheimers choose Trenton as their new *Heimat*?

In this study I have identified 85 male Hessian immigrants, singles and heads of families; they appear at least four times in official records during this 22-year period. I will focus on these 85 men and their families. In addition, I have recognized more than 180 men whose names appear only once on official records in Mercer County; they will be included in some of the discussions of this paper. There were also approximately 50 women married to non-Hessians, single women and widows born in Hesse-Darmstadt. Since they were listed usually as "housewife" or "servant," except for the widows, their assets and mobility are difficult to ascertain. Furthermore, the census did not attribute any property to them, except for widows. By 1870 about 900 Hessian-born lived in Trenton and suburbs, or approximately 15% of the German-born population.[5]

The number of arrivals in Trenton between 1848 and 1856 was extraordinary. Among them were four extended families from Bechtheim, six single men and at least four single women, totaling 38 persons. Grouped with these four families were another eight single men. Unfortunately, the Bechtheimer Archives and queries in Trenton do not reveal the motives for the city's attraction. The first to arrive, in 1848, were George Kleinkauf and George Hoffmann with his family. The former found employment with the state asylum as an engineer or machinist, the latter worked as a mason. Both must have realized the potential of Trenton's economy and communicated their enthusiasm to friends and relatives in Bechtheim. Most of the men who arrived later were skilled craftsmen, exactly what Trenton needed. Hoffmann's three sons were also masons. The Bechtheimers, however, realized their success at different times. All but three of the men purchased land; the first was George Hoffmann, in 1854; the other Bechtheimers waited until the 1860s. Eighteen men listed assets on the 1870 Census; only the young men were without property that year. John P. Freudenmacher married Rosana Fischer in 1853, and Georg Kleinkauf married Helena Kuchler in 1854. Both women were from Bechtheim. The others remained single or married non-Hessian or non-German women. The surprising conclusion from some of these numbers is that the Bechtheimers reflect in many ways the overall experience of other Hessians in Trenton between 1848 and 1870. The percentage differences in some of the above-mentioned statistics between Bechtheimers and other Hessians in Trenton are small and suggest similar experiences.[6]

By 1840 Trenton's location between Philadelphia and New York and its role as state capital and county seat stimulated growth. The building of the Raritan and Delaware Canal, its feeder and a water power supplier for factories, and three railroads—the Camden and Amboy, the New Jersey, and the Belvedere Delaware Railroad—boosted the commercial and retail establishments and, ten years later, initiated the industrialization of the city. Rail and canal affected the town's growth and its population patterns.[7]

Men and women seeking employment generally faced several occupational prospects in Trenton. They could work for the canal or railroads, in the pottery, iron or rubber industries, or in the many retail and service businesses. Both skilled and unskilled labor were in great demand by 1860. The establishment of machine shops and foundries before the outbreak of the Civil War made the city a hub for the production of iron, including locomotives, anvils, wire ropes and agricultural equipment; and the war contributed to an unprecedented expansion of these and related industries. Industries attracted immigrants, increasing population and stimulating further industrialization. The city grew by industrial sectors, delimited variously by a river, a creek, canals or rails as boundaries.[8]

Trenton's geographical position afforded advantages which few other cities in New Jersey could wrest from it. The trains brought immigrants and raw material and left town with finished products to be sold in eastern states and, by 1890, in other parts of the world.

Trenton's population in 1850 was 6,461 persons, with less than 20% foreign-born. By 1860 the city had grown to 17,774, and its foreign-born population had also increased to more than 25%, mostly Germans and Irish. The 1870 count was 22,872, and the percentage of the Irish- and German-born population remained about the same during the ten-year period.[9] Improvements to the city began in the 1850s, and by 1875 the capital enjoyed a public transportation system, piped water, sewers, pavements and street lights. Trenton had become a success story.

The industries grew along these communication and transportation lines as well as the water power supplier, and these attracted residential areas. The workers stayed close to their factories. The city was dissected by five water channels and three rail lines, over which many bridges allowed the movement of people and goods. The overall residential and industrial composition, however, did not change much during this 22-year period. Not one of the seven wards was considered an exclusively residential area in 1870, although the western part of the Second Ward was mostly residential. Mixed into these residential/industrial nodes were many retail and service stores. Therefore there was little need for most residents of these enclaves to leave their neighborhoods. The city had become a place of many, almost self-sufficient, areas confined by rail and water.[10]

It is thus not surprising that the geographical mobility of Germans, and especially of Hessians, was limited. Their movement, or the lack thereof, is documented by censuses and city directories. Their socio-economic mobility, however, is more difficult to ascertain since immigrants tended not to state the exact value of their personal and real estates on censuses. The only true indicator of wealth is evident in the records of sales of land and houses. Even wills do not always reveal true financial worth. Too many Hessians avoided these formalities and when they wrote their wills they spoke in general terms rather than listing specific assets. However, Lutheran and Catholic church records do at times shed light on the mobility of male Hessians.

Trenton's Hessian population consisted of fewer than 100 persons in 1850; ten years later it had grown to almost 800; and in 1870 there were approximately 900 Hessian-born in the state capital.[11] Hessian emigration to Trenton slowed down considerably during the 1860s: first, it was difficult to travel to America during the war period; second, the American draft did not sound attractive; third, the Hessian government had realized its responsibilities toward the populace so that economic conditions had improved over those of the 1850s. The uneven quality of available sources made a systematic analysis of the Hessian population difficult. Still, based on the existing records, certain trends and patterns may be detected among the 85 Hessian-born living in Trenton between 1848 and 1870.

All seven wards are considered in this study. Trenton's street system followed a colonial street pattern lacking symmetry. Since Trenton's expansion was geographically limited, additional streets were added within the city by subdividing, thus allowing the construction of new houses and creating a denser population. In the 1850s two "land sales" occurred in the Second and Fifth Wards, and many Germans, including Hessians, purchased these small lots on which to build their future homes. Three lots in 1854, for example, cost $80.

The Third and Fourth Wards, and parts of the Fifth and Seventh, could be classified as "immigrant" in 1870. Some of the areas within these four wards contained nearly 500 foreign-born and included mostly German and Irish. They were unskilled and skilled laborers, and their families lived in row houses, or as boarders with other families. The hub of the city included the eastern part of the Second District and the western sections of the Fifth and the First Wards. The center contained most of the hotels, boarding houses, retail and service businesses, as well as family houses. Germans in this area lived either in boarding houses or in apartments above commercial establishments. Small industrial nodes existed in the northern section of the Second and Fifth Wards; in 1867 these two sectors were included in the newly created Seventh Ward. These areas attracted primarily unskilled laborers and skilled craftsmen and their families. No Hessians lived in the western residential sections of the Second and Seventh Wards in 1870. Only one male Hessian and one married Hessian woman lived in the Sixth Ward in 1870, which was the smallest among the seven districts.[12]

Continuing the social and religious patterns of the old country, Germans built their churches and social clubs in the center of town. In the 1850s German-speaking groups founded Lutheran and Catholic churches, and in 1867 a Lutheran church for an English-speaking congregation was founded; it, too, attracted German immigrants. In the two oldest churches services were exclusively held in German; the Catholic church even included "German" in its official name. The first *Sängerbund* was founded in 1847, and in the following decade, Germans founded the Turnverein, limiting membership to Germans. However, within a few years the discriminatory clause was removed and the club opened its doors to all citizens of Trenton. By 1870 more than five social and fraternal societies existed.[13]

The choice of Trenton by the immigrants does not seem to have been planned, but made at random. More than 35 villages and towns of Hesse-Darmstadt are represented in the state capital according to church records. The Lutheran marriage records are the only documents revealing the birth places of Germans. Thus, this number is based on younger Hessians married in Trenton between 1853 and 1870. Only one Hessian community is heavily represented, namely Bechtheim. Two Hessian regions are dominant: the wine producing area of Rheinhessen and the eastern regions of Starkenburg. Craftsmen came from various rural counties, but none predominating.

By 1870 Trenton's proportionate number of foreign-born was equal to that of New Brunswick, Middlesex County and remained stable for several decades. Germans and Irish continued to arrive in the state capital in large numbers until the 1880s, but fewer Hessians as explained earlier. Hessian newcomers were attracted to those neighborhoods where Germans, and specifically Hessians, were already living, and after the creation of the new ward, to the Seventh. Yet these areas were neither exclusively Hessian nor German. Irish and American-born shared the neighborhoods. The most dominant Hessian/German area was located around Five Points along Greene, Willow, and Pennington Streets, and Princeton and Brunswick

Turnpikes with their many side streets and alleys. A second Hessian neighborhood was in the coal port area, or the northern section of the Fifth Ward, east of the Raritan and Delaware Canal. Here small industries and many craft shops were located, generating jobs and residential housing. The third concentration of Hessians occurred along Centre Street in the Third Ward, with its iron manufacturing industries. The continuous flow of immigrants to these areas is not surprising, since newcomers experienced cultural and geographical disorientation, and sought refuge among those with similar ethno-linguistic background.

The residential segregation never reached ghetto proportions. The Germans seemed to realize that assimilation was in their best interest. The change in the Constitution of the first Turnverein does reflect this notion, so do intermarriages with Irish or American-born. And in 1867, when Anglo-Americans founded the Lutheran Church, many German-born, including Hessians, joined this English-language congregation. These are some examples of the early assimilation in process, but it did not reach major proportions until the second generation.[14]

No ward in Trenton could be totally identified with any particular nationality. Large numbers of Irish were dispersed throughout the industrial districts. Neither the Germans nor the Irish ever constituted a majority in any ward, but combined they constituted pluralities in certain areas. Their neighborhoods one could readily identify. Within German neighborhoods there existed Hessian clusters but never representing a majority. By 1870 the concentration of Hessians was reflected, e.g., by 25 families living in five clusters next to each other, and by seven others sharing three houses in the Seventh Ward. It is not possible to discern from the 1870 Census whether Hessians were also living on the opposite side of the street or around the corner. The families of Georg Hoffmann and Peter Fabian were next door neighbors on Princeton Turnpike in 1870. It was not uncommon for families to rent space to single persons, especially when one of them was an apprentice with that householder such as Louis Grealing, living above the store with butcher Frederick Müller in the Seventh Ward. Among the 85 families eight widows were living with their children. During this 22-year period there seems to have been little urge to move out of the neighborhood. The permanence rate was moderate: 27 out of the 85 families (=32%) remained more than five years in a given ward; 19 (=22%) moved once; 5 (=5%) changed residence twice; and the remainder consists of persons leaving for the suburbs while still working in the city, or whose address is only recorded once. They account for 180 males, singles or heads of families, who resided among other Hessians. Shifting within single wards occurred on a frequent basis. Elisabeth Rosbach moved in the summer of 1870 from

Greene Street to Behm Street within the Fifth Ward, and Peter Keit moved his family from 9 Front Street to Number 26. And in the Fifth and Seventh Wards, where the development of row houses was under way by the end of the 1850s, a family having purchased a lot waited in an apartment within the ward until construction was completed.[15]

Although the new immigrants were faced with few *social* barriers, the *communication* barrier was real. This may in part explain the fact that almost a third of the 85 Hessian families chose to remain in their neighborhoods. William Fark lived on 47 Warren Street for more than 20 years. Work was plentiful and local housing available. Children of immigrants, whether born in Hesse or in Trenton, generally remained near their parents after marriage. Three Fischer families lived within four blocks of each other, and Nicholaus Fabian's two adult sons resided within easy reach of his house in the Seventh Ward. Sons of first-generation immigrants stayed in the same neighborhoods for security or simply for the social comfort. Only later would they move to different wards or leave the city. Still, while there was geographic mobility among Hessians in Trenton, the permanence rate of these Hessians was moderate for this period. The mobility rate of unskilled and skilled workers does not show any particular pattern except that when the opportunity arose, Hessians were willing to move, and in an expanding city, these moments occurred frequently.

Most of the 85 families lived in the Seventh (25 families), Fifth (22) and Third (12) Wards. The remaining Hessians lived in three wards. No Hessian families resided in the Sixth. But were these Hessians trapped in their environment because of poverty, as Oscar Handlin argued for the immigrants in Boston? Most of these 85 families seemed to be content with their occupations and wages; they lived comfortably and resided near churches and fraternal organizations. Trenton, a relatively small city in 1870, offered jobs, retail stores, and social and religious activities within limited areas easily accessible by foot, and by horse-drawn trolley after 1860. Hessian-owned retail stores were located in each of the Hessian-dominated clusters of the five wards, as were stores owned by Germans as well. Grocery stores were found on Lamberton Street dividing the Third and Fourth Wards, two were on Greene Street near Five Points in the Seventh Ward, and one at 115 Willow Street. Four Hessian-owned bakeries, such as Frederick Greiner's on Esher Street, were in the ethnic neighborhoods. Two variety stores were located on opposite ends of the city. Barber shops seemed to be everywhere in Trenton. There was no need for Hessians to walk far to purchase basic staples for the family. Hessian and other German stores were an integral part of each German/Hessian-dominated neighborhood.[16]

Besides the bakers John and Joseph Fritz, only one other unidentified Hessian commuted from Hamilton, a Trenton suburb. John Jammer, an iron worker, lived east of the Raritan and Delaware Canal in Chambersburg within walking distance to the factory. By 1870 public transportation had not yet reached Mercer County suburbs.

The various occupations of Hessian immigrants differed from, yet resembled those of, other Germans. These occupations matched the needs of the city. I identified four basic occupational groups among the Hessians in Mercer County: unskilled laborers, skilled workers, retailers and farmers. The largest group consisted of 40 craftsmen and tradesmen, representing seven different vocations (10 bakers; 4 butchers, 6 masons; 5 carpenters; 1 machinist; 6 barbers; 5 shoemakers; and 3 tailors). There were 21 Hessian laborers; 2 farm hands; 11 store owners; 2 farmers and 4 semi-skilled laborers. The 11 masons and carpenters reflect the needs of a growing industrial city in the construction of both factories and houses. There were no office clerks or associated professions among the Hessians. The language barrier seems to be the obvious reason. The same might be said about the absence of large proprietors, executives and professionals, since in these categories money and/or culture-specific education are usually prerequisites.

Occupational changes have always affected residential mobility. In turn, if Hessians remained in their neighborhoods, one might conclude that work was plentiful during this period. However, if immigrants changed their occupations, was it because of an upward move? The growing industries, especially during the Civil War, attracted hundreds of immigrants to Trenton, a trend which had been well under way during the 1850s. Among the 85 Hessians, 13 changed their occupation once, and Martin Dapper twice. Of 21 laborers identified, 10 sought a better living in the city. Their moves reflected the American dream of success through hard work leading to upward mobility. Nine of the ten became skilled workers and one a grocery retailer. There was a definite upward mobility for those unskilled laborers. One clerk bought a grocery store, and Martin Dapper went from boot maker to saloon keeper and then to cigar maker/dealer. Two others became store owners and one a saloon keeper. While ten of this group definitely upgraded their jobs, one could argue that job changes of the other three might not represent upward movement, e.g. from shoemaker to saloon keeper. Five occupational changes also involved residential movement within the city, including Martin Dapper's, who had lived in the West Ward in 1850 as a boot maker. In 1860 he sold lager beer on South Warren Street in the Fourth Ward and ten years later he worked as a cigar maker in the Fifth Ward. It would be interesting to determine if those Hessians appearing only once in the records were only passing through town, seeking better places—"floaters," as they are sometimes called. Or were they simply not picked up consistently by the census takers and city directories, which did happen in a number of cases. There was no downward movement among Hessians, the economy was expanding and jobs were plentiful.[17]

Extended families tended to live within easy reach of each member, and there was also a tendency for sons to follow their fathers' occupations. Jacob Hoffmann's three sons also were masons in Trenton, and Nicholaus Fabian's two sons became cigar makers. Passing father's trade to the next generation was particularly pronounced among craftsmen, a characteristic of that time.

Marriage records tend to show that Hessians married primarily non-Hessians. The records of the Lutheran Church from 1857 to 1870 are quite revealing in this respect. As listed by place of birth of brides and grooms, 25 German principalities were represented in Trenton; the four largest immigrant groups came from Württemberg, Mecklenburg, Baden and Hesse-Darmstadt. A total of 37 Hessian marriages were registered: 5 (=13%) both partners Hessians; 23 (=62%) with other Germans; and 9 (=24.1%) with non-Germans. Almost the same percentages apply to Lutheran German immigrants in Trenton marrying someone from the same state, or other Germans, or non-Germans. The percentage difference for each group is less than 2%. About 25% of the Hessians and Germans were willing to marry non-Germans. Half of the Germans, however, chose their spouses from different parts of Germany, a result quite understandable, since the population of young men and women from any one state was small.[18]

The assimilation process did not seem to be a major concern for the Hessians. Their motives cannot be discerned on the basis of official documents, since these do not reveal any personal reasons. Of the 85 Hessians identified in this paper 33 were naturalized before 1870, as were an additional 55 persons whose names appear only once in county records. These numbers do not represent a large group. The immigrants probably felt secure in their neighborhoods, and there was no governmental push for naturalization. Ownership of land, for example, was not restricted to citizens. By 1870, 681 of the Hessians owned land or houses, an extremely high percentage for a group of immigrants who had arrived between 1848 and 1865. In some cases Hessians bought land within five years of their arrival, as did George Hoffmann and John Bechtel. To be sure, young men in their 20s who are included in the 85 persons did not purchase property. This makes the percentage even higher when limited to persons above age 30. Land speculation was also prevalent among the Hessians. Between 1854 and 1870, land purchases were enacted more than three times by 19 of them or 38% of the 58 property holders. Speculation became possible when the two previously mentioned tracts of land were sold cheaply in the 1850s. Martin Weismar bought one lot on Behm Street in 1858 and three additional lots several years later; on one of these he built his home. The assets of the 85 Hessians were also quite impressive. Counting only a net worth of more than $1,000, there were 34 persons (=40%) enjoying wealth. This figure does not include widows who are not counted among the 85 persons. Charles Keeler had his land assessed at $30,000 on the 1870 Census, an extremely high figure. The other 33 Hessians claimed under $10,000. There is no discernible relationship between becoming naturalized and owning property and other assets.[19]

We can conclude that, encouraged by letters from friends and relatives in *Nordamerika* to break the shackles of destitution in Hesse-Darmstadt and to improve their lot in the New World with its freedom of movement and commerce, the *Auswanderer* availed themselves energetically of the great opportunities in Trenton. To be sure, not all experienced material improvement; many worked hard and never enjoyed affluence. Even some of their children did not achieve material success. However, compared with the homeland, this was not due to socio-economic strictures.

The Trenton experience of the 85 families studied here shows that many of the newcomers achieved upward mobility. Almost half were home owners. They enjoyed the prosperity of an expanding city that offered employment opportunities and made available open land for housing development. Most of the children of these families had a good chance to reach for the American dream.

NOTES

[1]The Bechtheimer Draft Board records are located in the Archives of the Town of Bechtheim under the call number XI. No catalog exists.

[2]According to official ducal records slightly more than 100,000 Hessians emigrated during this period. A careful study of local and county records reveals that many emigrants were not recorded by officials. It is my estimate, based on local reports and not mentioned in ducal records, that an additional 35% emigrated secretly, or as they were labeled *heimlich*.

[3]Most researchers support this thesis. Ingomar Bog, "Die Industrialisierung Hessens," in *Hessisches Auswandererbuch*, ed. Hans Herder (Frankfurt, 1984), 190ff., and Robert Müller, *Die industrielle Entwicklung Offenbachs* (Offenbach, 1932), 59ff. make convincingly similar statements. When comparing Hessian railroad construction with that of other German states, Hesse-Darmstadt ranked far below average during this period.

[4]*Beiträge zur Statistik des Grossherzogthums Hessen* (Darmstadt, 1862), 112ff.

[5]I counted slightly more than 900 Hessian-born men and women living in Mercer County in 1870. More than 2,700 residents of the county were born in German states.

[6]The above information is based on various documents located in Trenton: The records of St. John's Cath. Church (now Sacred Heart), St. Francis of Assisium German Cath. Church, St.

Johannis Gemeinde (now Trinity Church) and the Ev. Luth. Christ Church (records now at Trinity Church). I also made extensive use of the U.S. Bureau Census Records of 1850, 1860 and 1870; county property transaction records for Mercer Co.; and the annual city directories.

[7]Francis Bazley Lee, *History of Trenton, N.J.* (Trenton, 1895), 134ff.

[8]Jessie Rose Turk, "Trenton, N.J. in the 19th Century: The Significance of Location in the Historical Geography of a City" (University Microfilms, Inc., Ann Arbor, Mich.), 222- 338.

[9]The Trenton Hist. Soc., *A History of Trenton, 1679-1929* (Princeton, 1929), 919-944. Hereafter THS.

[10]THS, 523ff.

[11]My count, based on U.S. Census Bureau Records and local church records.

[12]Turk, 238ff. and Lee, 260ff.

[13]THS, 859ff.

[14]The discussion of Hessian neighborhoods in the wards is based on actual numbers of individuals and families living in these districts as recorded in the U.S. Census Bureau Records (my count).

[15]Ibid.

[16]Ibid. and the annual city directories.

[17]Ibid.

[18]I examined all baptism, marriage and death records of the four German churches in Trenton.

[19]I checked all property transactions (immigrants buying land and houses) for this period at the Mercer Co. Court House.

14 | Culture Island in the City: A Case Study of Frisian Migration to the USA (1880-1914)[1]

Annemieke J.B.E. Galema, *University of Groningen*

A well-known Frisian-American philosopher writing about Frisians in the United States once stressed the usefulness of finding a general motif or connecting idea when undertaking a survey of historical events. Without a motif, a historical survey can be no more than a chronology of dates, names and places—especially when one works with large data bases.[2]

I would like to create a motif from two peculiarities. First, it seems to be evident that Frisians generally like to describe themselves as "Frisians" rather than as "Germans" or as "Netherlanders." Professor B. Fridsma, a Frisian immigrant himself and an ardent promoter of Frisian language and culture, once put it this way: "Calling a Frisian a Dutchman is like saying an Armenian is a Russian or Basque is a Spaniard or telling a Welshman or a Scotsman he's English."[3] Second, history tells us that in 1782 the legislature of the autonomous state of Friesland voted to recognize the independence of the American colonies, the first official and formal recognition of the new republic by any governing body. The Frisians have been known for independence and individualism, and because in the popular mind they are often seen as "stubborn," the origin of the motif is obvious: one can suggest that 19th-century Frisian emigrants to the U.S. must have had some of those characteristics. Individualistic and independent behavior are thus recurrent themes in aspects of Frisian migration.

The Frisian homeland lies along the coast and adjacent islands of the North Sea and stretches from the province of Friesland in the Netherlands through Germany up to the border with Denmark. After 1579 the area of West and Mid Friesland became a province of the Netherlands. The area of East

Friesland is marked by the Ems and Weser Rivers, while the North Frisians' land is near Germany's Danish border. The Frisian language is closely related to English. Fridsma once said that telling a Frisian his language is a Dutch dialect gets about the same reaction as telling Muhammed Ali his name is Cassius Clay. Considering the fact that today an estimated 400,000 persons in the Netherlands speak Frisian, this kind of reaction may be less surprising. Germany has about 2,000 Frisian speakers in East Friesland and 10,000 along the coast and islands of North Friesland.[4]

Frisians and Their Migration to America

The first Frisians came with the colonial settlement of New Netherland (1624-1664) in the Hudson River Valley and northeastern New Jersey. Peter Stuyvesant (1592-1672), for example, nicknamed "hardheaded Pete," was from West-Friesland.[5]

Frisian emigration to America did not increase significantly until the middle of the 19th century when, after 1845, the number of the Dutch in general showed a steady and across the board increase. Some of these emigrants were discontented with the Dutch Reformed Church; others sought economic challenges. The growth of their group was reflected in the number of Holland-born residing in New Jersey, up from 357 in 1850 to 12,698 in 1910. By that year the Garden State ranked just behind Michigan and Illinois in terms of Holland-born residents. Naturally, they did not match the numbers of the principal ethnic groups, but they were more numerous than, e.g., the French, Belgians, Greeks and Scandinavians.[6] During the 19th century the majority of Frisians settled in rural communities in Michigan, Iowa and Wisconsin, others went to industrial centers like Chicago, Grand Rapids, Mich., and Paterson, N.J.[7]

Let us now focus on a group of Frisian emigrants from the Dutch province of Friesland, who went to Paterson and vicinity between 1880 and 1910. Paterson had a large Dutch center, estimated to have comprised more than 10,000 souls in 1920, the first American-born generation included.[8] A large part of this ethnic group was made up of emigrants from two provinces in the Netherlands: Zeeland and Friesland. The exact number of Frisians is hard to determine. This is due to the general problem with research in Frisian migration to the U.S.: Frisians are not distinguished from the Dutch in either American, Dutch or German statistical compilations. Although they had established their own communities and ethnic organizations, they were virtually invisible to the American public at large, for the once cherished great melting-pot USA contained only a small ingredient of Frisians. Outside of academia, for most Americans the Frisians were not a separate ethnic group, but simply 'Dutchmen,' 'Hollanders,' or 'Germans.' This is true also for the migration records in the Netherlands: the Frisians are considered a part of the Dutch population.

My research on Frisian migration to the U.S. focused on the northern part of the province. The heaviest emigration came from the municipalities of Het Bildt, Oost- en West Dongeradeel, Barradeel, Ferwerderadeel, and Wonseradeel (see map Figure I).[9] These are all agricultural regions with fertile clay soil. The agricultural depression in the late 19th century made a deep impression in this area.[10] Although in the second half of that century northern Friesland was already closely tied into the international agricultural market, their particular agrarian-oriented conjuncture did not fit in the development of the general pattern of market mechanisms after 1875. By 1879 the stagnation became clear in the drop of grain prices, caused by surplus production and the emergence of the world grain market which was very disadvantageous for Western Europe. There was also high unemployment among the farm workers. This was caused when farmers tried to raise their declining incomes by increased mechanization, specialization in profitable products, and by working with fewer hired hands.[11] In other parts of the province, where there was more mixed farming, this led to a shift from arable farming to dairying. Closely linked to the agricultural crisis and mechanization was the disappearance of the patriarchal labor relations of the 18th century between farmers and farmworkers. The hired hand was no longer considered part of the farmer's family. This resulted in class contrasts and worsening conditions for the workers. We may say that social conflict between landowners (farmers) and laborers was part of the complexity of motives for migration of the farm labor force. For some contemporary scholars the agricultural crisis of the 1880s and 1890s was a push factor of the emigration wave to the U.S.[12] Others think this was hardly the case, especially if Dutch migration is put into international perspectives; compared, e.g., with the Germans and the English, it is of much less significance. In addition, so the argument goes, if one considers Dutch emigration over time, the average annual emigration was considerably higher between 1905 and 1915.[13] This observation might be true for the Netherlands as a whole, but some regional emigration patterns differ from this time frame.

Sketch of Passaic County

As with other immigrant groups, the Dutch have shown a tendency to locate near and among their own. In the case of New Jersey, G.F. de Jong showed—on the basis of the census reports of 1920—that 60% of the Holland-born in New Jersey in 1920 were living in one county, namely Passaic, making it the home of the largest community of Holland immigrants in the East in those days.[14]

The city and the vicinity of Paterson are part of Passaic County, the most irregularly shaped in all of New Jersey. It shares its northern county line with

Figure I

The province of Friesland in the Netherlands and its municipalities around 1900.
Source: T. van der Wal, *"Op zoek naar een nieuwe vrijheid,"* diss. (Univ. Leiden, 1972), 50.

New York State's Orange County, and in the west, south, and east it borders on four New Jersey counties. In 1901 J. Whitehead remarked that the county looked somewhat like an old-fashioned hour glass, very unsymmetrical, however, and with ill-shaped sides.[15] In 1890 the county had a total of 106,734 acres; a large part of that is hilly, especially in the north and west.

Aukjen Pruiksma, a Frisian who arrived in Paterson in 1895, wrote about his new environment, *"het is hier in deeze omgeefing wat bergachtig en het loopt zwaar als men er bij op loopt"* ("the surroundings here are somewhat hilly and its quite a walk going up").[16] Mrs. Pruiksma had probably never seen anything but the flat countryside of FriesIand. Pieter Westerhuis, who migrated to Paterson in 1881, also expressed his astonishment with New Jersey's terrain:

> Gij zout verwonderlijk op zien zoo als gij hier ook eens kwam men kan het zen zoo niet voor stellen die en holland woont dat het hier er zoo uit ziet want varten en slotten ziet men hier niet zoo als in holland maar hoge bergen daar het water uit loopt en dan zoms een riever daar het water en langs loopt dat uit de bergen komt maar ander ziet men hier geen waters want het land dat aan eigenaaren behoort daar zijn allemaal stekken om maar geen slotten zoals bij u . . ." [You would really be surprised if you came here, and if one comes from Holland one cannot imagine that it looks like this because one doesn't see canals and ditches like in Holland but high mountains from which water runs down and sometimes a river where the water from the mountains runs into no other waters here while the land that belongs to the owners has fences everywhere no ditches like yours.] [17]

Although Westerhuis missed the canals and ditches, Passaic County was certainly well watered. Besides big rivers like the Passaic, the Pequannock, and the Wanaqua, the county has numerous small streams. Around the turn of the century many railroads also intersected the county in almost every direction, including a good connection between New York City and Paterson. Nearly all the people in Passaic in those days followed mechanical and manufacturing pursuits commensurate with the county's character as a leading manufacturing area in the state. In deciding on New Jersey as their new home, Frisian immigrants must have been attracted by the Dutch (and also Frisian) atmosphere that still lingered in parts of the state ever since the colonial period. The so-called Old-Dutch was still spoken, but newly arrived immigrants could hardly understand it. Frisian influence was also perceptible. J. van Hinte, in his work on the Dutch in America, relates the story of an American lady who wanted to show her devotion to the Dutch language, and referred to her grandmother as *"een sterke frommes,"* which means, in pure Frisian, "a strong woman."[18]

Other evidence of the Dutch-Frisian spirit in New Jersey is preserved in the many letters sent back home to the old country. These written accounts about the new environment were very influential. A single letter could swing the opinion of numerous villagers to emigrate, as George Schnuecker relates about East- Frisians from Neermoor. He noted that an 'America-letter' in the 1830s and 1840s was considered so unusual that it would be printed and distributed for the benefit of the entire community. This also happened with the letters of Sjoerd Aukes Sipma from Iowa to the province of Friesland in mid-19th century. Later, when postage rates decreased and letters became more numerous as more friends settled in America, they were still a good source of information for potential emigrants, though their novelty value had decreased.[19]

Although the preservation of Dutch-Frisian colonial and early 19th-century habits, manners, and customs was obvious in New Jersey at the turn of the century, the industrial boom that the state experienced after the Civil War was a greater attraction to Frisian immigrants. Industry was the inducement for many newcomers to settle in ever increasing numbers in cities like Paterson, and also Roseland, Ill., Rochester, N.Y., Cleveland, Grand Rapids, and Chicago.

In the early 19th century, Paterson was one of the two largest cotton cities in America. Iron industry also settled there, similarly attracted by the water power sites at the Passaic River Falls. Silk came later and would make Paterson into the Silk City 'par excellence.' According to J. van Hinte, there were many Dutch immigrants who, upon arrival in New York, stayed on the other side of the Hudson in the Paterson area for a while. There they usually found work immediately. Van Hinte also mentions that Paterson was the place where the trains to "The West" started.[20] Situated only a dozen miles from Hoboken, which subsequently became the terminal of the Holland-America Line, Paterson (together with the cities of Lodi and Passaic) was obviously destined to attract Dutch-Frisian immigrants.

In 1890, C.A. Shriner also mentioned that Paterson had experienced a steady increase of industries. The city's proximity to New York City, the trade and commercial center of the country, assured obvious advantages that were virtually bound to give her a choice industrial position.[21]

Frisian Migration to Paterson and Vicinity

Like other immigrant groups, the Dutch followed the typical 19th-century settlement pattern of ethnic clustering in culture islands. In many cities, though, Dutch neighborhood development followed the path of even further subdividing according to provinces of origin. In the case of Paterson an exclusive Frisian island came into being.[22] According D.G. Vanderstel, the Dutch residential concentrations were not based upon a common Dutch identity, but reflected the immigrants' diverse provincial origins, denominational affiliation, and time of arrival in the city. In his study on the Dutch in Grand Rapids, Mich., he shows churches, schools, the press, and various organizations upholding the notion of Dutch unity. However, he also points to differentiation among the Dutch immigrant population, based upon ideologies, beliefs, and perceptions of relations with the surrounding American society.[23]

From the group of Dutch-born in Paterson in 1900 (4,893 persons) and 1910 (4,929)—according to the U.S Census manuscripts—I was able to create a linkage group of 287 Frisian immigrants representing six municipalities in the northern part of the province of Friesland. For lack of exact emigration data, no attempts were made to link in all of Friesland. My main systematic information sources were the Netherlands Population Registers from 1880 to 1914, and the U.S. Census manuscripts of 1900 and 1910. The Dutch Registers cover place of birth, present hometown, civil status, religious affiliation, occupation, date of emigration and destination of the head of household and all the family members and servants living in the same home before departure. After arrival in the U.S., the census taker, in ten-year intervals, was supposed to record name, age, sex, nativity, citizenship, occupation, education, ownership of the house, and location in the area of settlement.

The linkage procedure is often quite difficult, but it can yield meaningful results. The following describes some aspects of occupational structure and occupational mobility based on the linked data. Since the linked file contains information about occupations of potential Frisian migrants and actual settlers, this allows comparisons of the labor forces in both countries and we can ascertain the extent to which—if any—migration actually led to upward mobility. In an essay on Dutch international labor migration, R.P. Swierenga says that "there is no better way to understand the complexities of individual situations and migration decisions than to work on the scale of small groups or individuals and follow these groups through the whole migration process."[24] We might augment Swierenga's small-group notion with that of regional groups.

Clearly, there was a relation between a region's occupational structure and the exercising of the emigration option. Looking also at regional aspects of labor relations, as in the Frisian experience, may further illuminate general international labor migration. The Dutch Population Registers (1880-1914) reveal that a very large percentage of the emigrants, older than 14, (i.e. the active work force of the population) found a source of income in agriculture. According to R.P. Swierenga, of all the emigrants to overseas countries between 1835 and 1880, 80% left rural municipalities. For

Friesland this does not mean that the Frisian emigrants to Paterson were farmers or landowners: most were unskilled day laborers and farmhands—no farmers included; and there were only three 'gardeniers,' whose socio-economic position was roughly between farmer and farm laborer. The 'gardenier' owned or rented a small piece of land and made a living by growing vegetable crops that were not profitable for the bigger farmer.[25] It should be noted that the emigrants' home area in northern Friesland was very rural and experienced a rather belated economic "take-off." With only a few small-scale industries there, the majority of the emigrants came from the agricultural occupations.

Another sizeable percentage of the labor force, according to the Population Registers, was made up of people who were not classified as to their occupation, or who did not have any at all. We may assume that most of the unclassified were probably unemployed, at least temporarily so.

Diversity in the emigrant labor force was obviously lacking. Hardly any white collar workers emigrated to Paterson between 1880 and 1914—my linkage group includes none. Unskilled workers outnumbered skilled craftsmen three to one (see Figure II).

In the comparison between pre- and post-migration occupations of the Frisians in the Paterson area we find one-third of the settlers of the linkage-

Figure II

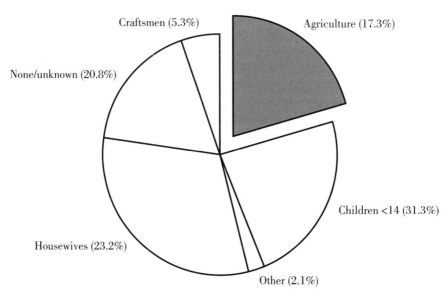

**Occupations of Frisian Emigrants
Linkage-Group Paterson 1880-1914**

Craftsmen (5.3%)

Agriculture (17.3%)

None/unknown (20.8%)

Children <14 (31.3%)

Housewives (23.2%)

Other (2.1%)

Figure III

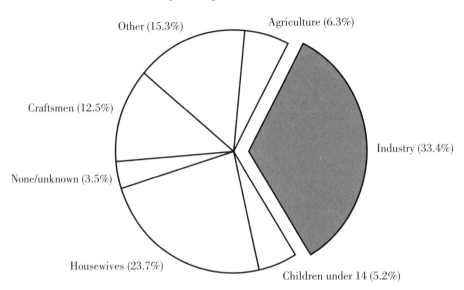

**Occupations of Frisian Immigrants
Linkage-Group Paterson 1880-1914**

Other (15.3%)

Agriculture (6.3%)

Craftsmen (12.5%)

Industry (33.4%)

None/unknown (3.5%)

Housewives (23.7%)

Children under 14 (5.2%)

group working in industry (see Figure III). This is especially striking, because we know that none of them had been working in industry before. Agriculture, on the other hand, absorbed only about 6% of them, although their backgrounds were typically rural. This suggests the conclusion that the effect of emigration on occupational status was largely determined by the economic nature of the receiving community. Paterson, a very industrial town, attracted blue collar workers, and the Frisian settlers had to take jobs that were available. Looking at the graph, two more striking matters have to be explained: First, the percentage of children is much higher before the Frisians' departure for America. This difference appears as the migrants of the linkage-group are traced in the U.S. Census manuscripts of 1900 and 1910. At that point they had been in the U.S. for some years and the children had grown beyond 18 years of age and consequently belonged now to the adult working population. Secondly, the occupationally unclassified group of migrants appears to be much larger before they left than after settlement in Paterson. Only 3.5% of the Frisians did not have a job in Paterson. This is an extremely low percentage considering the fact that one-third of this segment were older than 65. This low percentage was also due to Paterson's continuous growth and development providing plenty of work. Many of the immigrants mentioned in their letters back to the province of Friesland that wages were really good, even better than in Friesland. Pieter Westerhuis, for example, who emigrated in 1881 from Het Bildt in Friesland, stated in a letter that "work" and "bread" were his argument for staying in the U.S. and in Paterson.[26] F. Ramella found the same motivation for a group of Italian workers who migrated to Paterson and the nearby silk centers in the 1890s. For them America seemed to be synonymous with good wages and a variety of jobs.[27]

Many of Paterson's Frisians made a living as factory workers, especially in the silk mills. In the silk industry before World War I, particularly in dying and weaving, the Netherlanders were only outnumbered by Germans, Italians and Irish.[28] The Frisians, like the Germans and Czechs, distinguished themselves as hard workers and were, therefore, generally considered as desirable employees. The jobs of the Frisians in my linkage group were very often in precision work. But, it must be said, they rarely ever made it to 'foreman' or any other higher position in the silk industry. Quite the opposite was true for the comparable Italian immigrants. They came as skilled workers and stayed in the same crafts after migration to Paterson.[29]

The Frisians were largely responsible for the finishing touches in the Paterson silk mills. Many women and girls were employed there. The very exacting task of degumming the silk was often assigned to Dutch-Frisian immigrants. It involved the boiling of the raw silk in a soap solution to dissolve the layer of sericin. This process imparted a beautiful softness and sheen to the silk. This was a very hot job requiring close supervision to prevent part of the sericin from sticking to the silk. Around the turn of the century the average pay was $12.50 per week. Two decades before, J.G. Boekhout, an immigrant from Het Bildt, wrote to Friesland:

> "Ik werk nu niet meer aan het spoor ik werk nu in een siede molen en verdien daar 7 gulden en de week en dat komt mij niet zo slim an. . ." [I don't work on the railroad anymore. Now I work in a silk mill and I make seven guilders a week and that doesn't sound too bad to me. . .] [30]

H. Sannes, in his history of Het Bildt, mentions that day laborers with a permanent job earned 5 to 6.5 guilders a week during the summer, and 3 to 5 guilders during winter. These amounts were averages for the Frisian clay areas.[31] A field laborer only made 180 to 290 guilders a year, due to the fact that 'rain hours' were subtracted. In the last decades before 1900, temporary or seasonal laborers were very often unemployed during the winter. We may conclude, that the Frisian immigrants considered their wages in the silk industry as good. The same results are found in research on the Italian skilled textile workers Paterson. F. Ramella states that the local factory workers of Biella in Italy believed that wages in the silk mills of New Jersey were very high.[32] Regarding social status and hierarchy, the labor force in the silk mills seems to have been structured along the lines of skill and ethnic origin, with the English- and German-speaking workers at the top, followed by the skilled Italian weavers and the unskilled Frisians.

Figure IV

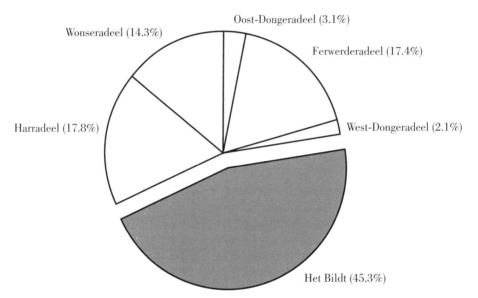

**Municipality of Departure
Linkage-Group Paterson 1880-1914**

Oost-Dongeradeel (3.1%)

Wonseradeel (14.3%)

Ferwerderadeel (17.4%)

Harradeel (17.8%)

West-Dongeradeel (2.1%)

Het Bildt (45.3%)

We recall that many of the Paterson Frisians had been day laborers in agriculture. Most of them were from the area of Het Bildt (see Figure IV) that had been in a deplorable economic state, felt especially by the field laborers—the biggest part of the work force. In his letters, J.G. Boekhout, emphasizes again and again the fact hat he and his fellow immigrants all had jobs. In 1883 he writes: "... *en nu ik werk noch in het verbriek . . . dus wij hebben het werk nog dicht bij huis en broeder Sjoerd is nu weer aan het kel ergrafen*" [and I still have a job in the factory . . . so we do have work close to home and brother Sjoerd again started to dig cellars].[33] Some immigrants tried to justify their decision to leave Friesland in every one of their letters. In 1882 Pieter Westerhuis wrote 'home' that he had heard Frisian field laborers were again experiencing a miserable year, so he thought:

"... voor een mensch die het van werken lebben moet is er geen beeter plaas dink ik als Paterzon, want die kinders heeft kunn en allemaal in het fabriek. . ." [For a man who needs work to make a living, I think there is no better place than Paterson, because those who have children can let them all work in the factory.][34]

But Pieter also had other ideas about finding his fortune. In the same letter he wrote:

> maar die geld heeft kan beter en de West gaen. Iege Mulder heeft daar een plaas gekogt en de staat Iowa die is daa gelukkig geweest wandt daar is bij de zomer een spoorweg doo zijn plaas gelegd en daar kreeg hij zoo veel voor dat hij zijn heele plaas betaalen kon. [But if you have money you can better go West. Iege Mulder bought a farm in the state of Iowa and he got very lucky because in the summer they put a railroad through his land and for that he got so much money that he at once could pay for his whole farm.][35]

There have been indications that the denominational preference of the Dutch settlers sometimes determined their chances of getting certain jobs. Van Hinte mentions that, although Hollanders were generally looked upon as desirable employees, employers sometimes preferred members of the Christian Reformed Church, an affiliation that included most of the Frisians of my linkage group.[36] Employers liked the idea that these workers considered strikes to be in conflict with their religious beliefs. Van Hinte points out how great this preference of employers could be. He had found out that a well-known Paterson manufacturer hired only employees who belonged to this denomination.[37]

In sum, Frisian labor migrants took jobs that were available in the receiving community of Paterson, N.J. The economic opportunities that this city offered were more important than clinging to their prior occupational backgrounds in the province of Friesland. In their choice of work, the first generation of Paterson's Frisians did not show the 'all important goal' of becoming the owner of a piece of land. The Frisians seemed to have been permanent emigrants whose transition from rural agricultural to urban industrial life and work seems to have been a definitive step. From an international perspective, Frisian migration shared the pattern of the proletarian mass migration that started in the 1880s and was characterized by the fact that a very high percentage of the migrants had been unskilled agricultural laborers or proletarianized small landowners, all ending up in the expanding industries of the U.S. In this respect we cannot speak of very individualistic behavior by Paterson's Frisians. Their individualism expressed itself more in aspects of cultural affiliation. And there were many reports on Frisians of the third generation still speaking the language of their ancestors. Of course, they also had their own cultural society, "Utspanning troch Ynspanning" (Diversion through Exertion). When the Frisian poet and orator Sjouke de Zee visited Paterson in 1928, he found a flourishing cultural *selskip* (society).[38] Although stubbornness, independence and individualism may be attributed to Frisians, we can also say that their individual occupational behavior was mainly determined by the need of their stomachs.

NOTES

[1]I would like to thank Robert P. Swierenga, George Welling, Horst Roessler, and Walter Kamphoefner for comment on earlier drafts of this paper, and also the Dutch Organization for Scientific Research (N.W.O.).

[2]M. ten Hoor, "Frisians in the U.S.," *Michigan Alumnus Quarterly Review LVIII* (Dec. 1951), 50-56.

[3]"Doch dyn plicht en lit de ljue rabje," *The Grand Rapids Press,* Jan. 19, 1975.

[4]"The Frisians," *Harvard Encyclopedia of American Ethnic Groups* (Cambridge, Mass., 1961), 401ff.

[5]M. ten Hoor, "Frisians", 51.

[6]H.S. Lucas, *Netherlanders in America* (Ann Arbor, 1955), Table II.

[7]*Harvard Encyclopedia,* 401ff.

[8]J. van Hinte, *Netherlanders in Amerika* (Groningen, 1928), II, 376.

[9]The data of all the emigrants from these six municipalities during 1880-1914 are stored in: A.J.B.E. Galema, *"Computer Compilation: Frisian Immigrants to the U.S.A. 1880-1911"* (Kent, Oh., 1985), unpubl.

[10]H. de Vries, *Landbouw en Bevolking tijdens de Agrarische Depressie in Friesland 1878-1895* (Wageningen, 1971).

[11]H. de Vries, "The labor market in Dutch agriculture and emigration to the U.S.," in R.P. Swierenga, ed., *The Dutch in America* (New Brunswick, 1985), 79.

[12]H. Blink, "De landverhuizing uit Nederland", *Vragen ven den dag* 30 (1915), 179-194.

[13]H. de Vries, "Labor Market", 78.

[14]G.F. de Jong, "Dutch Immigrants in New Jersey before World War I," *New Jersey History* 94 (Summer-Autumn 1976), 69-88.

[15]J.LL.D. Whitehead, *The Passaic Valley, New Jersey* (New York, 1901), 229.

[16]Letter of Aukjen Pruiksma, May 16, 1895, from Paterson to the province of Friesland. Collectie Rijksarchief Leeuwarden.

[17]Letter of Pieter Westerhuis, June 6, 1881, from Paterson to J.J. Hoogland, St.Anna Parochie, in *Collectie Hoogland,* Rijksarchief Leeuwarden.

[18]J. van Hinte, *Nederlenders I,* 65. For the Dutch colonial spirit in New Jersey see also: A.C. Leiby, *The Early Dutch and Swedish Settlers of New Jersey* (Princeton, 1964), 109-121.

[19]G. Schnuecker, *Die Ostfriesen in Amerika* (Cleveland, 1917), 5ff.; trans. of Sipma's letter by Robert P. Swierenga in *Annals of Iowa XXXVIII* (Des Moines, 1965) II: 81-118.

[20]J. van Hinte, *Nederlanders I,* 374.

[21]C.A. Shriner, *Paterson, New Jersey* (Paterson, 1890), 28,

[22]Culture island is a term used mainly in geogr. research, see B.L. Anderson, in his study *The Scandinavian and Dutch rural settlements in the Stillaguamis and Nooksack valleys of Western Washington* (Ann Abor, 1957).

[23]D.G. Vanderstel, *The Dutch of Grand Rapids, Mich., 1848-1900: Immigrant neighborhood and community development in a 19th century city* (Ann Arbor, 1986), 539.

[24]R.P. Swierenga, "International labor migration in the 19th century: the Dutch example," paper at the 7th Int. Econ. Hist. Congress (Edinburgh, Scotland, 1978).

[25]J.J. Spahr van der Hoek, *Geschiedenis van de Friese landbow* (Drachten, 1952), 648ff.

[26]Letter of Pieter Westerhuis, Jan. 3, 1882, from Paterson to J.J. Soogland, St. Anna Parochie. *Collectie Hoogland.*

[27]F. Ramella, "Across the Ocean or over the Border: Experiences and Expectations of Italians from Piedmont in New Jersey and Southern France," in D. Hoerder and H. Roessler, eds., *Distant Magnets: Migrants' Views of Opportunities in Industrializing Areas in Europe and America* (New York, 1993), 105-125.

[28]J.W. Jenks and W.J. Lauck, *The Immigration Problem* (New York, 1917) 516f.

[29]F. Ramella, "Across."

[30]Letter of J.G. Boekhout, Dec. 1, 1881, from Paterson to J.J. Hoogland, St. Anna Parochie, *Hoogland Collectie.*

[31]Amounts based on research of the "Friesch Comite van de Volkspartij" of 1891 and described by H. Sannes, *Geschiedenis van Het Bildt* IIIB, 1795-1955 (Franeker, 1956), 371f.

[32]F. Ramella, "Across."

[33]Letter of J.G. Boekhout, March 19, 1883, *Collectie Hoogland.*

[34]Letter of Pieter Westerhuis, Nov. 21, 1882, *Collectie Hoogland.*

[35]Yge Mulder was an immigrant who also came from Het Bildt and migrated in the early 1880s.

[36]The first period of 19th-century Dutch migration to the U.S. really started with the settlement of groups of Separatists who went with the their reverends B.P. Scholte and A. van Raalte to Iowa and Michigan, respectively. Initially, these Separatists joined the existing Ref. Church of America (a creation of earlier Dutch settlers), but many devout persons had begun to wonder whether or not Van Raalte and his closest friends had "sold the churches to an impure denomination." The result was that in 1857 a permanent separation occurred and a denomination of secessionists was formed. The new church was named The Christian Ref. Church. See A. Hyma, *Albertus C. van Raalte and his Dutch Settlements in the U.S.* (Grand Rapids, 1947), 193-239.

[37]J. Hinte, *Nederlanders*, II, 378.

[38]Sj. de Zee, *Myn Twadde Amerika-reis*, (Heerenveen, 1929), 64.

15 | Land and Marriage: German Regional Reflections in Four Texas Towns, 1845-1860

Lauren Ann Kattner, *University of Texas*

According to sociologist Milton Gordon, an important aspect of becoming "American" in the 19th century involved the marriage of couples of different national origins. He points out several factors which affected spouse selection. Obviously, wealth and religious preference influenced marriage choices. The ability to move freely from one place to another also provided the potential for women and men from two different ethnic groups to marry. In addition to these components, Gordon points out the importance of an economic hierarchy within individual German-American communities, the size of an ethnic community in a city/town, and U.S. regional location. The intersection of class (based on wealth), ethnicity, and religion appear in a label such as upper middle class white German Protestant.[1]

While acknowledging American regional differences, Gordon overlooks German regional identities in American towns and cities prior to the Civil War. Many young adults expressed their regional identification through intraregional marriage: they chose spouses from their own region. Andrew Yox tells of this phenomenon among Catholics in antebellum Buffalo, New York. Wealthy men from the southern German-language region who lived in Buffalo before the Civil War married women from their own region more often than did other German men of that city. Although coming from areas having different political boundaries, these Bavarians and Alsatians had an affinity through the overarching southern German communality. Their marriage choices suggest that they shared attitudes about family life as well.[2]

This paper investigates the potential for German-American cultural and economic unification despite regional differences in the Texas towns of Fredericksburg, New Braunfels, Yorktown, and Galveston between 1845 and 1860. The locations of these towns appear on Fig. 1. The first three of the towns were located in the antebellum fourth congressional district, a district composed chiefly of counties along the Indianola Trail. Small-scale tobacco farming, cattle ranching, and water-powered industries provided this district's economic base. In contrast, Galveston was the gateway to the third district, a district comprised primarily of plantation-run, cotton-growing counties in east-central Texas. Galveston's own economy depended on cotton exports and on a thriving publishing industry. Whereas only four counties in the third district included populations with 15% or more persons from German-speaking countries, 14 counties of the fourth district had this high a percentage or greater by 1860.[3]

Figure 1

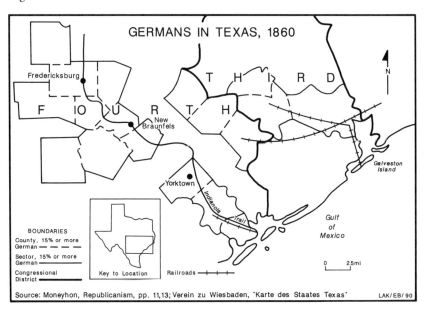

GERMANS IN TEXAS, 1860

Fredericksburg

T H I R D

F O U R T H

New Braunfels

Yorktown

Galveston Island

Gulf of Mexico

BOUNDARIES
County, 15% or more German — — — —
Sector, 15% or more German ——————
Congressional District ————

Key to Location

Railroads ++++

0   25mi

Source: Moneyhon, Republicanism, pp. 11,13; Verein zu Wiesbaden, "Karte des Staates Texas"   LAK/EB/90

Fig. 2 shows how the towns appeared both different and similar in the nature of their lot arrangements, going from a simple plan for small-sized Yorktown to a complex one for the large town of Galveston.[4] In the case of Galveston, Anglo-Americans—the town's chief developers—determined the spatial design in 1837. Within this complex setting, German immigrants and their children made up about 45% of the white population and concentrated in wards 1 and 2 between 1845 and 1860.[5] For New Braunfels and Fredericksburg, immigrant colonial councils chose neo-classical spatial schemes in 1846 and 1847 that included uniform street patterns and market squares. Such councils worked under the direction of a philanthropic—though entrepreneurial—German nobility, the *Texasverein*. In Texasverein-

Figure 2

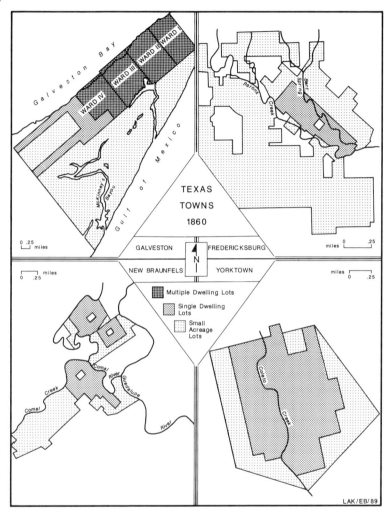

sponsored towns, German-Americans composed about 90% of the whites. German-Texan Franz Hoppe also selected a neoclassical arrangement for the streets of Yorktown in 1857. Germans and their Texas-born children made up that town's entire population. Regardless of each town designer's national origin, small acreage lots (generally around 10 acres in size) bordered all four towns.[6]

In these antebellum Texas towns, social and economic expectations, and religious differences colored reflections of regional identity. As this paper proposes to show, settlement patterns hindered German-American cohesion;

settlement choices, in part, influenced the extent of intraregional marriage. Yet Protestant-affiliated regional subgroups contributed most toward German-American fragmentation in the counties between New Braunfels and Fredericksburg. Subgroups tried to maintain social and economic power within the heavily German-populated fourth district. In so doing, they did not allow the formation of a strong and unified force which might have checked the statewide, secessionist power of Anglo planters and railroad developers from the third district. Settlement patterns and subsequent marriage selections prior to the Civil War highlighted the problems and prospects for German-American unity.

A three-step analysis aids in determining the extent of intraregional marriage and German regional segregation in Texas towns. First, the paper outlines regional identities among people living in early 19th-century German-speaking areas of Europe. It also describes reflections of those identities in immigrant marriages as it asks about the singular importance of regional background in preventing German-American cohesion. The second step of the analysis adds together important influences which favored intraregional marriage and regional segregation. Here we find that coming from a certain region and living in a particular Texas town added up to form one of several combined factors which influenced marriage choices. Various combinations moreover affected the continuation of German regionalism in antebellum Texas. During the final step of the analysis, we may see the special effects of an individual's religious affiliation: alone, acting in combination with other factors and, most importantly, interacting with regional origins to produce an extensive deterrent to German-American unity.[7]

I. Regionalism: How Important Was It?

Immigrants and their children in mid-19th-century Texas towns readily recognized the broad dimensions of regionalism. Wilhelm Hermes, a young, well-educated bachelor from Hamburg, provides us with a glimpse at regionally-related expressions. Visiting Fredericksburg in 1846, he wrote: "sometimes fandangos ended in quarreling. Two parties were usually formed at the beginning of each quarrel: the North Germans (called Hanoverians) and the South Germans (called Nassauers)."[8] That is, although called a Nassauer, a person's nativity may have been the Electorate of Cassel; and someone called a Hanoverian might well have arrived from Brunswick. As Hermes explained later in his letter, this situation existed because people from a general region, sharing a close proximity of culture and dialect, found identification with the principality or kingdom from which the majority in that region hailed. For the purposes of this paper, I call the people of the "Hanoverian" region *northwestern* Germans; those of the "Nassauer" area *west-central* Germans, except in situations where the precise states were involved.

The regional outlines of Fig. 3 provide the framework for classifying the specific provinces, kingdoms, and other German-speaking areas from which immigrants to Texas towns originated. The origins of German-Texan town dwellers are listed on Table 1.[9] Contrasting regions portrayed distinct social, cultural, and economic characteristics between the initial formation of the *Deutscher Zollverein* (1834) and the Austro-Prussian War (1866). On the one hand, a region like the northeast included mainly Protestants and based its economy on grain exported by large-scale Junkers who had utilized the serf system until about 1811. On the other hand, the southern German region included mainly Catholics and based its economy on a variety of food and manufactured products produced by small-scale family enterprises. Other regions likewise portrayed special characteristics.

Figure 3

Table 1 **Major Origins of German Speakers to Texas Towns, 1845-1860**

Region Areas	City/State	Kingdom Principality/Electorate	Prussian Province	Other German-Speaking Areas
North-West	Bremen Hamburg Luebeck Magdeburg	Brunswick Hanover Mecklenburg Oldenburg	Prignitz part of Brandenburg Lower Prov. Saxony Schleswig-Holstein Westphalia	
West-Central	Frankfurt/M	Elect. Cassel Grand duchy of Hesse (Mainz, Darmstadt, Rhine-Hesse) Lippe-Detmold Duchy of Nassau Waldeck	Rhineland	
South		Baden Bavaria Wuerttemberg		Austria Alsace & Lorraine Switzerland
East-Central	Dresden	Saxony 2 Thuringian states: Saxe-Altenburg Saxe-Weimar	Brandenburg south of Warthe Posen Silesia	Bohemia
North-East	Berlin Frankfurt/O	Anhalt-Dessau	Mittelmark part of Brandenburg Pommerania E. & W. Prussia	

Source: Kattner Project and Texas Demography Project databases.

Table 2   **Distribution of All Sample Marriages by Region in Four Texas Towns, 1845–1860**

%Grooms
% Brides

	(N)	Bride's Region					All Grooms:	
		NW	WC	S	EC	NE	%	(N)
		50.38	23.31	5.26	7.52	13.53	30.64	(133)
	NW	54.03	20.00	14.58	32.26	23.68		
		(67)	(31)	(7)	(10)	(18)		
		18.79	54.36	11.41	6.71	8.73	34.33	(149)
	WC	22.58	52.26	35.42	32.26	17.11		
		(28)	(81)	(17)	(10)	(13)		
Groom's		20.37	33.33	35.19	1.85	9.26	12.44	(54)
Region	S	8.87	11.61	39.58	3.23	6.58		
		(11)	(18)	(19)	(1)	(5)		
		27.03	18.92	8.11	21.62	24.32	8.53	(37)
	EC	8.07	4.52	6.25	25.80	11.84		
		(10)	(7)	(3)	(8)	(9)		
		13.11	29.51	3.28	3.28	50.82	14.06	(61)
	NE	6.45	11.61	4.17	6.45	40.79		
		(8)	(18)	(2)	(2)	(31)		
All Brides:								
	%	28.57	35.72	11.06	7.14	17.51	100.00	
	(N)	(124)	(155)	(48)	(31)	(76)		(434)

Phi coefficient =.602 (stastically significant)
   Source: Kattner Project and Texas Demography Project databases using 2x2 table analysis.

Table 2 frames regional reflections as seen in German-Texan town marriages. This table represents the experiences of a sample of 434 couples for whom both regional origins and religious preferences are known. The otherwise unbiased sample includes 51.7% of the 839 German-American couples whose marriages were performed between 1845 and 1860 in the four towns of this study.[10] Percentages on Table 2 show regional marriage combinations; a measure called the "Phi coefficient" also appears on this table. The Phi coefficient indicates that 60.2% of the variation in marriage choices can be explained by all of the different combinations shown on the table.[11]

The underlined percentages on Table 2 reveal a continuation of regional affiliation. All of the diagonal percentages are higher than their respective row and column numbers. For example, 54.36% of the west-central German grooms selected brides from their region of origin. This percentage is higher than the row total of 34.33% (the west-central grooms' portion among all German-speaking men in the sample). Also, 52.26% of the west-central

Figure 4   **Distribution of Intraregional Marriages by Region and Sex in Four Texas Towns, 1845-1860**

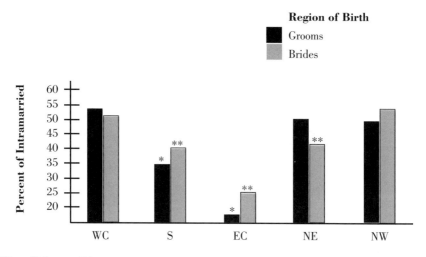

R² coefficient = .039
*Statistically significantly different from west-central grooms
**Statistically significantly different from west-central brides

German brides had husbands from their home region. This percentage is higher than the column total of 35.72% (the percent of west-central brides among all German-speaking women in the sample). Statistically, these higher percentages indicate that many young, newly married individuals continued to identify with their respective regions of origin. Indeed, the intraregional marriages of 206 couples account for almost half (47.5%) of all marriages in this sample.

A close-up comparison of male and female experiences is illustrated by Fig. 4—which is based on a "regression analysis." A regression analysis tells us proportional differences among people from diverse backgrounds.[12] Asterisks above the bars on the figure indicate statistically important differences which were discovered through the regression analysis. Using the asterisk indicators, we see that southern Germans of both sexes and northeastern women made substantially different marriage choices from west-central Germans. By limiting our view to a range of percentages between 20 and 60, Fig. 4 accents the lowest intraregional marriage percentages among women and men from east-central Europe. Northwestern people and northeastern men more likely followed the west-central path toward marrying someone else from their own respective regions. As among west-central Germans, their potential contribution toward German-American cultural homogeneity was relatively weak. Like Table 2, this figure reports a coefficient measure. The R^2 coefficient on Fig. 4 lets us know that only 3.9% of the intraregional marriages can be explained by the region of birth for either the bride or the groom.[13]

Views of regional identity, as reflected in marriage choices, imply that feelings about German-American homogeneity differed by specific regional groups. Statistics and the Hermes observation strongly suggest that some northwestern and west-central Germans in Texas towns favored German regionalism. Most east-central German-Texans apparently did not. Texans from the southern German region also differed significantly from west-central German immigrants. Yet we cannot assert that the southern Germans in Texas towns contrasted drastically with those in Buffalo, N.Y. who favored regionalism. To provide a more convincing argument, we need to consider several other factors which, when added together, could have influenced intraregional marriage, and which might have formed a deterrent to German-American homogeneity in Texas.

II. Adding Together the Potential for Intraregional Marriage and Regional Segregation

Gustav Seekatz and Anna Luise Elisabeth Lenz were typical of a German-Texan town couple who decided on an intraregional marriage. The same regional origins, their ranking within the New Braunfels economic hierarchy, and the extent of their ability to move from place to place—all of these circumstances together seemed to contribute toward their decision to marry. Both were born in the west-central region: Gustav came from Rennerod, Nassau; Elisabeth, from Offenbach, Hesse-Darmstadt. Gustav came to Texas as a bachelor. His father was a baker; his brother a butcher. Gustav fit into the lower-middle class. During his initial years in the state, Gustav worked temporarily as a wagoner until he could accumulate the capital needed to start his own butcher shop. Elisabeth's father became a lower-middle class farmer. Gustav and Elisabeth lived in separate town sectors before their marriage. By the time they married at the German Protestant Church in 1855, Gustav likely had visited his brother in New Braunfels' town center on different occasions for four to seven years. Elisabeth had lived with her parents and other family members for around eight years in a New Braunfels suburb. She depended on her father for transportation into the town center and did not go into town regularly each spring until her confirmation in 1853.[14]

Table 3 reflects the economic advantages and disadvantages of Gustav Seekatz and other immigrants. The family leaders and independent

Table 3   Aggregate Distribution of Family Heads and Independent Bachelors
           by Socioeconomic Classification and Region of Birth, 1850 and 1860
           (in percent)

Region of Birth	Upper	Socioeconomic classification: Upper-Middle	Lower-Middle	Upper-Working	Lower-Working	Region Total
		1850 (N=133)				
North-West	1.50	3.01	8.18*	1.50	6.77	20.96
West-Central	3.01	4.51	13.43*	3.01	9.77	33.73
South	-0-	2.26	3.01	.75	5.46*	11.48
East-Central	-0-	-0-	3.01*	.75	.75	4.51
North-East	-0-	5.46	13.43*	3.01	7.42	29.32
Overall	4.51	15.24	41.06*	9.02	30.17	100.00
		1860 (N=346)				
North-West	2.60	4.05	6.35*	2.89	5.78	21.67
West-Central	2.31	1.45	9.54*	2.31	5.78	21.39
South	.58	1.73	4.34*	1.45	4.34*	12.44
East-Central	-0-	.87	2.31*	1.16	1.16	5.50
North-East	2.89	6.35	12.71*	4.34	12.71*	39.00
Overall	8.38	14.45	35.25*	12.15	29.77	100.00

*regional peak
   Note: This table does not include independent persons or family heads whose region
and/or occupation are unknown.
   Source: Chiefly censuses for years indicated, suppl. by other information within Kattner
Project and Texas Demography Project databases.

individuals represented by this table emigrated from a variety of regions and
worked in numerous jobs. The table does not refer to specific occupations
like butcher or baker, or to a category such as "artisan/craftworker." Offering
a better way to determine the extent of German unity within mid-19th-
century Texas, the classification here cuts across occupational lines to take
into account varying degrees of property ownership and employer/employee
relations.[15] For example, a town-dwelling farmer like Franz Hoppe who
owned two lots in Yorktown and over 100 acres outside could hardly be
classified equally with a farmer such as Karl Meisner who merely rented a
small house located on a town lot.[16] In this case, Hoppe would rank in the
upper economic class; Meisner, in the lower working class. Both wealth and
employer/employee relations separated the two men despite their joint
occupational title of "farmer" during the summer months. On the one hand,

Meisner could have depended on the seasonal work offered by either town shop owners or independent farmers. On the other hand, Hoppe more often had opportunities for economic and political control. If not supervising the work on his acreage, Hoppe could have been elected or appointed to handle town or government affairs.[17]

The largest percentage of family leaders and independent bachelors, regardless of regional origin, fit into the lower middle-class category during the summers of 1850 and 1860. Percentages tagged with asterisks on Table 3 suggest this.[18] As in the case of Gustav Seekatz, not all artisans and craft workers envisioned an immediate future in which they could apply their skills. In fact, some chose farming over shop work when demand for their skills remained low. Thus, many independent town-dwelling farmers like Elisabeth Lenz's father also fit into the lower middle-class category.

Since a large portion of the family heads and independent men from a variety of regions were of the same lower-middle classification, we should not be surprised that regional origin and economic rank together usually did not influence intraregional marriage. A regression analysis involving the backgrounds of 257 men substantiates this point. According to an analysis of regression, the additive elements of regional origin and economic rank made no significant contribution toward intraregional marriage in most cases. Returning to the case of Gustav Seekatz, we can add that his lower-middle classification and west-central heritage did not necessarily ensure that he would select a bride from his own region. Gustav easily could have chosen another woman of his same economic class but from another region.

Table 4 portrays summer snapshots for sample subpopulations as they appeared in 1850 and in 1860. This table accounts not only for family leaders and self-supporting bachelors but also for children and other dependents. It omits individuals whose records or whose parental documents indicate the region of birth as "Prussia" or "Germany". Each town's sample involves persons whose addresses and/or lot numbers have been proven and people positioned on census lists between verified names. Asterisks on Table 4 designate the region with the largest percentage in each sample subpopulation. Thus, an asterisk appears beside northeastern Germans who composed about three-fourths of Yorktown's population.

Within towns like Yorktown, some regional groups outnumbered others for a variety of reasons. Several settlers of Yorktown and Galveston during the 1850s had come to Texas in the 1830s as the children of former Prussian Junkers and well-to-do northwestern German merchants and professionals.[19] The earliest settlers of New Braunfels and Fredericksburg had responded to the mid-1840s recruitment efforts of the *Texasverein* that had aimed mainly at

Table 4   Regional Distribution of German Population by Town

Town:		Region of Heritage for Sample Population [1]				
		North-West	West-Central	South	East-Central	North-East
Galveston	1850					
[2]	(N=173)	28.3*	15.6	17.3	15.1	23.7
	(1860)					
	(N=101)	24.8	15.8	6.9	24.8	27.7*
NewBraunfels						
& suburbs	1850					
	(N=613)	40.6*	40.4*	11.9	4.1	3.0
	1860					
	(N=877)	39.2	42.1*	13.2	3.3	2.2
Fredericksburg						
	1850					
	(N=176)	20.5	48.9*	6.3	5.1	19.2
	1860					
	(N=497)	19.7	37.0*	9.5	4.8	29.0
Yorktown	1860					
	(N=259)	10.5	2.3	11.2	5.4	70.6*
Overall	1850					
	(N=962)	34.7	37.5*	11.9	6.2	9.7
	1860					
	(N=1734)	28.5	33.2*	11.5	5.3	21.5

*largest regional group(s) in town for year indicated.
1—Does not include the heritage of Texas-born children whose parents came from different regions although the birthplaces of all parents in sample appear on this table.
2—Information for Galveston mainly represents Catholics in St. Joseph's parish, and Lutherans who either lived in one of the other three towns by 1910 or had relatives who did so.
    Source: Chiefly censuses for years indicated, suppl. by other information in Kattner Project and Texas Demography Project.

artisans and craftsmen of the northwestern and west-central regions. These men sought security away from the unstable social and economic conditions of central Europe. A few professionals who had arrived in the 1830s were recruited as local administrators for the society. Many professional men had already established their families by the 1840s; they brought their wives and children to the two towns. The majority of the society's members remained in Europe.[20] Unlike the other three towns, Galveston saw a large influx of unmarried laborers, dock workers, and domestic servants in addition to members of the lower middle class. Most Protestants arrived in Galveston during the 1850s from the northeastern region; Catholics generally hailed from the southern German region.[21] Between 1848 and 1854, a number of new residents in New Braunfels, Fredericksburg, and Galveston included well-educated men and women, together with their children, who fled the social and political turmoil of both central regions.[22]

The case of east-central Germans provides an exceptional situation among all regional groups who settled in, or passed through, the four towns of this study. We have already seen on Fig. 4 that east-central Germans were the least likely to intramarry. As Table 5 has shown, other regional groups outnumbered them in all towns during both census years except in Galveston in 1860. Ordinary circumstances placed east-central German young people at a distinct disadvantage in terms of finding a spouse from their own region. When east-central German men did marry intraregionally, their economic situations often influenced their selection of brides. In fact, the variation in intraregional marriages among almost one-fourth of the east-central German men in a sample of 32 can be explained by a highranking economic situation.[23] According to the information on Table 3, most east-central European workers in 1850 and 1860 came as members of the lower middle class. By 1860 some upper-middle class people from the east-central region had also moved into towns from nearby acre-lots. These and other well-educated east-central German men carefully selected wives from their own regional and economic group.

Census-based descriptions of individual towns like Galveston and Fredericksburg give the impression that each town's regional makeup during the summer was typical for the entire year; perhaps, for the years in between censuses. The year-round effects of town and region, when added together, were statistically significant in determining intraregional marriage. Nonetheless, such an effect influenced marriage selections very little. A groom's regional background, when considered with his adopted town's general characteristics, accounted for less than one-tenth of his chances for selecting a woman from his own region.[24] If we add in his economic rank, we may be disappointed to discover that the effects of "region + town + rank" equaled only 7.6% of the reasons for a groom's marrying intraregionally.[25]

The experiences among the young people in Galveston and Yorktown differed dramatically from those marriage choices made by persons in New Braunfels and Fredericksburg. Whereas half of the persons who married intraregionally in New Braunfels and Fredericksburg did so due to the general characteristics of the towns in which they lived, only one-third of the persons marrying intraregionally in Yorktown and Galveston did so for this reason.[26] Contrasting transportation situations provided the same low percentage of intraregional marriage. A lack of horses and a slowdown in the state's railroad development within the fourth district almost isolated Yorktown. Whether due to poverty or choice, few men owned horses within the town. Having such transportation limitations and with few familial

connections among Germans in the other towns of this study, anyone except
northeastern German men likely could not help but marry someone from
outside his or her regional group. As shown on Fig.1, extensive railroad
transportation by 1860 linked Galveston with moderately German-populated
counties within east-central Texas. A favorable transportation system
provided contact with eligible Germans outside the town limits. In-coming
immigrants expanded marriage choices.[27]

Local assurance of intraregional marriage in New Braunfels often
depended on geographic segregation. Regional groups settling in and passing
through this town and its suburbs utilized the water barriers shown on Fig. 2
to segregate themselves and to provide environments which favored
intraregional marriage among persons dominating particular town and
suburban neighborhoods. Landowners and speculators often encouraged
regional segregation. Immigrants from west-central Europe mainly lived in
the town center; northwestern Germans usually preferred—or were encouraged by west-central Germans—to live in the suburbs northwest of the Comal
River.[28]

The male control of transportation and women's usual restriction to
movement on foot influenced the incidence of intraregional marriage in
Fredericksburg as well as New Braunfels. Although men could travel on
horseback beyond both towns, most single women had no form of
transportation when fathers or male employers were gone. Only the daughters
of political refugees and well-to-do businessmen had access to horses and
buggies. Except among these young women, female participants at various
courtship activities depended in a large measure upon the willingness of
male household members or prospective grooms to transport them when
events were held outside the immediate geographic area.[29]

As we have looked at different scenarios in New Braunfels,
Fredericksburg and elsewhere, we have found little variation. Two
combinations of factors significantly affected intraregional marriage: region +
town, and region + town + rank. Yet each of these combinations accounted for
less than 10% of the reasons behind intraregional marriage. We also found
that east-central Germans continued to differ substantially from the men of
other regions. When, on rare occasions, they chose wives from their own
region, east-central German men did so somewhat due to their preference for
east-central German women of their own economic rank. In contrast with
these German-Americans, and with wealthy southern Germans in Buffalo as
well, southern Germans of the upper and upper-middle classes in Texas
towns did not seem to link wealth and region when selecting spouses.
Nonetheless, most German-Texan townspeople had limited resources and

married accordingly. Therefore, we may speculate that economic rather than regional or ethnic ties could have bound most of them together. Before reaching a conclusion regarding German-American homogeneity, we need to examine the role of religion.

III. The Special Effect of Religion

Table 5 reveals the overall importance of religion to German-Texan newlyweds. This table explains 80.2% of the variation in marriage choices.[30] Knowing the religion of both spouses thus increases our understanding of all marriage choices by 20% over only knowing their regions of birth. Diagonal percentages underscore religious attachment in that these percentages are higher than their corresponding row and column figures. We may also note that Catholic grooms more often chose brides outside their religion than did other men. Although Catholic men made up five-sixths of all Catholics who married, they selected Catholic brides only three-fourths of the time.

Table 5   Distribution of All Sample Marriages by Religion in Four Texas Towns, 1845-1860

%Grooms
%Brides

	(N)	Bride's Religion		All Grooms:	
		Protestant	Catholic	%	(N)
		98.26	1.74	79.49	(345)
	Protestant	94.17	8.11		
Groom's		(339)	(6)		
Religion		23.60	76.40	20.51	(89)
	Catholic	5.83	91.89		
		(21)	(68)		
All Brides:					
	%	82.95	17.05	100.00	
	(N)	(360)	(74)	(434)	

Phi coefficient=.802 (statistically significant)
    Source: Kattner Project and Texas Demography Project databases using 2x2 table analysis.

Aside from the Catholic groom exception, we may inaccurately assume that most people would sacrifice regional homogeneity to maintain religious unity. Additional information leads us to question this supposition. According to a regression analysis, religion alone did not significantly influence German-Texan men's decisions to select wives from their own regions or vice versa. Randomly adding a knowledge of regional background with the religious preference of a prospective spouse did increase the likelihood for intraregional marriage. However, such a random combination accounted for less than 3% of the instances where an individual chose a marriage partner from the same region.[31]

An examination of the social relations among the people of New Braunfels and Fredericksburg suggests a more deliberate attempt to match brides and grooms having the same region and religion. Although Catholics from many regions could settle in or near New Braunfels, unmarried west-central German Catholics were encouraged to settle in Fredericksburg.[32] Dominican Sr. Felicity (Bach) challenged the leadership among west-central Protestants in New Braunfels who likely caused the problem. She did so by opening a Catholic school in 1860 which provided a formal education for wealthy Protestant and Catholic, Anglo- and German-American girls. Although she also accepted west-central German orphans, Sr. Felicity probably did so with an aim toward training nun-teachers. The town's leaders reacted to the opening of the school by physically and mentally harassing Sr. Felicity until, within less than a year, she left.[33] By their actions, the leadership seemed to indicate that they did not want potential Anglo-American daughters-in-law to acquire a Catholic education. More importantly, town representatives wanted no young Protestant bachelor from the west-central region to be influenced by a Catholic wife. Contrary to the state of Nassau ideal, at that time, of Catholic and Protestant cooperation, the social and political leaders of New Braunfels reverted to 16th- and 17th-century religious antagonism that had plagued the west-central German region.[34]

New Braunfels and Fredericksburg were not the only towns where regionalism and religious devotion were closely linked. Not one of the regional groups in any of the towns of this study differed on this point. Therefore, being from the same region and having the same religion provided the most important reason for marrying intraregionally. Such a special effect accounted for 87.8% of the incidence of intraregional marriage.[35] This extremely high percentage is eight times greater than any other single or combined set of circumstances affecting intraregional marriage.

Our findings substantiate those of Yox who found close ties between regional affinity among southern Germans and their dedication to Catholicism. In Texas, southern German Protestants separated themselves from southern German Catholics just as west central Protestants and Catholics lived separate lives. As in other towns of the U. S., religion by itself provided little cause for unity in densely populated German-Texan areas.

Protestants did not marry Protestants just because they had the same religion. Likewise, Protestant town leaders did not segregate non-Protestants simply due to religious differences.

IV. Germans in Texas and the South

This paper has revealed instances in which German-Texans did not form one distinct cultural group. East-central German men, in particular, made marriage choices that differed from other regional groups. Among regional subgroups, the intersection of regional and religious ties prevented unification throughout the fourth district. Such separation of groups among German-Texan town dwellers probably prevented German men of the third and fourth districts from forming a powerful political force on the state level as well.

Unlike the divisive outcome of combining regional background with religious affiliation, economic circumstances did provide some potential for lower-middle-class unity. Members of this class clearly outnumbered other economic groups in heavily German-populated towns. Nonetheless, linkages between religious preferences and regional identities, as reflected in the marriages of almost half of our sample, likely contributed toward the failure of this class from reaching its full potential. In addition, women and men of the lower-middle class did not have access to policy-making power: women, because they had no right to vote, and men, because most voted for state representatives who stood behind the profit-seeking secessionists of the third district.[36]

A brief analysis of secession in 1861 underscores the inability of German-Texans to form an homogeneous ethnic group. When the direct vote concerning secession was taken, all of the four German-populated counties in the third district supported the cause. In the fourth district, 6 out of 14 counties with a large percentage of ethnic Germans did so. Of the four towns of this study, only Fredericksburg opposed the movement.[37]

Outside of Texas, German-Americans of the U.S. South faced additional problems in forming one homogeneous cultural unit that could have prompted social and economic reforms prior to the Civil War. German immigrants and their children composed about 25% of the whites who lived in antebellum ports like New Orleans, Natchez, Charleston, Richmond, and Baltimore. Among these people, professionals, moderately wealthy merchants, and other members of the upper-middle class had to decide if they would continue the prevalent socialization and economic support of young unmarried German women. Customarily, upper-middle class families hired German youths as domestic servants before these young women married. However, fairly well-off families from the northwestern and southern regions decided to buy and rent female slaves instead. In so doing, well-to-do people from Hanover, Mecklenburg, Oldenburg, and Bavaria—while thereby attaining social and economic stature among Anglo-Southerners—were failing to aid German-Americans of lower classes.[38]

Lower-middle class German-Americans, whose predominant region is yet to be discovered, also decided to live in southern ports. However, these families and independent bachelors had no economic or social use for slaves. Port life offered German men the prospects of financial security through their own ability to pursue their usual occupations as self-supporting artisans and craftsmen.[39]

Within ports and other towns of the antebellum South, the absence of a coalition based on ethnic identity may have significantly influenced the nature of formal and informal political participation among both men and women. If so, then intraregional marriage and regional segregation probably played important roles in the politics of everyday life. Both within and outside of Texas, social and economic advantages and disadvantages resulting from marriage selections and settlement patterns likely contributed toward regional variations in ethnic/black interaction and in the maintenance of economic power. If so, the secession crisis in particular, and German attitudes about racism in general, may need re-interpretation to uncover conflicts and compromises as two kinds of regionalism intersected. As a result of such a re-interpretation, we may provide a greater understanding of long-term similarities as well as differences between German-American regional affinities and "white" Southern cultural identities.

Notes

For support with this project the author thanks the Jane Blaffer Owen's Scholar Fund, the Henry DuBois Scholarship Committee, and the Llano Branch of the American Assoc. of Univ. Women. Thanks also to Walter Kamphoefner, Myron Gutmann, Shearer Davis Bowman, Thomas Pullum, and Robert Frizzell for their comments, and to Harry Vernon Kattner, Elaine Bargsley, Myron Gutmann, Kenneth Fliess, and Jane Zachritz for technical assistance.

[1]Milton Gordon, *Assimilation in American Life: The Role of Race, Religion, and National Origins* (New York, 1964), 27, 32f., 63ff., 71, 76, 97ff., 121-131, 202, 212.

[2]Andrew Yox, "Ethnic Loyalties of the Alsatians in Buffalo, 1829-1855," *Yearbook of German-American Studies* 20 (1985): 105-121.

[3]*Karte des Staates Texas* (Wiesbaden, 1851), printed map, at Univ. of Texas, Barker Texas History Center (herein: BTHC); Carl H. Moneyhon, *Republicanism in Reconstruction Texas* (Austin, 1980), 10ff; J.D.B. deBow, *Statistical View of the U.S. Compendium of the 7th Census*

of the U.S.: 1850, Report prep. for the Bureau of the Census (Washington, D.C., 1854), 310, 514ff; Joseph C.G. Kennedy, *Agriculture of the U.S. in 1860*, Report prep. for the Bureau of the Census (Washington, D.C., 1864), 73.

[4]For Fig. 2, I utilized maps found in BTHC, including: New Braunfels and Fredericksburg printed maps contained in Verein zum Schutze dt. Einwanderer nach Texas, *Instruktion f. dt. Auswanderer nach Texas nebst der Neusten Karte dieses Staates: nach dessen Grenzbestimmungen durch Congress Beschluss vom Sept. 1850* (1850); S.V. Pfeuffer, "Map of New Braunfels" (1889); Sanborn Fire Ins. Co., *Man of Yorktown, Texas* (1887), printed map; William H. Sandusky, *Plan of the City of Galveston, Texas* (1845), printed map. Ward boundaries for Galveston are explained in city codes for 1854.

[5]David G. McComb, *Galveston: A History* (Austin, 1986), 43; U.S. Bureau of the Census, Galveston Co., Tex. Census, 1850 (Washington, D.C.: Nat. Arch. Microfilms Publ., 1964), microfilm, M-432; U.S. Bureau of the Census, Galveston Co., Tex. Census, 1860 (Washington, D.C.: Nat. Arch. Microfilms Publ., 1964), microfilm, vol. 3, M-653; Sandusky, *Plan.*

[6]Lauren Ann Kattner, "From Immigrant Settlement to Town: New Braunfels, 1845-1870," *Amerikastudien/American Studies* 36.2 (Summer, 1991): 155-177; Nellie Murphree, *A History of Dewitt County*, ed. by Robert W. Shook (Victoria, Tex., 1962), 57; U.S. Bureau of the Census, DeWitt Co., Tex. Census, 1860 (Washington, D.C.: Nat. Arch. Microfilms Publ., 1964), microfilm; U.S. Bureau of the Census, Gillespie Co., Tex. Census, 1850 (Washington, D.C.: Nat. Arch. Microfilms Publ., 1964), microfilm; U.S. Bureau of the Census, Gillespie Co., Tex. Census, 1860 (Washington, D.C.: Nat. Arch. Microfilms Publ., 1964), microfilm.

[7]This paper uses two computerized sets of information about families as its main source of evidence: the Kattner Project and the Texas Demography Project. For sources and methods on New Braunfels, see Lauren Ann Kattner, "Growing Up and Town Development: Social and Cultural Adaptation in a German-American Town," M.A. thesis (Univ. of Texas at Dallas, 1987). Sources and methods for Galveston research in Kattner, "Ethnicity, Race, Gender, and Class: Shaping Society, Culture, and Politics in 19th-Century New Orleans and Galveston," book in progress. The construction and use of databases for the Texas Demography Project appear in Myron P. Gutmann/Kenneth H. Fliess, "Reconstructing a Hist. Community: Fredericksburg, Tex., 1846-1910," in *Proceedings of the 1986 IBM Academic Information Systems University AEP Conference "Goals for Learning,"* ed. by Frederick P. Dwyer (Milford, Conn., 1986).

[8]Wilhelm Hermes, Letter, Galveston, ca. 1848?, in *Jahrbuch 1941* (New Braunfels, Tex. *Neu-Braunfelser Zeitung*, 1941), my trans.

[9]Regional boundaries derive from the following: R. Priebsch and W.E. Collinson, *The German Language*, 6th ed. (London, 1964); William W. Hagen, "The Junkers' Faithless Servants: Peasant Insubordination and the Breakdown of Serfdom in Brandenburg-Prussia, 1763-1811," in *The German Peasantry: Conflict and Community in Rural Society from the 18th to the 20th Centuries,* ed. by Richard J. Evans/W.R. Lee (London, 1986), 71-101; Hartmut Harnisch, "Peasants and Markets: The Background to the Agrarian Reforms in Feudal Prussia East of the Elbe, 1760-1807," trans. by Bernd Feldmann/Richard J. Evans, with assistance from William W. Hagen, in Evans and Lee, *The German Peasantry*, 37-70; Lutz K. Berkner, "Inheritance, land tenure and peasant family structure: a German regional comparison," in *Family and Inheritance: Rural Society in Western Europe, 1200-1800,* ed. by Jack Goody, Joan Thirsk, and E.P. Thompson (Cambridge, England, 1976), 71-96; Hilke Guenter-Arndt/Juergen Kocka, eds., *Geschichtsbuch 3: Die Menschen u. ihre Geschichte in Darstellungen u. Dokumenten, Ausg. A: Das 19.Jahrhundert* (Berlin, 1986), 59, 112, 129.

[10]Except as otherwise noted, all statistics in this study come from analyses of information in the Kattner and Texas Demography projects. To complete these analyses, I used PC-SAS software (a product of SAS Institute, Inc.).

[11]For a specific definition and formula for the Phi coefficient, see: George W. Bohrnstedt and David Knoke, *Statistics for Social Data Analysis*, 2nd ed. (Itasca, Ill., 1988), 333ff., 356, 497.

[12]For a specific definition and illustrations of regression analysis, see Bohrnstedt and Knoke, *Statistics*, 253ff., 403ff., 495, 499.

[13]For discussion and examples of the R coefficient, see Bohrnstedt and Knoke, *Statistics*, 266ff., 392ff., 490.—Throughout the rest of this essay, R^2 and the corresponding general formula will be reported as a source for most percentages. In the present paragraph, e.g., an R of .039 times 100 equals 3.9% when intraregional marriage was influenced by the origin of the spouse (NIG=region). Regional categories correspond with those shown on Fig. 3.

[14]Protestant Church (New Braunfels), marriage records for 1855, entry #21, 28 Oct. 1855, confirmation list for 1853, and communion lists for 1847-1855; Comal Co. Censuses, 1850-1860.

[15]For further details on the classification used here, including occupational ranking, gender differentiation, agricultural classification, and merchant divisions, see Kattner, "Growing Up and Town Development."

[16]It is assumed that Meisner rented a lot because another person owned the lot on which he resided.

[17]Esp. see: Amy Elizabeth Holmes, "You Win Some, You Lose Some: The Social Bases of Local Political Office in Fredericksburg, Tex., From 1848 to 1910," B.A. honors thesis (Univ. of Texas, 1987).

[18]Adam Struve's analysis of passenger lists for Galveston between 1846 and 1850 reveals that 39.3% of a sample of 1,112 immigrant men were artisans and craftsmen. See his ms. essay, "Artisans among Galveston-Bound Immigrants, 1846/1850" (1985).

[19]Flora von Roeder, with Carol von Roeder Hamilton, Constance von Roeder, and Robert G. von Roeder, *These are the generations: A biogr. of the Von Roeder Family and its role in Texas history* (Houston, 1978), 24ff., 41ff., 55ff., 70ff., 91; Rosa von Roeder Kleberg, autobiogr., trans. by Rudolph Kleberg, Jr., in *The Golden Free Land: The Reminiscences and Letters of Women on an American Frontier*, ed. by Crystal Sasse Ragsdale, 21-33.

[20]Kattner, "Immigrant Settlement"; Myron P. Gutmann, "Denomination and Fertility Decline: The Catholics and Protestants of Gillespie Co., Texas," *Continuity and Change* 5.3 (Dec., 1990): 393, 400f.

[21]Kattner Project database.

[22]For examples see: William W. Newcomb, Jr., with Mary S. Carnahan, *German Artist on the Texas Frontier: Friedrich Richard Petri* (Austin, 1978), 13, 15, 19, 65, 69, 77, 82, 84, and James Patrick McGuire, *Herman Lungkwitz: Romantic Landscapist on the Texas Frontier* (Austin, 1983), 6-19.

[23]The appr. standardized coefficient is .245 for east-central German men when NIG=region. It is statistically significant.

[24]R^2 =.068 when intraregional marriage was influenced by randomly combining town of marriage with regional origin (NIG=town+region). Town and region categories correspond to those found on Fig. 2 and 3.

[25]R^2 =.076 when intraregional marriage was influenced by the addition of the town of marriage, regional backgrounds, and groom's economic rank (NIG=town+region+rank). Town

and region categories correspond to those found on Fig. 2 and 3 respectively; rank categories were numbered 1 to 5 with 1 being the highest.

[26]R^2 =.033 when intraregional marriage was influenced by the characteristics of the town of marriage (NIG=town). Percentages intramarrying due to town characteristics were: New Braunfels, 53.33; Fredericksburg, 48.82; Yorktown, 29.16; and Galveston, 29.41.

[27]Regarding railroad development, see: Charles S. Potts, *Railroad Transportation in Texas* (Austin, 1909); St. Clair Griffin Reed, *A History of the Texas Railroads and of Transportation Conditions under Spain and Mexico and the Republic and the State* (Houston, 1941); Moneyhon, *Republicanism*, 7ff., 12ff.

[28]Kattner, "Growing up Female in New Braunfels: Social and Cultural Adaptation in a German-Texan Town, 1845-1885," *Journal of American Ethnic Hist.* 9.2 (Spring, 1990): 1-24.

[29]Kattner, "Growing up Female"; Mathilda Doebbler Gruen Wagner, oral history, transcr. by Winifred S. Cade [ca. 1940], in Ragsdale, *Golden Free Land*, 157-168.

[30]Phi coefficient =.802 when marriages of all religious combinations are considered.

[31]R^2 =.0398 when intraregional marriage was affected by the random addition of regional background to religious preference (NIG=region+religion).

[32]Kattner and Texas Demography project databases.—The verb "encouraged" is used here because family stories indicate that Catholics were asked to leave New Braunfels.

[33]Sr. Mary Generosa (Callahan), *The History of the Sisters of Divine Providence San Antonio, Tex.* (Milwaukee, 1955); Shiela Hackett, *Dominican Women in Texas: From Ohio to Galveston and Beyond* (Houston, 1986); *New Braunfels, 1860 Census.*

[34]Wolf-Heino Struck, "Die nassauische Simultanschule," *Herzogtum Nassau 1860-1866: Politik. Wirtschaft. Kultur* (Wiesbaden, 1981), 253f.; Gerald Strauss, *Nuremberg in the 16th Century*, rev. ed. (Bloomington, 1976); Gerald Lyman Soliday, *A Community in Conflict: Frankfurt Society in the 17th and early 18th Centuries.*

[35]R2 =.878 when intraregional marriage was influenced by the interaction of the same regional background and the same religious preference for each couple (NIG=same region+same religion).

[36]Walter L. Buenger, *Secession and the Union in Texas* (1984); Moneyhon, *Republicanism*, 7ff., 12ff.—For upper middle-class German-Texan women's politically-related views on republicanism and slavery, see the following in Ragsdale's *Golden Free Land*: Kleberg, autobiogr., 25f., 29ff.; Louise Ernst Stoehr, autobiogr. [1884], 4; and letters by Elise Kuckuck Willrich to Georg Ludwig Kuckuck, Mt. Eliza (Fayette Co.) Tex., 18 April 1848 and 21 April 1848, 55, 58ff.; Elise Kuckuck Willrich to Gretchen Keuffel, Mt. Eliza, 26 Sept. 1849, 62; Amanda Fallier von Rosenberg to Rev. Theil, Galveston, 9 Dec. 1849, 117f.; Amanda Fallier von Rosenberg to Johanna Fallier, Farm Nassau (Fayette Co.), 29 March 1850, 120f., 125ff.

[37]Buenger, *Secession;* Moneyhon, *Republicanism*, 7ff., 12ff.

[38]Kattner, "Status, Cost, or Ethnicity? A reexamination of immigration and urban slavery, 1836-1850" (1988); "Race, Ethnicity, and Single Parenthood in the South, 1845-1885," presented at the Social Science Hist. Assoc. Annual Meeting, Washington, D.C., 1989.

[39]Kattner, "Status"; Kattner, "Race"; Michael P. Johnson and James L. Roarck, *Black Masters: A Free Family of Color in the Old South* (NY, 1984), 173-187.

16 | Paths of Urbanization: St. Louis in 1860

Walter D. Kamphoefner, *Texas A & M University*

Pencilled into the margin of the 1860 census manuscripts of the Second Ward of St. Louis is the wry comment, "This is the enumerator who gave such a fuss." The enumerator was Edward Thierry, a civil engineer and draftsman from Saxe-Meiningen in Germany, the census taker for the Second Ward. The fuss that he gave was to take the census with Teutonic thoroughness, recording not just state of birth but also the home town or county for most ward residents. In Thierry's own case, for example, we know that his wife's origins were in the big city of Bremen, miles and miles away from his native Thuringia. Perhaps they had married in America, since they had no children born in Europe. But their path to St. Louis was in any case quite indirect. Around 1843 when their first child was born they were living in McCracken Co., KY, the Paducah area. In 1849 they had their second child, this time in St. Francis Co., AK, a little southwest of Memphis. They had probably been in St. Louis about ten years, since their eight-year old and all subsequent children were born in the Gateway City. Information such as this is available for most of the inhabitants of the Second Ward.

The census taker's over-zealousness gives us the opportunity to pursue several questions that normally remain inaccessible on the basis of U.S. census data. First of all, one can gain a much more precise picture of the degree of homogeneity or heterogeneity of the immigrant population, and the extent of local and regional clustering as a result of chain migration. By comparing the birthplaces of household heads with that of their spouses, children, and other household members, one can measure the strength of regional loyalties, the amount of migration experienced by married couples before emigration, and the effects that such factors exerted on social mobility in the American city. We can also ask how many inhabitants of American cities were of urban backgrounds, and what difference did this make with regard to their position on the economic and social scale.

The Second Ward presented a good cross-section of the St. Louis population in 1860 in terms of social class. It was in no sense a neighborhood, just a long, narrow strip drawn arbitrarily from the riverfront to the western city limits; it spanned the social scale from the rough levee district and the literally floating population living on steamboats, to the fashionable neighborhoods around Lafayette Park and the mansions of the recently annexed suburbs, housing the likes of James Eads, who even before his bridge building feats was worth $400,000. Eads was among the small minority of Anglo-Americans in his ward, which forms part of the heavily German south side of St. Louis.

In its ethnic composition, Ward Two was highly skewed. About two-thirds of all inhabitants over age 21 had been born in the Federation of German States, and besides these there were substantial numbers of German speakers from Switzerland, Alsace, and the Austro-Hungarian Empire. Irish, making up 7%, were the largest immigrant group besides Germans, and together with a scattering from Britain and the Western Hemisphere they brought the proportion of English-speaking immigrants up to 10%. Out of an adult population of over 3,200 females and nearly 3,700 males, there were barely 300 adults of each gender, less than 10%, born in the U.S.[1]

One of the questions that I am pursuing on the basis of Second Ward data is to what extent an urban environment broke down the regional loyalties of German immigrants, which persisted to a considerable extent in the rural Midwest, as my earlier research has shown. I have attempted to identify all the German places of birth of Second Ward residents and used the four-digit German postal codes (replaced by a five-digit code in 1993) to systematize this information. It became immediately clear that the makeup of this urban immigrant population was of diverse geographic origins, but there are some distinct clusters that can be identified as well. Moreover, there are entire districts of Germany that were virtually unrepresented in the ward.

Although St. Louis as a whole had more than its share of North Germans, two of the largest clusters in the Second Ward were from South Germany (see Fig. 1). The largest concentration was from the adjacent 75 and 76 postal zones in Baden, which together accounted for over 300 immigrants or 9.5% of all with specified birthplaces. In fact, 64 of those or nearly 2% hailed from the town of Forbach alone, though it was a town of less than 2,000 inhabitants. There was another large cluster, 190 people or nearly 6%, from the Bavarian Palatinate, postal zone 67, on the opposite side of the Rhine. The postal zones are further subdivided by two more digits, and 25 towns of the first 50 in the 6700 range were represented in Ward Two, and 36 of the

Figure 1   Pre-1993 German Postal Codes

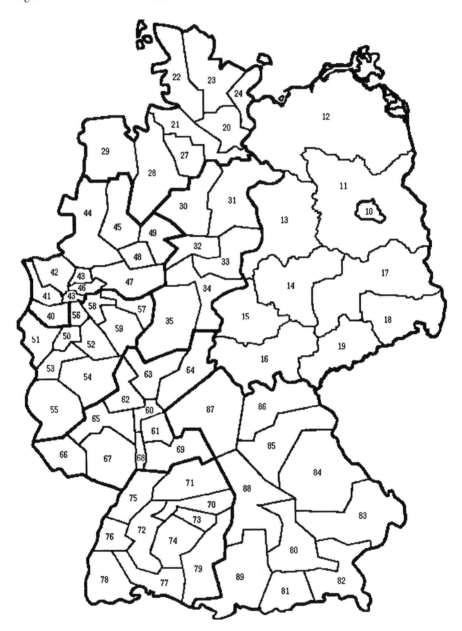

100 all told, though no single zip code accounted for more than the 22, 27, and 20 respectively claimed by Landau, its surrounding villages, and Edenkoben.

Another of the larger clusters was from the northwest German area around Osnabrück, the 45 postal zone on Fig.1, which was also the source of several chain migration communities in rural Missouri. In Ward Two there were 164 immigrants (5% of all those who gave exact birthplaces) from the Osnabrück zone, and 78, 50, and 63 immigrants respectively from the adjacent 44, 48, and 49 postal zones around Münster, Bielefeld, and Minden in Prussian Westfalia. Moreover, many of the 240 immigrants who merely listed their home state of Hannover were probably from the Osnabrück area as well.[2]

The degree of local and regional clustering in urban areas, however, pales by comparison with that in rural immigrant communities, both in relative terms and even in absolute numbers. The tiny Duchy of Brunswick, about 0.3% of Germany's population, accounted for over one-fifth of all Germans in Cape Girardeau Co., MO, a total of nearly 500 people or 100 more than in all of St. Louis.[3] One single Westfalian town, Westerkappeln, could claim over 200 immigrants in the adjacent Missouri counties of St. Charles and Warren. Warren Co. was also home to 343 immigrants from the tiny principality of Lippe Detmold, compared to just 81 in all of St. Louis.[4]

In contrast to the clusters mentioned above, some parts of Germany were virtually unrepresented in the Second Ward. The Bavarian areas in the extreme southeast of the Federal Republic, (zones 80 through 84 and 89), were represented by just 18 towns, and only 44 individuals all told. Similarly, except for 33 people from the immigrant port of Hamburg, the extreme north of Germany, zones 20 through 24, accounted for just 27 persons from 14 scattered towns. The same is largely true of the East German coastal plain that extends out from Hamburg; there were only 41 Mecklenburgers in the ward, and except for Thuringia and Saxony, East German areas in general were lightly represented.

A similar pattern emerges with the Irish and Swiss populations of the ward: a broad field of recruitment, but considerable clustering. These immigrants usually specified only the county or canton of birth. Every one of Ireland's 32 counties was represented in the ward, but of the nearly 600 Irish, over 10% hailed from Tipperary. Similarly, present in the Second Ward were immigrants from all of Switzerland's 21 cantons except three of the smallest, but of the 475 Swiss, over 100 had origins in Canton Aargau, right along the German border adjoining Baden, or just south of the 78 postal zone in the extreme lower left of the Fig. 1.[5]

The exact birthplaces reported in the Second Ward can also be used to reconstruct, at least for families with children, the paths immigrants followed to St. Louis and the places they stopped along the way. One can compare different immigrant groups, or Germans from various regions, in this respect.

Of all American-born children of German parentage in the Second Ward, 11.6% had been born outside St. Louis, suggesting that most German families wasted little time on their way to the Gateway City. Their Irish neighbors, by contrast, were more than twice as likely to have made stops along the way. One-fourth of all Irish-American children in the ward had been born outside St. Louis, and the rate was even higher for British-Americans.[6] Swiss and Bohemians, however, fell into a similar range as Germans.

Germans from different regions showed different propensities and patterns of stopping along the way. Groups that were heavily concentrated in St. Louis were most likely to have migrated directly there. While the overall stopover rate (proportion of German-American children born outside St. Louis) was 11.6%, it was 9.4% for natives of Hannover, below 6% for neighboring Westfalia, and a mere 3% for immigrants from the Osnabrück region (postal code 45), the core of a chain migration community. The migration clusters from the Palatinate and central Baden (postal codes 67, 75 and 76) also showed below average stopover rates, about 8.5%. By contrast, areas that were sparsely represented in St. Louis, such as Württemberg and the East Elbian region, showed considerably higher stopover rates, both at 19%. This suggests that immigrants of these origins made their decision to locate in St. Louis only after arriving in America.[7]

Regional origin also influenced *where* immigrants stopped off. For example, 8 of 15 stopovers in Wisconsin were made by East Elbians, who were heavily concentrated in that state though they made up only 15% of Second Ward Germans; 8 of 19 stopovers in Philadelphia were made by Württembergers, who accounted for triple their nationwide share of that city's Germans. Baltimore, by contrast, had a heavy concentration of Hessians, who made 4 of the 10 stopovers there. Overall, states on the Eastern seaboard accounted for one-third of all stopovers, but only for 5 of 33 (15%) by natives of Hannover. Of course, with the small numbers involved not every city or state has such easily explainable stopover rates. But these patterns do provide additional evidence that random, Brownian motion is not the appropriate metaphor for immigration; rather, its paths were structured by the ties of personal contacts, family and friends who had gone before.[8]

Moves by immigrant families from rural to urban America were relatively rare, judging by Second Ward data. For the majority of Germans, American cities constituted the way-stations on the road to St. Louis. In 1860, 35% of all German-Americans outside St. Louis lived in cities of over 20,000, but at least 54% of all German children born on the way to St. Louis listed such big cities as birthplaces, (one and one-half times the expected rate). Even most of the stops along the way outside such major urban centers apparently were in smaller towns rather than on farms. Only 25 of the nearly 350 German children born on the way to St. Louis listed a county rather than a city or town as their birthplace.[9] There were only 21 German children born in Missouri outside St. Louis Co., fewer than in Cincinnati alone. It appears that Latin farmers may have been especially prone to such rural-urban migration. For example, the Latin settlement of Belleville and several nearby towns were the leading source of German in-migration from Illinois.

The concentration of German-Americans along water routes was also very evident despite the advances in railroad building by 1860. Of the 25 German children born in Iowa, all hailed from towns or counties on the Mississippi except five from the Iowa City area and one from Council Bluffs on the Missouri. Thirteen of the 17 born in Kentucky hailed from Louisville, and at least two others from river towns; Indiana, lacking a big river town, accounted for a mere four stopovers.

Table 1   Extrafamilial German Household Members by Birthplace of Head of Household

	Male Boarders		Female Domestics	
Birthplace of Head	**N**	**%**	**N**	**%**
USA	6	1.7	15	12.8
Europe outside Germany	34	9.6	25	21.4
Different German State	224	63.9	54	46.2
Same German State	65	18.4	18	15.4
Same District	9	2.5	1	0.9
Same County	2	0.6	1	0.9
Same Town	14	4.0	3	2.6

If provincial loyalties and associations based on common origins influenced the paths immigrants followed to St. Louis, how important were they in shaping the ethnic community once people arrived at their destinations? A look at the two most common forms of extrafamilial household members, male boarders and female domestics, showed very little evidence of any local or regional ties (Table 1). True, relatively few Germans resided under American roofs, not even 2% of male boarders and only one-eighth of the female domestics in the Second Ward (though the proportion might well have been higher in more fashionable Anglo wards). Non-German Europeans were much more popular than Americans as landlords or employers. Most German boarders and servants, however, resided with fellow Germans, though regional origins in the homeland played little or no role in their location. Only one-fifth of the women and one-fourth of the men lived with someone from as near as the same state, and only 3 or 4% lived with someone from the same town. But since boarders and domestics make up such a small proportion of the German population, and since they tended to be recent arrivals in the city, perhaps this is not the best test of regional loyalties.

Intermarriage patterns are among the best clues to cultural affinities and antipathies. This analysis is restricted to couples who had no children born outside the U.S. and for the most part presumably married after immigration. Over 1,500 German men fell into this category, and nearly 1,400 German women. This imbalance made a certain amount of intermarriage unavoidable for German males, but the question was, with whom? Certainly not the Irish: despite a considerable contingent from Catholic areas of Germany in the Second Ward, there was not a single German woman married to an Irishman, and only 8 German men who took Irish brides. Although Bohemians had endogamy rates as high as the Irish, over 80%, the foreign partners they took were mostly German. (Some of the Bohemian-born may have been Jews or *Sudetendeutsche*, but family names and the ward's St. John Nepomuk church, founded in 1855 as the nation's first Czech-language parish, leave little doubt that the majority were Slavic.) About half of all Swiss chose partners of their own kind, but of those who did not, all the Swiss women and a majority of Swiss men turned to Germans, particularly south Germans. The group that had the highest rates of intermarriage with Germans, however, were the Alsatians. Only 35 to 40% of them stayed within their own group, a smaller proportion than married Germans (particularly south Germans, as with the Swiss). The same held true for the handful of Lorrainians in the ward.

Intermarriage patterns also reveal something about the cohesiveness of German regional groups, and the strength of dialect and other regional barriers. German women, being in scarce supply, ventured outside their own group less frequently than their male counterparts: 4% of the men and barely 1% of the women took American partners; in fact only 3.3% of these women and less than 10% of the men ventured anywhere beyond German-speaking circles for partners. Still, less than half married someone from the same German state, just 42% of the men and 46% of the women. The rates were lowest for the relatively small groups from the east and far north of Germany or from the Rhineland. Nor did the Elbe River or the *Mainlinie* prove to be an insurmountable barrier where love was at stake: there was considerable intermarriage across these traditional tripartite divisions of Germany. Not surprising because of their heavy male surplus, East Germans had the highest tendency to seek partners from other German regions. South Germans stuck most to themselves, but were also the ones most likely to reach out to other Germanophones in neighboring Switzerland and Alsace.

Table 2   **German-born Heads of Household Married in the U.S.,**
Social Indicators by Birthplace of Spouse

Birthplace of Spouse	Mean Wealth	Mean Occ. Strata*	Mean Age	% Urban	N	%
USA	$3611	2.8	33.4	31	59	4.0
Europe outside German	1751	3.2	33.4	13	108	7.4
Different German State	2054	3.1	35.8	14	583	39.8
Same German State	2138	3.2	36.7	5	422	28.8
Same District	1476	3.3	37.6	2	57	3.9
Same County	1652	3.1	34.8	0	24	1.6
Same Town	1237	3.4	38.3	14	210	14.4
All	**1972**	**3.2**	**36.2**	**11**	**1463**	**100**

*high white collar, professional = 1; low white collar, proprietor = 2; skilled = 3; unskilled = 4; occupational data was missing for 181 cases.

This raises the more general question of the relationship between intermarriage and social mobility. Whether one attributes it to ambitious men or mercenary women, one would expect that immigrant men who married native women were among the most prosperous, but as was seen above, this was a relatively small group. More interesting would be to see if the same contrasts held true between men who married outside or inside their own German regional group. Table 2 analyzes the birthplaces of spouses of all German heads of household in the Second Ward who showed no children born in Germany. It compares the mean wealth level and an index of occupational strata of immigrants in relation to how far afield or how close to home they had gone, figuratively speaking, to seek a mate.[10] Although seven-eighths of all German men found brides from among their compatriots, (like census taker Thierry) they often married someone whose German roots were quite different from their own. Regional endogamy was relatively low, with not quite half marrying someone even from the same German state. It is also clear that men who were "provincial" in their choice of marriage partner were also for the most part less progressive economically than their exogamous counterparts. Men who married American women had the highest levels of wealth and occupational strata of any group; moreover, nearly a third of them hailed from German cities. There is a fairly regular progression downward, men with spouses from the same state outranking those with spouses from the same district or county. The lowest levels of both wealth and occupation were shown by men who married women from their own home towns, and this despite the fact that they included a sizeable number of urban-born. Nor were these contrasts simply a matter of age and greater opportunity to accumulate wealth; those with spouses from the same town in fact averaged five years older than those marrying Americans. Both the American melting pot and also the German-American one seem to have absorbed the most progressive immigrants first. For example, of 26 men native to Germany's free cities of Hamburg, Bremen, and Frankfurt, only two married women of the same origins.

Comparing these results with my earlier findings suggests that rates of out-group marriage generally were higher among Germans in urban than in rural America. My previous work examined the marriage patterns in three rural Missouri counties of immigrants from Lippe-Detmold, a tiny principality smaller than many midwestern counties, and constituting just one German county in the Federal Republic. Out of a group of 145 men with no German-born children in 1860, 101 or nearly 70% married someone else from Lippe-Detmold. In the Second Ward, not even half of the Germans married someone from as nearby as the same state (and usually much larger states such as Baden or Hannover). Thus urban immigrants exhibited a clear contrast with their rural counterparts in their choice of spouses.

A contributing factor in urban exogamy was the age and gender makeup of the immigrant community. The population pyramids of rural immigrants generally show a more balanced sex ratio and a broader age distribution characteristic of family immigration. Urban immigrants, on the other hand, show a concentration in the young adult age groups and a larger surplus of males typical of individual migration. The same groups that dominated among urban newcomers back in Germany were also contributing most heavily to German-American urbanization. The decision to locate in urban America was perhaps as much a function of life cycle stage as it was of occupation or previous urban background. Not only was a greater proportion of immigrants arriving in rural areas already married, but those young Germans who did marry in rural America were doing so more often under parental auspices and under the stronger influence of chain migration communities than those in the immigrant city.

The Second Ward data also allow us to pose the question of the importance of background factors in the economic arena. To pursue this issue I used both a "rifle" and a "shotgun" approach. The "rifle" approach simply involved pinpointing all immigrants who came from the Ruhr industrial region (defined as the districts of Arnsberg and Düsseldorf), and seeing how they compared with Germans as a whole. As it turned out, men from the *Ruhrgebiet* were much more heavily concentrated in the skilled trades than St. Louis Germans generally. Overall, about 45% of German men in the Second Ward labor force fell into the skilled labor category, compared to 60%

of Ruhr natives. However, a look at individual birthplaces and occupations reveals only one cluster clearly based on an imported specialty. Of seven gainfully employed men from the metalworking center of Solingen, famous for its cutlery fabrication, two called themselves cutlery and knife manufacturers, two others were blacksmiths, and another was a laborer in a foundry. Such skills notwithstanding, all were probably employees since none owned any real estate. In general, the industrial background of immigrants from the Ruhr did not appear to put them at much of a financial advantage. While their mean wealth was nearly $2,100, again half that of the average German male over 21, their median wealth was only $150, the same with Germans overall, indicating that a few wealthy individuals were pulling up the average. One reason for this unspectacular showing was that immigrants from other regions, even rural areas such as the Westfalia-Osnabrück district, were much more likely to be shopkeepers and grocers than those from the Ruhr.

I also used the "shotgun" approach to pursue on a more systematic basis the influence of urban background, isolating all Germans from cities of 20,000 and larger and seeing how they compared with their compatriots of rural or small town origins. Besides looking at census figures on wealth, I constructed an occupational index, using the Philadelphia Social History Project's code and scoring High White Collar occupations *one*; Low White Collar, *two*; Skilled Labor, *three*; and Unskilled Labor, *four* (thus the lower the index, the higher the prestige).

Among the questions posed were: how many Second Ward Germans were of urban backgrounds, and how much of an advantage did they enjoy over their compatriots from rural areas. As it turned out, relatively few had been born in urban areas. Only 15.5%, or less than one in six were from cities of 20,000 inhabitants or larger. Such cities made up 12.5% of total German population in 1871, indicating that American cities were not recruiting that heavily from German cities in absolute or relative terms.[11]

Table 3 examines the influence of urban background on German men aged 21 and over who reported an exact birthplace in the 1860 census. Immigrants with urban roots were at some advantage in the city; their mean wealth was about half again as high as that of rural immigrants. Such figures, however, are often inflated by a few extreme cases, as is indicated by the large standard deviations, over four times the size of the mean. It would be more accurate to say that the rich were disproportionately urban in origin than that those of urban origins were disproportionately rich. This becomes clear when one looks at the median, which is probably a better measure of wealth. Here, too, the city-born come off better, but the contrast is not so striking, $200 against $150 for all immigrants, and $250 vs. $200 for family

Table 3   German-born Adult Male Immigrants in Ward Two, Social Indicators by Place of Birth

	Mean Wealth	Mean Occ. Strata*	Mean Age	Median Wealth	Birthplace N	%
All Adults						
Urban	$1,893	3.0	36.8	$200	260	16.1
Rural	1,348	3.1	37.2	150	1356	83.9
Family Heads Only						
Urban	$2,325	3.0	38.0	$250	209	15.7
Rural	1,599	3.2	38.3	200	1123	83.3

* high white collar, professional = 1; low white collar, proprietor = 2; skilled = 3; unskilled = 4; occupational data was missing for 204 cases, among them 147 family heads.

heads. The occupational index also shows people of urban origins to be slightly higher on the prestige scale, but only by one or two tenths of a point.

More revealing than this overall figure is the distribution over the various occupational categories (Table 4). A scant 16% of Germans overall, the city-born were most heavily represented in the professional and high white collar strata, where they made up 24%, or about 50% more than their share. Their lowest concentration was in the common laborer category, where they accounted for 8.5%, just over half their share. In the rest of the occupational categories, deviations were not striking, amounting only to a couple of percentage points. In fact, the skilled artisan category and one of the unskilled groups consisting largely of factory workers had a slightly higher share of urbanites than the low white collar group.

Of course, such nominal occupational categories do not tell the whole story, so I also compared the average wealth of urban- and rural-born

Table 4   German-born Adult Male Immigrants in Ward Two, Occupational Strata and Mean Wealth by Place of Birth

	Cities over 20,000			Rural, Small Town		
	N	%	Wealth	Wealth	N	%
Prof., High White-Collar	6	24.0	$6875	$5426	19	76.0
Propr., Low White-Collar	41	17.4	3090	1719	195	82.6
Skilled Crafts	128	18.5	935	1034	565	81.5
Unskilled Specified Task	22	14.7	741	756	128	85.3
Unskilled,Unspecified	22	8.5	81	250	238	91.5
Other Unskilled	9	18.8	372	429	39	81.3
Site or Product Only	10	11.5	10945	6636	77	88.5
All	**238**	**15.9**	**$1758**	**$1353**	**1261**	**84.1**

Germans within each occupational level. If one breaks down wealth figures on the rural- and urban-born by occupational strata, one sees that in both white collar categories, and with those (usually proprietors) who merely listed worksites, urbanites were better off than their rural compatriots, but in the skilled and unskilled labor categories, immigrants from the country showed a slight edge in wealth. There was one area where practically no difference showed up between urban- and rural-born Germans: the sector of the economy in which they were employed. The secondary (manufacturing) sector employed practically the same proportion of urbanites as the tertiary (sales and service) sector. In summary, then, the evidence presented above shows that immigrants of urban backgrounds were at some advantage in American cities, but the contrasts with their rural counterparts were in no sense drastic. This may also reflect the fact that the most highly qualified or skilled urbanites were unlikely to emigrate in the first place.

This by no means exhausts the list of insights that can be gained from Edward Thierry's feat of census taking. An additional possibility would be to use address books to retrace the census taker's steps and spatially plot each family on a map of the city. This would allow us to identify smaller clusters based on *Landsmannschaft* and assess the influence of common origins in neighborhood formation. More work of this kind would help us gain a better understanding of migration processes, of the way that various environments influenced the process of immigrant acculturation, and particularly of rural-urban contrasts. While the organized colonies of Germans in America have been rather well studied, the investigation of unorganized colonies that made up the great bulk of the immigration is still in its beginnings.

DATA BASE

The St. Louis Genealogical Society generously granted me access to a machine readable version of their 1860 St. Louis census index, so that I could start with a page-by-page list of all inhabitants of the Second Ward giving full names and ages.[12] To this was added from the original census the line number (to reconstruct the original census order), the family number, race, sex, occupation, real and personal property, and state and town of birth. Relation to head of family is not normally listed in the 1860 census, but was often noted by the census taker where it was not obvious from the sequence of persons, allowing a sharper distinction between in-laws and boarders than is normally possible.[13] Occupations were coded using the system of the Philadelphia Social History Project, which classifies not only strata, but also sector, industry, function, worksite, and where given, life cycle stage; a few occupations not covered by the code, such as "fur trapper in Rocky Mountains," were coded on the same principles.[14]

The classification of over 3,000 different birthplaces listed by the 13,500 inhabitants of the ward proved challenging. The West German and East German *Postleitzahlen,* the former 4-digit equivalents of U.S. Zip Codes, were used to compress and systematize birthplace information.[15] The West German code uses 1000 for West Berlin and runs from 2000 through 8999 for the original Federal Republic. For West Germany I adopted this postal code outright; for former East Germany I took the first three digits of their code, preceded by a I. West Germany is thus fitted into a somewhat finer grid than East Germany, but the East has less than one-third the population and less than half the area of the West, so the discrepancy is not great, and East Germany was in any case lightly represented in the migration before 1860. The few German places of origin east of former East Germany were also fitted into the code in the 1000 category. An additional variable was created flagging all birthplaces with populations of over 20,000 in 1861,[16] all cases where state or province but not town was identified, and all towns for which postal codes could not be determined. Misspellings, phonetic spellings, and misreadings of initial letters in the data entry process made coding challenging, but birthplaces for all but about 600 individuals could be determined with a reasonable degree of confidence. With place names like "Neuenkirchen" or "Holzhausen," the "Meyers" and "Smiths" of German towns, the German state of birth often helped in determining which of several possibilities was the correct one.

American birthplaces were assigned numbers under 1000 in the coding scheme. For most analyses, only state of origin was used, except for cities of 20,000 and above and communities within a fifty mile radius of St. Louis. European nationalities outside Germany were assigned codes in the 9000 and above range. Swiss were coded only by canton, Irish and British only by county since the census was usually no more specific than that. French birthplaces were divided between Alsace, Lorraine, and other, flagging the larger cities.

Using the sort and merge capabilities of SPSS-X, information for the head of a family and his wife were attached to all cases in the family. Then, by using sorts, lags, and "select if" statements, it was possible to identify families where the oldest child was born in America, or to identify the last child of a family born abroad, and conduct the head and spouse birthplace comparisons only for those cases. In a few instances where family members are listed in unusual order in the census, misclassifications may have resulted, but these would be exceedingly rare.

NOTES

[1]David Ward, *Cities and Immigrants: A Geography of Change in 19th Century America* (New York, 1971), 22. There has been surprisingly little work done since Ward on the sources of recruitment of urban populations or the selectivity of migration to urban areas. One piece of empirical work that parallels the present study is John Modell, "The Peopling of a Working Class Ward: Reading, Pa., 1850," *Journal of Social Hist.* 5 (1971): 71-95.

[2]Similar urban concentrations of immigrants have been found in other cities. Of 503 emigrants from Bergzabern County who listed destinations, 186 were headed for Cincinnati; moreover, 135 of these stemmed from just three neighboring villages, where they made up about one-fifth of all emigrants. Sigrid Faltin, *Die Auswanderung aus der Pfalz nach Nordamerika im 19. Jh.: Unter bes. Berücksicht. des Landkommissariates Bergzabern* (Frankfurt/M., 1987), 296.

[3]Walter D. Kamphoefner, "Chain Migration and Local Homogeneity of Immigration: Cape Girardeau County Germans in Comparative Perspective," in Michael Roark, ed., *French and Germans in the Mississippi Valley, Landscape and Cultural Traditions* (Cape Girardeau, MO, 1988), 179-89.

[4]Walter D. Kamphoefner, *The Westfalians: From Germany to Missouri* (Princeton, 1987), 86ff.

[5]The only cantons not represented were Uri, Obwalden, and Appenzell-Innerrhoden, which together made up less than 3% of the Swiss population in 1860. *Schweizer. Statistik*, I. Lfg., (Zürich, 1860), 41.

[6]Similar patterns were found in Milwaukee by Kathleen Neils Conzen, *Immigrant Milwaukee, 1836-1860* (Cambridge, MA, 1976), 39ff.

[7]Statements on national distribution of Germans are based on the 1870 U.S. census, which was most complete in reporting German state of birth. See also the figures in Kamphoefner, *The Westfalians*, 74ff.

[8]Over 70% of the emigrants from Bergzabern County in the Palatinate, 1816-1914, gave to protocol that they had relatives in America. Faltin, *Auswanderung*, 295.

[9]Urban-rural migration of German immigrants within America probably took on greater dimensions than the opposite flow. Even if one regards all children born outside cities of over 20,000 as rural, they account for only 5% of all German-American children born outside St. Louis. By contrast, over 10% of all German families in two southern Illinois counties had at least one child born in Missouri, presumably St. Louis. Kamphoefner, *The Westfalians*, 83.

[10]The occupational index was calculated by adapting the Philadelphia Project's vertical code: 1) high white collar, professional; 2) low white collar, proprietor; 3) skilled labor; and collapsing codes 4 to 6 into 4) all unskilled labor. Technically, these are ordinal rather than metric data, and thus it is inappropriate to calculate means for them, but this at least gives a rough indicator of average occupational status.

[11]G. Hohorst, J. Kocka, G.A. Ritter, *Sozialgeschichtl. Arbeitsbuch II* (München, 1978), 52; 4.8% of all Germans resided in cities of over 100,000.

[12]St. Louis Genealogical Soc., comp., *Index to the 1860 St. Louis and St. Louis County Federal Census*, 4 vols., (St. Louis, 1984).

[13] Kamphoefner, *The Westfalians*, 204.

[14]Theodore Hershberg and Robert Dockhorn, "Occupational Classification," *Historical Methods Newsletter* 9 (1976): 59-98.

[15]Sources for coding German birthplaces include Deutsche Bundespost, *Verzeichnis der Postleitzahlen* (Bonn, 1973); *Shell Touring Atlas* (Stuttgart, 1975-6); *Der Grosse ADAC General*

Atlas (Ostfildern, 1985). An earlier edition of the postal code guide was preferred to a later one because of the number of independent villages that have since been annexed by larger towns.

[16]Ernst Lutter, *Geograph.-statist. Untersuchung über die Lage der Städte des Dt. Reiches mit mehr als 20 000 Einwohnern u. ihre Entwicklung im Laufe des 19. Jhs.* (Bonn, 1909), appendix.

VI.
Aspects of Ethnic Culture

17 | "Still, They Were All Germans in Town"—Music in the Multi-Religious German-American Community

Philip V. Bohlman, *University of Chicago*

The language and concepts with which we represent the historical and cultural experiences of German-Americans have traditionally employed a discourse of constraint and caution. In establishing a place for a German-American reality, our recourse to and discourse of nostalgia have often called attention to an evidence provided by boundaries, survival, and the seemingly unequivocal insistence of the past not yet expunged from the present. The most convenient measurements of German-American culture are therefore quantitative, that is the numbers and statistics which signify not just an ethnic ontology, but provide the imperative for studying it.

The study of German music in North America has generally provided some of the most incontrovertible evidence for the maintenance of this patina of pastness. Whether one invokes the censuses of symphony orchestras, the history of music printing in America, or the evolution of mass urban song festivals, Germans and German music are there in numbers far exceeding those any other ethnic group might muster. The claim that German music was an omnipresent artifact of survival—a symbol of the old country that German-Americans refused to relinquish—would surely be a reasonable candidate for one of the root metaphors of German-American culture.[1]

When I first considered the title of the New Harmony conference on "Emigration and Settlement Patterns of German Communities in North America" and then reconsidered it as the special theme for the volume in which this essay would appear, I confess that I found the lingering presence of this discourse of constraint and caution more than a little discomfiting, if not troubling. First, I found the emphasis on *emigration* and *German communities* implicitly weighted toward old-world Germanness. It followed, therefore, that *settlement patterns*, obviously in the central position of the theme, was itself weighted toward Europe, suggesting at the very least that settlement patterns were generated primarily by experiences and conditions in Germany. The patterned and utopian communities examined by conference speakers—the Harmonist settlements, Ephrata, and communal communities of various kinds were surely notable, not least because of their distinctive German music cultures. But, in fact, the German music from such communities has had virtually no impact on a broader German-American community. The destinies of such communities belonged less to the mainstream of American ethnicity than to the valiant efforts of preservationists primarily concerned with providing Americans with a way of "remembering how it once was."

So, finally, and most troubling, I did not quite see how music fitted the pattern of patterns that predominated in the conference theme. I had long maintained that German music in America was one of the cultural symbols that most quickly became German-American during the process of immigration and therefore could function most trenchantly in ways quite distinct from the *patterns* that had characterized the music cultures of Central Europe (see Bohlman 1985). The real power of German-American music lay in its ability to wrench itself free of these patterns and to establish new meaning for the radically transformed community in America. In the process of creating German-American culture, music was malleable and polysemous; it belied and defied patterns. Well, at least some patterns, at least those that it conceivably could have inherited from old-world experiences. In fact, its role in German-American culture depended also on patterns that were immanent in the music itself, that is in the ways music encoded culture through an oral and aesthetic experience. Simply stated, music withstood the pressures of immigration because it responded with change and all the while continued to sound German.

Bonduel, Wisconsin: A German-American Settlement Pattern

Lest the reader think I'm a terrible curmudgeon and that I'm out to bash the theme of the New Harmony conference and this volume, let me offer some assurance that I take the challenge posed by the theme very seriously, indeed so much so that I should like to draw upon its inherent perspectives while looking at the musical life of a single German-American community in northeastern Wisconsin. Bonduel is a village whose patterns are hard to define, though, perhaps better stated, I might say hard to pin down. It is a village in which Germans settled rather early for northern Wisconsin, having already established a fundamentally German *Vereinswesen* by 1860 and retained this until the 1970s and 1980s, when I conducted intensive ethnomusicological research. Even in Wisconsin, Bonduel is remarkable for the persistence of its German-Americanness. It has an extraordinarily high percentage of residents with German ancestry—in the state with the highest percentage of residents with German ancestry. One would think that Bonduel would be rich in identifiable patterns that preserved the past and that the music in the community would bear witness to these.

In fact, I encountered something quite different in Bonduel. On the one hand, there was no questioning the essential German-Americanness of the town; on the other, the town was redolent with paradoxes that encumbered me from understanding its music and culture and, consequently, from ascribing patterns to these. The paradoxes were of several kinds. First of all, settlement itself had occurred in various stages, and accordingly the residents of Bonduel traced their German heritage to different regions of Germany. Aware of these regional distinctions and distinct family histories, the residents held very different notions of German-Americanness and could articulate these clearly in the narratives they constructed about themselves and their town. Second, the people of Bonduel have relied on German religious organizations for many aspects of their cultural life, but religion in the village was highly fractional, even characterized by a history of internecine disputes. Secular Germanness, therefore, was highly inflected by religious Germanness, as well as religious Americanness. Third, German musical life was still thriving, but there was no single German repertory that the town shared. Sacred and secular traditions mixed with *volkstümliche Lieder* and classicized ballads in 19th-century settings. There was remarkably little reticence about singing "German songs," but each individual or family construed such a category in personal, if not idiosyncratic, terms. Bonduel was multicultural, multireligious, and multi-musical; but it was at the same time remarkably German-American.

If there is a consistent settlement pattern that one can observe in Bonduel's history, it is that the town has characteristically fallen along the periphery of several distinct patterns. The town itself lies between the two largest rural areas of German settlement in Wisconsin, the eastern and north-central parts of the state (see Fig. 1).

Bonduel's earliest inhabitants arrived during the first significant wave of immigration to the state, in the 1850s, and the population swelled during the 1880s, when lumbering opened new farmland in northern Wisconsin and German immigration was peaking in the 19th century. First evidence of village organization dates from 1859-60, when attempts to organize schools

Figure 1   Distribution of Germans in Wisconsin 1890

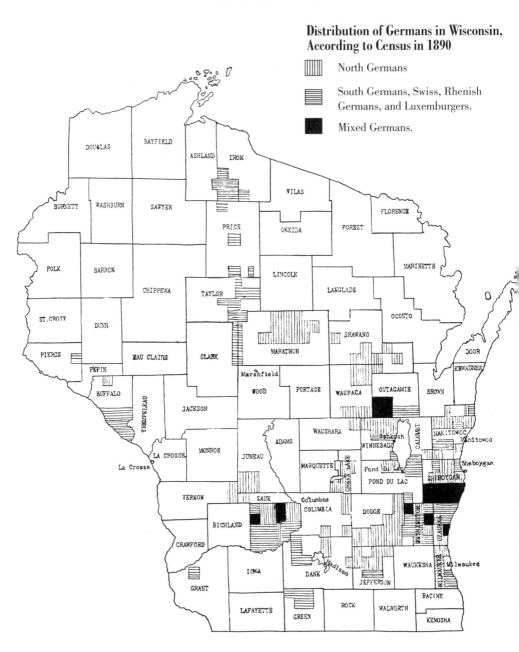

Distribution of Germans in Wisconsin, According to Census in 1890

▥ North Germans

▤ South Germans, Swiss, Rhenish Germans, and Luxemburgers.

■ Mixed Germans.

North Germans are strong in La Crosse, Columbus, and Shawano.
South Germans are strong in Appleton, Madison, and Marshfield.
Mixture of North and South Germans in Manitowoc, Oshkosh, Fond du Lac, Sheboygan, and Milwaukee.

Source: Wisconsin Historical Collections XIV (Madison, 1898), 340 [insert].

and incorporate a township appear (Monroe 1977:1). The early settlers all have German names, and there can be no question that they envisioned their village coalescing around German *Vereinswesen.* Rather striking to me as I undertook fieldwork over a century later, about half of the names mentioned in accounts from the first decade of settlement are found in the village today, and, in fact, all those who were kind enough to allow me to interview them intensively between 1977 and 1985 could trace their families back to the original founding mothers and fathers.

Throughout its history, Bonduel was rather more subject to isolation than other small towns in northern Wisconsin. In part, this isolation is explained by physical and geographic circumstances. Bonduel did not lie on a waterway that was either navigable or suitable for moving felled trees from the vast forests of the area to mills and urban markets. The railroad, too, a creator of boom towns in northern Wisconsin, reached Bonduel only in 1905, long after it could have transformed the town into an industrial center of regional significance. There were also internal reasons for this relative isolation, which we can trace to the density of German settlement, and the extent to which a fairly small number of families remained the primary inhabitants of Bonduel and the chief stewards of its history. The settlement pattern, therefore, would by no means contradict the language of pastness and unbroken connections against which I cautioned in my introductory paragraphs.

Bonduel's settlement pattern, nonetheless, was not characterized by sameness. Quite the contrary, it both admitted and provided the historical conditions necessary for fostering differences. Difference is perhaps most distinctive in the religious makeup of the village. Bonduel also lay at the boundaries between major areas of 19th-century German religious influence, with Missouri Synod Lutheranism predominant to the west, Wisconsin Synod Lutheranism to the south, and Catholicism to the southeast. German Methodists, rarely a major presence among Midwestern German communities, had established themselves in Bonduel before the end of the 19th century. Doctrinal and ideological differences among these various congregations were sharply drawn. Sectarian differences not only produced a variety of social patterns within the village itself, but it marked these with different social and cultural and musical traits. Several religious musical repertories came into being. The members of each congregation surely recognized these as German; residents whom I interviewed in the 1970s and 1980s unanimously agreed that the church had been the primary force for the preservation of German in the community. But each repertory also contained abundant markers that distinguished it from other repertories. With each doctrinal disagreement over the course of the past century, both in Bonduel and at the level of national religious polities, these markers became increasingly important, and the differences became increasingly more significant than similarities. In their abundant differences, however, they also became more German-American.

Documentary evidence and family histories suggest that Bonduel attracted individuals or small families, and that most of these were attracted by the possibility of the independent well being that inexpensive land and rich soil promised. Immigrant guides to the area attempted to woo potential settlers almost entirely on this basis:

> Karl Sumnicht, der im Kreis Hartland [Bonduel], in diesem County wohnt, kam arm hier an, und lebte einige Jahre in einer Blockhütte. Jetzt eignet er 640 Morgen Land, wovon 45 Morgen urbar sind, und versieht das Amt eines Registrators und Schatzmeisters. Heinrich Lücke, aus demselben Kreis, kam als armer Mann hier an und eignet jetzt 500 Morgen Land, wovon 45 Morgen urbar sind, und versieht das Amt eines Supervisors (County Behörde 1870:12).

The same immigrant guides stressed the presence of an active religious life in the area, not so much because it would appeal to specific groups, but rather to those in search of German neighbors; in other words, it was the fact that the churches were German, not Lutheran, Evangelical, or Catholic, that distinguished them (ibid.:19). Education, too, was extolled because it was German, public, and therefore open to all immigrants:

> In jedem Kreis des Bezirks herrscht das Freischulen System, das dem Einwanderer ausgezeichnete Gelegenheit bietet, seine Kinder zu erziehen. Diese öffentlichen Schulen werden hauptsächlich durch Einkünfte von verkauftem Schulland erhalten, ausserdem durch Steuern, und stehen unter der Aufsicht eines Schulsuperintendenten, der alle zwei Jahre vom Volk erwählt wird. Unter den Deutschen gibt es deutsche Schullehrer, was als grosse Wohlthat zu betrachten ist (ibid.).

The settlers of Bonduel came almost entirely to purchase small farms and to live relatively independently, with the village less a locus for shared beliefs and cultural background than a financial, educational, and social center. It was not until the late 19th century that the name of the township, Hartland, was replaced by that of the village forming its political nucleus, Bonduel. Settlement stretched over many decades, with most settlers choosing Bonduel only after arriving at a Lake Michigan port and traveling to the regional land office, Mayville, in eastern Wisconsin, where they received what must be understood as little more than an assignment to a rural area with adequate and cheap land (Bohlman 1980:289).

The farm economy of Bonduel also offers further explanations for the unexpected juxtaposition of isolation and internal diversity in the town's pattern of settlement. During the 19th century and early decades of the 20th century, Bonduel was the most productive agricultural township in the region immediately surrounding it. State census figures from 1885, 1895, and 1905 reveal that Hartland possessed more acres of farmland than any other township in the county at the turn of the century, thus corroborating the rhetoric of immigrant guides from several decades earlier (cf. *Tabular Statements of the Census Enumeration . . .* 1885, 1895, 1905). Census statistics further demonstrate a tremendously diversified approach to agriculture in Hartland township. For example, in 1885, the township led the county in the number of sheep and work animals (horses and mules), and in the production of wheat, oats, potatoes, and "beans and peas" (ibid. 1885, part I:520ff.). The township was either second or third in its report of hogs and cattle on hand, and in the production of corn. Hartland township's penchant for agricultural diversity continued into the 20th century, even intensifying in the state's two remaining census reports of 1895 and 1905 (publ. state census reports ceased after 1905). In the last report, the township led the county in numbers of work animals, cattle, hogs, sheep, and poultry, and in the production of barley, apples, beans and peas, and wool. It was ranked either second or third in the number of milk cows and in the production of wheat, oats, corn, hay, and cheese (ibid. 1905, part II:passim). The diversity of agriculture in the Bonduel settlement area appears in even brighter light when it becomes apparent that this extensive production was intended largely for the township itself, for large-scale transportation from Bonduel to other parts of the state or the Midwest was not yet possible at the time of these reports.

Bonduel's farm economy was in many ways similar to that of other fairly isolated German settlements, for example, those of Texas studied by Terry Jordan (cf. 1966:198). The coupling of isolation with high levels of diversified productivity, moreover, reflects similar processes of combining cultural practices. To underscore Germanness, a community needed to diversify, but diversifying did not necessarily signal assimilation. Indeed, diversification might well mean that the community's distinctiveness was even greater than had the community chosen preservation of old-country ways as a means of retaining its German culture. Diversification was an aggressive strategy of both adaptation and the creation of new patterns of identity and ethnicity, which, it would seem, we have no choice but to call German-American.

If we are generous, we might regard the settlement pattern for Bonduel as random in its juxtaposition of differences and diversification. It seems to me more reasonable to see it falling between other patterns, for Bonduel's settlers were largely those who immigrated with sufficiently open plans to move to wherever the best opportunities were readily available. The core of families that remained in the village for over a century would therefore not explain a pattern of chain immigration, for which substantial evidence is lacking, but rather resulted from an absence of outward migration made possible by relatively stable agricultural practices, that is, the ability of families to stay with their farms generation after generation.

During the lives of 20th-century Bonduel residents cultural boundaries within the community have retained the flexibility that they acquired in the first half century of settlement. Marriage is largely among German-Americans, but religious and regional admixture is the rule. The town was essentially trilingual until at least the 1950s, when many families spoke dialect German at home and on the street, *Hochdeutsch* during church and school, and English in their dealings with the outside world. The function of these three languages, which would be more properly interpreted as a continuum of language styles and uses stretching between the institutionalized extremes of English and Standard German, was again to afford flexibility. A distinctly German-American linguistic freedom, therefore, abrogated religious and regional differences. There can be no question that historical patterns do emerge from the processes of cultural negotiation that have accompanied life in Bonduel for some 140 years, but increasingly during this period these patterns have depended on conditions unique to Bonduel.

The Musical Amalgam of Bonduel

The musical life that I found in Bonduel during the 1970s and 1980s is exactly the sort that any ethnomusicologist or folk music scholar counts him or herself lucky to stumble upon. In other words, from the beginning of my fieldwork in Bonduel I was fortunate to find musicians who actively maintained German musical repertories and social activities in which these repertories had a position. I should even add that my initial decision to work in Bonduel was the result of residents writing to me after I had placed a query in a statewide literary magazine, *The Wisconsin Regional Writer*. In short, there existed already in Bonduel an awareness that the maintenance of German musical traditions in the town were distinctive. There was, moreover, what I might call a folk taxonomy of German musical traditions, a shared concept of the role of German music in the past and present of the town. The initial response of Bonduel residents to my inquiries about their musical life

therefore indicated that I might expect German music to undergird a
conscious pastness and a related pride in maintaining Germanness. Folk
music scholarship, particularly the burgeoning interest in ethnic folk music
that began in the 1960s, generally sought out and valorized the preservation
of pastness, and in this sense its general notions of music as a symbol for
ethnic maintenance would fit conveniently with the conservative language of
German-American history.

Bonduel lent itself, so it seemed during exploratory visits, extraordinarily
well to the convergence of these two models: the abundance of German music
would justify sweeping claims for the town's connection with the past. Soon,
however, it became necessary to question these early assumptions.
Abundance in itself, though welcome in any field study, was not the trait that
most distinguished music in Bonduel. Rather, it was diversity that fulfilled
such a role. Diversity was evident at every level of music and music-making.
Repertories demonstrated diversity, both in the songs known by individual
musicians and in the larger repertory characterizing the entire town. An
individual's repertory tended to grow as the result of participation in different
social activities or institutions, for example, the church, parochial school, or
musical organizations. Individuals knew the songs that were a part of small
groups, and most associated the songs with the specific activities of these
groups. Even to the extent that the repertories of these small groups
overlapped, individuals did not necessarily regard this as a significant
pattern that yielded a larger repertory for the entire town or region, much less
an ethnic group that I might call German-American.[2] The hymn repertory of
the Wisconsin Synod Lutheran Church is not substantially different from that
of the Missouri Synod Lutheran Church if one creates a concordance from
their hymnals, but to the parishioners of these two churches, the repertories
are, in fact, vastly different.[3] It was hardly surprising that the terminology I
used to describe Bonduel's musical life—not least in this jargon—the
concept of "German-American music" was quite meaningless to the people of
Bonduel.

German musical traditions had been all-the-more resilient because of the
role of musical literacy, which benefited from the use of certain standard
songbooks in the community. These songbooks are notable because they
conflated diverse traditions: sacred and secular; dialect and standard;
children and adult; indeed, German and American. The most common
songbooks were printed by religious music presses in America, but were not,
in fact, intended for sectarian uses (cf. *Unser Liederbuch* 1894). Songbooks
printed by synodical publishing houses, e.g., the well-known *Lieder-Perlen*
(1905) of the Missouri Synod's Concordia Publishing House, also found their
way into the homes of many German-Americans who did not belong to the

Missouri Synod. Again, these songbooks are notable because of the extensive concordances they share: their contents are not vastly different, and yet they expand the sense of musical diversity at both community and ethnic group levels. On the one hand, they provided a consistent store of beloved German songs; on the other, they made it possible for any given group or community to reshuffle and recombine these songs into repertories that were distinctive and characteristic of the group or community, rather than the ethnic group as a whole, to which we might presume they belong.[4]

The presence of different songbooks in Wisconsin also reveals larger settlement patterns. In contrasting areas of Missouri Synod or Wisconsin Synod concentration I have generally observed contrasting preferences for one songbook or the other. In rural Marathon County, lying northwest of the area in which Bonduel is located, the most common home songbook is the *Lieder-Perlen*, and other songbooks by religious presses are relatively scarce. I have not similarly examined the use of German songbooks in the home in eastern Wisconsin, core of Wisconsin Synod settlement, but Wisconsin Synod publications, in general, are more common in that part of the state.[5] The difference in songbook use is, I feel, significant, for it meant in Bonduel, where both Missouri Synod and Wisconsin Synod churches are found, that the repertory of the most widespread songbook was not tied to a particular church, nor did it suffer the consequences of sectarian strife. Its meaning and the function of individual songs, instead, resulted from a sense of Germanness that was inclusive rather than exclusive. Songbooks, too, came to be understood as repositories of German songs that could be used in very flexible ways. The diverse songs in these books, therefore, became a common aesthetic lingua franca, providing a sense of German culture that belonged in certain specific ways to the community itself.

The religious German songs of Bonduel are filled with abundant metaphors, intentional in their religious texts, but specified by the town residents in such a way that individual personalities and a local worldview can be extrapolated, or at least surmised. "Wo findet die Seele die Heimat der Ruh'?" is one of the best-known songs in the Lutheran traditions of the town. In Bonduel, the song has very specific functions, primarily as a funeral song, and it belongs in a specific way to the repertory of two of the most knowledgeable singers in the town, Meta Brusewitz and Clara Stuewer. Not only do they sing this song in their personal traditions as a duet—they preferred to sing it for me *only* as a duet—(see Fig. 2) but they have created their own harmonic variant of the song. This variant relies on a parallel movement of the two voices in thirds, with a marking of points of structural importance by smaller or wider intervals (for example, the minor second at "hier" in the fifth line of the first verse). My point here is not as complicated

Figure 2

"Wo findet die Seele die Heimath der Ruh?"*

Originally sung in C Major
♩ = 126 mm.

Meta Brusewitz, Soprano
Clara Stuewer, Alto
Recorded January 11, 1978
Bonduel, Wisconsin

TRANSLATION

1 Wo findet die Seele die Heimath der Ruh?
Wer deckt sie mit schützenden Fittigen zu?
Ach, bietet die Welt keine Freistatt mir an,
Wo Sünde nicht kommen, nicht anfechten kann?
Nein, nein, nein, nein hier ist sie nicht:
Die Heimath der Seelen ist droben im Licht.

2 Verlasse die Erde, die Heimath zu sehn,
Die Heimath der Seele, so herrlich so schön,
Jerusalem droben, von Golde gebaut,
Ist dieses die Heimath der Seele, der Braut?
Ja, ja, ja, ja, dieses allein
Kann Ruhplatz und Heimath der Seele nur
sein.

3 Wie selig die Ruhe bei Jesu im Licht!
Tod, Sünde und Schmerzen, die kennt man dort
nicht.
Das Rauschen der Harfen, der liebliche Klang
Bewillkommt die Seele mit süssem Gesang.
Ruh, ruh, ruh, ruh, himmlische Ruh,
Im Schoosse des Mittlers, ich eile dir zu!

1 Where does the soul find a home of peace?
Who covers it with protective wings?
Alas, does the world offer no sanctuary for me,
Where sin does not come, and cannot trouble?
No, no, no, no, here there is none:
The home of the soul is in the light above.

2 Leave the earth behind, to be in the home,
The home of the soul, so splendid, so
beautiful,
Jerusalem above, built from gold,
Is this the home of the soul, the bethrothed?
Yes, yes, yes, yes, this alone
Can be the resting place and home of the soul.

3 How blissful the peace near Jesus in light!
Death, sin and suffering, one no longer knows
them there.
The music of harps, the lovely sound
Welcomes the soul with sweet song.
Peace, peace, peace, peace, heavenly peace,
In the lap of Christ, the mediator, I hasten
toward you!

*Spellings employ the conventions in the songbooks found in Bonduel

as my musical-analytical description might imply; rather, I mean to point out that the singers have succeeded in creating their own harmonic language, not vastly different from that of the German original, but clearly a musical idiolect that belongs to Bonduel.

The function of "Wo findet die Seele" in Bonduel also reflects the accretion of new meaning and the transformation of musical genre through the personalizing actions of the singers and the generalizing function of the song's metaphors in the community. The primary setting for the song's performance is a funeral, a moment when family members often prefer music with German texts.[6] The singers of "Wo findet die Seele" interpret its meanings in a strikingly optimistic sense. At a religious level, death represents a release from the toil and misery of earthly life, and Christ is seen as the direct mediator between mortality and immortality. The reference to "Heimat," however, suggests another level of interpretation, one far more secular in its highly symbolic construal of the metaphors for "homeland." The song essentially conflates several metaphors for *Heimat*, in effect giving the song several layers of meaning. The singers and listeners in Bonduel pick and choose from these, depending on the occasion for which the song is performed.

Secular German music also continued to thrive in Bonduel. Rather unusual for a town of its size in rural Wisconsin, classicized ballads survived in oral tradition (cf. the recording of "Es steht eine Linde im tiefsten Tal" on Martin et al. 1986). Again, musical literacy and the special role for *Hochdeutsch* (i.e., as the language of learning and literature) may account to a considerable degree for this tenacity. The story in a narrative ballad, therefore, symbolizes the importance of literary metaphors in German Romanticism. Secular ballads are important because they underscore the reasons for maintaining a German musical repertory. The precise repertory for achieving this is far less important. Rather than belonging to small groups, secular ballads tend to circulate within the family or to belong to the repertory of a single individual who learns them specifically to employ their symbolic importance in her or his own decisions about the maintenance of German-American ethnicity. Again, Bonduel's musical life demonstrates specific idiolects. More commonly, the secular musical traditions enjoying favor in rural Wisconsin have been instrumental and urban, namely the polkas and Dutchman bands that were virtually ubiquitous, except, that is, in towns like Bonduel.

Just how does one grow up musically in the German-American culture of Bonduel? What are the rites of passage that ensure one's participation in the music-making of the community? What qualifications determine a musician, and who becomes one? I have posed these questions to shift this essay away from a discussion of music *per se*, music as a sound phenomenon, to music as a human activity; by extension, I return to my assertion that it is not abundance alone that is significant in Bonduel's German-American musical life, rather the variety and freedom available to the individual to transform German music into something personal and freighted with different meanings. One becomes a musician in Bonduel not by learning certain pieces and building certain repertories, but by participating in events or institutions where German music is a viable communication skill. The most active musicians in the town traditionally sang at home, at school, and in the church. They understood the importance of musical literacy and combined that with an elevated use of German music. Acquisition of musical skill resulted from both formal study and trial and error, but the individual became a musician by responding to the expectations and needs of the town itself. This process of music education was eloquently described to me by one of Bonduel's outstanding musicians, Clara Stuewer, during a 1978 interview.

> To me there [are] no sharps or flats. I mean, if you want to transpose, you go up a little higher all the way through. That's the way I do it. I do it that way when it's too high for me, or too low . . . I never learned to read all the notes, you know. I know 'C'. But then I played by ear . . . I know one time . . . I was supposed to entertain them on the piano; so, I played all kinds of comical [pieces], any kind of song that came. Then I ran out of songs; I didn't know what to play anymore. Then they'd always tell me what to play next. But now—I'm not trying to brag it wasn't an accomplished [performance]. But I could play the melody. I don't care: there could be a hundred people singing in church, unless they'd sing wrong together, if they'd sing the regular melody, I could harmonize it by alto if I wanted to. It wouldn't be that the very first verse of second would be altogether correct. Maybe, one or two or three notes would be wrong, but I could do it, it's so easy.

In general, becoming a German-American musician in Bonduel resulted only from active decisions, made because of specific musical demands on individuals whom the community recognized as particularly talented. One did not become a musician simply because one maintained a repertory from the old country or because one sang from a single, representative repertory. Becoming a musician in Bonduel meant, instead, actively becoming German-American in ways patterned and sanctioned by the community itself.

Just how does this suggestion that German-American music demonstrates variety and multiple functions reflect the attitude toward music expressed by the residents in Bonduel? Do they recognize some of the same processes of change and juxtaposition? My view of musical life in Bonduel and that of the town's own residents probably differ more in kind than in substance. Both views emphasize the role of religion, which certainly undergirds many facets of musical life. Religion is therefore widely accepted as a quality of complex forms of expression. Many residents regard all German music as essentially religious and firmly reprimanded me when I suggested that a song was secular because it was sung at a social event not directly associated with the church. Clearly, the category, "multi-religious community," in the title is more mine than Bonduel's, and in my successive visits to the town I found that residents and I disagreed about the different ramifications this can have.

But we were in agreement in our recognition of musical diversity ; moreover, in this respect, we shared a belief that musical diversity has buttressed the vitality of German-American music in the town. In fact, it is through Bonduel's own sense of its musical diversity that its residents articulate a concept of German-Americanness. It was far less important to the residents of the town that they knew certain songs than that the songs they knew worked, that is, reinforced their sense of the town's German-American history, their own ancestry, and the distinctive cultural life that marks Bonduel today. The musicians of Bonduel have long ago ceased regarding German-American music as the product of Germany; rarely do they claim that music preserves the past, and when it does, that past encompasses the experiences of America. Music is, therefore, a means of cultural negotiation, a measure of the processes of change. Music does not recuperate a specific and frozen past, rather it participates in the making of a dynamic present.

German-American Music: Patterns and Processes

To some degree the music history of Bonduel only confirms one of the most commonly accepted, yet misunderstood platitudes in the study of German-American culture: music is very important. Music is very important in Bonduel's pattern of German-Americanness. Arguably, German music has outlasted the German language; it is surely practiced with greater vitality. Residents in the town are far more likely to sing something in German than to converse in the language. But why music? What does music achieve that other cultural activities, say painting or monumental architecture, have not achieved? My own admission that German-Americans employ music as a means of cultural identity notwithstanding, I do not subscribe to the facile explanation that Germans are especially musical people or that they have a special love for music; there are musical communities, ethnic groups, and national aggregates throughout the world. Rather, I think the answers lie in the more complex functions that music can and does play in German-American culture. Music, in short, has become one of the mechanisms for the transformation of old-world products into new-world processes, or patterns, to bring this essay full circle to the theme of this volume. Not only do repertories of German-American music tend to develop as amalgams of diverse parts, but musical genres have also taken shape as conflations of style and form, some of them leading to unlikely and unpredictable combinations.

Despite my attention to the single case study of Bonduel, I should also like to speculate that the creation of German-American music by juxtaposing disparate, if not previously unrelated, parts has characterized the entire music history for the ethnic group. Accounts of the performances of popular music in the German-American community, for example, the tours of German musicians that introduced the concertina in North America, reveal a tendency to market repertories by forging—or better, cobbling together strings of tunes called "medleys." The Schmidt Brothers, to take the case of the earliest hawkers of the concertina, produced demonstration records that crammed as many tunes as possible onto a three minute side (cf. March and Leary 1989). It was no more requisite that a tune be presented as a whole than it was that some sort of German repertory serve as the musical font for these records. Throwing American popular tunes into these demonstration records and performances was, in fact, an effective marketing strategy.

The popular music of German-American Dutchman bands today is no less eclectic, with styles no less mixed. A band surely chooses to emphasize its German tunes—at least when playing in German-American communities—although Polish, Bohemian, and Slovenian tunes also abound. LaVern J. Rippley's research into the music history of the New Ulm, Minn., Dutchman bands, particularly Hans ("Whoopie John") Wilfahrt's band, similarly uncovers a wealth of styles, a tendency to traverse European stylistic boundaries, and a remarkable adaptability to American audiences who had formed their own aesthetic of German-American music.

The juxtaposition of various parts also characterizes individual tastes and styles. The version of "Zum Lauterbach hab' ich mein' Strumpf verlor'n" that appears in Fig. 3 is a striking case of some five different pieces that are assembled for a performance lasting little more than a minute. We recognize "Zum Lauterbach" and "Mein Hut, der hat drei Ecken" as German chestnuts, "Where, Oh Where Did My Little Dog Go?" as an American popular tune, and the yodeling as a Swiss vocal technique modified to sound like America's "Blue Yodeller," Jimmie Rodgers. This compact little mosaic is even more remarkable because it has been collected in several different types of German-American community and in different regions of the U.S. The version transcribed below was sung by a resident of eastern Wisconsin; Brigitte Bachmann-Geiser has found the same song in a version containing the same five parts assembled in the same way in Amish communities of northeastern Indiana (Bachmann-Geiser and Bachmann 1988:93); and

Figure 3

Singer: Albert Kolberg

Sheboygan Co., Wisconsin
December 13, 1984

Source: Martin et al. 1986, cut 1, side 1
Transcribed by Christine W. Bohlman

Collected by Philip Martin
Published in Bohlman 1988:136-37

Rudolf Pietsch has found the song to be common among Burgenland immigrants to eastern Pennsylvania (Pietsch 1989).[7] We can conclude, therefore, that the song has formed into a distinctively American species, has entered into widespread oral tradition in different German-American communities, and has come to exhibit a life of its own that would be quite unpredictable from the diverse components it combines (cf. also Bohlman 1988:135-38.).

As a mechanism, music makes it possible to forge new patterns, to invent new ethnicities. Kathleen Neils Conzen has observed that German-Americans were perhaps the first and surely one of the earliest groups to invent an effective ethnicity (1985). I should like to posit here that this propensity for creative invention is related to the penchant for maintaining a distinctly German-American musical life. "Invention," in fact, is a concept with a special resonance for music, having been borrowed from the process of *inventio* in classical rhetoric to describe the processes of creation in which the form and substance of a musical composition are immanent in the musical material that one chooses as a starting point. Just as invention in music depends on exactly what one chooses to bring to the piece at the moment of its inception, so too the invention of German-American music depends on a carefully chosen cultural baggage: just which symbols and sounds one selects out of a vast number of possibilities. How these combine to produce the musical repertories in a town like Bonduel thus relates directly to the town, its people and history, and the very possibilities they open for invention. Bonduel and, for that matter, thousands of other multi-religious and multicultural communities offer abundant paradigms for this fundamental inventiveness. Music in Bonduel has bridged differences; it has provided a common language; it has taken its place in activities shared by the entire community; it has per persisted because it could respond with change to the pressures of assimilation. The music one encounters in Bonduel is not redolent of the symbols of a stereotyped Germany; any drinking, student, or wandering songs that might once have been part of the town's repertory had disappeared long before I worked in the town. To the extent that remnants of a European repertory survived, they had assumed new functions, which embodied new cultural meanings and symbols. These, in turn, represented something shared by the people of Bonduel and associated by them with their own past. They and their ancestors had, in effect, invented a particular and distinctive German-American ethnicity. Music had provided a common voice for and a means of expressing that ethnicity; it had given the residents of the multi-religious community the assurance that, whatever their other differences might be, "still, they were all Germans in town."

Notes

[1]For an example of the use of statistics and censuses to establish the Germanness of American music, see Bohlman (1985; 1986). The special qualities of German-American festival culture are examined from two different perspectives in Conzen (1989) and Vitz (1986), the intricate relation between immigrant German-American musicians and the history of American orchestral life in Schabas (1989).

[2]Theories of "group song" as the most appropriate basis for folk song had as their chief exponent Ernst Klusen. His most complete work on the subject is *Volkslied: Fund u. Erfindung* (1969); although relatively little of Klusen's work has appeared in English, Klusen (1986) provides a tightly argued summary of his notion of group song.

[3]The hymn repertories of both churches included almost entirely texts that were in English, although the indebtedness of Lutheran hymn repertory to earlier German versions is generally acknowledged by the hymnals and recognized by those who use them. For two different histories of transitions from German to English texts in German-American hymnody see Schalk (1965) and Hinks (1986).

[4]Both *Unser Liederbuch* and the *Lieder-Perlen* appeared in numerous reprintings and achieved enormous popularity. A study of their publication and distribution during the second half of the 19th century and the first of the 20th century, a study no one has yet undertaken, would contribute enormously to the social history of German-Americans.

[5]I rely unscientifically on the name of purchaser and place and date of purchase appearing inside the cover of books I have examined from eastern Wisconsin for this observation.

[6]In general, community residents specify rites of passage and religious holidays as the events for which German music is most desirable, even necessary. The requisite use of German music, thus, counterbalances the widespread presence of music in English in the town. Intense associations of meaning, therefore, explain the maintenance of German songs far more than the encroachment of English would explain away that maintenance.

[7]The extent to which the component parts are not drawn from European repertories is abundantly evident in the Burgenland-American example, for Burgenland is the only province in Austria in which yodeling is not traditional.

Bibliography

Bachmann-Geiser, Brigitte, and Eugen Bachmann, *Amische: Die Lebensweise der Amischen in Berne, Indiana* (Berne, 1988).

Bohlman, Philip V., "Music in the Culture of German-Americans in North Central Wisconsin." M.A. thesis (Univ. of Illinois at Urbana Champaign, 1980). " 'Viele Einwanderer aus der alten Welt': German-American Rural Community Structure in Wisconsin," *Midwestern Journal of Language and Folklore* 8 (1982) 1: 8-33. "Hymnody in the Rural German-American Community of the Upper Midwest," *The Hymn* 35 (1984) 3: 158-64. "Prolegomena to the Classification of German-American Music." *Yearbook of German-American Studies* 20 (1985): 33-48. "European-American Music: 3. German," in H. Wiley Hitchcock and Stanley Sadie, eds., *The New Grove Dictionary of American Music* (New York, 1986), Vol.2, 772. *The Study of Folk Music in the Modern World* (Bloomington, Ind., 1988).

Conzen, Kathleen Neils, "German-Americans and the Invention of Ethnicity," in Frank Trommler and Joseph McVeigh, eds., *America and the Germans: An Assessment of a Three-Hundred-Year History*, (Philadelphia, 1985), Vol. I, 131-47. "Ethnicity as Festive Culture: 19th-Century German America on Parade," in Werner Sollors, ed., *The Invention of Ethnicity* (New York, 1989), 44-73.

County Behörde, eds., *Erwerbs-Quellen, Vorzüge u. Erzeugnisse welche die Counties Brown, Door, Oconto u. Shawano, im Staat Wisconsin dem Einwanderer bieten* (Green Bay, 1870: Fr. Burkard, Druckerei der *Wisconsin Staats Zeitung*).

Hinks, Donald R., *Brethren Hymn Books and Hymnals, 1720-1884* (Gettysburg, Pa., 1986).

Jordan, Terry G., *German Seed in Texas Soil: Immigrant Farmers in 19th-Century Texas* (Austin, 1966).

Klusen, Ernst, *Volkslied: Fund u. Erfindung* (Köln, 1969). "The Group Song as Object," in James R. Dow and Hannjost Lixfeld, eds. and translators, *German Volkskunde: A Decade of Theoretical Confrontations, Debate, and Reorientation (1967-1977)*, (Bloomington, Ind., 1986), 184-202.

Lieder-Perlen (St. Louis, 1905).

March, Richard, and James P. Leary, "Concertinas," weekly program in "Downhome Dairyland," special radio series for WERN, Wisconsin Public Radio (1989).

Martin, Philip, et al., *Ach Ya! Traditional German-American Music from Wisconsin* (Dodgeville, Wis., 1986).

Monroe, (Mrs.) Reuben, *The History of Bonduel*, rev. and updated by (Mrs.) Charles Stern, (Bonduel, 1977), 1st publ. 1944.

Pietsch, Rudolf, Personal communication, (1989).

Rippley, LaVern J., *The Whoopee John Wilfahrt Dance Band* (Northfield, Minn., 1992).

Schabas, Ezra, *Theodore Thomas: America's Conductor and Builder of Orchestras, 1835-1905* (Urbana, Ill., 1989)

Schalk, Carl, *The Roots of Hymnody in the Luth. Church-Missouri Synod* (St. Louis, 1965).

Sollors, Werner, "Introduction: The Invention of Ethnicity," in idem, ed., The *Invention of Ethnicity* (New York, 1989), ix-xx.

Stuewer, Clara, Interview. Bonduel, Wis., Jan. 11, 1978.

Stuewer, Hugo, "Oral Autobiography" (1966), transcr. by Clara Stuewer as a typescript.

Tabular Statements of the Census Enumeration and the Agricultural, Mineral, and Manufacturing Interests of the State of Wisconsin, 3 Vols., (Madison, 1885, 1895, 1905).

Unser Liederbuch (Reading, 1894).

Vitz, Robert C., " 'Im wunderschönen Monat Mai': Organizing the Great Cincinnati May Festival of 1878," *American Music* 4 (1986).

18 | Women's Lives in New York City, 1890-1910: The Women's Pages of the Middle-class *New Yorker Staats-Zeitung* and the Socialist *New Yorker Volkszeitung*

Agnes Bretting, *Verlag Gruner & Jahr, Hamburg*

In 19th-century New York City, Germans had always constituted an impressive element. In 1890 more than 200,000 German-born persons were listed in its census, accounting for roughly 14% of the total population and one third of all foreign-born people in the city. The German community enjoyed an astonishingly high number of publications in its own language. By 1850 there were already four daily German-language papers—more than German cities like Berlin or Leipzig could boast at that time. Eight other papers appeared either weekly, fortnightly or monthly; and due largely to the arrival of the politically active and outspoken 48ers—many of whom became journalists or editors—numbers mushroomed in the 1850s and after the Civil War.[1]

The two leading German-language dailies were the conservative *New Yorker Staats-Zeitung (SZ)* and the socialist *New Yorker Volkszeitung (VZ)*. The *SZ* had been established as a weekly in December 1834. Politically it was opposed to the Whig Party, and the paper was clearly aimed at the German middle-class, which favored the Democrats.[2] The paper flourished and appeared as a daily only ten years later. Under the editorship of both Oswald Ottendorfer who took over in 1858, and Hermann Ridder, editor after Ottendorfer's death in 1900,[3] its circulation increased rapidly. In 1872 the *SZ* had the highest circulation (55,000) of all German-language newspapers printed in the U.S. and in Germany. Since 1885 the paper maintained its own correspondent in Berlin thus being the first paper printed in the U.S. no longer to rely on London news agencies. The *SZ* survived both world wars and is still in circulation today.

Founded in 1878, as the official organ of the Socialist Labor Party (SLP), the *VZ* became the major 19th-century voice of organized Marxism in the U.S. It was produced by a non-profit Socialist Co-operative Publishing Association; the first editors were Alexander Jonas (1878-1889) Sergius Schewitsch (1890), Julius Grunzig (1890-91) and, until 1919, Hermann Schlueter.[4] The paper started with a circulation of 5,500—included in this number were 4,000 subscribers—going up to 10,000 in 1880 and 20,000 in 1890, thereafter fluctuating between 17,000 and 23,000. Due to financial difficulties caused by the worldwide depression the paper ceased to exist in October, 1932.[5]

The Introduction of Women's Pages

The first magazine in the U.S. written especially for women was printed in 1837.[6] After the Civil War the number of women's journals increased rapidly. Women had been "discovered" both as readers and as consumers. In order to attract female readers, pages or columns written especially for women were introduced by most major papers in the 1890s.

In March 1891 the first page entitled *Unter uns Frauen* (Among Us Women) was published in the Sunday edition of the *SZ*. In 1892 a women's page became part of the newly founded evening edition, and two years later a column aimed at the interests of women, *Für Haus und Heim* (For House and Home), was added to the morning edition Wednesdays and Fridays.

Not until January 1900 did the second largest German-language daily in New York City, the *VZ*, offer a special page for women. This comparatively late introduction finds its explanation in socialist ideology, which had a great impact on the make-up of the women's page as well. The editors of the *VZ* simply did not see the necessity for a special page for female readers. Since the Socialist party propagated class struggle as the means of liberating men and women alike, equal rights for both were theoretically implied. Agitation against capitalism left no room for an independent, separate women's movement; the so-called "women's question" would be solved as soon as the social question was taken care of.

For a long time Socialist women quietly accepted this line of argumentation. However, in the 1870s and 1880s they became more aware of their own problems and the political implications thereof. Women began to organize into socialist women's clubs, and through their activities they eventually forced their male comrades to "strive for a new attitude toward the women's question. The men now had to reconcile their traditional, paternalistic, family-oriented ideology with the new reality of the women's movement in their own ranks".[7]

So in 1900 the editors of the *VZ* granted space for a special column *Für Frauen* (For Women), as requested by the politically active *Sozialistischer Frauen Bund* (Socialist Women's League). Here, women were to "exchange their thoughts and wishes, concerning economical or political topics, or questions on education and household."[8] The column *Für Frauen* appeared in the Sunday paper and was reprinted in the weekly edition.

However, issues concerning women were not now reduced to a women's page; they were already being well covered in the *VZ* from its beginning. The paper's first editor, Alexander Jonas, had actively promoted the idea of equal rights for women, in lecturing as well as in writing.[9] Thus even though the women's pages in these two papers paralleled each other only for ten years of the period under consideration, it is nevertheless possible to compare the image of the German-American woman as it was propagated in the *SZ* and the *VZ* between 1890 and 1910.

The *VZ* women's column—it rarely developed into a full page—was meant to be a forum for women, one which reflected their daily lives. Women asked for it because they felt that their situation did not and could not receive sufficient coverage in a paper dominated by male editors. Unfortunately, the authors of the women's column rarely signed their articles or used initials only. It is therefore difficult to assess the independence of the editresses in their choice of articles printed. Johanna Greie-Cramer, long-time activist in the SLP, was editress in charge of the women's page. In October 1906 she was followed by Meta Stern, the American-born daughter of Augusta Lilienthal, a radical freethinker strongly advocating women's emancipation. Meta Stern published under the assumed name of Hebe; Johanna Greic-Cramer probably was the author of many articles signed by *Kathie or Käthe.*

The purpose of the column *Für Frauen* clearly was information and agitation; women should become aware of their own vital interests in the Socialist movement. The column did not appeal to a larger audience: an editorial, just a few letters, and one or two long thematic articles, mostly reprints from other newspapers or from books, made up the column. No illustrations, recipes, fashion or the like were printed.[10] Rarely could the female reader find something like hints for a moderate make up for working girls.[11] Except for the caption *Für Frauen,* there was no eye-catcher whatsoever. Much space was given to announcements by, and reports of, socialist women's clubs, especially the Sozialistischer Frauen Bund.

The women's pages of the *SZ* were quite different in their outer appearance. Topics centered around the home and the question of how to please men. Exhaustive illustrated coverage was given to fashion trends, which even included the so-called "reform fashion"—bloomers, white blouses, the giving up of the corset—actually a concern of the women's liberation movement. Society news was allotted more and more space, until in April 1904 a special column called *New Yorker Frauenleben* (Women's Life in New York) was introduced for this kind of information. For weeks, readers and Frau Anna, editress of the page, corresponded on questions like: Why do young girls today prefer much more to stay single than they used to a generation ago?—Is this true for German-American girls as well?—What can be done to get domestic help by decent, honest maids?[12] Most subjects were treated for several weeks; one reason was that Frau Anna wrote her editorials on important questions as series, and because she successfully called upon her readers to express their opinions or experiences on certain subjects. Since editorials were not signed, we cannot be sure sure that all of them were written by Frau Anna. But judging from the style and concluding from frequent hints as to personal experiences, many of them were, and others were chosen by her for publication.[13]

Frau Anna, whose real name was E. C. Dittmar, had joined the staff of the *SZ* in 1891. She was the only female staff member and in charge of everything concerning women, home and family. The women's pages of the Sunday paper and, since 1892, of the evening edition, as well as the biweekly column *"Für Haus und Heim"* since 1894, appeared under her editorship. Mrs. Dittmar had come to New York in 1879 at the request of her fiance—as she once told her readers. He had migrated to America earlier and "needed a home" (*"bedurfte einer Häuslichkeit"*).[14] The couple had to struggle from the start, and she had to work to make ends meet. Not until the mid 1890s could she and her family—she had two children—afford the middle-class lifestyle she believed she was entitled to by background and education.[15]

At first glance it seems as if the content of the women's page of the *SZ* was nothing but "aimless chatter and cozy nonsense," as Robert Stein, publisher and editor of *McCalls* magazine once had characterized print media for women.[16] A closer look at the topics treated reveals that there were some striking similarities with the content of the lecturing women's column of the *VZ*.

Women and Family

The natural sphere of activity for women was the family and the home. On this point, male Germans—bourgeois and Socialist alike—agreed. Actually, this attitude very much corresponded with the reality of German-

American families.[17] Compared to other ethnic groups few German-American women worked in factories, sweatshops or offices.[18] They were housewives, often trying to add some cash to the family income by taking in boarders, or doing some paid labor like washing or sewing in their home. The majority of German women who were gainfully employed worked as domestic servants.[19]

The *VZ* upheld this picture of women as housewives and mothers; no new perspectives were added. The first women's page published the letter of one Frau Helene, who complained about her husband who wanted her to stay at home when she was interested in attending socialist meetings.[20] The following issue published an answer by another woman who agreed with the husband's point of view. Housework, so she argued, had to be finished by the time the husband came home from work, so that by then she could afford the time to be his companion (*Gesellschafter*).[21]

The editors either ignored the situation of women or they discussed it rather theoretically. Up to the 1870s the *VZ* had, at best, treated the problem of women's position in society in some minor articles or "back columns."[22] And even though the women's page started discussions on marriage or the question of "free love," the underlying conviction was that Socialist women were members of the "big party-family," they were—once educated to the proper understanding of socialism—the subservient, but understanding, helpmates of their active male partners. Johanna Greie-Cramer "continually reminded her readers of the integral relationship between the emancipation of women and the Socialist revolution."[23]

Female readers questioned their role within the family. Reading their letters on the one hand and the editorials on the other, one gets the feeling that the discussion on topics like marriage, love and the family was a result of pressure by the readers. Readers were well aware of the fact that Socialist men propagated equal rights for both sexes but acted otherwise. "There are a lot of enlightened men for whom the emancipation of women is a thorn in the flesh, in fact, they even work against it with all their strength," one Mrs. Bertha wrote.[24] "The woman as mother, the woman bringing up her children, is she supposed to be left in the dark, supposed to serve the man like a maid? How does that go with socialism?" another female reader complained.[25] There clearly existed an awareness of specifically female problems and a need to discuss them with other women.

Frau Anna of the *SZ*, in contrast, stressed the view of women as guardians of home and family. In her March 1891 programmatic editorial for the first women's page she wrote, "The whole world belongs to the man, the woman has as her sphere what she establishes for herself. . . . There are mothers and housewives, wives and young girls, ladies of society and feminists, writers and teachers, workers and artists in many fields."[26] But she left no doubt that happiness could be achieved only by choosing their natural sphere of activity; time and again she urged her readers to be satisfied with their "true mission," namely the role of housewife and mother given to them "by nature, world order, and civilization." "Would not or cannot those women who are trying to extend women's activities into the field of politics understand that there is no calling which is so supreme, so sacred, of such important consequences as that which is fulfilled by a conscientious mother, wife and housekeeper?" One of the editorials had this kind of admonition for women.[27]

Frau Anna was convinced that the Bible was perfectly right in telling women, "And he shall be your master."[28] For her this was basic for the functioning of society. The constant discussion of the so-called *Heirathsfrage* (on getting married) did not question the institution of marriage as such—the *SZ* women's page never seriously considered the possibility of "free love"— but rather focused on the problem of how to find the right partner. Readers, male and female, responded enthusiastically; the topic had touched upon a real problem. Women complained that most men were looking for rich spouses, men accused young girls of asking for too luxurious a life style, thus ruining their husbands instead of being modest, industrious and thrifty.[29] Sometimes, almost the whole page was taken up by letters concerning this problem, for instance when readers started to organize a "marriage brokerage."[30]

The articles on fashions and recipes, on education and housekeeping were all written for women who were married or for young girls preparing to be married some day. Editorializing on problems like unhappy marriages or unruly children, Frau Anna always blamed women. Women were either undutiful in their natural calling or they did not know better, because they had not been educated for it by their mothers.[31]

Marriage, family life and housekeeping were seen as a fulfillment by Frau Anna and then by editresses associated with the *VZ*.[32] But wage earning for women could be a necessity, and the question of gainful employment for women shows that another consensus existed between the two papers of such different political orientation.

Women as Wage Earners

Socialists strongly rejected the idea of women working for wages. In articles like *"Die Befreiung der Familie"* (Liberation of the Family) or *"Die Stellung der Frau in der Gesellschaft"* (Women's Position within Society), *VZ* editors insisted on this view.[33] They maintained that women in the work force kept men's wages down, and men were the ones who had to care for a family; and, of course, gainful employment also kept women from their important task of taking care of, and educating, their children.[34] The fight against capitalism and for better pay was also necessary in order to enable families to live according to this "natural" pattern.

Many women, however, were forced to earn money, and this had to be accepted. But the resulting tension between the facts of life and the "natural" calling of women as housewives could not be resolved. "That women were subjected to a massive double burden was evidently seen as an unfortunate, but inevitable, fate."[35] Sympathetic coverage was given to strikes of female laborers or to intolerable sweatshop conditions,[36] but the underlying creed always was that the so-called women's question was just one expression of the conflict between capital and labor. Authors writing for the women's page did not query this position, nor did they offer any help by challenging traditional role models. Nowhere was it suggested, for example, that men might share the duties of housekeeping.[37] Instead, women were urged to change their plight by actively participating in the Socialist struggle, that is, by taking up another, a third burden.

Even though Frau Anna in the *SZ* mainly addressed the woman as housewife and mother, she could not deny that the number of women in the city's work force was increasing, and that married and single women stood their ground in all kinds of jobs and professions. She was aware that in many German-American families the struggle to make ends meet made discussions on the recruitment of decent maids or the proper age for marriage rather absurd. Girls growing up under these social conditions were forced to work, she told her readers, they had to strive for some economic independence so that they would not have to desperately look for a husband—however, "if there comes a man who fetches her away from her workplace to his home, so much the better."[38] The real problem was, according to Frau Anna, that many, if not most girls, went out to work not because of need but for the want of extra money which was to finance an extravagant, luxurious lifestyle. Again and again Frau Anna criticized this attitude. It was morally wrong, she said, because these women pushed men and needy women out of their jobs or brought down their wages.[39] It was much better, she argued, to keep a young girl at home, even if she had to give up dreams of luxury and be content with a simple woolen dress, because "this would help her poor sister to cover herself with a cotton dress without being forced to give up her self-respect."[40] Women who could afford to stay at home should do so; for them there was social work to do. The gap between rich and poor was deplorable and dangerous. However, Frau Anna did not demand political action—at least not by women—but appealed instead to charity.[41] Charity was the task, or rather the duty, of wealthier women, Frau Anna insisted.[42]

She herself followed this advice in the "Letter Box" of the women's pages, by turning it actually into a kind of employment and welfare agency. In this 'Letter Box'[43] she not only dispensed comfort and advice, recipes and helpful hints for housekeeping, she also tried to bring together those who wanted to do work at home, like laundering, sewing, embroidering, even babysitting, with those who needed these services. In some cases she collected money and clothing for worthy poor. The "Letter Box" made up a considerable part of the women's page, and apparently many needy women applied to Frau Anna for help. From time to time she had to devote the whole page to answering letters sent to her. "I am unable to abolish poverty," she once wrote, "but some readers do expect just that. Those who do not receive an answer—and there are many—do have to believe me that I was not able to help."[44]

Women and Education

Since the proper role of women was defined in such stringent terms in the *SZ* women's page, education for women logically was to focus on this role only. The educational goal was so obvious that not too many articles actually dealt with this issue. As to the education of boys, Frau Anna had nothing beyond general admonitions like: teach your children to always tell the truth, respect the parents, be modest—values which she felt were being disregarded in many American homes.[45] The American educational system could be a danger for girls. "In grammar- and high schools our girls are taught everything that will keep them away from home and enable them to displace men in the labor market. This means turning the tables on oneself. We need housewives in the future just as we have needed them in the past," Frau Anna wrote.[46] Therefore keep your daughters at home if possible, if not, let them take a job in the domestic sphere. On the question of intellectual training for girls, *SZ* readers were advised to let them learn something, but to take care that they don't grow too ambitious. But even though college education should not be for boys only, for girls it was dangerous because it afforded power, and very often knowledge was achieved at the cost of a girl's health.[47] Frau Anna admonished mothers, "don't let your daughters strive above your own class . . . no college education, no profession can make good for an inner alienation from one's family."[48]

In the *VZ*, on the other hand, women's education was a topic of high priority. However, the paper did not stress preparation for the "proper" gender role but rather the teaching of the Socialist creed. "The inferior education of so many German women is one of the greatest and most serious obstacles in the workingmen's movement. How often does his wife's scolding . . . keep a man from fighting his enemy, and her intellectual and moral narrowness becomes his own in the end," another Socialist paper, the *Chicago Vorbote*, stated in 1874.[49]

This assessment of women not being educated enough to take part in the progressive movement clearly was the underlying assumption of the editorials in the *VZ* as well. For Johanna Greie-Cramer one means of educating women towards this end was the radical press itself.[50] However, she knew that only few women were reading it. "The very paper . . . which fights for improving the situation of women belonging to the working class . . . is rejected by them," she wrote in 1903, "and instead a trivial paper, pleasing their curiosity only, is relished."[51] Men were responsible for their wives' education, "Take care of what your wives are reading," Greie-Cramer warned husbands in an article printed in the women's page. Don't ask too much of them, teach them step by step.[52] Next to reading, active participation in Socialist women's clubs was of great importance.[53]

Much emphasis was put on questions concerning the education of children. Most articles on this topic on the women's page were reprints from male authors, often medical doctors, who treated the subject with scientific thoroughness.[54] But these articles apparently did not completely satisfy the readers, if the many questions and exchanged opinions are any indication. In 1900, for example, a discussion on the attitude of Socialists towards parochial education was forced on the paper. Some weeks after the women's column had been introduced, a letter was published in which a woman expressed regret that most children attending the Socialist Free German Schools in New York were only enrolled there in order to learn the language, but not out of interest in the progressive cause. "Very few of them (the children) are Socialists, most go to church,"[55] she complained. There was no immediate reaction to this letter, but some months later, after several complaints about readers showing too little interest in their column, one woman suggested that one cause for the apparent indifference could be the editors' narrow focus on Socialism; she "could not see any harm in having her children attend church."[56] This statement started a vivid discussion. Many women insisted that the churches, and especially schools connected with the German churches, often offered the best possible choice for children in the neighborhood. Frau Käthe immediately tried to stop this discussion. With "sisterly" care she asked, "Can a mother do anything more wrong than being liberal-minded herself and yet allow her children's brains to be filled with nonsense by a cleric?"[57] Despite her warning, more letters on this problem followed. Obviously, there was something that had touched upon a common experience of German-American mothers, something that was on their minds. In November, an article by Minnie Koehn, *"Zur Religionsfrage"* (On the Question of Religion),[58] explained at length why religious education could not be tolerated, but it still took weeks before women stopped commenting—or before the editors stopped printing their letters.

Women and the Vote

The one question causing controversies about women's rights and women's proper place in society was whether women should vote. Frau Anna gave an apodictic answer in the *SZ*. "There is no doubt that the majority of German women are determined enemies to the women's right to vote," she declared in a February 1896 editorial.[59] This was the first one of a series meant to explain why women "had to ward off the duty to vote." The franchise would be nothing but a new burden for women, one which they could not face since they were "different from men in their spiritual, organic whole."[60] It was an illusion to believe in social change by voting,[61] and there simply was no need to become active, since men cared for women's happiness; in fact, women were privileged to be allowed to leave the "ugly outside world" to men.[62]

Frau Anna was sure that she spoke not only for German women but for all, including Americans. But at the beginning of the 20th century, when the franchise movement intensified, Frau Anna modified her opinion. Her strict position had proven to be too old-fashioned. Women should show interest in politics, she conceded, especially young women, who were the ones for whom new territory was captured. But she insisted that it was most important not to infringe upon limits of decency basic to womanliness (*Weiblichkeit*).[63]

In the Socialist *VZ* surprisingly little was said about the franchise movement. Johanna Greie-Cramer voiced the official position of the paper: "The solving of the social question, the liberation of labor from capital, will bring full equality to women as well."[64] Readers were kept informed, but more coverage was given to the movement in Europe than in America. This changed, however, when Johanna Greie-Cramer retired for reasons of health. In October 1906 Meta Stern took charge of the women's column.

Born in the U.S., Stern spoke English fluently and was well informed on the American women's movement. Women should have equal rights, and the right to vote was a basic one, she argued. Progress could be achieved only by multi-ethnic cooperation within the U.S.; Europe no longer was the focal point. But by propagating cooperation with the American liberal women's movement she ran into official ideology and clashed with the male editorship of the paper. For years Socialists had declared liberal feminists to be adversaries, since they fought a bourgeois battle. And now Meta Stern not only considered those who opposed the women's right to vote as "the enemies of progress," [65] she even told her female readers, that "comrades who can afford the time should go to the meetings of American feminists." "Even though they are no Socialists," she argued, "they do stand for part of our wishes as well and we can, without being disloyal to Socialism, support them morally."[66] However, male Socialists were not yet ready to accept this attitude, and in 1910 Julie Romm took over the *VZ* women's page.

Acceptance by the Readers

An attitude of timidity and precariousness was to be felt in all women's pages of the *VZ*, be it in letters written by readers or in articles which always stressed the need to educate women. Editresses of this paper seem to have worked under the pressure of being closely watched by male colleagues. Johanna Greie-Cramer had to respond to complaints that the editor-in-chief did not print letters mailed to the *VZ* for the women's page or that he had cut down on them.[67] Women were advised to complain to the Sozialistischer Frauen Bund, who would take care of the matter.

But for women who wrote letters to the *VZ* it apparently did not come easy to pen their thoughts on matters which traditionally were seen as "male affairs." One woman suggested that all the existing women's societies should publish their announcements in the women's page, but only if "the editors of the *VZ* do not object to this idea."[68] Another one wrote, "I do hope the content of the women's column does not offend other *VZ* readers . . . we are just discussing things . . . we know that we still have a long way to go until we are equal to those progressive men."[69] Frau Anna did not seem to have any real disagreements with the male publishers or editors of the *SZ*, except that they sometimes complained that her page was growing too fast.[70] But what could men say against a women's page whose editress made women solely responsible for a good marriage and a happy family and who printed advice like the following, given to a distressed husband: it had been his fault to give in too much to his wife's wishes; he should take a firm stand against her, tell her what to do and then "you will see things change. A woman wants to see in her husband a man, not a worm."[71]

How then was such a page or column accepted by women? While the *SZ* page flourished and expanded several times, the *VZ* column, introduced comparatively late, always struggled for survival. After the enthusiastic welcome wore off, the discrepancy between expectations and content soon stopped the flow of responsive letters. As early as June 1900, barely in its sixth month, a woman from Chicago wrote, "Women, are you really giving up your page? . . . You need not talk only of Socialism, church and children's education. Write down what is on your mind. That, too, is part of agitation for freedom!"[72] Some weeks later Frau Kathie complained in an editorial about too little interest shown by her readers.[73]

One reader, writing under the name of "An enlightened Swabian," tried to point out deficiencies of the page, "The reason is that it offers too little diversity; I think that if women would learn something entertaining, something about cooking and housekeeping and about the newest fashion, it would be most stimulating without doing damage to our cause, which we will pursue at all times."[74]

Again and again women complained more or less directly that they were intellectually and physically unable to attain to that ever striving person they were urged to be. Those difficult economic lectures were of no interest to most, one "proletarian" wrote, for there was almost nothing to meet women's needs, to help their imagination. "By discussing practical, hygienic, moral affairs and, last but not least, food, our women's corner could be much more attractive. . . Politics can not be our sole aim in life . . . less scientific nourishment, but a more realistic fare" was needed.[75]

But did the *SZ* women's page offer this "more realistic fare"? Judging from its success, it appealed to German-American women in New York and all over the country. Apparently, the make-up of this page and its content did what the women's page was meant to do, namely, attract female readers. It would be too easy—and certainly too much biased by our own understanding of emancipation—to conclude that most German-American women at the end of the 19th century were satisfied with being housewives and mothers, that they did not show any interest or desire to take over new responsibilities and that their intellectual needs consisted of society news and shallow chatter.

German immigrant women in New York expected help and advice for their everyday reality: the daily chores, the care for food, making ends meet and helping their children grow up.[76] Women were confronted with acculturation problems in their homes and in their neighborhoods. They wanted advice for problems within this sphere. Whenever a paper offered help along these lines, they responded. To be sure, this seemingly narrow sphere was not so narrow after all; it required their commitment and energy, and within its confines women achieved a lot. These achievements, however, were not reflected in the women's pages.

The success of the *SZ* women's pages lay in the personal approach of Frau Anna towards her readers. By answering letters, by trying to help with material or other needs, by publishing recipes, addresses of home economics schools and other institutions on request of her readers, she communicated with them and offered German-American women a forum. By approving women's traditional role within the family she upgraded it. And her assurance that German values were something superior gave immigrant women the feeling of not always being the underdog; it gave them the feeling of being the better housewives. Frau Anna said nothing about the activities of women outside the home. She never challenged traditional sex roles, and she probably rather impeded the acculturation process by urging her readers to be the guardians of ethnicity.

As to the *VZ* authors, they did not find a way to get women involved, to really let them participate in "their" page. Certainly, this women's column, too, assured "the ordinary woman . . . that her life was important, her problems understood . . . [it] gave her the solace of knowing that her thoughts and feelings were shared by others," as Maxine Seller has put it.[77] But the column did not really offer help, since the discussion of topics and the way they were discussed were restricted to the educational goal of ideologically bringing women up to the standard of men. In the *VZ*, too, traditional sex-roles went unquestioned; the editresses left out the gap which existed between Socialist ideology and the reality of acculturation faced by women. Women repeatedly tried to point towards this discrepancy, and their letters cast some light on the reality of women's existence in New York City.

The comparison of the women's pages of these two important New York papers reveals an ideologically predetermined approach to issues of German-American womanhood, from both the conservative and Socialist camp. It was for different reasons, however, that both papers championed adherence to traditional female role models.

While these papers give some insight into problems of everyday living of their female readers, women's achievements outside their homes received little editorial attention. Problems faced by German-American women were determined more by the necessities of acculturation than by differences of class. However, much more research has to be done on this subject. Present research activities on the subject promise interesting results.[78] To come to a fuller view of German immigrant women's life in American cities means nothing less than to come to a better understanding of acculturation of Germans in the United States.

NOTES

For helpful comments on this paper I want to thank Christiane Harzig; to Ed McKenney I am grateful for having a close look at my non-native English.

[1]In the U.S. the number of German-language papers almost doubled between 1848 and 1852. See Wittke, Carl, *The German-Language Press in America* (Univ. of Kentucky Press, 1957), 75f.

[2]See Bretting, Agnes, *Soziale Probleme dt. Einwanderer in New York City, 1800-1860* (Wiesbaden, 1981), 136ff.

[3]Oswald Ottendorfer had participated in the revolutionary movement in Vienna, Prague and Dresden. He arrived in New York in 1850 and joined the *SZ* in 1851. As a staunch Democrat he actively participated in the city's politics; in 1874 he was running for the office of mayor of New York. He enjoyed the reputation of an independent, civic-minded man.—The journalist Hermann Ridder, son of immigrant parents, had joined the *SZ* as shareholder and member of the editorship in 1891.

[4]Born in Berlin, Alexander Jonas came to the U.S. in 1869. As an able Marxist he became a prominent speaker of the SLP. He was co-founder of the *VZ*. The nobleman Sergius Schewitsch was a refugee from Russia. Hermann Schlueter became known as the leading scholar of the German-American labor and socialist movement in America.

[5]For details see Hoerder, Dirk/Thomas Weber (eds.), *Glimpses of the German-American Radical Press. Die Jubiläumsnummern der "New Yorker Volkszeitung" 1888, 1903, 1928* (Bremen, 1985), 10ff.

[6]Godey's Lady's Book, printed in Philadelphia. Marzolf, Marion, *Up from the Footnote. A Hist. of Women Journalists* (New York, 1977), 12.

[7]See Harzig, Christiane, "The Role of German Women in the German-American Working-Class Movement in Late 19th-Century New York", *Journal of American Hist.* 8, 2 (1989), 87-107; quotation p. 97.

[8]*VZ*, 1 July 1900, 16. All quotations from the *VZ* as well as the *SZ* were trans. by the author.

[9]E.g., he had been writing articles for the first German-language women's paper in America, *Die Neue Zeit*, publ. by Mathilde Wendt and Auguste Lilienthal. See Hoerder/Weber (1985), 16.

[10]The first illustr. fashion advertisement was printed 22 Dec. 1907, 20.

[11]*VZ*, 31 July 1904, 16.

[12]Marriage ("Die Heirathsfrage") was treated extensively in winter 1891 and spring 1892; the problem of domestic help ("Die Dienstbotenfrage") was an issue which came up again and again.

[13]Some of the editorials must have come from some kind of agency, since they were printed in the women's pages of German-language newspapers in various cities in the U.S. The article on "Women's Calling," e.g., appeared in the *SZ* (22 March 1896) and in the Illinois *Staats-Zeitung* (9 July 1899). In this case, of course, it could possibly have originated from Frau Anna.

[14]Dittmar, E. C., *Die Einwanderung gebildeter weibl. Erwerbsbedürftiger in die Ver. Staaten* (Bielefeld/Leipzig, 1909), 2.

[15]Ibid.

[16]Quoted in White, Cynthia L., *Women's Magazines, 1693-1968* (London, 1970), 250.

[17]See Harzig (1989), 88.

[18]Dickinson, Joan Younger, *The Role of Immigrant Women in the U.S. Labor Force, 1890-1910* (New York, 1980), 209; see also Kessler-Harris, Alice, *Out to Work: A Hist. of Wage-Earning Women in the U.S.* (New York, 1982).

[19]Ibid. In 1900, 54.6% of all female Germans who were gainfully employed worked as domestic servants (p. 74); but only 12.4% of all German women in the city were working for

wages at all (p. 68). In 1870 every fourth household in the city employed a female help; that was a much higher percentage than in the German capital city of Berlin. See Helbich, Wolfgang/Walter D. Kamphoefner/Ulrike Sommer (eds.), *Briefe aus Amerika. Dt. Auswanderer schreiben aus der Neuen Welt, 1830-1930* (München, 1988), 494. On working conditions of maids see Katzman, David M., *Seven Days a Week, Women and Domestic Service in Industrializing America* (New York, 1978).

[20]*VZ*, 7 Jan. 1900, 16.

[21]Ibid., 14 Jan. 1900, 9.

[22]See Buhle, Mary Jo, *Women and American Socialism* (Urbana, Ill, 1981), 19.

[23]Seifert, Ruth, "The Portrayal of Women in the German-American Labor Movement", in: Keil, Hartmut (ed.), *German Workers' Culture in the U.S. 1850 to 1920* (Washington/London, 1988), 109-136; quotation p. 127.

[24]*VZ*, 12 Jan. 1902, 9.

[25]Ibid., 3 March 1901, 9.

[26]*SZ* , 22 March 1891, 5.

[27]Ibid., 22 March 1896, 14. See fn. 13.

[28]Ibid., 31 Jan. 1904, 18, Frau Anna told her readers, that she had started her career as a journalist by writing an essay on this word of the Bible for the *Evening Telegram*, which got printed as an editorial.

[29]Ibid., 20 Dec. and 27 Dec. 1891, 5.

[30]Ibid., 27 March 1892, 6.

[31]Ibid., 4 and 11 June 1893, 6.

[32]Very little is known about the perception German-American women had about housework. Welcomed and long overdue information on this important question can be expected from a dissertation by Monika Blaschke, Univ. of Bremen.

[33]Ibid., 27 July 1890, 4; 12 Feb. 1898, 2.

[34]See, e.g., *VZ*, 15 Feb. 1880, 3; 11 Feb. 1885, 2.

[35]Seifert (1988), 123.

[36]For instance *VZ*, 20 Nov. 1892, 9; 9 Feb. 1894, 2; 5 April 1895, 9; 5 Oct. 1899, 9.

[37]A similar conclusion is given by Seller, Maxine S., "The Women's Interest Page of the *Jewish Daily Forward:* Socialism, Feminism, and Americanization in 1919," in: Harzig, Christiane/Dirk Hoerder (eds.), *The Press of Labor Migrants in Europe and North America, 1880s to 1930s* (Bremen, 1985), 221- 242, despite the fact that in this paper wage work for women was seen as more than just a necessity, and housework was judged to be a drudgery.

[38]*SZ*, 29 March 1891, 5; 21 June 1898, 18.

[39]Ibid., 25 Sept. 1898, 18.

[40]Ibid., 18 Sept. 1898, 18.

[41]Ibid., 10 Dec. 1899, 18; 14 and 21 Sep. 1902, 18. On the question how wages were spent by working girls and what these girls expected by their "new" lifestyle Kathy Peiss has done valuable research: *Cheap Amusements. Working Women and Leisure in Turn-of-the-Century New York* (Philadelphia, 1986).

[42]Frau Anna did not believe in solidarity by the working class itself; see for instance her editorial in *SZ*, 3 Jan. 1904, 18.

[43]Only the answers were printed, applications and requests had to be deducted.

[44]*SZ*, 13 Dec. 1903, 22.

[45]Ibid., 13 March 1892, 6; 16 Sept. 1906, 22.

[46]Ibid., 19 Nov. 1899, 18.

[47]Ibid., 10 Nov. 1895, 14.

[48]Ibid., 28 Aug. 1898, 18.

[49]*Chicago Vorbote*, 16 Aug. 1874.

[50]*VZ*, 4 Feb. 1900, 9.

[51]Ibid., 21 Feb. 1903, 16.

[52]Ibid., 11 Feb. 1900, 9

[53]Many articles stressed that point, a programmatic one is, e.g., *VZ*, 2 June 1901, 9.

[54]E.g., ibid., 4 Oct. 1903, 16: "Das Geschlechtliche in der Jugenderziehung" (The Aspect of Sexuality in the Education of the Young).

[55]Ibid., 13 April 1900, 9.

[56]Ibid., 7 Oct. 1900, 9.

[57]Ibid., 28 Oct. 1900, 9.

[58]Ibid., 11 Nov. 1900, 9.

[59]*SZ*, 9 Feb. 1896, 14.

[60]Ibid., 16 Feb. 1896, 14.

[61]Ibid., 23 Feb. 1896, 14.

[62]Ibid., 1 March 1896, 14.

[63]Ibid., 4 Sep. 1910, 16.

[64]*VZ*, 21 Feb. 1903, 16.

[65]Ibid., 27 Oct. 1907, 20.

[66]Ibid., 5 Jan. 1908, 20.

[67]Ibid., 16 Sep. 1900, 9.

[68]Ibid., 21 Oct. 1900, 9.

[69]Ibid., 4 Nov. 1900, 16.

[70]*SZ*, 15 March 1908, 18.

[71]Ibid., 5 Nov. 1899, 18.

[72]*VZ*, 24 June 1900, 9.

[73]Ibid., 12 Aug. 1900, 9.

[74]Ibid., 23 Sep. 1900, 9.

[75]Ibid., 20 Dec. 1903, 16.

[76]See, e.g., Strasser, Susan, *Never Done: A Hist. of American Housework* (New York, 1982).

[77]Seller (1985), 231.

[78]In the U.S. a number of studies on immigrant women and various aspects of acculturation have been published in recent years; see the bibliogr. review on this subject by Donna Gabbaccia, "America's Immigrant Women: A Review Essay", *Journal of American Ethnic Hist.* 8, 2 (1989): 127-133. But research specifically on German-American women is still in the beginning. Recent studies include the diss. by Monika Blaschke (see fn. 32); Christiane Harzig's *Familie, Arbeit u. weibl. Oeffentlichkeit in einer Einwanderungsstadt: Dt.-Amerikanerinnen in Chicago um die Jahrhundertwende* (St. Katharinen, 1991); and the project on "Women in the Migration Process, a Comparison of German, Irish, Polish, and Swedish Women in Chicago" (Univ. of Bremen), chaired by Chr. Harzig.

19 | German Jewish Identity and German Jewish Emigration to the Midwest in the 19th Century

Carolyn S. Blackwell, *Indiana University-Purdue University at Indianapolis*

I

This essay attempts to define what constituted German Jewish identity during the 19th century and how it influenced German Jewish immigration in the Midwest, particularly in Indiana. Also to be considered is how German Jews were perceived by the American population. German or Jew? German Jew? German of the Jewish faith? This question of identity was debated among Jews during the 19th and 20th centuries. Scholars have commented that German Jews had two aspirations: one being to integrate themselves into the dominant culture and the other to retain Jewish identity.[1]

The question of German Jewish assimilation is still a controversial topic and is the central issue in defining individual or group identity of German Jews. From an historical perspective, the assimilation, which began in the late 18th and early 19th centuries, did not cause any integration into German society; it did, however, create a minority group (subgroup) which conformed to German middle-class characteristics.[2] German Jews used assimilation to diminish cultural boundaries and thereby lose their separate identity, a prerequisite for merging with the German culture to form one culture. But what occurred in reality was an incorporation of Jews into German culture without a change in the dominant group's perception of the Jews as being separate from Germans.

Ethnic distinctions do not depend upon an absence of mobility, contact, or information, but do involve the social processes of exclusion and incorporation.[3] German Jews faced varying degrees of exclusion in the professions, occupations, and in social interactions with the dominant group.

There is a need to rethink explanations concerning German Jewish identity and the process of assimilation. For this discussion, the phenomenon of assimilation and acculturation will be defined as follows: *Assimilation* refers to a loss of ethnic and religious identity, as exemplified by Jews who intermarried or were baptized and had social ties with Christians or other Jews like themselves. *Acculturation* refers to the acceptance of certain customs and cultural patterns of the majority while still remaining loyal to ethnic and/or religious traditions of one's group. This is seen in Jews who adopted styles of dress, manners, speech, and acquired middle-class attitudes and loyalty to the country of the majority.[4]

To investigate the merger tendency on the one hand and the forces that maintained German Jews as a separate group on the other, I will focus on the internal structure of the German Jewish community as well as the ethnic boundaries and the maintenance of boundaries.[5]

A boundary is used to maintain and/or diminish cultural differences. Factors that affect boundaries are marriage patterns, occupational specialization, politics, and demographic features.[6] Scholars for most of the 20th century have cited assimilation as the method used by Jews to diminish cultural boundaries. But assimilation was not a means the majority of German Jews embraced; for if one *assimilated* it meant the loss of Jewish ethnic and religious identity with Germanization the end result. Usually assimilated individuals became Christians by baptism and married within the dominant group. Their interactions were with Christians and Jews like themselves.[7] Uriel Tal speaks of the dual aspirations of many German Jews who struggled to integrate into the German culture and to maintain Jewish identity.[8]

Degrees of integration into the German social and occupational structure were influenced by the majority group's acceptance of Jews and the willingness and ability of Jews to take advantage of opportunities. What occurred in most Jewish communities was the *acculturation* of Jews. Characteristics of the German culture such as dress, language, loyalty to country, attitude of the middle-class about hard work and achievement were adopted by Jews. German Jews saw no conflict between their Germanness and their Jewishness as they still retained religious practices, celebrated holidays and continued to marry within their group.[9]

The difficulties encountered by German Jews attempting to establish a German Jewish identity resulted from differing perceptions of the German and Jewish communities. The perceptions of the German community ranged from seeing Jews as part of German society but with a different religion, to strong anti-Semitism in the form of economic and political sanctions. The Jewish perception of the German Jew reflected the needs and experiences of the individual. Diverse definitions of the identity of German Jews therefore came as no surprise.

Two major factors that influenced Jewish identity were the German Enlightenment and the unification of Germany in 1871. The Enlightenment brought improvement for both Germans and Jews, as well as new conflicts and tensions between the groups. Religious conflict and dislike decreased during the 19th century but was replaced by the growth of ethnic consciousness and national feelings.[10]

George Mosse sees the Enlightenment giving support to the ideal of self-education, *Bildung*, which became decisive for German Jewry.[11] The word *Bildung* evoked a meaning of more than education as it incorporated the concepts of moral and character development of the individual. *Bildung* was defined in Goethe's *Wilhelm Meister's Apprenticeship* (1795/96) as the "cultivation of my individual self just as I am."[12] The process of *Bildung* was seen as an individual inward process that continued all through life. This ideal appealed to Jews because it seemed to go beyond nationalism and religion, allowing development of the individual with assimilation being the outcome. Leo Baeck did not use the word *Erziehung* (education), but used instead *Bildung* by which he meant, "bringing someone to self-realization, not educating people but helping them to educate themselves." He expanded this definition in a lecture in 1926, when he described educating a person as "the most artistic accomplishment of man."[13]

During the Enlightenment, the religious relationship between Christians and Jews was changed from the religious to the secular arena. Jews used the rationale of the Enlightenment (reason, equal rights, and humanistic education), the development of modern industry, and change in social classes to further their integration into German society. Jews assumed a society would develop on the premise of man's achievements, not on the basis of his religion or his heritage. Therefore, Jews would not need to change their religion because religion (Christian or Judaic) would be valued in terms of its contribution to man's moral and ethical development. Also, nationality would be determined not on biological or ethnic origin, but on loyalty to the country of birth and/or adoption and the adoption of the language and culture of the majority group.[14]

The unification of Germany (1871) brought full emancipation of the Jews and created an atmosphere of hope. Individual Jews were able to hold official administrative, academic and legal positions. This expanded range of opportunities for Jewish ctizens led to increased energy in various fields, especially science and politics. During this period, Jews became more secular as they sought the unity of nature, not the unity of the invisible God.[15] H. I. Bach states in his work on German Jewish synthesis: "The trend toward secularization of Judaism meant its values were given new and creative applications."[16] The religious Reform movement had its origin in German Jewry.[17] The German community did not perceive these applications as Jewish community values and efforts, but as individual values and efforts. This perception led Jews to become more dependent on the German community for their identity; previously, Jewish identity had been taken from their relationship with God and the Jewish community.[18] While the unification brought about emancipation for the Jews, it also brought about a shift in the "Jewish problem" from the civic to the social field.[19] The loss of integrity of the boundary of the Jewish community accentuated the differences within and caused increased debate among Jews about German identity.

The unification of Germany not only allowed for increased participation by Jews in German life, but concurrently brought about increased hostility toward Jews.[20] Having achieved unification, the state wanted to maintain the nation-state and develop a wider base of popular support. The state used the concepts of *Volk* and *Kultur* to forge a strong spirit of nationalism among Germans. The word *Volk* had the inference of genetic identity and shared cultural traditions.[21] J. G. Herder (1744-1803) commented that each *Volk* must progress along its own historical path in order to maintain its individuality and to survive.[22] *Völkisch* Germans perceived themselves as a distinct group with blood ties and a shared history, rooted in soil, culture, and tradition. For these the German *Volk* represented those people who were of the "same blood."[23]

The German word *Kultur* was used in contrast to the word *Zivilisation*. *Kultur* evoked the meaning of stability and continuity of tradition. The themes of *Volk* and *Kultur* were permanence, rooted in the soil, common racial ancestry, land and traditions. These were seen as a bond between Germans and were used to unite Germans.

Zivilisation became equated with modernization, opportunism, and urban setting. *Zivilisation* did not signify the virtues of modern life, but its negative aspects: rural folk moving to overcrowded cities, abandoning traditional values, and elites prospering by exploiting others. This was seen by some German intellectuals as depicting Jewish life.[24]

The question was raised: Could Jews ever be considered part of the German *Volk*? The position of liberal Germans was that Jews could become German if they gave up Judaism. The more accepted German position was one of opposition and, with the growth of nationalism, anti-Semitism increased. While Jews were committed to the identity rooted in the values of *Bildung*, Germans tended to be more and more committed to the identity of the *Volk*. The two groups became even more distinct, though Jewish assimilation had yet to reach its peak during the Weimar Republic.

The Jewish goal of assimilation called for Jews to diminish cultural boundaries between the groups. But some factors that influence these boundaries—demographics and occupations—served to maintain and not to diminish the boundaries: About 33% of the German Jews lived in Berlin, while an additional 40% lived in other large cities. Occupations in the area of trade and commerce accounted for over 65%; 25% were employed in the industrial and manual trades, and about 15% in public service and the professions. Almost 50% of the gainfully employed were self-employed.[25] This profile increased the visibility of Jews, and anti-Semites perceived them as being not part of the Volk but people of *Zivilisation*.

The political spirit of Jews reflected their loyalty to Germany. As long as German nationalism portrayed the concepts of *Bildung* and democratic ideas, Jews could identify with German nationalism. But when German nationalism projected the ideas of *Volk* and *Kultur* and increased anti-Semitism, Jews felt that the true German spirit, as described by the poets and thinkers, had been repudiated by the anti-Semites.[26]

The historical phenomena of *Bildung*, emancipation, and unification questioned the validity of Jewish identity, thereby creating a crisis of identity. Previously, Jewish identity was one of belonging to a group whose values and traditions were part of a religious heritage. The events of the late 18th and 19th centuries were seen to have created a society which was not divided by religion but included all men. Confusion and controversy were generated among Jews as they sought to gain entrance into the German community.

There was no agreement on German Jewish identity. Some said, "follow your bent," others said, "remain inconspicuous," call yourself "a German citizen of the Jewish faith," or "call for a national home."[27]

The identity of German Jews was defined in part by the German society as Jews chose assimilation as the way to prove their Germanness. Those who did so gave up or modified part of their traditions and accepted German values and culture, hoping to erase the boundaries.

Nineteenth-century German Jewish identity thus was based on the ideals of *Bildung* and the perception held by Jews that they were an integral part of German society. Acculturated Jews did not reject their Jewishness or Judaism but attempted to redefine it in terms of their Germanness. Assimilated Jews sought to leave their Jewishness and to redefine themselves in terms of

European and/or German society, but they could not obliterate their Judaic origins.

II

The emigration of German Jews was an integral part of the large-scale immigration of Germans. In America, German Jews tended to remain culturally part of the German community. Prior to 1830 the Jewish population in the Midwest was small in number and scattered throughout various trading posts and small settlements. However, German Jewish emigration—begun in 1820 and lasting until the 1870s—increased the American Jewish population from 6,000 to 150,000. The new arrivals spread across the continent with many settling in the Midwest and western parts of the country.[28]

German Jews were not peasants; they lived primarily in cities and towns. Though many were from southern Bavaria, they did not work the land but were peddlers, horse and cattle dealers, traders in agricultural products, storekeepers, and artisans. Jews emigrated along with non-Jews and both groups settled in the cities, towns, and rural areas of the Midwest and Great Lakes region. The non-Jew became the customer of the Jewish peddler.[29]

Few Jewish immigrants, like most non-Jewish immigrants, arrived with money, as the majority of individuals had come to America seeking economic improvement. However, German Jews left Germany not only for economic reasons but also because of civil inequalities. After the failure of the 1848 Revolution in Germany, Jews lost hope for emancipation and German Jewish emigration increased. A large number of German Jewish immigrants came from Bavaria where their legal position was fragile. In a given locality, the number of Jewish families was held to a given quota. As a consequence, many second and third sons emigrated because the eldest son received his father's protection letter (*Schutzbrief*) which permitted him to marry and remain in the community. The other sons could not marry until a childless registered individual died. Therefore, many young, single Jewish males left Germany. The following observation was made by a German Jewish newspaper: "The Jewish emigration appears to be less due to greed for gain than to consciousness of being unable in any other way to achieve independence or to found a family."[30]

German Jews (*Ashkenazim*) did not blend (or unite) with American Jews any more than German Catholics did with American-born Catholics. Old American Jews were descendants of many nationalities but they stressed their Sephardic (Spanish) origins. After 1820, Americans perceived Jews as a nationality group. However, they were identified according to language. Thus German-speaking Jews were considered German.[31] Immigrant German Jews came to consider themselves to be German-Americans of the Jewish faith. However, Jews moving to the Midwest or West faced a major difficulty in maintaining their religious identity, for the Jewish population was scattered and not organized. Therefore, Jewish life was slow to develop. Many of the earlier German Jewish immigrants were assimilated through marriage with Christians and no longer practiced Judaism but raised their children as Christians.[32] German language and culture were preserved within the family.

Assimilation of German Jews decreased as Jewish marriages became more feasible and the practice of Judaism was resumed. By the 1840s German Jews dominated Jewish life in Indiana. Their allegiance to religious liberalism provided the basis for the success of the Reform movement in the U.S. (In 1824 the Reform movement had started independently in North Carolina.) It allowed for adjustment to American cultural patterns; the service was modified and reflected the standards of the Protestant middle class.

German Jews accommodated the majority group by obeying the Christian Sabbath as far as business practices were concerned. However, they maintained much of their German culture as exemplified by the close family ties kept with those still in Germany, stern discipline, and use of the German language. If German Jews were fluent in a language other than English, it was German, not Hebrew. The Achduth Vesholom (Unity and Peace) Congregation of Fort Wayne was established in 1848. The minutes of the congregation were written and the services conducted in German for over 20 years.[33]

If German Jews were to be found in a "cluster," it was not in their residences, but in their places of business which was the pattern in Germany. By the middle of the 19th century certain sections of New York's Manhattan were filled with wholesale and retail businesses of German Jews. A considerable number were involved in the garment trade, and as mass production and consumption of clothing grew, this trade became a specialty of German Jews. Businesses were concentrated along streets which connected the main areas of the German settlement on the lower East side with the main shopping areas—in the 1870s, Grand Street. Streets, such as Canal Street, which ran parallel then became sites for German Jewish wholesalers. This network formed the basis of a socio-economic phenomenon that coincided with the growth of the garment industry and the wave of Eastern European Jews in the 1880s. Garment production "was to run its veins through the surrounding tangle of residential streets into the tenements themselves."[34]

Many young single German Jews, though skilled in a variety of trades, chose to earn their livelihood by peddling. These individuals left the east coast and headed west with packs on their backs, each developing his own route and customers. The peddler often specialized and was called "basket peddler, custom peddler, pack peddler, wagon baron, and jewelry count."[35] One such peddler describes his first day:

> The first day I went towards the Bardstown Road, applied to many houses trying to sell some of my load, but were shown the door and in some houses were introduced to a big dog. So I tramped till I were out of the city and succeeded to sell a pair of hose for 30 cents. Was so fatigued could not proceed either way, so I sat by the roadside to rest. When about 5 p.m. a teamster hauling a load of cordwood into the city came by I applied for a lift, and paying him my 30 cents hauled me back to the city . . .[36]

The peddler looked forward to the day when he could have his own store. When he was able to begin his own business, he often chose a small community that offered less competition. Thus, German Jews remained scattered throughout the Midwest with the larger centers at Chicago and Cincinnati.

One such German Jewish peddler was Adam Gimbel, born in the Bavarian Palatinate in 1818. He arrived in the U.S. at New Orleans in 1836. For the next six years he peddled throughout the Mississippi Valley. In May 1842 he traveled to Vincennes, Indiana where he paid the Knox County treasurer five dollars for a "Peddler's License" to "retail Dry Goods until first Monday in June." The Knox County records show that licenses were issued to Adam Gimbel and his brother Solomon for the years 1843 and 1844.

After peddling for several years Gimbel and his brother rented a store and named it Gimbel & Brother. From this small beginning to 1966, the Gimbel family came to own 27 Gimbel stores and 27 Saks stores.[37]

Not all German Jews remained merchants or businessmen. Edward S. Solomon, born in Schleswig, was interested in military science. In 1848 he left Germany and worked in New York as a merchant for six months. Then he went to Chicago to study law and was admitted to the Bar in 1859. Solomon became active in Republican politics and was elected to the Chicago City Council in 1860. During the Civil War, he was in the 82nd Illinois Infantry which was made up of immigrants. He rose to the rank of Lieutenant Colonel and was with the Union army at Gettysburg. He also served under Sherman during the "March through Georgia." After the war he returned to public life and was elected Clerk of Cook County. In 1869 President Grant appointed him Governor of the Washington Territory which was undeveloped and the railway was being built. After two years he resigned and moved to California where he served two terms as a State Representative.[38]

The relationship between the German Jew and the non-Jewish American is seen in the Ligonier experience. In 1854, Frederick Straus and Solomon Mier, in their mid-twenties, arrived in Ligonier, Indiana from Germany. At that time Ligonier was a northeastern Hoosier village of 300 people. Probably the building of the Lake Shore and Michigan Railroad through Ligonier is what attracted the two young men to the village.

Straus opened a small general store and by 1860 was able to bring his two brothers, Mathias and Jacob, from Germany. In less than 15 years the store was sold and the brothers founded the Citizens Bank. In 1928 the bank merged with the banking house of Solomon Mier and became the American State Bank. The bank remained solvent through the depression years of the 1920s and 1930s. The Straus brothers became successful land brokers and bankers. They established banks in Ohio, Michigan, Illinois, Minnesota, North Dakota, and southern Ontario, Canada. Mier became one of the largest farm dealers in the Midwest.

German Jews worked with the Ligonier community and helped to introduce many improvements, one being a public elementary and high school. In 1876 Straus and Jacob Stahl, a Presbyterian, were the driving force behind the project. Mier was the "prime mover" behind the installation of the first sewerage system. He insisted the water works be publicly, not privately, owned.

In 1908 the building of a library became a reality for the town. This was accomplished through Carnegie funds and many donations in the form of money and books by Jewish community members of the Straus, Mier, Jacob Goldsmith families, and many others. In July 1974 the library's board of directors volunteered to set aside a room dedicated to the more than one hundred years of Jewish contributions to the town of Ligonier: "The city of Ligonier is proud to pay this tribute to the Jewish residents who were such an integral, vital, and forward looking segment of this small Midwestern community."[39] Today there are no Jewish families remaining in Ligonier. The decline began in the 1920s as young Jews went to college, married or moved to the cities. The last Jewish resident, Durbin Mier, died in 1981.

During the 19th century the relationship between German Jews and American non-Jews, including Germans, was one of cooperation and acceptance.

During the 1850s to the 1860s, German Jews settled throughout northern and central Indiana at Plymouth, Wabash, Huntington, North Manchester, and Indianapolis. There was little interethnic conflict and German Jews felt secure, particularly in Indianapolis where there was a large and active German community. Indianapolis German Jews supported, and participated in, the German associations of the city, such as the Maennerchor and the Deutsches Haus-Athenaeum.[40]

Mayer Messing, a rabbi from Prussia, became the first Jewish religious leader in Indianapolis to participate in civic life. He was a founder and president of the Indianapolis Humane Society, served on the boards of the Industrial Home for the Blind, the Fresh Air Mission, and the Indiana Red Cross.[41]

After 1871, German Jewish emigration from Germany slowed down to a trickle as the long-desired emancipation became a reality. The early and mid-19th century immigrants had achieved remarkable success by the 1880s: from back peddlers to well-to-do business people and civic leaders. The early German Jewish peddler helped further the economic growth of the areas where he settled and became involved in civic activities. Consequently he became well known in his community, and as his participation in civic matters increased, so did his respectability. Historian John Higham states that the prominence of Jews in the early history of a city may have affected the later status of Jewish-Christian relations. Since German Jews were involved in the early development of many towns and cities, they achieved a noted and respected place in the community.[42]

It appears that in the 19th century, over a relatively short period of time, German Jews in Indiana and other areas of the Midwest found a level of security, acceptance and respect never before accorded them. Yet their American acculturation and integration did not diminish their love of German culture and language.

NOTES

[1]For consideration, see Greshom Scholem, "German and Jews," lecture at Fifth Convention of the World Jewish Congress, Brussels, 1966. He states German Jews were prepared to give up their Jewish nationality but in some way wanted to preserve their Judaism, heritage, or religion. Uriel Tal in *Christians and Jews in Germany* (Ithaca, 1975) speaks of dual aspiration and explains if a person was proud he was a Jew and not a German, he had no right to complain about the Germans not accepting him. Also, to remain a complete Jew and a complete German was impossible.

[2]Jacob Katz, "German Culture and the Jews," in Jehuda Reinharz & Walter Schatzberg, eds., *The Jewish Response to German Culture* (Hanover, N. H., 1985), 85. In 1935 Katz stated in his dissertation, "Die Entstehung der Judenassimilation in Deutschland u. deren Ideologie" (Frankfurt/M), 32, "Jews have not assimilated into the German people, but into a certain layer of it, the newly emerged middle class." Fifty years later he still agrees with his statement but qualifies it by stating the entrance of Jews as a collective into German society did not achieve real integration, but created a separate subgroup.

[3]Fredrik Barth, *Ethnic Group and Boundaries* (Boston, 1969), 9.

[4]These definitions are based on work by: Milton M. Gordon, *Assimilation in American Life, the Role of Race, Religion and National Origins* (New York, 1964); Marion A. Kaplan, "Traditions and Transitions, the Acculturation, Assimilation, and Integration of Jews in Imperial Germany," *Leo Baeck Yearbook XXVIII* (London, 1982).

[5]Barth, 10.

[6]Michael Howard, *Contemporary Cultural Anthropology* (Boston, 1986), 288.

[7]Kaplan, 4.

[8]See fn. 1

[9]Kaplan, 6f.

[10]Alfred Low, *Jews in the Eyes of Germans* (Philadelphia, 1979), 409.

[11]George L. Mosse, *German Jews Beyond Judaism* (Bloomington, 1985), 3.

[12]Quoted in Mosse, 3.

[13]Quoted in Leonard Baker, *Days of Sorrow and Pain, Leo Baeck, and the Berlin Jews* (New York, 1978), 99.

[14]Tal, 16f.; Lucy Dawidowicz, The War Against the Jews, 1933-1945 (New York, 1975), 3-22; 169-196. She states that Jews committed to the Enlightenment identified themselves as Germans and contended Jews were not a nation, but only believers in a particular faith and had primary loyalty to the country in which they lived. This "split the atom of Jewish identity" which had been united by a sense of peoplehood and faith.

[15]H. I. Bach, *The German Jew, a Synthesis of Judaism and Western Civilization 1730-1930* (New York, 1984), 119.

[16]Bach, 121.

[17]Bach, 245; see also Yehuda Bauer, *A History of the Holocaust* (New York, 1982), 32. He states that during the second half of the 19th century German Jews adapted religious traditions to German Protestantism and saw themselves as another "German tribe."

[18]Bach, 21.

[19]Kaplan, 25; see also Eva G. Reichmann, *Hostages of Civilization* (Boston, 1957), 22ff; Jacob Katz, *Out of the Ghetto* (Cambridge, MA), 216; Jacob Petuchowski, "On the Validity of German Jewish Self Definitions," Leo Baeck Memorial Lecture 29, 4, states Jews in the 19th century faced anti-Semitic sentiments based on religion. If Jews would convert to Christianity they could be integrated into German society. It was in the last 30 years of the 19th century that anti-Semitism became racist and demanded Jews be expelled from German society. Many German Jews thought the "Jewish problem" solved because of recognized legal status, but equality was not achieved—discrimination persisted.

[20]Low, 410.

[21]Leonard Glick, "Types Distinct from Our Own, Franz Boas on Jewish Identity and Assimilation," *American Anthropologist*, 84 (Sept. 1982), 548.

[22]F. M. Barnard, *Herder's Social and Political Thought* (Oxford, 1965), 55ff.

[23]Werner E. Braatz, "The 'Völkisch' Ideology and Antisemitism in Germany," *Yivo Annual of Jewish Social Science*, XV (1974), 179ff.

[24]Glick, 549; Bauer, 41. Modernization brought changes in anti-Semitism as it shifted from one of Jews rejecting Christ to one of Jews being strangers to the past and starting capitalism. Braatz, 167, states the intellectuals fashioned a *Kulturkritik* which spoke against materialism and progress. They described the Jews as the makers of modernism and materialism. The main spokesmen for this thought were Paul de Lagarde and Heinrich von Treitschke.

[25]Esra Bennathan, "Die demograph. u. wirtschaftl. Struktur der Juden," Werner Mosse and Arnold Paucker, eds., *Entscheidungsjahr 1932: Zur Judenfrage in der Weimarer Republik* (Tübingen, 1966), 87-131.

[26]Bela Vago, ed., *Jewish Assimilation in Modern Times* (Boulder, 1981), 42.

[27]Peter Gay, "The Berlin-Jewish Spirit: A Dogma in Search of Some Doubts," Leo Baeck Memorial Lecture 15 (1972), 17.

[28]Henry Feingold, *Zion in America* (New York, 1974), 68f.

[29]Charlotte Baum, et al, *The Jewish Women in America* (New York, 1976), 34f.

[30]Joseph Blau, Salo Baron, eds., *The Jews of the U.S. 1790-1840: A Documentary History* (New York, 1963), Vol. III, 803f. Quote from *Allgemeine Zeitung des Judentums*, 28 Sept., 1839.

[31]Oscar Handlin, *Adventures in Freedom, 300 Years of Jewish Life in America* (New York, 1954), 74f.

[32]"The Jewish Experience in Indiana before the Civil War," in *Indiana Jew. Hist. Soc.*, *Fort Wayne, Publ. 6*, 2-10; Baum, 24.

[33]Ruth Zweig, "The First Hundred and Twenty-five Years," in *Indiana Jew. Hist. Soc.*, *Publ. 2*, Sept., 1973, 6.

[34]Ronald Sanders, *The Downtown Jews, Portraits of an Immigrant Generation* (New York, 1969), 5-47.

[35]Nathan Glazer, "Social Characteristics of American Jews, 1654-1954," *American Jewish Yearbook* (1955), 6f.

[36]Bernard Baum, "Recollections" 1903, Indiana Hist. Soc. Library, Indianapolis, (SC 1745), 8.

[37]Richard Day, "A Report on the Gimbel Buildings," *Memoirs and Reflections*, in *Indiana Jew. Hist. Soc., Publ. 17* (1983), 44-57. See also typescript history of the Vincennes Jewish community by Albert Rosenberg, on file at the Indiana Jew. Hist. Soc. The minutes of the Jew. Congregation are in the Byron Lewis Hist. Library at Vincennes Univ.

[38]Lee M. Friedman, *Jewish Pioneers and Patriots* (Philadelphia, 1945), 353ff.

[39]Lois Fields Schwartz, *The Jews of Ligonier, an American Experience, Indiana Jew. Hist. Soc.* (1978), 4-31.

[40]George T. Probst, "The Germans in Indianapolis 1850-1914," M.A. thesis (Indiana Univ., 1951), 64, 65, 69.

[41]Judith E. Endelman, *The Jewish Community of Indianapolis 1849 to Present* (Bloomington, 1984), 29.

[42]John Hingham, "Social Discrimination Against Jews in America, 1830-1930," in *Indiana Jew. Hist. Soc., Publ. 47* (1957), 26.

VII.
EMIGRATION AND IMMIGRATION IN CONTEXT: PROS AND CONS

20 | German Immigration and Settlement in Canada: English-Canadian Perspectives

Gerhard P. Bassler, *Memorial University of Newfoundland, Canada*

In 1989 German Canadians celebrated the 325th anniversary of German settlement in Canada. Exhibitions, films, public festivities, posters and mail stickers—all drew attention to Canada's German roots. German Canadians pride themselves on a German-language press and associational life dating back more than two centuries.[1] The celebration of such anniversaries is encouraged by the government of Canada whose official policy of multiculturalism since 1971 has been promoting the preservation of not only the English and French cultural heritages, but also those of all the other groups in Canada's population. In other words, Canada officially rejects the melting pot concept of Canadian culture in favor of the maintenance of a diverse mosaic.

If, inspired by the German-Canadian anniversary and the policy of multiculturalism, a layman wants to learn more about German Canadians from English-Canadian historical accounts, what will he find? What has been the effect of Canada's official policy of multiculturalism on the historical image of German Canadians? In short, how have German-speaking immigration and settlement been perceived in English-Canadian historical writing? The answer to these questions depends on whether one turns to pre-World War I first-hand English-Canadian historical accounts or to the standard post-World War I interpretations of Canadian history. In the first case one would be able to trace the presence of Germans to the opening up and development of every region in Canada; in the second case, however, one will be disappointed to find few, if any, references to German Canadians.[2] This paper examines the nature and reasons for these dichotomous English-Canadian perspectives.

English-language (and French-language) primary sources provide the basis for a small body of German-Canadian historical research in which amateur historians (journalists, teachers of German and chroniclers of various kinds) play a large part. This research has traced the presence of Germans to the beginnings of Canadian history in the mid-17th century. According to it, Germans appear as a recognizable, if not significant, element in the historical development of every region of the country. The record of German-speaking immigration to, and settlement in, Canada reveals striking parallels to the American record. Almost from the beginning, next to the British and French, Germans have formed Canada's largest group of settlers. Responsible for this has been the virtually continuous flow, coupled with a steadily increasing volume, of German-speaking immigration since the mid-18th century. The flow was steady, thanks to periodic influxes from the U.S. alternating with waves of migrants from central and eastern Europe. As a result, German Canadians have formed the most colorful mosaic imaginable of origins, denominations and regional adaptations.

English-Canadian primary sources show German-speaking immigrants to have been remarkably adaptable to Canada's challenges over the course of three centuries of Canadian history. They came as missionaries to Labrador, fought as soldiers in the British and French armies, worked as fishermen and boat builders in Lunenburg, and as farmers, artisans, skilled tradesmen, entrepreneurs, professionals and artists across Canada. Germans were indispensable in the defense of British North America against the threats of the American Revolution. Their record of loyalty to the Crown, of economic success and of socio-cultural assimilability has caused Germans—along with other north and west Europeans—to be ranked among Canada's preferred settlers. English-Canadian primary sources, in short, have led German-Canadian historiography to present the historical experience of German Canadians as an integral and vital part of the history of Canada's colonization, struggle for independence, economic growth and cultural development.[3]

In the standard works on Canadian history, however, readers will search in vain for a confirmation or a discussion of the findings of German-Canadian historiography. The reader may even be hard pressed to find in these works any references at all to German immigrants and settlers. Popular historical accounts, schoolbooks and the media either are uninformed or continue to rehash stereotypical assumptions which appear to be inspired by the perceptions of the foremost English-Canadian historians. Is it therefore surprising that English Canada has been ignoring the German-Canadian anniversary celebrations? This observation has triggered the questions raised in this paper.

To illustrate the dichotomy of English-Canadian perspectives, five cases of German immigration and settlement will be compared on two levels—the levels of a) first-hand accounts and pre-World War I local and regional history, and b) studies representing the main schools of national historiography. The five cases to be examined are: 1) the settlement of the so-called foreign Protestants in Nova Scotia in the 1750s, 2) the German United Empire Loyalists, 3) the "Hessian" defenders of British North America against the American Revolution, 4) the mid-19th century immigration to the Kitchener-Waterloo area, and 5) the opening up of the West between 1874 and 1914. These cases are among the most significant episodes of pre-20th century German immigration to Canada.

The first case involved the 2,400—almost exclusively German-speaking—'foreign Protestants' from the upper Rhine. They came to Nova Scotia between 1750 and 1753 where they initially settled in Halifax. Most of them soon established the nearby community of Lunenburg. Their immigration provided the first permanent pro-British population base in this newly annexed former French province of Acadia where they were originally to function as a Protestant buffer for the English Crown against the resident French Catholics. In the early 1750s, these Germans outnumbered the English in Nova Scotia, and after the expulsion of the francophone Acadians in 1755, Halifax and Lunenburg were the only European settlements left in Nova Scotia until the New England migrations started in 1760.

Contemporary English accounts are the main sources of information about the customs and ways of life of the Lunenburg Germans and their adjustment over the course of a century and a half. These sources yield a consistent picture of the Lunenburgers' unique character traits—stubbornness, thrift and industry—as well as of their defiant century-long retention of German religious affiliations and customs in conjunction with a thick German accent. Although arriving as farmers and laborers from the landlocked southwest of Germany, the Lunenburg settlers attracted new attention when, by the second generation, they developed new technologies in boat building and fishing in Atlantic Canada. Typical for the grudging amazement of English fellow-Nova Scotians is a Halifax editorial of 1859:

> These despised Dutchman have done more to foster the art of shipbuilding in Nova
> Scotia than any other class of people within our borders . . . The vessels these
> people build are marvels of neatness. We verily believe that they lavish a greater
> amount of money in ornamenting their craft—in carving and gilding—than they
> would be willing to disburse in decorating their frows [sic] and daughters.[4]

Throughout the 19th century, aspects of the cultural, economic and religious life of the Lunenburg Germans attracted the attention of local historians.[5] Yet a new national perspective in historical writing, which in 1900 became apparent in the publications of Montreal historian J.G. Bourinot,[6] highlighted the historic contributions of the province's French, English, American, Scottish and Irish settlers and relegated those of Nova Scotia's German element to insignificance. The precedent set by Bourinot of ignoring the Lunenburgers remained until after World War II, when local folklorists, high school principals and archivists tried to recapture their lost heritage.[7]

The American Revolution triggered the second wave of German-speaking migrants who, as part of the so-called United Empire Loyalists, chose Canada as a haven. The American United Empire Loyalists have been revered as the founders of British Canada. Their settlement in what was then exclusively French-speaking Quebec and sparsely populated Nova Scotia created Canada's distinct identity separate from the United States. It is significant that of the total number of 45,000 American U.E. Loyalist refugees, an estimated 10-40% were of German background. British-Canadian sources at the time and accounts of early local historians indicate that "half of those who came to the Niagara used the High or Low German and Dutch."[8] In the newly founded Loyalist townships along Lake Ontario at least half of the original settlers were reported to be German, and among the Loyalists in Quebec those of Anglo-Saxon origin were in the minority.[9] The best known and perhaps largest group among the German Loyalists who settled in what became the provinces of Quebec and Ontario consisted primarily of second-generation German-speaking Palatine settlers from the Hudson, Mohawk and Schoharie valleys. In the early 1930s, inspired by the prolific English-Canadian source materials, the German historian Heinz Lehmann wrote about the significant extent of the German Loyalists' settlement, socio-cultural life and linguistic retention in Ontario and Quebec.[10]

During the American Revolution, some 30,000 German auxiliary troops defended Britain's cause. Although these soldiers came from different parts of Germany, they were all named "Hessians" because the Hessian states supplied more than half of all the troops. An estimated 2,400 of them stayed in Canada. Had it not been for the arrival of these Hessians at a time when the British force of 8,500 was dangerously outnumbered by American rebel forces, the American Revolution would almost certainly have spread to Canada. That these German troops were crucial for the defense of British North America is confirmed by Canada's Swiss-born Gov. Frederick Haldimand. He noted that from 1779 to 1781 his "English" army was for the most part German.[11] Some of the primary evidence suggests that the Hessians were excellent soldiers and that desertion during the war was not as prevalent among them as among British, American and German-American troops.[12]

Despite their pivotal importance for Canada, however, most of the documentation on the Hessians is of American origin. Consequently, the prevailing contemporary image is that of the older American historical literature and popular mythology where "Hessians" is a derogatory term referring pejoratively to German mercenaries who deliberately fought for money instead of principles against the 13 colonies in the American Revolution.[13]

The fourth case in point is the Kitchener-Waterloo area where German-Canadian urban culture could be readily recognized in the 19th century. Immigrants from Germany were attracted to this area by Pennsylvania German Mennonites who had opened up the land in Waterloo County between 1786 and 1830. By the 1850s, Waterloo County had developed a self-sustaining German life which attracted national attention. Germans were acknowledged from the beginning as the charter group in the county seat of Berlin, Ontario—which became known as the German capital of Canada—and the surrounding area. The insistent pride and self-evidence with which these German Canadians reconciled German values with Canadian patriotism is well documented. On the occasion of a *Friedensfest* which the German citizens of Berlin organized in May 1871 to celebrate Germany's unification and victory over France, English-Canadian fellow citizens assured them of the "heartfelt" and "genuine esteem" in which they held them,

> not only as friends, but also as fellow workers with ourselves in the erection on this continent, of a great Canadian nationality . . . We will both be laying for our common country a foundation similar to that upon which now stands the powerful and united empire of Germany.[14]

Postwar generations cannot comprehend the virtually uncritical acceptance and even acclaim by the English-Canadian fellow citizens of Berlin of this openly paraded German-Canadian patriotism, because after World War I it was decried as an unacceptable divided loyalty.

Between 1874 and 1914 three Governors General of Canada visited Berlin, Ontario and lavished praise on its German character and tradition. In 1874 the Earl of Dufferin expressed "the general feeling of the British section and of every other section of the Canadian people, who all recognize in the German element a contribution of strength to our national constitution."[15] In 1879, Marquis of Lorne rejoiced at being welcomed in German and replied (in German) that the German settlers' esteem for the Queen was entirely compatible with speaking German and remaining good Germans.[16] As late as May 1914 the Duke of Connaught reassured Ontario's Berliners of his admiration for "the admirable qualities—the thoroughness, the tenacity and the loyalty—of the great Teutonic Race" which, as he put it, would "go far in the making of good Canadians and loyal citizens of the British Empire."[17]

In the building of a new society in the Canadian West from 1874 to 1914, the qualities of pioneers of German background—whether Mennonites in Manitoba, German Americans in Saskatchewan, Germans from eastern Europe in Alberta, or *Reichsdeutsche* in British Columbia—were consistently held in high esteem by contemporary English-Canadian observers. For all of these types of German pioneers, the depictions of Edmonton newspaper editor and Liberal MP Frank Oliver in 1901, the Liberal MP H.H. Miller from South Grey, and the Methodist director of the Winnipeg "All People's Mission," James S. Woodsworth, in 1909 may be considered representative of English-Canadian opinion. MP Oliver distinguished the German from the Slav ("Galician" and Doukhobor), whom he disliked, in these words: "He [i.e., the German] is a man of dominant race, of untiring energy, of great foresight; he is a man of sterling honesty and reliability, whether he comes from Germany, from Galicia, or anywhere else."[18]

Comparing German with French Canadians, MP Miller thought that "the German in Canada does not hold quite so tenaciously, it may be, to the use of the language of his fathers as do our French Canadian friends." Nevertheless, he suggested, that whatever their position in life, the Germans were law-abiding, family-oriented citizens with a high work ethic.

> There are no men in the Dominion of Canada who have made better settlers than these German people, whose names are rarely found on the lists of our courts and are seldom or never seen in any of our police records. The German as we find him in Canada is naturally a religious man . . . The German is a man of domestic habits, fond of his home and of his home life . . .The German people are brought up to work, and they all work, and are characteristically industrious."[19]

Favorable English-Canadian recognition was thus facilitated by the primarily economic nature of their contributions. Germans, furthermore, were considered easily assimilable. They were, as Woodsworth summed up prevailing English-Canadian opinion, viewed as "white people like ourselves." Woodsworth found the Germans "easily assimilated" but in such a way that "in the long run it would seem as if it is often the others who are Germanized."[20]

Despite their religious separatism and their preference for block settlement, in 1878 even Manitoba's Mennonite colonists from Russia gave the Governor General of Canada cause for expressions of "unmitigated satisfaction."[21] In the 1870s their previous experience on the Russian steppe enabled them to prove the viability of successful farming on the open treeless prairie. Government officials liked to refer to the Mennonite settlements as showplaces for what could be done with the untamed West. Woodsworth, who identified the Mennonites as Germans, prophesied in 1909 that "from a material, a social, an educational or a religious standpoint, the Mennonites will contribute no small share in the making of the Canadian West."[22]

These five cases reveal that English-Canadian first-hand accounts provide thorough documentation for the immigration and settlement of immigrants of German ethnic origin. Furthermore, this evidence indicates the compatibility of their cultural baggage with that of the host society, and it shows the positive portrayal of the German-speaking settlers' contributions. How is this primary evidence reflected on the level of academic English-Canadian historiography?

Uneven coverage is accorded to the Lunenburg Germans' role in the history of Atlantic Canada and to the German U.E. Loyalists in Upper Canada. Most of the main national historians do not mention them at all.[23] The nationalist Arthur R.M. Lower, however, credits the Lunenburgers with being the first English-speaking Canadians. He concedes that Loyalists of German and Dutch origin may have been more numerous than Loyalists of Anglo-Saxon background.[24] Timid recent attempts to explore the Loyalists' multicultural composition[25] have been offset by studies reaffirming the thesis that English-speaking Loyalists were the founding fathers of British Canada.[26] The deeply entrenched post-World War I Loyalist myth might be responsible for the distortion of the Loyalist image. According to this myth, the Loyalists founded Canada on the virtues of conservative British sentiment as well as on the allegedly pure "Britishness" of their heritage.[27] The attribution of Anglo-Saxon characteristics to all Loyalists was popularized as a corollary to English Canada's postwar Canadianization drive against so-called "foreign" settlers and settlements.

Similarly the "Hessians," despite their defense of Canada's cause against rebellious America, either have disappeared altogether from English-Canadian history[28] or are portrayed in the unfavorable light in which they are viewed in America. Canadian military historians, if they take note of the Hessians at all, view them only as "lazy" and "poor quality troops" who "lumbered" around.[29] No Canadian history book mentions the 2,400 Hessian settlers, who in 1783 formed 4% of Canada's male population and as musicians, physicians, artisans, etc. introduced skills in short supply or else unavailable.[30] In tracing the genesis of post-revolutionary Canadian society, English-Canadian historians occasionally recognized Tunkers, Moravians and Mennonites—along with French, English, Dutch, Scottish, Irish and American settlers—but rarely Germans.[31]

None of the major English-Canadian works of a national scope mention the growth of Waterloo County's (and esp. Berlin-Kitchener's) distinctly

German socio-cultural life. Until the publication of the scholarly Kitchener biography by John English and Kenneth McLaughlin in 1983,[32] all portrayals of Kitchener were either published in German or authored by German-Canadian amateur and local historians. English and McLaughlin view the demise of Canada's German culture, including the forced renaming of Berlin into Kitchener (the name of Britain's most famous World War I warrior), as a beneficial development.

With regard to the case to be examined—German-speaking migrations and colonization in the West—historian Heinz Lehmann observed in the early 1930s that even in scholarly monographs the role of Germans is ignored or belittled, while loving consideration is given to the extremely minute numbers of British settlers from the Channel Islands and the Isle of Man.[33] In post-World War II studies of western settlement, although German-speaking pioneers constituted by far the largest non-British group by the 1930s, they have continued to receive little attention or have remained concealed under such labels as "Russian Mennonites" and "other East Europeans."[34] Their German ethnicity, by the way, was easily identifiable before 1914 and in Saskatchewan, for instance, amounted to at least 15% of the population between the world wars.

A number of reasons may be given for the exclusion of German Canadians from academic English-Canadian historical accounts, despite the relative abundance of references to German Canadians in English-Canadian primary accounts.

The first reason may be traced to the nature of the German-Canadian group as a mosaic and to its postwar image as an invisible ethnic group. As a result of immigration patterns, Canada's German community became one of the most colorful mosaics of origins, denominations and regional adaptations brought together under the umbrella label of German. Unlike the American example, in Canada immigrants from Germany proper were but a minority compared with Germans from eastern Europe, and, in addition, Mennonites have constituted the second largest denominational as well as a leading cultural element of the German-Canadian community. Until the beginning of the 20th century Canada's German community was largely a rural one, with regional isolation, denominational divisions and dissimilar lifestyles promoting ethno-political disunity and separation. Prior to World War I, however, all segments of the German mosaic were united in their positive attitude towards the German culture. The maintenance of cultural legacies and treasured values was perceived as a matter of need of self-evident pride or of unquestioned principle. After World II, by contrast, German Canadians were found to aspire to be, as well as actually to be, one of the most assimilated of Canada's immigrant groups.

A second reason for the German Canadians' negative image or absence in English-Canadian historical accounts is attributable to the foundations of Canadian academic historiography. The main schools of Canadian historiography, which did not emerge in English Canada until around 1900 and did not reach its heyday until after World War I, focused on the formation of the nation's English-French community, on the evolution of self-government, on historical patterns conditioned by geography and economics and on the relevance of political biography. Virtually all its major representatives were English-born and ethnocentric. They were imbued with a strong sense of the significance of Canada's British heritage, her national unity and her position within the British Empire-Commonwealth. Some (Arthur R.M. Lower and his school) viewed the persistence of ethnic identifications other than British as an impediment to the development of a British-Canadian allegiance.[35]

The world wars, furthermore, had strengthened pro-British national feelings and anti-foreign sentiment, both of which fueled an aggressive campaign for so-called Canadianization in every aspect of life, including historical writing. For Canada's population of non-British origin, Canadianization implied actively embracing British traditions. It meant taking pride in being a British (rather than a Canadian) subject. In fact, Canada's national symbols were British, so this pride could be shown by flying the Union Jack and singing "God Save the Queen."[36] For the nationalist generation of historians inspired by the experience of World War I, the nation's German-Canadian heritage was understandably a particular embarrassment. They found German Canadians, stigmatized and disenfranchised as enemy aliens from 1914 to 1919 and again from 1939 to 1946, willing to cooperate in the deletion of their ethnic identity and historical record. After World War I ethnic pride and traditional self-esteem plummeted to a point where even those U.E. Loyalist families who before 1914 had been proud of their German descent suddenly sought to reject their ethnic origin.[37]

As a result of these various factors, 20th-century Canadian historical accounts have ignored the true role of German Canadians in Canadian history. When mentioned at all, the image is essentially that of foreigners whose allegiance is to Germany, and although since 1914 no more than one fifth of German Canadians have had their roots in Germany itself, German Canadians and their historical record (if considered at all) have been judged by Germany's past role in Europe. This tradition appears so deeply entrenched that it is being perpetuated not only by subsequent English-Canadian historians but even by academics of German-speaking background specializing in Canadian history.[38]

Despite nearly two decades of multicultural policy in Canada, Canadian historians have shown little inclination to reintegrate Germans into Canadian history. Nor has the English-Canadian academic establishment been interested in absorbing the findings of German-Canadian historical research. Like a self-perpetuating cycle, the historical place of German-speaking immigration and settlement in Canada, although well documented in English-Canadian primary sources, remains in limbo between the filio-pietistic writings of German-Canadian amateur historians and the Canadian historical profession.

NOTES

[1]Canada's oldest German society, the Hochteutsche Gesellschaft, was founded in 1786 in Halifax. Canada's first German-language paper, *Der Neuschottländische Calender*, appeared also in Halifax in 1787.

[2]A typical example is the newly published academic textbook by R. Douglas Francis, Richard Jones, Donald B. Smith, *Origins: Canada's History to Confederation* (Toronto, 1988). It is used in Canadian history courses across the country and does, in its 410 pp. not contain a single reference to Germans, Dutch, Swiss, Palatines, Mennonites, Hessians or any other German-speaking settlement in Canada.

[3]See Gerhard P. Bassler, "Germans in Canada: An Introduction to the Historiography," *The Immigration History Newsletter*, XX (May 1988) 1: 1-10.

[4]*Morning Journal and Commercial Advertiser* (Halifax, 14 Dec.1859).

[5]See Mather Byles DesBrisay, *History of the County of Lunenburg* (Toronto, 1870; 2nd ed. 1895).

[6]John G. Bourinot, *Builders of Nova Scotia* (Toronto, 1900) and *Canada Under British Rule, 1760-1900* (Cambridge, 1900).

[7]G.C. Campbell, *The History of Nova Scotia* (Toronto, 1948). Helen Creighton, *Folklore of Lunenburg County, Nova Scotia* (Ottawa, 1950); Winthrop Pickard Bell, *The "Foreign Protestants" and the Settlement of Nova Scotia* (Toronto, 1961).

[8]William Kirby, *The Annals of Niagara* (Niagara Falls: Lundy's Lane Hist. Soc., 1896), 28.

[9]E.C. Guillet, *Early Life in Upper Canada* (Toronto, 1933).

[10]Heinz Lehmann, *Zur Geschichte des Deutschtums in Kanada* Bd.1: *Das Deutschtum in Ostkanada* (Stuttgart, 1931).

[11]National Archives of Canada, Q Series, Vol. 19, p. 271, Haldimand to Germain, 23 Nov. 1781.

[12]See the documentation in Stephen Francis Gradish, "The German Mercenaries in Canada, 1776-1783," M.A. thesis (Univ. of Western Ontario, 1964); Rodney Atwood, *The Hessians: Mercenaries from Hessen-Kassel in the American Revolution* (Cambridge, 1980); Edward J. Lowell, *The Hessians and Other German Auxiliaries of Great Britain in the Revolutionary War* (New York, 1884).

[13]See e.g. Esther Forbes, *Paul Revere and the World He Lived In* (Boston, 1942), 322.

[14]Original in private possession of W.H.E. Schmalz, Kitchener, and repr. in Gottlieb Leibbrandt, *Little Paradise: Aus Leben u. Geschichte der Deutschkanadier in the County Waterloo, Ontario, 1800-1975* (Kitchener, 1977), 223ff.

[15]*Berliner Journal,* 27 Aug. 1974.

[16]*Daily News* (Berlin), 17 Sept. 1879.

[17]*Berlin Daily Telegraph,* 9 May 1914.

[18]Canada, Parliament, *Official Report of the Debates of the House of Commons, 1911,* vol. LIV, 2928 (12 April 1901).

[19]Canada, Parliament, *Official Report of the Debates of the House of Commons, 1907-08,* vol. XXXV, 6826ff. (14 April 1908).

[20]James S. Woodsworth, *Strangers Within Our Gates: or Coming Canadians* (Toronto, 1909), 89-101.

[21]Earl of Dufferin, *Speeches of the Earl of Dufferin, Governor General of Canada* (Toronto, 1878), 92.

[22]Woodsworth, 101ff.

[23]John G. Bourinot, *Canada Under British Rule, 1760-1900* (Cambridge, 1900); J.M.S. Careless, *Canada: A Story of Challenge* (Toronto, 1953); W.L. Morton, *The Kingdom of Canada: A General History from Earliest Times* (Toronto, 1963); Kenneth McNaught, *The Pelican History of Canada* (Harmondsworth, 1969).

[24]Arthur R.M. Lower, *Colony to Nation: A History of Canada* (Toronto, 1964), 106, 121.

[25]Joan Magee, ed., *Loyalist Mosaic: A Multi-ethnic Heritage* (Toronto, 1984); Nick and Helma Mika, *United Empire Loyalists: Pioneers of Upper Canada* (Belleville, 1976); Mary Beacock Fryer, *Loyalist Spy: The Experiences of Captain John Walden Meyers during the American Revolution* (Brockville, 1974).

[26]E.g.: Don Mills, *The Idea of Loyalty in Upper Canada, 1784-1850* (Kingston and Montreal, 1988); Wallace Brown and Hereward Senior, *Victorious in Defeat: The Loyalists in Canada* (Toronto, 1984); Donald Wetmore and Lester B. Sellick, eds., *Loyalists in Nova Scotia* (Hantsport, 1983).

[27]See L.F.S. Upton, ed., *The United Empire Loyalists: Men and Myths* (Toronto, 1967).

[28]In Desmond Morton's *A Military History of Canada* (Edmonton, 1985), 45, the author's only comment on the Hessians is that they were slow and "lumbered" around "with all the paraphernalia of European-style campaigning."

[29]J. Mackay Hitsman, *Safeguarding Canada, 1763-1871* (Toronto, 1968), 43, refers to them as poor quality troops, "lazy and inactive," and ready to desert anytime to join local German settlers; Hilda Neatby, *Quebec: The Revolutionary Age, 1760-1791* (Toronto, 1966), 175, characterizes the "German mercenaries" as fit only for garrison duty and "somewhat difficult guests, who were prone to desert and steal over the border to join their cousins in Pennsylvania."

[30]Jean-Pierre Wilhelmy, *Les Mercenaires Allemands au Quebec du XVIIIe siècle et leur apport a la population* (Beloeil, 1984).

[31]Jean R. Burnet, *Ethnic Groups in Upper Canada* (Toronto, 1972); J.M.S. Careless, *The Union of the Canadas: The Growth of Canadian Institutions, 1841-1857* (Toronto, 1967), 30f.

[32]John English and Kenneth McLaughlin, *Kitchener: An Illustrated History* (Waterloo, 1983).

[33]Heinz Lehmann, *Das Deutschtum in Westkanada* (Berlin, 1939), 8.

[34]E.g.: Barry Broadfoot, *The Pioneer Years: Memories of Settlers Who Opened the West* (Markham, 1978); Allan Anderson, *Remembering the Farm: Memories of Farming, Ranching and Rural Life in Canada, Past and Present* (Toronto, 1977); Richard Allen, ed., *A Region of the Mind: Interpreting the Western Canadian Plains* (Regina, 1973); Henry C. Klassen, ed., *The Canadian West: Social Change and Economic Development* (Calgary, 1977); Howard Palmer, ed., The Settlement of the West (Calgary, 1977); T.D. Regehr, *Remembering Saskatchewan: A History of Rural Saskatchewan* (Saskatoon, 1979).

[35]Carl Berger, *The Writing of Canadian History: Aspects of English-Canadian Historical Writing since 1900* (Toronto, 1986), 113, 129ff., 307.

[36]See David V.J. Bell, "The Loyalist Tradition in Canada," *Journal of Canadian Studies*, V (May 1970), 22-33.

[37]See introduction to W. Bowman Tucker, *The Romance of the Palatine Millers: A Tale of Palatine Irish Americans and United Empire Loyalists* (Montreal, 1929).

[38]See, e.g., Udo Sautter, *Geschichte Kanadas: Das Werden einer Nation* (Stuttgart, 1972). In its 317 pp. it contains no reference to immigrants and settlers of German-speaking background.

21 | Attitudes of German Socialists and Their Forerunners towards Emigration and Colonization Projects in the 19th Century

Horst Rössler, *Universität Bremen*

In the 1840s German emigration to North America became a regular occurrence. Starting in Southwestern Germany, this migration movement spread to the West and Northwest and by mid-century comprised all the German states, though to varying degrees. The structural causes of this movement lay in the marked population growth arising from the shift from agricultural production to a money economy and capitalist industrialization. This process was attended by the pauperization of peasant small holders and agriculturalists, of workers in domestic industries and of artisans who were increasingly threatened by proletarianization. In addition to these longer-term developments came short-term economic recessions caused by the crop failures of 1846-47 which, after the Revolution of 1848, recurred in the first half of the 1850s. These were also the first peak years of mass migration to North America[1] which increasingly gave rise to public reactions. From the mid-1840s, a number of emigration and colonization societies were founded, and periodicals especially devoted to questions of emigration came into being. As Mack Walker remarks, the public debate about emigration was a relevant aspect of the "political and social controversies with which Germany was buzzing" in the years before the Revolution.[2]

I

Quite early, representatives of communist societies took part in this debate. These societies had been established in the 1830s and 1840s by German political emigrants and traveling journeymen in Switzerland, France, Belgium and Britain and can be regarded as forerunners of the social democratic parties founded in the 1860s.[3] Exiled to Brussels, Wilhelm Wolff, a close associate of Karl Marx and Friedrich Engels and a member of the *Bund der Kommunisten* (Communist League) founded in London in 1847, repeatedly commented on the subject of German emigration. His views can be considered typical for this organization. In his opinion, emigration was caused by the development of European capitalism (with its concentration of wealth in ever fewer hands, the decline of the bourgeois middle-strata, and the exploitation of a growing proletariat) in general, and in particular by German particularism (with its police despotism, press censorship, and the burden of taxes and levies from which its subjects suffered).[4] Wolff also noted man's ancient aspiration to a happy life in a new and better world. However, the idea of achieving this better world by emigrating to America he considered a big mistake. His critical stance on emigration seemed to have been nourished by reports on the failure of obviously mishandled emigration and colonization projects, by accounts of the degrading conditions in which towns and villages in some cases had deported their poor to America, and by reports about the lack of welfare or absence of protection for the emigrants on the part of the authorities during the 1840s.[5] To Wolff's mind, no other emigrants were as pushed around, mistreated and cheated as were the Germans: while on their journeys, runners and hotel owners would swindle them out of their last penny; many die from diseases on overcrowded ships; no German consul cares about them in case of need; and, finally, the poorer migrants will have to offer their labor to the bourgeoisie in America where they are equally or even more exploited than at home—so Wolff asserted, but without producing evidence. His examination of German emigration was politically motivated and characterized by his endeavor to deter artisans and workers from joining emigration and colonization projects. Instead, he hoped to direct their attention to the struggle for a revolutionary change of society at home. "What would it be like," he addressed the workers and artisans among the emigrants in 1847, "if you were just once to put your heads together, instead of moving away to the distant republic of America and letting yourselves be pushed around and exploited on the way there. Put an end to the 'Christian German' nonsense; summon your most gracious sovereigns to travel to milder climes (such as Texas or Central Africa . . .) . . . then establish a republic in Germany in which everyone who is willing to work will be able to make a living . . . Proletarians, reflect on this!"[6]

Emigration was also debated by the German Left within the context of potentially establishing communities on the principle of collective ownership [*Gütergemeinschaften*] in the U.S.; and in the early 1840s this question came up for discussion among German communist artisans who had migrated to London.[7] However, this discussion was not confined to the German Left; it played an important role for many workers and artisans all over Western Europe. Great Britain—asylum for many of these radicals and birth place of the modern labor movement—became a center for such discussions. In fact, there was a lively debate about socialist emigration schemes. Various detailed propositions for founding communist settlements were being put forward by some followers of Robert Owen and the German utopian communist Johann Adolphus Etzler, then residing in England.[8] These debates at the meetings of the German Communist Workers' Educational Association (founded in London in 1840) and the Société Démocratique Française, with whose members the Germans regularly met for discussions,[9] show that among them (as well as among the British Owenites) there were conflicting views in regards to establishing communist colonies in America. Some, like the French bookbinder Charles Sully[10] or the German tailor Albert Lehmann, were in favor of such projects. We do not know their exact arguments, but what they probably had in mind were small settlements which were to demonstrate to the world the advantages of communist living and working conditions and thus, by example, form the nucleus of a new and better society. The majority, however, as will be shown, were quite opposed to such ideas. Among them were the tailor Wilhelm Weitling, the most famous of the early German communists, who in 1845 participated in the discussions of the Workers' Educational Association, the shoemaker Heinrich Bauer, and the former student and now composer Karl Schapper. The latter two were leading figures in the Workers' Educational Association and the Communist League.[11]

In 1847 the French Communist Étienne Cabet announced his intention to emigrate with his followers to America and found a colony there. His project met with biting criticism not only from sections of the French Left, but also from the English Chartists and the French and German Communist artisans in London.[12] Disputing Cabet's plan, an article in the *Kommunistische Zeitschrift*, probably written by Schapper, made the arguments of those hostile to Communist emigration projects quite clear. In their opinion, a Communist colony would more than likely be doomed to failure from the beginning.[13] These were their reasons: first, because the emigrants, by virtue of their origin and education, were still too greatly influenced by the errors and prejudices of the Old World to prevent squabbles and frictions from prevailing among the settlers who would not yet be in a position to live and work in a Communist way; second, because the majority of the emigrants, namely urban craftsmen, would be unfit to cultivate the land and clear the forest; and third, because privation and disease caused by the change of climate would discourage settlers. The essential argument brought forward, however, was that small communities based on joint ownership, if they survived at all, would inevitably assume an exclusive and sectarian character, like that of Georg Rapp's Harmonie Society. This could not be in the interest of Communists, as the article stated. On the contrary, it was seen as "the duty of every champion of justice and truth to stay in the country, to enlighten the people, to instill sinking hearts with new courage, and to lay the foundations of a new organization of society." Wolff's comments had been meant as advice to emigrants weary of Germany, whereas Schapper's article was meant to set forth imperatives for revolutionary behavior: it was not his duty to establish sectarian communities in the backwoods of America, but to fight the struggle for the overthrow of society in Germany and in Europe.[14]

II

Only a few months after the dispute with Cabet, the revolutions broke out on the Continent, including Germany. Within this new context the debate on emigration continued to play a certain role. Popular assemblies called for state-directed emigration for those too poor to support themselves at home, while the Frankfurt Parliament decided in favor of freedom of emigration and protection for the emigrants. The influential German Agricultural Congress, however, disapproved of any encouragement of emigration, fearing a shortage of labor that would be detrimental to their interests.[15] For the radical Left who had returned from exile, and for the emerging working class organizations (mainly composed of skilled artisans), the emigration question was not among the most important problems they had to struggle with during the Revolution.[16] Those expressing their opinion on this subject seem to have been hostile to emigration. The Central Committee for Workers in Berlin agreed with the British Chartists' rejection of emigration and colonization projects and demanded a new state which would guarantee the right to work instead, thus making emigration unnecessary.[17] Here the influence of Stephan Born, a typesetter and former member of the Communist League, became apparent. As a leading figure of the Central Committee and the *Arbeiterverbrüderung* (Workers' Brotherhood, a national organization composed of some 100 workers' organizations with a total of 12,000 to 15,000 members), he warned the working classes against looking at emigration as a way out of social misery. Discussing the problem of so-called overpopulation, Born also objected to the idea of government-assisted workers' emigration and settlement in America, because the money for such an expensive project could be put to better use for the benefit of workers at home. Besides, Germany was exporting grain, as the *Arbeiterverbrüderung* asserted, which seemed to contradict the notion of absolute overpopulation. In the end, the solution to this problem would require not useless emigration and colonization projects, but a radical change of society and of the mode of production based on the antagonistic relationship between capital and labor, to one based on free, associated labor.[18]

Born was not the only one among the influential spokesmen of the revolutionary Left to be concerned with the emigration question. Weitling, who had emigrated to America at the end of 1846, also hurried back to Germany as soon as the news of the Revolution had reached him. However, by the time he arrived in Berlin, the Revolution was already well past its peak, and Weitling was under no illusions that a radical transformation of Germany in the interest of artisans and workers could be achieved[19]. This was probably one of the reasons why Weitling, who by that time had joined the *'Arbeiterverbrüderung,'* differed with Born and paid considerable attention to the emigration problem in his short-lived periodical *Urwähler*. He even recommended himself as an emigrants' guide. Referring to his own experience as traveler to and through the U.S., he warned prospective migrants of agents and loafers, and he recommended particular lodging houses. He gave detailed advice on provisions (see illustration) and other matters, including the hint not to board a ship without arms, in order to be able to defend one's rights against despotic captains, if necessary.[20] After his return to New York in 1849, he even came up with a proposal to establish immigrants' houses supported and financed by workers' associations. These houses were to provide German migrants with better and cheaper lodging than hotels and boarding houses operated by profit-hunting owners.[21] However, this plan never materialized.

Supporting the emigration movement, Weitling pursued larger goals than merely advising emigrants on the ins and outs of traveling to America. As early as 1847, during his first stay in New York, he founded the *'Befreiungsbund'* (League of Emancipation) which he intended to propagate also in Germany. Among the Bund's objectives were those which called for support of emigration and colonization projects.[22] In fact, Weitling had obviously turned away from the negative position towards Communist emigration schemes which he had held in the mid-1840s. In 1852 he founded the *Arbeiterbund* (Workingmen's League, successor to the *Befreiungsbund*) for which setting up Communist colonies was an essential aspect of radical social reform. In doing so, Weitling joined the tradition of a communitarian reform movement which at the time was of some importance in the U.S.[23]

In America, Weitling carefully followed the fate of various communal and Communist experiments. He observed with critical sympathy the development of the 'Icarian' community at Nauvoo, Ill., which had been founded by Cabet's followers; he even took a favorable view of the Rappites' 'Economy' community in Pennsylvania—despite their lack of interest in social revolution and their religious sectarianism.[24] With great hope he viewed an attempt by emigrants from Mecklenburg at Liberty, Ia. in 1851—with some of his own followers among them—to set up a colony based on

Illustration: Excerpt from Wilhelm Weitling, "Auswanderung. I," *Der Urwähler* no. 4, (Berlin, Oct. 1848)

— 29 —

Schiffsprovision
für fünf Leute auf vier Wochen.

		l.	s.	d.
1)	Verschiedene Geschirre, als: einen eisernen Kochtopf, eine Bratpfanne, zwei blecherne Schüsseln, eine Kaffeekanne, 5 Becher, 5 Näpfe, alles von Blech, damit es nicht zerbricht, eine Reibe, einen großen hölzernen Löffel, fünf Eßlöffel, fünf Gabeln und Messern, eine Wasserflasche, mehrere Säcke und Beutel für das abgesonderte Aufbewahren der Victualien, einen steinernen Buttertopf, ein blecherner Kaffeebehälter, ein Nachtgeschirr, Handtücher und Lappen zum Abwaschen, zusammen	4	—	—
2)	Ein Faß voll Kartoffeln, nicht von den schlechtesten	2	2	—
3)	Einen halben Sack Aepfel	1	2	—
4)	30 Pfd. Schinken à 13 d.	3	4	2
5)	2 Rinder-Zungen oder Rindfleisch an deren Stelle	1	—	—
6)	Trockenes Obst, Zwiebeln und etwas Grünes	1	—	—
7)	20 Pfd. Mehl à 3½ d.	—	5	8
8)	6 Brode (solche, welche bei uns zusammen 15 Sgr. kosten)	—	4	6
9)	4 Quart Salz	—	—	10
10)	15 Pfd. Reis à 5 d.	—	6	—
11)	75 Pfd. Schiffszwieback vom nächst feinsten	3	5	—
12)	2 Pfd. gedörrte Pflaumen (sind in Amerika sehr theuer, weil sie von Europa kommen und viel Eingangszoll kosten	—	4	—
13)	15 Pfd. Butter à 24 d.	2	6	7
14)	200 Eier	2	—	—
15)	4 Pfd. Käse	—	4	—
16)	2 Pfd. Zucker	—	4	6
17)	2 Pfd. Kaffee	—	2	4
18)	¼ Metze Erbsen	—	—	11
19)	¼ Pfd. Thee	—	2	—
20)	¼ Metze Bohnen	—	—	9
21)	Senf (wir erhielten aber Sägespäne mit Essig, Gummi Gutti und Pfeffer angemacht in einer versiegelten Krufe)	—	1	—
22)	Seife, Pfeffer, eine Flasche Essig eine Flasche Salat-Del, Gewürze u. dgl.	—	4	—

Fünf Mann, welche nicht viel seekrank werden, brauchen dies in 4 Wochen rein auf. Man thut daher wohl eher mehr als weniger zu kaufen, weil die Reise im unglücklichen Falle auch 6—8 Wochen ja noch länger dauern kann und man dann mit dem vorlieb nehmen muß, was der Kapitain liefert, mit Reis, Salzfleisch und Mehl. Im glücklichsten Falle dauert die Reise 14 Tage, meistens aber 4 Wochen. Als Bett wird gewöhnlich eine mit Seegras ausgestopfte Matraze nebst gleichen Kissen gebraucht, welche sehr billig in den Hafenstätten zu haben sind, sie sind aber auch herzlich dünn und hart, wenn man eine Weile darauf gelegen hat. Da die Betträume so abgetheilt sind, daß immer vier und vier zusammenliegen, so thut man wohl, wenn man seine Nachbarn noch nicht kennt, sich mit zwei Matrazen zu versehen: denn wenn man Nachbarn bekommt, welche mit guten Unterbetten versehen sind, so liegt man auf der schmalen Matraze tiefer als sie. Sie fallen daher bei dem Schaukeln des Schiffes Einem stets auf den Leib, was leicht begreiflich, höchst unangenehm ist.

Die frischen Brode und die Schinken lasse man nicht in den Kisten eingepackt, sondern hänge sie in den Schiffsraum, oder noch besser einige Zeit des Tages ins Freie, wenn dies möglich ist. Ueberhaupt verwahre man seine Sachen so, daß nicht das Trockene mit dem Feuchten sich vermische und eines das Andere verderbe. Aus eben diesem Grunde lege man sich das nahe zur Hand, was man am meisten braucht und verpacke tief, was man erst später, oder selten braucht, denn der Raum im Schiff wird von den vielen Menschen und Kisten gar eng vollgepfropft. Auf dem Schiffe werden des Schmutzes und der Nässe wegen die Kleider sehr ruinirt, man ziehe daher auf dem Schiffe die schlechtesten Kleider an.

Man schaffe sich einige gute weiße Hemden an. Kann man sich keine feine leinene anschaffen, so kaufe man gut fassonirte baumwollene Hemden, denn in Amerika sieht man Niemanden in schmutzigen und groben Hemden, als einige ganz Arme und Fremde, die sich aber auch bald reinlicher gewöhnen. Der Tagelöhner selbst zieht ein paar Mal die Woche ein reines Hemd an. Die weißen Brustlappen, welche bei uns so schmutzigen Hemden bedecken, sind drüben nicht Mode. Wir Deutsche würden schon dann in besserm Ansehen bei den Amerikanern stehen, wenn wir immer in reinlicher Kleidung vor ihnen erschienen. Ueberhaupt vermeide man die Farrenmacherei in Kleidungsstücken als geschnürte Röcke, Polonaisen, Jagdanzüge, Reifröcke und Frauenröcke mit Falten bis herunter, eben so die verschiedenen nationalen Kopfbedeckungen. In Amerika trägt jede Frau einen Hut, im bloßen Kopf gehen nur einige, der erst kürzlich angekommenen irischen und deutschen Mädchen. Ich rathe unsern

property held in common. The anti-industrial and utopian character of such experiments in community building becomes obvious in the case of Liberty. Inspired by the desire to leave the Old World with its "heaps of stones called towns" which "should wither and rot away," the initiators of the project saw in their colony nothing less than a lever "by which we shall shake the world to its foundations." It would take only ten years, so they hoped, "when our colonies will rule all along the Mississippi from north to south and the commerce of the West will be ours."[25] However, the Mecklenburgers' project collapsed after a few months. It was as abortive as the plan of some German socialist workers who, also in 1851, attempted to establish a colony called 'Teutonia' in the Saginaw Valley of Tuscola County, Mich. along the lines of Weitling's ideas.[26]

In the end, Weitling's special efforts were directed at the propagandistic and financial support and development of the 'Communia' colony in Clayton County, Ia., which had joined the *Arbeiterbund* in 1853. As early as 1852— never before had so many Germans emigrated to America as in that year— Weitling had made an appeal "To The German Emigrants" in the *Republik der Arbeiter* (the organ of the *Arbeiterbund*). Those he had in mind, however, were probably not so much the German emigrants but rather the likes of the shoemaker from Esslingen who in 1848 wrote on his departure:

> The aristocracy of money is unrestrained now. Reliance on the honest working man
> has declined; the capitalists and the rich have little or no heart for the destitute . . .
> therefore I preferred to go to a land where I shall, in any case, find what the
> Württemberger hopes to attain in the future. There a worker is still worth his wage.[27]

Weitling warned such emigrants about having any illusions in regards to living and working in the U.S.: many would find only low-paying jobs or even none at all; and the American freedom of which emigrants were dreaming was only for those who had enough money. The only opportunity for emigrants to enjoy a free and happy life would be to organize in the *Arbeiterbund* and join the 'Communia' colony.[28] In the final analysis, Weitling's efforts at advising German emigrants in 1848 have to be placed in the context of his plans for social reform. By the mid-1850s the 'Communia' broke up from inner dissension and the lack of financial support—a problem which also led to the demise of the Arbeiterbund.[29]

III

After emigration had subsided in the latter half of the 1850s, it took nearly a decade until a new wave hit Germany between 1865 and 1873. The wars Germany had gone through in those years were one probable cause. But generally, from the mid-1860s on, American developments strengthened the pull factors: the passage of the Homestead Act (1862) and the booming economy of the post-Civil War years. This was also the time when Midwestern states made considerable official efforts to attract European emigrants.[30] M. H. Allardt, the Immigration Commissioner for Michigan residing in Hamburg, was especially active. In 1872 his advertisements offering free pamphlets for *Auswanderungslustige* (prospective settlers), describing opportunities for emigrants in Michigan in very attractive terms, even found their way into some social democratic newspapers.[31]

Allardt was also one of the initiators of an emigration scheme that evoked the greatest interest in certain segments of German Social Democracy. While the Lasallean General German Workers' Association (ADAV) took no notice of it,[32] the central organ of the Eisenacher Social Democratic Working Men's Party (SDAP), the *Volksstaat,* reported regularly on the 'Saxonia' colony, an emigration society established in Dresden in 1872, whose purpose was to settle German families on Lake Superior in Schoolcraft County, Mich. The SDAP's particular interest finds its explanation first in the fact that Saxony was a stronghold of the party in terms of membership and electorate; second, the 'Saxonia' project was not concerned with the emigration of agriculturalists and rural laborers, but with urban industrial workers whose representation of interests lay at the heart of the SDAP's policy;[33] and third, a considerable number of prospective settlers were spinners and weavers, and Saxon hand loom weavers were said to be 'altogether Social Democrats.' To the party leadership's great regret, there were indeed quite a few Social Democrats among the emigrants.[34]

For all these reasons it was imperative for the SDAP to take a position on the 'Saxonia' society. The colony's fate was regularly commented upon and its ultimate failure analyzed in the sense that the site of the settlement lay in northern Michigan where the winter lasted up to seven or eight months, making it totally unsuitable for farming. Furthermore, the urban workers were thought to be unfit for the exacting task of clearing the land. Worse still, not only had the settlers paid more than twice the going price per acre, they also found to their dismay that their contract with the American Iron Company—the seller of the land—was null and void. The *Volksstaat* thus came to the conclusion that it had been in the American company's ultimate interest to lure as many workers as possible in order to scale down wages in that area.[35] The SDAP reasoned that the emigrants had obviously fallen into the hands of "unscrupulous agents of unscrupulous American capitalists" and that the whole affair smacked of slave trade (*Seelenverkäuferei*). This criticism was shared by Friedrich Kapp, a member of the Reichstag for the liberal Progressive Party, an old Forty-Eighter who had fled to America, where, prior to his return to Germany, he became Immigration Commissioner for New York.[36]

For the SDAP the 'Saxonia' affair was more than the exposure of a burst emigration bubble. When discussing it, Wilhelm Liebknecht, editor of the *Volksstaat* and an old member of the London Communist Workers' Educational Association, first coined the dictum, in imitation of Goethe: *"Our 'America' is in Germany!"*[37] This summed up the attitude of Social Democracy toward the complex issue of emigration to America. From the 1870s onward, the Social Democrats firmly criticized views which regarded emigration and settlement schemes as a general remedy for social misery at home. Emigration to them would distract people's thinking from the real causes of social misery, namely political and economic oppression under capitalism, and thus would divert attention from the true solution of the problem: the struggle for socialist change at home.[38]

With regard to *individual* emigration, the German Socialists took an ambivalent stand. On the one hand, they did not object; on the contrary, they opposed any possible restrictions and even assisted labor migrants by reporting in their press about favorable American labor market conditions or by warning workers not to emigrate during periods of strikes.[39] On the other hand, they did nothing to encourage emigration and rather tended to advise workers against it. After all, there were principles at stake. Socialism called for focusing workers' attention to the necessity for change at home.[40] By contrast, the party leadership's attitude toward the emigration of party members was unequivocally negative. However, this did not stop socialists from leaving for America, particularly during the years of the Anti-Socialist Law (1878-1890).[41]

The Social Democrats' party line also rejected the founding of socialist communities in the transatlantic republic. A project of the Danish Socialist Party to establish such a community was severely criticized as utopian by German socialists in 1877.[42] Although discussing the problem of Communist colonies at the beginning of the last great wave of German emigration in the early 1880s, the socialists conceded that such New World communities could serve as examples demonstrating the superiority of the Communist over the individualist mode of production. But at the same time they stressed that it was not the task of modern social democracy to establish them. "Our final end is not emigration, not colonization, but revolution!"[43]

From the early Communists to modern social democracy, most leaders opposed the founding of settlements in the U.S., Communist or otherwise. Only a few—most notably Weitling—were, like other European Communists and socialists, prepared to experiment and test Communist ideas in New World colonies. These few wanted to use these colonies as models for future communal forms of living and property ownership (in a mainly agrarian setting). However, the majority of the early Communists and, later, the social democrats—who continued the tradition of Wolff, Schapper or Born—advocated improvement through struggle at home; they judged emigration to America from a rather hostile point of view. But the social democrats could not maintain their rigorous position. When agrarian and utopian projects faded they had to accept the individual migration of workers in what became a proletarian mass migration (Willcox/Ferenczi) at the turn of the century.

NOTES

[1]Peter Marschalck, *Bevölkerungsgeschichte Deutschlands im 19. u. 20. Jh.* (Frankfurt a.M., 1984), 29ff.; Marschalck, *Deutsche Ueberseewanderung im 19. Jh.* (Stuttgart, 1973), 34ff.; Mack Walker, *Germany and the Emigration 1816-1885*, (Cambridge, Mass., 1964), 70ff.; LaVern J. Rippley, *The German-Americans* (Lanham, 1976), 74, 79.

[2]Walker, *Germany*, 102; ibid., 122f.; Marschalck, *Ueberseewanderung*, 19ff.

[3]Georg Fülberth, "Die Entwicklung der dt. Sozialdemokratie von ihrer Gründung bis zum Ende des Sozialistengesetzes", in Jutta von Freyberg, Georg Fülberth et al, eds., *Geschichte der dt. Sozialdemokratie 1863-1975* (Köln, 1975), 11ff.

[4]See *Deutsche-Brüsseler-Zeitung* (4 Apr. & 27 May 1847).

[5]See Walker, *Germany*, 74-102.

[6]*Kommunist. Zeitschr.* (London, Sept. 1847); repr. in *Der Bund der Kommunisten. Dokumente u. Materialien*, vol. 1 (Berlin, GDR, 1983), 521ff.; the article was repr. in *Deutsche-Brüsseler Zeitung*, 19 Sept. 1847; for a biting criticism of emigration agents, captains, colonization societies and public authorities, see ibid., 6 May 1847.

[7]Even before 1840, L. Gall (1819) and J. A. Etzler (1832) had tried in vain to found socialist settlements in the 'Free Republic of the West,' see Gian Mario Bravo, "Wilhelm Weitling, Die 'Republik der Arbeiter' u. die Polemik gegen Marx (1850-1855)," *Einleitung* to *Die Republik der Arbeiter*, repr. in *Topos* IX-X (Vaduz, 1979); Gregory Claeys, "Johann Adolphus Etzler, Technological Utopianism, and British Specialism: the Tropical Emigration Society's Venezuelan Mission and Its Social Context, 1833-1848," *English Hist. Review* CI (1986), 352.

[8]Ibid., 351-375; in 1831 Etzler emigrated from Thuringia to the U.S.; after having failed to establish a utopian community near Cincinnati, he traveled through North America and to the West Indies and returned to the Old World, to England, in 1843. Here his followers founded the Tropical Emigration Society (1844) and later, after a split, the U.S. Emigration Society (1846). There seems to have been no direct link between Etzler and the German Communist emigrants who were organized in the Workers' Educational Assoc.

[9]Alexander Brandenburg, *Theoriebildungsprozesse in der dt. Arbeiterbewegung, 1835-1850* (Hannover, 1977), 134.

[10]Sully was a follower of Owen and Cabet; at a meeting of the Société Démocratique Française in May 1843 he had commented quite critically on a project to establish a socialist colony in North America; however, only a few months later he became an ardent advocate of Communist settlement schemes and was secretary to the Democratic Co-operative Society for Emigrating to the Western States of North America; in 1847 he became an organizer for Cabet's emigration project and in 1851, in America, he made propaganda for the organization

of workers and farmers in cooperatives; see London periodicals: *Northern Star* (23 March 1844), *Movement* (29 June 1844), New Moral World (5 Oct. 1844), *Spirit of the Age* (2 Dec. 1848); Arthur Lehning, "Discussions à Londres sur le communism icarien", *Bulletin of the Internat. Institute of Social Hist.* 7 (1952), 98f.; Christopher H. Johnson, *Utopian Communism in France. Cabet and the Icarians* (London, 1974), 255f.

[11]See Lehning, "Discussions à Londres," 97ff.; Lehning, "La Réponse de Cabet à Schapper," *Bulletin of the Internat. Institute of Social Hist.* 8 (1953), 7ff.; Max Nettlau, "Londoner dt. kommunist. Diskussionen, 1845. Nach dem Protokollbuch des C.A.B.V.," *Archiv f. d. Geschichte des Sozialismus u. der Arbeiterbewegung* 10 (1922): 366f., 370, 373f., 376ff.; Carl Wittke, *The Utopian Communist. A Biography of Wilhelm Weitling, 19th-Century Reformer* (Baton Rouge, 1950), 103, asserts falsely that Weitling in the mid-forties was quite interested in emigration societies and model colonies and that this was one of the major differences between him on the one side, and Bauer and Schapper on the other. However, discussing the question of what would be the best possible way to establish Communism (meeting of the Workers' Educ. Assoc., 15 & 22 July 1845), Weitling not only criticized the Owenites' model colony in England, Harmony Hall, but also Communist emigration schemes. He called those who wanted to found communities with jointly held property in America "foolish" and argued that people could "do something better here in Europe" than clearing forests in America (see Nettlau 376f.). Besides, Wittke himself gives evidence that Weitling at that time was not in favor of Communist colonization, mentioning that in 1843 he did not join the emigration and settlement project of fellow utopian Andreas Dietsch, a Swiss brushmaker, because Weitling "seems to have had little faith in the success of such a scheme" (Wittke, 240).

[12]*Deutsche-Brüsseler-Zeitung* (30 Sept. 1847); Johnson, *Utopian Communism*, 235-259; however, Cabet's plan met with some response in English radical circles, see [R.], "The British Section of Icarian Communists," *Bulletin of the Internat. Institute of Social Hist.* 1 (1937): 84-88.

[13]In fact, the Icarian colonies of Cabet's followers turned out to be among the longest-lived Communist settlements in the U.S., see Shalom Wurm, *Das Leben in den histor. Kommunen* (Köln, 1977), 187-244.

[14]*Kommunist. Zeitschr.* (Sept. 1847).

[15]Walker, *Germany*, 133, 138ff.; P. H. Noyes, *Organization and Revolution. Working-Class Associations in the German Revolution of 1848-1849* (Princeton, 1966), 251ff.

[16]Significantly, the daily *Neue Rhein. Zeitung* (Köln, 1848-49), ed. by Marx, did not discuss the problem at all, though it did publish farewell addresses by emigrants and ads for the Central Verein für Auswanderung (Köln & Düsseldorf) and ads for shipping companies targeted at prospective migrants.

[17]*Das Volk* (Berlin, 8 July 1848); for the Chartists' view of emigration at that time see e.g. *Northern Star* (23 Sept. & 2 Dec. 1848); *Chartist Tracts for the Times* 6 (1849).

[18]*Die Verbrüderung* (Leipzig, 24 Oct. 1848 & 8 Jan. 1850); Weitling had already argued in the early 1840s that the solution to social misery and so-called overpopulation would not lie in extensive emigration, but only in a radical reconstruction of society based on Communist principles of "equality and association," *Die junge Generation*, Dec. 1842.

[19]Bravo, *Einleitung*, x.

[20]Prospectus of *Der Urwähler* (Sept. 1848), repr. in Wolf Schäfer, "Die Verdrängung des Anderen . . . mit einem Anhang: Neue Materialien zum 'Urwähler,' " *Internat. wissenschaftl. Korrespondenz zur Geschichte der dt. Arbeiterbewegung*, (IWK) 17 (1981): 333; *Der Urwähler* (Berlin, no. 4, Oct. & no. 5, Nov. 1848).

[21]*Die Republik der Arbeiter* (New York, July 1850).

[22]*Der Urwähler* no. 1 & 2, Oct. 1848.

[23]*Die Republik der Arbeiter,* Jan., May, Nov. 1850; 13 Dec. 1851; 3 Apr. 1852; Bravo, *Einleitung* XVI-XVII; Hans-Arthur Marsiske, "Wilhelm Weitling u. die amerik. Sozialreformer, 1848-1856," *IWK* 25 (1989), 1-10.

[24]*Die Republik der Arbeiter,* 8 Nov., 6 & 13 Dec. 1851; Wittke, *Utopian Communist,* 176-180.

[25]*Die Republik der Arbeiter,* 18 Apr. 1851, also 14 June & 18 Oct. 1851; Wittke, *Utopian Communist,* 176.

[26]*Die Republik der Arbeiter,* Nov. 1850, Feb. 1851; this seems to have been a still-born project; it is not listed in Robert S. Fogarty, ed., *Dictionary of American Communal and Utopian History* (Westport, Conn.,1980).

[27]Quoted in Walker, *Germany,* 155.

[28]*Die Republik der Arbeiter* (22 May 1852).

[29]Hermann Schlüter, *Die Anfänge der dt. Arbeiterbewegung in Amerika* (Stuttgart, 1907), 110ff.; Wittke, *Utopian Communist,* 237-275.

[30]Rippley, *German-Americans,* 80, 90; for the changed regional background, demographic and social structure of this and the next emigration wave (1880-1893), see Marschalck, *Bevölkerungsgeschichte,* 45ff.

[31]*Neuer Sozial-Demokrat* (Berlin, 14 July 1872); *Braunschweiger Volksfreund* (14 June 1872); publishing of such ads was severely criticized in the *Volksstaat* (Leipzig, 14 Aug. 1872).

[32]For the negative attitude of this party toward emigration, see e.g. *Sozial-Demokrat* (Berlin, 8 Feb. & 12 June 1870).

[33]However, the SDAP also tried, though in vain, to organize agricultural workers; one purpose connected with these efforts was to discourage them from overseas migration. See *Volksstaat* (7 Jan 1874).

[34]*Concordia* (Berlin, 18 Apr. 1874); *Volksstaat* (7 Sept. 1873), and farewell addresses of Saxonia colonists (ibid., 5 Apr. & 17 Sept. 1873.

[35]*Volksstaat* (29 March, 4 June, 27 July, 3 Aug., 7 Sept., 5 Oct., 1873).

[36]Ibid., 21 May & 4 June 1873; *Dt. Auswanderer-Zeitung* (Bremen, 2 June 1873).

[37]*Volksstaat* (4 Dec. 1872); ibid., 7 Jan 1874; *Hamburg-Altonaer Volksblatt* (28 Jan. 1877); *Sozialdemokrat* (Zürich, 16 Jan. 1881). In 1847, disgusted with political conditions in Germany, Liebknecht and some of his friends had intended to leave Giessen for Wisconsin and found a co-operative agrarian colony there; however, he abandoned that plan, participated in the Revolution and afterwards emigrated to London. See W. Liebknecht, *Erinnerungen eines Soldaten der Revolution,* repr. (Berlin, GDR, 1976), 47ff.

[38]*Volksstaat* (4 Jan. 1873); *Sozialdemokrat* (16 Jan. 1881); *Neue Zeit* 9 (1981), 121f.

[39]Dirk Hoerder/Hartmut Keil, "The American Case and German Social Democracy at the Turn of the 20th Century, 1878-1907," in Jean Heffer, Jeanine Rovet, eds., *Why is there no Socialism in the U.S.?* (Paris, 1988), 145f.

[40]*Braunschweiger Volksfreund* (8 Sept. 1872); *Volksstaat* (4 Dec. 1872; 4 Jan. & 7 Sept. 1873; 7 Jan. 1874); and esp. 17 May 1873); addressing the German workers, the party organ declared: "It is not emigration, not desertion that will save us. Struggle for victory—that is our answer." See also H. Keil, "An Ambivalent Identity: The Attitude of German Socialist Immigrants Toward American Political Institutions and American Citizenship," Marianne Debouzy, ed., *In the Shadow of the Statue of Liberty* (Paris, 1988), 252.

[41]See *Volksstaat* (26 Feb. 1873); Hoerder/Keil, "American Case," 151f.; H. Rössler, "Amerika, du hast es besser'—Zigarrenarbeiter aus dem Vierstädtegebiet wandern über den

Atlantik, 1868-1886," *Demokratische Geschichte. Jahrbuch zur Arbeiterbewegung u. Demokratie in Schleswig-Holstein* 4 (1989).

[42]*Sozialdemokrat* (3 Apr. 1881); ibid., 22 Sept. 1886.

[43]*Hamburg-Altonaer Volksblatt* (28 Jan., 11 & 14 Feb. 1877); Kristian Hvidt, *Flight to America. The Social Background of 300,000 Danish Emigrants* (New York, 1975), 143ff.

[All translations of German quotations are mine.]

22 | The "Trained Observer" and the Common Immigrant: Differences in the Perceptions of "the Americans"

Wolfgang J. Helbich, *Ruhr-Universität Bochum*

Emigrant letters, or at least those of emigrants who had no claim to fame or prominence, are relative newcomers to the group of generally recognized sources in immigration and ethnic history, or more generally in American social history. Lack of availability was one of the reasons for neglect of this source by historians. Until recently, it was impossible to find a major collection of emigrant letters in most European countries. The few letters that could be located were generally not transcribed; and only rarely was anything known about the writer and the addressee. An even more important reason for their neglect was the somewhat precarious position of social history as a discipline and in particular the opinion long prevalent among historians that one might write about the common man, but need not bother to find out what he himself had said, thought or written.

Increased interest in "history from the bottom up," in biographical methods, and in ethnic history contributed to the rediscovery of emigrant letters (after their original discovery just before World War I in Denmark, Poland, and the USA) in the 1960s. Collections were started and editions published in several countries.[1] Germany, country of origin for the largest number of 19th-century immigrants to the USA, joined the group during the 1980s. Roughly 6,000 letters have been collected, transcribed, and made accessible at the University of Bochum, and they formed the basis for two major and two minor publications.[2] A Volkswagen Foundation grant made it possible to do archival research on the German background and the actual living conditions of the majority of the letter writers in the U.S. The bulk of German emigrant guides and travel descriptions—here understood as nonfictional German-language books printed and sold in Germany, offering information to potential and actual emigrants about America and ways of getting there—have been similarly neglected by historians and only recently been made the subject of serious research.[3]

Emigrant letters and emigrant guides have at least two more things in common. During the 19th century, they were competing for the attention of people interested in emigration—together with the many emigration agents and agencies, shipping and railroad companies, emigrant newspapers and oral reports of visitors or return migrants. Whereas it is easy to establish that letters had a far greater impact on individual decisions for emigration than all the other information media combined,[4] it appears impossible to measure the relative importance of the latter, to say nothing of establishing a rank order of effectiveness.

The fact that emigrant guides and travel accounts seemed profitable to publishers and that more than 400 different ones appeared during the 19th century, a good number of them in several editions,[5] would make it appear likely that at least a segment of the emigrants—probably the more affluent and more literate—had read one or more of them or learned about their content. Yet it is also a fact that virtually no German emigrant letter-writer ever refers to such a book, neither recommending nor criticizing it. If such guides had played a significant part in the usual long family discussions about emigrating for a considerable number of poorer and less literate people, it would seem more than likely that something was said about such a book; comparisons between expectations in Germany and the American reality were constantly made in the letters. But there may be other explanations for this silence, and even if the great majority of emigrants had not read any of the guide books, it seems quite plausible that some of the information or opinions given there (but hardly the name of the author) filtered down to the less articulate from the minority that could afford books and could read them without great effort.

The second aspect letters share with emigrant guides does not concern their impact on individual and family decisions made in the 19th century, but their quality as sources of American social history. (Both genres shed light on German social history as well, but that aspect shall not be pursued here.) The role of the accounts of America experiences by foreign visitors for writing traditional American social history needs no elaboration here. And although some 400 German, Austrian, and Swiss authors never reached the prominence and fame of de Tocqueville or Charles Dickens, their ability to write books that found publishers would put them in the category of the educated minority and—though with different degrees of expertise—that of the "trained observer."

In a somewhat similar context, Schmidbauer arrives at a conclusion that rings partly true and partly false: "The authors of the travel accounts were mostly persons of higher social rank who remained true to their own cultural framework. This social predetermination of the author's background determined his image of America. It is therefore subjective and needs being complemented by the less literate emigrants to America, whose 'oral cultural history' would have to be discovered in the few existing sources."[6]

The basic idea is certainly sound, but it is less than clear why that cultural history should be *oral*, and the claims that sources are scarce can make sense only if letters are entirely ignored. But whether the main idea is that of complementing the printed works, or a comparison in the sense of finding agreement and differences between "trained observers" and the untrained, or more specifically examining which parts of the image of America conveyed by the information literature, or which expectations created by the books were found to be true by the actual emigrant—a comparison of the two genres appears worthwhile.

To keep the task manageable, several selections had to be made. Of the 6,000 letters, I have confined myself to the about 3,800 that have been transcribed *and* indexed according to subject matter. Of the over 400 guide titles, with at most 300 available, I made a somewhat subjective selection of 45 titles.[7] A final selection was necessary with regard to the subject matter to be compared, since the whole spectrum of America and the Americans would require a book-length study. Singling out "the Americans," their mentality or "national character," seemed less arbitrary than cutting out some slice of the society and its institutions.

One final introductory remark: While it is obvious that not every letter has something to say on American traits, the same goes for information literature as well. In fact, only 25 of the 45 works consulted contain pronouncements on "the American"—male or female.[8] It is impossible, of course, to make meaningful quantitative comparisons between books and letters, but if one puts 45 authors on one side and some 420 letter writers on the other, the result is clear: an ordinary immigrant has much less to say about "typical traits" than an author. In fact, letter writers comment more frequently on Negroes than on white Americans, and American men are outscored by American women as to the quantity of statements.

I

Having analyzed almost a hundred German 19th-century emigrant guides, Ruth Roebke summarizes the characterization of American women in those books as follows: they are skinny rather than Rubenesque, and therefore no beauties; they dress alike in the city and country; they dress well—hat, veil, and parasol are a must—love luxury, and are expensive to maintain and entertain. They never work in the fields and some of them never work at all. In fact, here is one of the few controversial points: some authors cultivate the rocking-chair image or claim that American women spend little time on cooking and housework, whereas others hold that they work from morning to night, and some point out that the degree of cleanliness produced by them is unsurpassed anywhere in Europe. They have a practical bent and concentrate on the essential rather than the ornamental in the house. They rarely become servants, leaving that sort of employment to Blacks and immigrants; and they like to get married early. Men respect them highly, and brutality or even rude manners toward a woman can easily land the offender in prison.[9]

So much for the trained observers. In this context, easily the most striking thing about the letter writers is that the bulk of their comments on American women were penned by men, and that very rarely did a woman report anything about her American sisters.

The physical features, pleasant or not, are practically not mentioned at all in the letters. That they dress well, and elaborately, and that there is little difference between town or country, is rarely stated directly, but frequently indirectly, like when a husband writes that his wife or daughters sport this or that accouterment, since such is the fashion in America. For the practical rather than ornamental bent observed by authors, there is virtually no echo. And it is only by implication that the statements about not tending to being servants but getting married early are confirmed by letter writers.

One encounters the rocking chair quite frequently:

> What does the American woman do and work? Nothing but rock in the rocking chair all day and, just to pass the time, indulge in a bit of reading or sewing.
> It's rare that American women work, they spend much time dressing up, stroll about and reportedly know neither how to knit nor how to sew.[10]

Such remarks are often coupled with the assurance that never, ever would the letter writer marry such a useless and costly creature. The hard-working American woman, and particularly her admirable thoroughness when cleaning house, are almost totally absent from the letters; on the contrary, it is not difficult to find disparaging remarks about the lack of cleanliness not only in the streets, but also in the house and the front yard.

Quite frequently, and with expressions of amazement, it is reported that women don't work in the fields. There is much ambivalence in the feelings expressed about that shocking custom. It is similar to what is written about luxury—it's good to have, and yet a bit frivolous; and the farmers, who need the help, tend to prefer reserving this privilege to Anglo-Americans.

But it is women's legal and customary prerogatives that fascinate male letter writers most—and even more than the authors of emigrant guides: it may not be too surprising that wife beaters end up in prison, but more so that they might be joined there by men who approached a lady in the street a trifle too directly, or by men convicted because one female testimony outweighs that of half a dozen males. If it is not prison, it may be a similarly deplorable fate; simply going out with an American girl, or vaguely mentioning marriage to her, will be construed as a promise of marriage. Then the poor man doesn't have a chance, the law being entirely on her side.

While the hitherto unheard-of legal protection of women is reported like an exotic aberration that may be very virtuous, the male letter writers can rarely hide their anxiety about such a situation. They quite clearly feel threatened. So Martin Weitz, 32 years old, a master craftsman and sober and solid as can be, writes in 1855, after a year in the U.S.:

> How many German fellows take American or Irish girls one is not allowed to have much fun, or they go straight to court then the marshall gets the fellow and then they are married then there is no more fun they go to the factory together and work both of them and board with other people.[11]

It is entirely consistent that a year later he successfully asks a girl from the vicinity of his home town to come over and marry him. It would seem reasonable to infer that such fears of being forced into marriage (interestingly, this could apparently not happen with German or German-American girls) reinforced the strong tendency towards endogamy and was also played up to rationalize the apprehension or insecurity felt in any case vis-a-vis women of non-German backgrounds.

Another "privilege" frequently noted, and obviously the consequence of that legal protection plus male chivalry: women, young or old, frequently travel alone, even over long distances. That is considered quite normal, they write, and nothing untoward ever happens to them. This is one of the instances where we can be sure that letter writers are not just passing on what they have heard, not really bothering whether a colorful item is true or not (as we may assume in the case of the rocking chair-cum-sewing quotes), since the news about safe travel for unaccompanied women is often conveyed in the context of advice to family members planning to cross the Atlantic and having to travel on in America.

One can offer a number of explanations, though none of them really convincing, why the letters contain almost nothing on the physical appearance of American women (or men, for that matter), which attracts considerable attention in the guides; it might be added that Indian, Irish and Black women are similarly passed over in silence. On the other hand, it is entirely obvious why the hard-working American woman of the guidebooks virtually does not exist in the letters: everybody in the old country knows that women work from early morning to late at night—there is nothing exotic or astonishing about such a report from America, and thus it is not worth mentioning.

The clear contradiction between those authors who describe American women as paragons of cleanliness and the letter writers, who either express no opinion or make more or less drastic negative comments, might be interpreted plausibly. Fairly early, at least since the 1850s, cleanliness, order, and reliability appear in the letters as specifically German virtues or strong points—with the corollary of frequent snide remarks about the lack of such traits with Americans.

If a convincing explanation for the silence of female letter writers on the different—more protected and somewhat more equal—position of American women exists, I am not aware of it. More than a fifth of the letters in Bochum were written by women, so the sample is quite large. The topic cannot have been taboo in any way, since men—whether writing to men, women, or both—discussed it freely. And there are many articulate, strong-willed female letter writers. Perhaps it takes a psychologist to untangle this, or perhaps further work by historians—including a comparison with letters from other immigrant nationalities. The suspicions and fears aroused in German male immigrants certainly deserve further examination.

Still, despite some differences and contradictions, the pictures drawn by guide authors and letter writers appear remarkably similar, remarkably so at least by contrast to the wide divergence that exists with regard to American men.

II

German emigrant guides have a lot more to say about American men than about American women—in stark contrast to the letter writers. Though there are two general book-length studies of emigrant guides and travel literature, none of them provides a concise and yet fairly comprehensive picture of "the American" like the one presented by Roebke for American women. Schmidbauer not only describes a wide spectrum of aspects of American society, as reflected in the 26 books he examines, but he also has a chapter on "Americans" and subchapters on "American mentality," "mobility," "family life," "social life," or "morality." Yet he has a tendency to compile colorful quotations, while keeping analysis and interpretation to a minimum, and he desists from even such quantification as might make clear to the reader what the majority opinion is, or if there is one.

Görisch, on the other hand, writes an admirable dissertation on important social, economic, and communications aspects of the genre, but makes only three contributions as to content: A 12-page chapter on "Americanization," i.e. the dire warnings against giving up one's language and culture in America; a rough content analysis showing how much space is devoted to a dozen items ranging from preparations for the voyage to culture in America; and the assurance that the content is fascinating and that he will go into that in his next publications, starting with Native Americans.[12] Thus, neither Schmidbauer's nor Görisch's study can offer any help—or corrective—to the work at hand.

For the 25 books described above and listed in fn. 8, I tried to draw up a list of all characteristics attributed to "the American," selecting those that were advanced by more than one author and sorting them according to the explicit or obvious value judgment that almost inevitably comes with the description. I arrived at a roster of six positive traits, ten negative ones, and three more or less indifferent. Of course, there is not a single point on which all 25 authors offer a comment (17 is the maximum), and though there is far more unanimity on many traits than one could reasonably expect, some differences of opinion do exist and will be duly noted.

On the affirmative side, there is the great decency and tact that Americans show in public. Five authors agree on that, and eight of them point out that this is particularly noticeable and unfailing vis-à-vis women. Two or three authors each point out that Americans value personal cleanliness highly and are elegantly dressed; very religious; generous rather than miserly; and—an idea difficult to comprehend at first sight—that common people in America are no more educated, but still more intelligent than those in Europe.[13]

The letter writers seem to see the American from a different angle. If one or two agree about the decency and tact, there are definitely more who put the contrary rather bluntly: "Uncouth and uneducated is the American. . ."[14] Only the respect for women is frequently confirmed, and occasionally his being religious—a very shaky compliment if weighed against the frequency with which he is accused of hypocrisy (see infra). Personal cleanliness and elegant attire are virtually not mentioned. Their generosity is not confirmed by any letter writer, but there is a passage in one letter that both supports and at least partly explains the claim of high intelligence for the common people. Immigrant Wilhelmina Stille writes about her immigrant brother in 1837:

I am pleased to see that. . . Wilhelm is so much more intelligent than he used to be in Germany. It is hard to believe but I think it has a lot to do with his having so little to do, and easy work at that, and his walking about and talking with all kinds of intelligent people in various trades, and so forth.[15]

As to physical appearance, there is a lone critic who feels:

Physically speaking, nature has not treated the American with any preference. He is of middle hight, and his body, though tough and enduring, is neither particularly strong nor well-formed.

But four authors do not agree. Bromme finds that "the inhabitants of the U.S. are, generally speaking, a strong, sturdy race." Douai and Arends share his opinion, and Streckfuss is outright enthusiastic when he describes the American male's "splendid physical proportions" and "noble bearing."[16]

But while the guide authors go about describing the looks of American men at different lengths and with different results, though always very seriously, the letter writers disagree with all of them: not a single one of them considers the appearance of American men worth commenting on—there is total silence.[17] One might speculate whether it was because they felt Americans looked just like people in Germany and thus any comment was superfluous, or because they simply had more important things on their minds than something so entirely irrelevant to their lives as the physical appearance of males of the host society.

As to the three "neutral" statements in the guides—everybody, everywhere reads newspapers, and usually more than one; Americans always gulp down their food or at least eat hastily; and their most striking habit is ". . .to position their feet as high as possible while sitting"[18]—the letter writers simply seem not to have noticed, or not to have cared.

On the negative side of the balance sheet, proceeding from the bottom to the top with regard to the number of authors mentioning a specific characteristic, there is aversion to hard physical labor; Americans like to reserve it for Negroes or Irishmen or Germans. Similar observations, explicit or implicit, tinged with self-pity or slightly critical or simply matter-of-fact, can occasionally be found in emigrant letters as well. But the value judgments are generally subdued; the stereotypical "that's the way things are here" tends to neutralize criticism of all but the most blatant abuses. The familiar complaint of numerous Forty-Eighters that for American politicians ideas are unimportant and what counts is only success at the polls, often coupled with the accusation that office-holding serves one purpose above all, amassing riches, is presented by no more than two authors, and is occasionally echoed by a letter writer blasting political corruption or biased judges.

Two authors mention matter-of-factly that Americans are indifferent to the beauty of nature or "attractive landscape gardening." A third one prefers a more aggressive stance. A beautiful flower, or Niagara Falls? The American's interest is strictly confined to how one makes money with or through or from them. He concludes accordingly: "With a Yankee, it is never, ever a question of *admiring* nature but rather of *exploiting* it. . ."[19] Here again, the letter writers remain silent. They seem to be "like Americans" in that they do not express admiration for nature, let alone criticize Americans for not doing so. Only in a more comprehensive sense of "nature" are there some comments. A few very convincingly voice their horror at the pervasive blackness of mid-century Pittsburgh or the frightening sight of downtown Chicago; but for the majority, even for those living in Pittsburgh, ecological disasters do not rank highly enough to write about, as they do at length about "natural" ones like hurricanes, floods or fires.

Recklessness and low regard for human life are described as another negative trait. While Ziegler very generally lists "low esteem of human life" among the faults of the American, Kirsten is very specific. He sees him as reckless, risk-prone, and not at all interested in questions of safety.

> If a stranger expresses his astonishment at the fact that in those steamboat races human lives are put in jeopardy without any cause [or if he demands more safety for the railroads]. . . such a statement encounters incomprehension or indignation.[20]

This is one of the few aspects where guidebooks and letters are in almost total agreement. It is a ubiquitous stereotype in the letters that Americans do not care about human lives, whether in bridge construction, in running railroads or riverboats, or in mines and factories. A particularly lurid example is offered by a German Union army surgeon in 1863. Commenting on the construction of a bridge, "which is being conducted with American recklessness," he continues:

> How little the American government cares about a soldier breaking his neck you can see in the fact that on this trip our two divisions, 5,000 to 6,000 men, had lost 25 dead when we arrived [the boxcars being overcrowded, soldiers traveled on the roof—and fell off. But during the whole time nothing at all was being done to remedy this incredible situation, which 25 fellows had to pay for with their lives.[21]

Some guidebooks inform their readers that "help yourself" is the American's most important motto or guideline. Vulpius interprets the slogan as "no one helps anyone else unless there is a profit in it," and Griesinger agrees that an American would not help anyone out of simple friendship if there were no prospect of profit. And Wander hits really hard:

> The American principle, "*help yourself!*" embodies such a cold cruelty, such a negation of all humanity, that the individual is, like in black heathen days, confronted with every human being in hostility, whereby the crudest, most materialistic egotism is recognized as the highest principle.[22]

In the letters, "help yourself" is a stereotype, and one occuring very often. But it is also an oddity in that it is a stereotype with three different meanings: in the USA, there is no obligation to go out of your way for other people; here you must help yourself, since no one else will, but here you are also given a chance to do so; in America you are on your own, you can expect help from nobody, with the consequence that "if you don't have any money, you're almost worse off than in Germany."[23]

This latter version—the interpretation advanced by the guidebooks—can be found in the letters most often. The point, frequently with the corollary that it was imperative to accumulate considerable savings in order to be able to deal with all kinds of crises, may occasionally have been used to minimize expectations of financial help from the letter writer. There is no doubt, however, that most of them experienced and recognized a distinct contrast between a more paternalistic or communitarian—or more "caring"—old country and the one that came to make "rugged individualism" a term connoting admiration.

Six authors expand on the coolness and lack of cordiality of Americans: "A coolly polite behavior and a certain taciturnity are so deeply ingrained in the American that he is not receptive for cordial relations and *true* friendship."[24] This is a mild version of the general idea that not even the family, let alone friends, mean anything to the Yankee. Another author puts this more bluntly—and more romantically:

> This coldness appears most strikingly in conjugal life. There one finds. . . no sign of sympathy or fondness between parents and children. . . Nothing of the depth of feeling, the cordiality and mutual empathy which makes the life of two loving spouses so wonderful, a veritable paradise on earth.[25]

One cannot help wondering if such highly developed middle-class idealism is echoed by less elevated letter writers. The theme is occasionally taken up in a letter, but usually one written by an educated person, like Sophie Meinecke: "Here, i.e. in American families, it occurs very rarely that parents and children are sad when they have to separate for a considerable period," after having explained that "the Americans are known to be rather unfeeling and indifferent."[26] But it is anything but a favorite topic, and one can easily find contrary statements as well:

> This is an example of genuine American friendliness, as one encounters it almost every day. . . These people seemingly so cool and calculating, are really more kindhearted than they want to show.[27]

But easily the most significant fact about the letter writers is that they largely ignore the problem and seem unaware of any controversy.

Again six authors attribute chauvinism of one shade or another to the American: "This haughtiness and conceit is born with him, and therefore there simply is no Yankee boy who is not fully convinced of being the *non plus ultra* of creation."[28] This is said to be coupled with their disdain for other people, their refusal to learn anything about them or even to study foreign languages—all resulting in dismal ignorance of other countries and cultures. It is obvious that the resentment of such myopia, freely expressed by several authors, results from their slighted feelings as Germans and self-appointed representatives of German culture. It comes as a surprise that this idea is picked up in the letters by a few of the educated immigrants. It is virtually ignored, however, by the great majority of the letter writers. Common people might feel hurt by being looked down upon, though they rarely wrote about it. It did not occur to them, however, to attribute such condescension or worse to American chauvinism.

Another complex on which eight authors elaborate is what one of them calls a "gypsy-like migrating instinct"[29] that contrasts with the ideal of cultivating one piece of land and staying on it for the rest of one's life. Others place more emphasis on the aspect of restless activity for gain that the American indulges in, or the furious pace at which he operates, never slowing down except at home with his family. Arends draws the logical and, as of 1838, still somewhat prophetical conclusion:

> Americans are. . . a migrating people, never resting; once the present states are more or less peopled, they will take over the lands conceded to the Indians and next fill up the prairies or, skipping those, the beautiful valleys beyond the Oregon river all the way to the Pacific Sea.[30]

Letter writers comment endlessly on Americans not staying on and with their land—usually without any value judgment; and some of the more astute ones have quickly grasped the idea of land values increasing with time. But the remainder of the concept—the hectic pace of gainful life—either goes unnoticed or is not considered worth noting.

Considering that one of the most persistent *American* clichés about *German* immigrants was that—as businessmen—they were too solid, too unimaginative, too shy of risks, it is both ironic and logical that a guidebook criticism of Americans was their being too risk-prone, too much given to speculation, and highly unreliable. Letter writers usually find this idea too abstract to mention it, but some of them do, and if so, they agree, like this remarkable immigrant in Washington City, Ill., in 1842, who sees a remedy for economic misery and low prices for agrarian produce in "the establishment of factories and manufactures," but feels rather pessimistic: "But there is little hope for this being done. The restless, irresponsible character of the American is not at all suited for such endeavors and in any case much prefers getting rich quickly by taking risks to taking the safe, slow way."[31]

To the weightiest point made by the guidebooks, no less than 17 out of 25 authors make a contribution. Somewhat surprisingly, most of them avoid the term "materialism," which from the last quarter of the 19th century became almost ubiquitous in a context such as this. Instead, we have "greed," along with "heartlessness" and "egotism," the deification of making money, "addiction to gain," and the claim that "wealth" is valued more highly than "erudition."[32]

While none of the 17 deny that money and moneymaking plays a key role for the American, two of them tend to be apologetic. Duden rejects any reproach concerning "addiction to gain" by claiming there is just as much of it in England or France or Germany. Fleischmann makes a similar statement with a similar argument, but then continues by giving various reasons why making money is more important in America than in Europe, and offering mitigating circumstances.[33]

The remaining 15 authors differ only in the intensity of their condemnation of American money-mindedness and in the fertility of their imagination in expressing their shock and disgust. There are mild statements about a dominating drive to get rich or on cheating in business being permitted.[34] But it is easy to improve on that. To Löher, cheating is not only tolerated but considered "smart," whereas Griesinger finds that the Yankee's "sense of fraud" is "infallibly developed very strongly."[35] There is also invective, or what amounts to it. Arends claims that for love of money Americans deny the noblest of feelings; Gall curtly writes about "dirtiest, most ruthless greed," whereas Vulpius does not hesitate to speak about a "people of swindlers" and a "robber country."[36]

There is nothing remarkable in the *manner* in which money-grubbing as a prominent trait of "the American" is described—with one notable exception. No less than six, or better than a third, of the 17 authors apparently believe they can clarify or illustrate the concept by using a common cliché about Jews. Vulpius is somewhat outside this group when he claims a similarity that goes unnoticed by the other authors: "The American also loves to eat raw onions, just as one can in fact notice a similarity with the Jew in quite a few points [the greed theme follows here]."[37] And a certain originality is shown by Kirsten who seems to pretend having interviewed some of the persons concerned. Americans, he writes, are well-versed in trade:

> Most badly hurt by this are the Jews who come over from Germany in great numbers and typically begin to work as peddlers all over the country. They all claim that the Americans are their betters with regard to cunning and say they need an apprenticeship with the Americans.[38]

One author uses the cliché but with a different twist. Griesinger states that people have called the Yankee "oftentimes the Jew of the West," and in a footnote he adds the "proverb": "You can turn one Yankee into two Jews, and still have a Christian left over." But then he points out that the comparison is valid only to a small extent, since the life of most Jews consists only of "bargaining and fast talking," whereas the Yankee is adept at any trade and occupation.[39]

While one might summarize Griesinger in the sense that Jews are like Americans, only worse, the other three authors agree with Kirsten and depict the American as a sort of "Super-Jew". Hesse calls money-making the god that rules North America, and continues: "Therefore the Americans in all trading cities possess a cunning and slyness unmatched by the German Jews' proverbial adroitness in trade."[40] Menzel calls the American a superb speculator, particularly in trade. "In this, he far surpasses the European Jew, whom he strikingly resembles as a businessman with regard to integrity and reliability, a point passed over in silence by the glorifiers of the Americans."[41] Steinert, finally, makes the strongest statement as far as quantification is concerned: "The Jews of the Old World were never as bad as these people. The Yankees are five-fold Jews, says an old proverb."[42]

This use of the "Jewish analogy" allows two safe conclusions: the authors concerned took for granted that every reader was familiar with the cliché, and that none harbored any serious doubts about its validity. It seems less certain that their making the comparison betrays an anti-semitic attitude, let alone implies an attempt to turn anti-semitic emotions against Americans. The Jewish cliché is not necessarily a negative value judgment, but can imply admiration or at least respect, and the characterization of the American resulting from the comparison is not always hostile. A "proverb" preserved in Grimm's *Wörterbuch* seems to warn against simplistic labeling: "It takes nine Jews to cheat a Baseler, and nine Baseler to cheat a Genevan."[43] The quotation also shows that the comparison of Jews to some nationality was not altogether original.[44]

As one may expect, the chase for the dollar—materialism (frequently coupled with *Kulturlosigkeit* or lack of *Gemüt*, not to speak of *Gemütlichkeit*)—is a stereotype in the letters, though not a particularly frequent one. But even though they abound with references to Jews in Germany as well as German Jews in America (usually, though by no means always, with negative connotations), and also to "the Jew" as the epitome of sharp business practices, not a single letter writer refers to Jews in describing the American penchant for money-making. Only one gets close, after trying his hand at peddling, when he writes about the "basic principles of a genuine American (as well as the Jew)" about earning money and concludes: ". . . yet I do not want to earn money the way the American and the son of Abraham think fit," explaining: ". . .earn money, justly or unjustly, but do earn money."[45]

A number of character traits have been pointed out which, while presented by the guidebooks, are entirely or virtually ignored by the letter writers. But the inverse constellation exists as well. For two stereotypes in the letters, no real counterpart can be found in the book sample. One of them is—somewhat unexpectedly—hypocrisy:

> The Americans go to *Schochs* [church], that means *Kirche*, 3 times every Sunday and 3 evenings a week, and they think they're so holy but when they can take the skin off the back of someone else they don't mind at all. These people just pray to get what they want, that's what the Americans are like. . .[46]

The accusation of hypocrisy appears rather frequently, though in different contexts—religion and business, blue laws and prohibition, festivities, politics, and minorities.

As to the other stereotype, it may come as a surprise that Yankees are accused of rather un-Puritanical behavior. Instead of unremitting work, thrift, and laying up for tomorrow, "The Americans are strong and quick, they can do more in one day than the Germans, but they don't want to work every day" and the men here are like this, what they earn one day they have to drink up the next."[47] The following blast comes from Arkansas in 1833: "The Americans are all an indolent people, and in the towns, of which there cannot be more than half a dozen in all of Arkansas, a very dissolute one, too."[48] And the writer does not seem to confine himself to poor whites either.

With some simplification, the quantitative result of a comparison between the opinion of guide books on the one hand and emigrant letters on the other, would be that out of 30 topics discussed in the books, there is a range from basic to complete agreement between the two types of writers on eight points. They concern women's attire, differences between town and country, the rocking chair, women and field work, the protected position of women; the American's being religious; his leaving hard work to others, and his recklessness.

A second category would comprise such items proposed by the guidebooks as are not ignored in the letters, but viewed from a different angle, dealt with only in part, attributed a differing value judgment, or mentioned only by one single letter writer. Again, there are eight of them: American women don't become servants, and they get married early; the higher intelligence of common people; politicians; "help yourself"; the "migrating instinct"; excessive risk-taking; and the role of making money.

The final category of 14 items is made up by one guidebook's claim ("great decency") that is flatly contradicted by the majority of letter writers, and 13 items on which there are no comments at all from the letter writers.

One might, of course, try to weigh the 30 items, considering some of them very important and others less so, and by so doing arrive at a different evaluation. I do not believe in such weighing, because in this present context the question "important to *whom?*" can simply not be eliminated. Without it, the purely numerical result is that actual emigrants fully agree on only one out of four guidebook statements, and with very severe reservations or restrictions on an equivalent proportion. To the supposed readers of the guidebooks, almost one half of the explanation of "the American" seem totally irrelevant.

Even a superficial look at those 14 items will show that they are either abstractions (practical bent, decency, generosity, coolness, chauvinism) or esthetic statements (appearance of women and of men, nature) or oddities in behavior that could hardly find the interest of laboring people (newspaper reading, feet up, gulping food) or, finally, traits that would appear either entirely normal to common people from Germany or, perhaps, irrelevant (hard-working women, cleanliness in housekeeping, neat dressing and personal cleanliness).

This attempt at an interpretation of the differences in subject-matter between books and letters seems so clear, neat, and convincing that some suspicion seems in order, simply because things usually don't fit so perfectly in history. But not being able to find anything seriously wrong with it, I would like to add two ideas that are based on distinct impressions but not on anything like analysis.

Generally speaking, the guidebooks present a more negative picture of America (and the Americans) than the letters do. In view of the mass migration—despite the dire warnings of so many books—one might want to keep in mind that the letters, taken as a body, always had an immensely greater readership than all the books (one could easily make a case for 10:1 or better).

And whereas I have always set books against letters here, just occasionally mentioning letters from middle-class or educated people, it should at least be pointed out that the division could and possibly should be refined by drawing the line not simply between books and letters but—as a closer examination of the middle category (neither agree nor ignore) would illustrate—between books and the letters of "intellectuals" on the one side, and the great bulk of the letters from writers with little education.

I would like to conclude with two more remarks. I believe that the question as to which of the two sorts of writing represents the *better* sources for German emigration, ethnic history, or American social history cannot even be asked, let alone answered, since there would be as many answers as there are purposes for which they are used. But I hope it has become clear that in some respects at least more can be gained from considering books and letters side by side than from examining either by themselves. Consequently, and after having chosen a rather small and perhaps not quite ideal slice of the image of America presented by different media, I feel that a few similar studies on concrete political or social or other matters might enhance our understanding of phenomena and processes that still elude our grasp.

Thus I had been intrigued for years about the unanimous, enthusiastic reports on "equality" not just as an ideal, but as a reality in their lives, by dozens of German immigrants writing home. I occasionally commented briefly on the strange phenomenon of what looked like a collective illusion being, except for appearances, entirely at odds with reality.[49] My attempts at interpreting this were necessarily partly speculative, and I was never quite sure whether I had the full answer—or even the right one.

So it was with something like relief that I found, besides some people who agree with the letter writers[51], several authors who do not hesitate to call American society even less equal than German. Steinert writes about "a plutocracy that could not be worse anywhere." Bauer agrees: "There the caste spirit dominates far worse than in old Europe. Money, wealth is what differentiates human being from human being here." And perhaps the most perspicacious comment and certainly the most balanced one is given by Wander: "It is true that one does not bow to rank and money, but the latter does not rule any less for that."[52]

Thus, not all Germans let themselves be taken in—if such a gross simplification is permitted for argument's sake; and 19th century immigrants did not need the hindsight of 20th century historians if they really wanted to see through flattering appearances; yet, of course, the subjective validity of the letter writers' belief in equality is not in any way diminished by debunking intellectuals at the time or by critical scholars several generations later.

Notes

[1]See Wolfgang Helbich, Walter D. Kamphoefner, Ulrike Sommer, eds., *Briefe aus Amerika. Dt. Auswanderer schreiben aus der Neuen Welt 1830-1930* (München, 1988), 46ff.; American ed. by Cornell Univ. Press, *News from the Land of Freedom: German Immigrants Write Home*, ed. by Kamphoefner, Helbich, and Sommer, trans. by Susan Carter Vogel (Ithaca, 1991).

[2]Helbich, ed., *"Amerika ist ein freies Land. . ." Auswanderer schreiben nach Deutschland* (Darmstadt, 1985); Helbich, *"Alle Menschen sind dort gleich. . ." Die dt. Amerika-Auswanderung im 19. u. 20. Jh.* (Düsseldorf, 1988); Helbich, *Briefe.*

[3]Apart from smaller pieces, there are three more comprehensive studies: Ruth Roebke, "Informationen f. Frauen u. das Frauenbild in den Auswandererratgebern aus dem 19. Jh.," MA thesis (Marburg: Europ. Ethnologie u. Kulturforschung 1986); Georg Schmidbauer, "Das Amerikabild in den dt. Reisebeschreibungen von 1776 bis 1860," MA thesis (München: History 1988); Stephan W. Görisch, *Information zwischen Werbung u. Warnung. Die Rolle der Amerikalit. in der Auswanderung des 18. u. 19. Jhs.*, in *Quellen u. Forschungen zur hess. Geschichte* 84 (Darmstadt, 1992)

[4]Helbich, *Briefe* 32f.

[5]Görisch lists 394 titles, pointing out that 128 of them could not be located by him; but Schmidbauer alone has examined 15 titles that Görisch does not mention.

[6]Schmidbauer, 11 (my trans.).

[7]I chose titles in standard bibliographies that clearly indicated the author's intention of giving advice to emigrants to America, and stopped when I had about 50.

[8]I have listed only those 25 titles that offer some comment on "the American": Friedrich Arends, *Schilderung des Mississippithales, oder des Westens der Ver. Staaten von Nordamerika nebst Abriss meiner Reise dahin* (Emden, 1838); F. Anton Bauer, *Taschenbüchlein f. Auswanderer u. Reisende nach den Ver. Staaten von Nordamerika, oder: Rathgeber f. Alle, welche nach den Ver. Staaten von Nord-Amerika übersiedeln u. daselbst sich häuslich niederlassen u. eine sichere Existenz gründen wollen* (Augsburg, 1854); L. von Baumbach, *Briefe aus den Ver. Staaten von Nordamerika in die Heimath. . .* (Cassel, 1851); Moritz Beyer, *Das Auswanderungsbuch oder Führer u. Rathgeber bei der Auswanderung nach Nordamerika u. Texas in Bezug auf Ueberfahrt, Ankunft u. Ansiedelung. . . Grösstentheils nach eigener Auffassung während eines zweijähr. Aufenthalts in Amerika* (Leipzig, 1850); Traugott Bromme, *Hand- u. Reisebuch f. Auswanderer nach den Ver. Staaten von Nord-Amerika* (Bayreuth, 1848); Adolf Douai, *Land u. Leute in der Union* (Berlin, 1864); Gottfried Duden, *Bericht über eine Reise nach den westl. Staaten Nordamerika's oder Das Leben im Innern der Ver. Staaten* (Elberfeld, 1829); C.L. Fleischmann, *Wegweiser u. Rathgeber nach u. in den Ver. Staaten von Nord-Amerika* (Stuttgart, 1852); Julius Froebel, *Aus Amerika. Erfahrungen, Reisen u. Studien,*

2 vols. (Leipzig, 1856); Ludwig Gall, *Meine Auswanderung nach den Ver. Staaten in Nord-Amerika im Frühjahr 1819 u. meine Rückkehr nach der Heimath im Winter 1820*, 2 vols. (Trier, 1822); Theodor Griesinger, *Land u. Leute in Amerika. Skizzen aus dem amerikan. Leben* (Stuttgart, 1863); U. Hesse, *Das westl. Nordamerika, in bes. Beziehunq auf die dt. Einwanderer in ihren landwirthschaftl. Handels- u. Gewerbeverhältnissen* (Paderborn, 1838); A. Kirsten, *Skizzen aus den Ver. Staaten von Nordamerika* (Leipzig, 1851); Karl Kohler, *Briefe aus Amerika f. dt. Auswanderer. Mit fünf Ansichten nach der Natur.* . . (Darmstadt, 1852); Franz v. Löher, *Land u. Leute in der alten u. neuen Welt. Reiseskizzen*, vol. 1 (Göttingen, 1854); Gottfr. Menzel, *Die Ver. Staaten von Nordamerika mit bes. Rücksicht auf dt. Auswanderung dahin* (Berlin, 1853); Friedrich Münch, *Der Staat Missouri* (New York, St. Louis, 1859); W. Steinert, *Nordamerika vorzüglich Texas im Jahre 1849. Reisebericht. Ein Buch f. Auswanderer, bes. f. Auswanderungslustige* (Berlin, 1850); G.F. Streckfuss, *Der Auswanderer nach Amerika oder treue Schilderung der Schicksale, welche mich auf meiner Wanderung nach Amerika, während meines dortigen Aufenthaltes oder auf meiner Rückreise trafen; nebst Bemerkungen über die Landschaften, welche ich kennen lernte, die Sitten ihrer Bewohner u. die Lage der dort eingewanderten Deutschen* (Zeitz, 1836); Gustav Struve, *Kurzgefasster Wegweiser f. Auswanderer mit bes. Rücksicht auf Nordamerika, die brit. Kolonien, Mexiko, die südamerik. Republiken, Brasilien u. Australien* (Bamberg, 1867); Friedr. Vulpius, *Amerik. Erfahrungen, Winke u. Warnungen f. Auswanderungslustige* (Vlgsbh. zu Belle-Vue, 1847); K.F.W. Wander, *Auswanderungs-Katechismus. Ein Rathgeber f. Auswanderer, bes. f. Diejenigen, welche nach Nordamerika auswandern wollen, in Bezug auf Kenntniss des Landes, Abreise, Ueberfahrt, Ankunft, Ansiedelung, Lebensweise usw. u. ein belehrendes Volksbuch f. die Hierbleibenden* (Glogau, 1852), repr. ed. Wolfgang Mieder (Bern, 1988); Alexander Ziegler, *Der dt. Auswanderer nach den Ver. Staaten von Nordamerika. Ein Lehrbuch auf seinen Weg* (Leipzig, 1849).

[9]Roebke, 66-105. What has been said above about the 25 out of 45 authors does not apply here. For the image of American *women*, I did not refer to the guides directly, since Roebke's findings appeared fully satisfactory as a foil for the immigrant letters, and I have no reason to doubt the validity of her results.

[10]*"Was thut u. wirkt die Amerik. Frau? Anders nichts als sich den ganzen Tag in den Schaukelstuhl zu wiegen, u. sich aus Zeitvertreib ein wenig mit Lesen oder Nähen zu beschäftigen."* *"Arbeiten tun selten die amerik. Frauen, sie putzen sich, schlendern herum u. sollen oft weder Stricken noch Nähen können"* (Helbich, *Amerika*, 131, 132).

[11]". . .*wie viele Deusche Bursche nehmen sich Ameriganer u. Eurische viel spass darf man nicht machen sonst gehen Sie gleich auf die Curt das heisst vor das Gericht da wird der Bursch gehot vom Gerichtdiener u. da werden Sie koppaliert da ist der spass aus da gehen Sie miteinander in die Fecktori u. arbeiten zusammen u. gehen in Board bei andere Leute"* (Helbich, *Briefe*, 329).

[12]Görisch, 316-28; 329-33; 333.

[13]". . .a high degree of intelligence pervades even the lowest classes, which therefore stand in odd contrast to the European masses." ". . .*ein hoher Grad von lntelligenz durchdringt selbst die niedrigsten Klassen, die deshalb mit der Masse der europ. Bevölkerung einen sonderbaren Gegensatz bilden"* (Bromme, 84).

[14]*"Roh u. ungebildet ist der Amerikaner. . ."* (Groth/Groth series, Milwaukee, 8-12-1890, in the Bochum letters collection: Bochumer Auswandererbrief-Sammlung, cited infra as BABS). These letter writers are supported by one author who attests "an apparent uncouthness, lack of sensitivity". *"Eine anscheinende Rohheit, Mangel an zartem Gefühl"* (Arends, 199).

[15]". . .*das freuet mich.* . . . *das der Wilhelm so sehr viel klüger ist als er in deutsland war das hätte ich nicht geglaupt aber ich glaube das es viel macht das er so wenig leichte arbeit hat u. gehet so herum u. spricht mit alle kluge Leute von allerlei Handel u.s.w.* . . ." (Helbich, *Briefe*, 73).

[16]"*In körperl. Beziehung ist der Amerikaner von der Natur nicht bevorzugt. Seinem Körperbaue von mittlerer Grösse ist wohl ein ziemlich hoher Grad von Zähigkeit u. Ausdauer, aber weder besondere Kraft noch Wohlgestalt eigen*" (Menzel, 94); "*Die Bewohner der Ver. Staaten sind im Allg. ein starker kräftiger Menschenschlag.* . ." (Bromme, 50); Douai, 121; Arends, 438; *Schöne Körperformen*", "*edle Haltung*" (Streckfuss, 81).

[17]Whites, that is; reports on the phys. appearance of African and Native Americans are rather common when those groups are described.

[18]". . . *ihre Füsse während dem Sitzen so hoch als möglich zu postiren*" (Menzel, 103).

[19]"*Schöne Garten-Anlagen*" (Beyer, 81); "*Von Bewunderung der Natur kann also bei einem Yankee nimmermehr die Rede sein, wohl aber von deren Ausbeutung*" (Griesinger, 16).

[20]"*Geringschätzung des Menschenlebens*" (Ziegler, 34); "*Gibt ein Fremder seine Verwunderung zu erkennen, dass bei den Wettfahrten der Dampfboote das Menschenleben ohne alle Ursache auf's Spiel gesetzt wird,*" oder fordert er mehr Sicherheit bei der Eisenbahn, "*so wird eine solche Aeusserung gewissermassen mit Befremden aufgenommen*" (Kirsten, 39).

[21]"*der [Bau] mit amerik. Leichtsinnigkeit geführt wird*". "*Wie wenig sich übrigens die amerik. Regierung um einen gebrochenen Soldatenhals bekümmert kannst Du daraus sehen, dass wir auf unsrer Reise von unseren beiden Divisionen fünf bis sechs tausend Mann—25 Tote hatten, als wir ankamen [bei überfüllten Waggons fuhren Soldaten auf dem Dach—u. stürzten ab]. Es ward aber auf der ganzen Reise nicht das Geringste gethan, diesem heillosen Uebelstand abzuhelfen, den 25 Burschen mit dem Leben bezahlten*" (Ohlerich/Uterhard series, 10-9-1863, BABS).

[22]"*Keiner hilft dem Anderen, wenn kein Profit dabei zu erlangen ist*" (Vulpius, 67); Griesinger, 29; "*In dem amerik. Prinzip: 'Hilf dir selbst!' liegt eine so kalte Grausamkeit, liegt ein solcher Widerspruch gegen alle Humanität ausgesprochen, dass das Individuum, wie im grauen Heidenthum, sich jedem Menschen feindlich gegenübergestellt sieht, wodurch der roheste, materiellste Egoismus als höchstes Prinzip anerkannt wird*" (Wander, 39).

[23]"*Wer hier kein Geld hat, der ist fast schlimmer ab, wie in Deutschland*" (Helbich, *Briefe*, 183).

[24]"*Kalthöfliches Benehmen u. eine gewisse Einsylbigkeit sind dem Amerikaner so sehr eigen, dass sie ihn f. herzliches Entgegenkommen u. eigentliche Freundschaft unempfänglich machen*" (Hesse, 118).

[25]"*Jene Kälte zeigt sich besonders auffallend im ehelichen Leben. Da bemerkt man.* . . *kein Zeichen von Zuneigung oder Anhänglichkeit zwischen Eltern u. Kindern.* . . *nichts von der Innigkeit, der Herzlichkeit u. gegenseitigen Theilnahme, welche das Leben zweier sich liebenden Gatten so entzückend, zum irdischen Paradiese machen*" (Arends, 443).

[26]"*Hier d.h. bei Amerikanern sind auch höchst selten Eltern und Kinder traurig, wenn sie sich auf längere Zeit trennen müssen.*" "*Die Amerikaner sind f. ziemlich gefühllos u. gleichgültig bekannt.* . ." (Kaper/Meinecke series, 6-7-1861, BABS).

[27]"*Das ist ein Beispiel ächt amerik. Freundlichkeit, wie es einem fast täglich vorkommt.* . . *Diese anscheinend so kühlen, berechnenden Menschen sind im Grund gutherziger als sie zeigen wollen*" (Bauer/Württemberger series, 11-4-1910, BABS).

[28]"*Dieser Hochmuth u. Selbstdünkel kommt schon mit ihm auf die Welt u. es gibt deshalb keinen Yankeebuben, der nicht in der Ueberzeugung lebte, das Non plus ultra der Schöpfung zu sein*" (Griesinger, 6).

[29]*"Zigeunerartiger Wandertrieb"* (ibid, 15f.).

[30]*"Die Amerikaner sind überhaupt. . . ein wanderndes Volk, das nie rastet; sind die jetzigen Staaten einigermassen bevölkert, so werden sie die den Indianern eingeräumten Besitzungen einnehmen und demnächst die jenseitigen Steppen oder, diese überspringend, die schönen Thäler jenseits des Oregon bis zum stillen Meer anfüllen"* (Arends, 198).

[31]*"Anlegen von Fabriken u. Manufakturen"; "Allein obiges lässt sich nicht hoffen. Der unstätige leichtsinnige Character des Amerikaners. . . eignet sich dazu durchaus nicht u. zieht überhaupt das gewagte schnelle reich werden dem sichern langsamen Weg bey weitem vor"* (Engstfeld/Spannagel series, 9-4-1842, BABS).

[32]*"Geldgier, Herzlosigkeit, Egoismus, Gewinnsucht, Reichtum, Gelehrsamkeit."*

[33]Duden, 126f.; Fleischmann, 64f.

[34]Kirsten, 42f.; Donai, 81.

[35]Löher, *Aussichten*, 8; *"Betrugssinn. . . regelmässig sehr stark ausgeprägt"* (Griesinger, 4).

[36]Arends, 449; *"schmutzigste, rücksichtsloseste Habsucht"* (Gall, 14); *"Volk von Schwindlern", "Räuberstaat"* (Vulpius, 9).

[37]*"Auch rohe Zwiebeln sind eine Lieblingsspeise des Amerikaners, so wie er überhaupt in gar Manchem Aehnlichkeit mit dem Juden verräth"* (Vulpius, 45).

[38]*"Am übelsten empfinden dies die in grosser Zahl von Deutschland herüberkommenden Juden, die meistentheils anfangs hier Hausirhandel treiben u. das ganze Land damit überschwemmen. Insgesammt behaupten sie, von den Amerikanern in der Schlauheit noch übertroffen zu werden und bei diesen noch in die Lehre gehen zu müssen"* (Kirsten, 48).

[39]*"Schon vielfach den Juden des Westens."* *"Sprüchwort"*: *"Aus einem Yankee kann man zwei Juden machen u. dann bleibt immer noch ein Christ übrig"* (Griesinger, 14).

[40]*"Darum wohnt dem Amerikaner in allen Handelsstädten eine List u. Verschlagenheit bei, die von der zum Sprichwort gewordenen Handelsgewandtheit dt. Juden nicht erreicht wird"* (Hesse, 132).

[41]*"Hierin übertrifft er weit den europ. Juden, mit dem er als Geschäftsmann überdies in Hinsicht der Redlichkeit u. Verlässlichkeit eine auffallende Aehnlichkeit hat, welchen Punkt die Lobredner der Amerikaner mit Stillschweigen übergehen"* (Menzel, 94-5).

[42]*"Die Juden der Alten Welt waren nie so arg wie diese Leute. Die Yankees sind 5fache Juden, ein altes Sprichwort"* (Steinert, 269f.).

[43]*"Es gehören neun Juden dazu um einen Baseler u. neun Baseler um einen Genfer zu betrügen"* (*Dt. Wb. von Jacob u. Wilhelm Grimm*, Leipzig 1854-1960, 33 vols., München, 1984, vol. 10, 2353).

[44]It would probably be worthwhile to probe more deeply into what the common roots were for German middle-class, mid-19th-century authors to be suspicious of a supposedly common trait of Jews and Americans, and whether their ideology predisposed them to a more general rejection of Jewish and American culture.

[45]*"Grundprinzipien eines echten Amerikaners (so wie des Juden)." ". . .doch auf dem Wege wie der Amerikaner u. der Sohn Abrahams denkt, mag ich kein Geld* erwerben. . ."; "verdiene Geld per fas oder per nefas, nur verdiene Geld" (Gronemeyer/Gronemeyer series, 6-23-1837, BABS).

[46]*". . .da gehen die Amerikaner jeden Sonntag 3 mal in die Schochs d.h. Kirche u. jede Woche 3 mal Abends da wollen sie so Heilig sein aber wenn sie jemandem die Haut herunter können ziehen da nehmen sie nichts vor übel das sind Menschen die beten Blos um Ihre Zwecke erreichen zu können so sein die Americaner. . ."* (Helbich, *Briefe*, 331).

[47]*"Die Amerikaner sind stark u. geschwind, die können in einem Tag mehr thun wie die Deutschen, aber nur wollen sie auch nicht jeden Tag arbeiten"; ". . .die Mannsleuthe die sind hir soh, was sie den einen Tag verdienen das muss den andern Tag wieder versoffen werden"* (ibid., 69, 72).

[48]*"Die Amerikaner sind durchgängig ein träges u. in den kleinen Städten, wovon ganz Arkansas nur ein Halbdutzend zählen kann. . . ein sehr liederliches Volk"* (Helbich, *Amerika*), 193, cf. 194.

[49]E.g. in "Letters from America: Documents of the Adjustment Process of German Immigrants in the U.S.," *Anglistik & Englischunterricht* 26 (1985): 205f.; "The Letters They Sent Home: The Subjective Perspective of German Immigrants in the 19th Century," *Yearbook of German-American Studies* 22 (1987): 5-8; "Stereotypen in Auswandererbriefen: Die USA im 19. Jh. aus der Sicht dt. Einwanderer," in *Exotische Welt in populären Lektüren,* ed. Anselm Maler (Tübingen, 1990), 71.

[50]Bromme, 83; Menzel, 96.

[51]*"Ein Geldadel, wie man ihn nirgends schlimmer haben kann"* (Steinert, 277); *"Es herrscht dort selbst der Kastengeist noch in einem schrofferen Grade, als im alten Europa. Das Geld, der Reichtum ist hier, was den Menschen vom Menschen unterscheidet"* (Bauer, 17); *"Man bückt sich freilich nicht vor Stand u. Geld, aber das letztere herrscht dessenungeachtet nicht weniger"* (Wander, 31).

23 | The Harmonists: Two Points of View. A Tribute to the 175th Anniversary of New Harmony, Indiana

Eberhard and Ruth Reichmann, *Indiana University*

Migrants to the New World are cast in a many-faceted dual role as *Auswanderer* and *Einwanderer*, legally (by the bureaucracies of the discharging and receiving governments), psychologically (by unavoidable self-classification of the migrating persons), and perceptionally (by those from whom they departed and by those in whose midst they begin their new life).

This paper's focus is on perceptional aspects of the *emigrant/immigrant* phenomenon as demonstrated in the case of the religious separatist and millenarian Johann Georg Rapp and his Harmonie Society on the one hand, and the people of the town of Wiernsheim, Baden-Württemberg, past and present, on the other.

In 1979, through Ruth Reichmann's function as Indiana state representative of Sister Cities International, we became involved in forming a town affiliation between New Harmony, Ind.—Rapp's second settlement— and Wiernsheim with its incorporated townships of Iptingen, Serres, and Pinache, the core area of Harmonist emigration. The belief held by Sister Cities International, which educates informally through town affiliations worldwide, is that only when people get directly involved with people can one really understand the others' point of view. In the case of the Harmonists, American and German perspectives yielded two radically different points of view with commensurate consequences for human relationships.

In America, Father Rapp and his Harmonists have been seen primarily as founders of three thriving communities and, compared with all other communal societies, as having achieved unparalleled economic success.[1]

People in the Harmonist home territory in Württemberg saw in the weaver Rapp and his followers, "the Rappites," a bunch of impudent disturbers of peace and order in church and society.

We will sketch the genesis of these positions and pinpoint some outcomes and lessons of the partnership between New Harmony and Wiernsheim.

I

The year is 1803. The weaver Johann Georg Rapp, spiritual head of possibly up to 20,000 separatist followers and sympathizers, now age 46, sails to America with three of his associates. The goal: to find and acquire an appropriate settlement area for his flock. He buys 6,000 acres on the Conquenessing in Butler County, Pa. In 1804, some 600 Württembergers from the then Oberamt (county) Maulbronn follow Father Rapp. The Town of Harmony, Pa. comes into being.

By 1814 the communal society of the Harmonists—meanwhile augmented by new arrivals to over 700—sells the town and moves to the southwest corner of the Indiana Territory. They constitute the largest and earliest organized group of Germans to settle in Indiana. New Harmony on the Wabash, their second town, is carved out of the wilderness and becomes, if you will, the first German "economic miracle" or—in contemporary appraisal—"the Wonder of the West." Living up to the proverbial Swabian work ethics: *Schaffa, schaffa, schaffa; spara, spara, spara; Häusle baua. . .,*" (Work, work, work; save, save, save; build a little house. . .), combined with the Benedictine principle of *ora et labora,* New Harmony, within just ten years, advances to the rank of the wealthiest (per capita) community in America. No less than 20,000 acres, with 3,000 fenced and producing bumper crops, surround their community with its prosperous economy that is based on advanced planning, building and manufacturing concepts, with its first coeducational public school, its kindergarten, its public library, and its rich musical life. And all this despite a catastrophic malaria epidemic claiming numerous lives during their first year on the banks of the Wabash.[2]

In 1824 Rapp sells the communally-held Indiana town to Robert Owen, British industrialist and social reformer, for the latter's short-lived but noteworthy utopian experiment of "the community of equals." The

Harmonists move back to Pennsylvania and build their third town, named Economy, of which a part is now a State Historic Site in Ambridge, Pa., known as Old Economy. It is here that they become a major economic force in the industrial development of the Pittsburgh area; it is here that the collective worth of the millenarians reaches $16 million; it is here where Rapp dies at the biblical age of 90, convinced to his end that Christ's coming is imminent; it is here where his celibate society—replenished over the years by adopted orphans—dies out in the early 20th century.[3]

But the legacy of Harmonist achievements in the New World continues to be appreciated and admired in America by the thousands of visitors to the towns the Swabians built. Their sectarian faith has enjoyed protection under the law in the land of separation of church and state.

II

Back in the Old World the long-time and generally shared perception of the four Wiernsheim communities centered on the Harmonists' irreconcilable conflict with the Protestant state church and on their disruptive challenge to traditional village ways. Beyond villages near Wiernsheim, the spirit of Rapp had made itself felt particularly in the rural area marked by the town triangle of Pforzheim—Ludwigsburg—Böblingen, north and northwest of Stuttgart. Rapp was born in 1757 in Iptingen, now a township of 800 in the consolidated community of Wiernsheim which, together with the townships of Serres (500) and Pinache (700), has a population of 4,500.

We do not mention the latter two communities as contributing to Rapp's cause, but they are of some significance for the understanding of differences in the perception of the emigration/immigration phenomenon. The village names of Serres and Pinache not only *sound* French, they are. Both were founded in 1699 when hundreds of Waldensian refugee families from the French Piedmont valleys accepted the invitation of Duke Eberhard Ludwig of Württemberg whose land had been devastated and depopulated during the Thirty Years War. The process of cultural integration of the Waldensians was not accelerated until the post-Napoleonic 1820s when, by government fiat, German replaced French as the language of school and church, and when their church became part of the Evangelische Landeskirche. Not counting post-WWII *Hereingeschmeckte* (semi-unwelcomed newcomers) and *Gastarbeiter* (guest workers), the Wiernsheim area has thus experienced both group *immigration* and group *emigration*, about equal in numbers and motivation, and all within the span of a century. Later we shall see how these two migrations have been perceived and valued differently by the people of Wiernsheim.

But first we must return to Rapp himself, then a young weaver and vinedresser, who had devoted his spare time to the intensive study of the Bible and the literature of radical Pietism. His championing of an intense *inner* religious experience—as opposed to observed routine practices—estranged him from the ecclesiastical establishment, i.e. the Evangelische Landeskirche, from its rituals and some of its fundamental tenets. At age 24, Rapp began presenting his Bible interpretations to ever-growing audiences who eventually became his flock and, with him, separated formally from the church to start their own "Church of Brethren" with Rapp functioning as their *de facto* Bishop. His "Lomersheim Declaration of Faith" (March 1798),[4] and again "The Oehlbronn Declaration of Faith" (Nov. 1799),[5] both required by, and submitted to, state authorities, unleashed unacceptable criticism of church life and spelled out social disruption if left unchecked. A brief summary of these Declarations must suffice:

a. The first-century church of the Apostles is the model: a church of the spirit, not of stone. God's omnipresence needs no buildings.

b. Group experience of like minds is stressed, aiming at harmony and brotherly love in unity.

c. The practice of child baptism has no biblical basis. With St. John, penance is seen as the prerequisite for real baptism. Through prayer the newborn is taken into the covenant with God.

d. Communion makes sense only as an inner, spiritual experience. The mechanical weekly practice of the established church caters to outer instead of inner experience. Total and absolute harmony among all members must precede the act of communion.

e. Harmonist children are to be educated in the home. For in the schools they lose their simplicity of mind and get distracted from their ultimate destiny. The merely outward form of school prayer is a farce.

f. Confirmation, likewise, has lost its spiritual significance. It has turned into a materialistic exercise with new clothes and gifts playing the primary role, and this misguided development excludes the poor from equal participation.

g. Government as an institution is confirmed. For "if it had not been for the government, the people of Wiernsheim-Iptingen would long ago have driven us to the end of the world." Obedience to government, however, is not unconditional. "We will pay our dues and due respect to government, as long as we are tolerated." But the practice of swearing an oath is rejected on biblical grounds.

h. Military service for "born-again Christians"—in the Rapp sense—is rejected. For it is utterly absurd for a Christian to raise arms against fellow Christians. Taxes and, if necessary, penalties are offered as alternatives to soldiering.

These articles of faith and their expressed or implied criticism of church and society were clearly dynamite to the existing order. A break of some sort was inevitable, especially since the number of Rappites had passed the point of a possibly tolerable dissent. The signals showed a clear tendency toward a mass movement. Lower level church and secular authorities conducted interrogations and wrote numerous reports to a surprisingly enlightened and relatively tolerant state commission.

What took place must be seen as a genuinely tragic conflict. On the one side: the Rappites with the classical Luther posture of not being able to retract, save on biblical grounds, a minority with their quest for religious freedom and certain human rights. On the other side: the local folk and the lower clergy and officials firmly standing by the traditional ecclesiastical and secular order and defending the religious and civic homogeneity of rural communities against cultural revolutionaries.

In Rapp's analysis, persecution of his faithful was quite certain—after all, he himself had already been temporarily incarcerated in Maulbronn. Combining this with the political developments of the Napoleonic era convinced him that the second coming of Christ was imminent. With St. John's Revelation as his guide, his flock became the sunwoman who had to flee into the wilderness. The wilderness was in America. There they would prepare for the Millennium with prayer and labor for the divine economy of the New Jerusalem. Their travel songs[6] repeatedly praise America as "the promised land," as in these excerpts:

Let us go, let us go.
In America, the great sheep pasture
we shall find.
There the sunwoman is to flee
that at the time of evil safe she shall be.
Then Judgment will break out to avenge.

Onward to America,
there is our Father's land. . .[7]

Brethren, the time is at hand.
To North America, the promised land!
Come on, ye friends, with trust and courage.
Do not tarry, God will carry and strengthen your spirit.
Soon better days we will enjoy,
without the pains we face today.

Happy day, with Babel behind us,
in America, God will govern us
with His hand. . .[8]

Brethren, dear Brethren, rejoice.
Sing new songs unto the Lord.
He will build His new kingdom in America
and destroy all of Europa.
Brethren hurry!

Now, fare well, you Württembergers.
Your day of judgment
in the sinister prison of fire
will not harm us,
but it will destroy you altogether. . . [9]

And so they left, never to return, and leaving behind in the Wiernsheim area and elsewhere deeply disturbed and broken-up families and communities.

As time went on and word about the Harmonists' miraculous success reached the villages in the Oberamt Maulbronn, there was icy silence. For unlike the generous donations to the home town of Iptingen by the former shoemaker Johannes Huber, who had made his good fortune in France, there was not one penny coming back from the "promised land." And when after World War I distant relatives of the then extinct Harmonists took legal action to get their share of that American fortune—but failed—the Harmonists were totally eradicated from collective memory.

III

In New Harmony, on the other hand, the 900 people living there today represent the typical Midwestern small-town blend of various European ethnic strands. They have always been fond of their founding fathers and cogniszant of Rapp's place of origin, especially since extensive historic preservation in the 1960s and 1970s has transformed the town into "historic New Harmony," with equal attention paid to the heritage of the Harmonists and their immediate successors, the Owenites. But there were no personal contacts with Wiernsheim and Iptingen, Rapp's birthplace. The occasional visiting American historian doing research in the Wiernsheim area would not understand that there was no marker, no museum, no street named after Rapp, nor anyone talking about the contributions their distant relatives had made to America.

Things began to change in 1979 when New Harmony aimed at a town affiliation. A resolution was drafted and signed by literally everybody in town, extending a warm invitation to Wiernsheim for a Sister Cities relationship. That resolution is now on display at the Town Hall of Wiernsheim. Preliminary negotiations were conducted by the Reichmanns.

What did we find in Wiernsheim? A great initial reluctance on the part of the mayor, who happened to be also a deacon on the Protestant church council, which reflected the seemingly unpardonable religious and social disturbance caused by the "no-good" Rappites and their subsequent "defection" to America. In contrast, he spoke warmly and proudly of the Waldensians, Wiernsheim's own immigrants and settlers of the incorporated villages of Serres and Pinache, as "our religious refugees." Arranging a partnership in the face of religious difficulties, he felt, was a thankless job. Pinache had tried so hard with Pinasca, but the Catholic church there did not want to have anything to do "with these apostates," he sighed, and "if the religious ideas of Rapp are still alive in New Harmony today, there is no use even discussing a partnership." We assured him that the Rappite's utopian dream was now safely buried in the annals of history. But while in our conversation he could not deny principal parallels between the Waldensians and the Harmonists, he certainly did not realize his—and the community's— application of dual standards to the emigration/immigration phenomenon in their own history. He was nice enough, though, to call a town meeting.

When the surprisingly large audience of several hundred heard an American professor address them in their own dialect, the ice melted quickly. We showed a professionally-made film, *New Harmony—A Beacon and a Light*, for which we spoke the original English-language text of the sound track in German translation. Interest began to emerge. Talking about Rapp, however, consistently yielded a stereotyped negative image. For the folk there he was simply a "trouble-maker," "no-good," "religious nut," "fanatic," "heretic" and, at best, a "dissident," or "separatist." We realized that we were confronted with a persistence of historically-rooted collective grudges and that today's professed acceptance of the notions of self-determination, self-fulfillment and the right to dissent was meaningless for the moment. Nevertheless, a willingness toward a Sister Cities arrangement did surface. The phase of trust formation had begun. The particular challenge for us now was to bring both communities to understand and appreciate the divergent perceptions of Rapp, the rebel, and Rapp, the American pioneer—to reconcile the dichotomy inherent in the *emigrant/immigrant* phenomenon.

Back home in Indiana, New Harmony's intercultural willingness was great but didn't quite match the needed Germany-specific competencies in language and cultural knowledge. This led to the appointment of Ruth Reichmann as "intercommunal" adviser who also acted on behalf of Wiernsheim as a quasi ambassador. Person-to-person contacts on a broader scale did not begin until a large delegation headed by Mayor Rolf Gockeler of Wiernsheim arrived in New Harmony for the signing of the Sister Cities charter.

The people of New Harmony prepared themselves for the big event of the summer of 1980. It was also to be an act of reconciliation after 175 years, uniting the two towns in a newly won friendship. Help came from the German Fulbright Commissioner Uli Littmann, who provided a teacher from Germany to re-introduce the German language for both high school students and adults, and to serve as a cultural representative. The Wiernsheimers, in turn, brushed up their English.

Then came the visit of the Wiernsheimers, 40 persons of all ages and backgrounds interested in finding out first-hand "what these Harmonists were all about" and how they had applied the Swabian "work-work-work" philosophy in America. The visit culminated in the signing of a Twinning Charter by the two mayors, and in the symbolic act of placing bricks from the former Rapp house in Iptingen into the wall surrounding the old Harmonist cemetery. Those who witnessed the ceremony felt the wheel of local German-American history turning. Reconciliation at last, and the beginning of an understanding of differing points of view, appreciation of members of another culture, and friendship from people to people. Enthusiastic travel reports of the Wiernsheimers made the press in their county, the Enzkreis. Significantly, the former negative *emigrant* perception with the associated rebel image was altered by the *immigrant* perception with its image of the American frontier pioneer. Former rejection had turned into pride about the Harmonists' remarkable achievements and contributions to the building of America, and many a native Iptinger and Wiernsheimer suddenly rediscovered a relationship to the emigrants of 1804. Similarly, in New Harmony there was suddenly a willingness to acknowledge German descent openly.

Other notable community events in the process of reconciliation were the 1982 concert of the Harmonist Chorale Ensemble in the Maulbronn Monastery (Rapp had been incarcerated in Maulbronn just prior to his emigration) and the performance of Harmonist hymns in a fully-packed bilingual German/English service at the Church of Iptingen. Again, a significant symbolic act, infinitely more important than the Ensemble's other well-attended concerts in Baden-Württemberg. Later that year, Johann Georg Rapp himself made a "re-appearance" in Wiernsheim at the "Festparade" in honor of the 125th anniversary of the *Gesangverein*. He and a group of Harmonist men, women and children rode on a wagon waving the Hoosier and the American flag. There is nothing like "coming home!"

Anniversaries are milestones of historical consciousness. In 1983 the Tricentennial of German Immigration brought an Indiana concert tour of the Kloster Maulbronn Chamber Choir, including a week-long participation in the New Harmony Music Fest; and for the 175th anniversary of New Harmony in 1989 the Pinache Men's Choir gave a musical tribute from the Old Country.

IV

What lessons can be learned from this town affiliation experience? *Emigration* and *immigration* perceptions can be very different: In Wiernsheim, the Waldensians who settled in Serres and Pinache had long been positively regarded as "our religious refugees," while the departed Harmonists were simply "scoundrels and rebels," with a double negative rating for Rapp. In New Harmony, Rapp and his followers were perceived as pioneers, hard-working, economically successful newcomers and founders of three thriving villages. The positive or negative viewpoint, it turns out, is clearly derived from the respective cultural/religious and economic impact of the migrants.

For us authors, intercultural interpretation had become a major activity, far beyond explaining and clarifying the historical role of Rapp and his followers.

We were also reminded of the limits of objectivity in interpretation. No matter how objective we think we are, our experientially determined coordinates of reference, time and place do color our vision. Borrowing the natural sciences' tenet that *objectivity* equals *replicability*, tells us that we must seek agreement on the interpretation of data, documents and artifacts, so that our experience might be more correctly interpreted. Applied to the topic at hand, neither the emigration point of view, nor the immigration point of view—if solely relied upon—provides a sufficient basis for objectivity. Only when these two halves are put together can the whole experience find a balanced interpretation.

It also became clear that interpretive sites like New Harmony and Old Economy are venerable historical landmarks of considerable significance, not only for Americans but also for Germans. In visiting such sites, Germans can become better aware of the migrant's dual role as the *Auswanderer* who left and the *Einwanderer* who arrived. And both sides will better appreciate that it took generations of immigrants to build this nation—a "nation of immigrants."

Notes

[1] In 1840 Gideon B. Smith, editor of the *Journal of the American Silk Society*, praised one particular achievement of the Harmonists, namely to "have brought the art [of silk making] to a state of perfection equal to any establishment in Europe. . ." They proved, he further observed, that the silk business "is both a practicable and profitable business for the people of the U.S." For Smith, the Harmonists' economic reputation includes "the well known fact, that these people never pursue any branch of business that they do not find profitable." See Karl J.R. Arndt, *George Rapp's Harmony Society 1785-1847*, rev. ed. (Cranbury, NJ, 1972), 582f.

[2] For those venturing into Harmonist studies, the fundamental and indispensable research has been the lifelong work of one scholar, Karl J. R. Arndt, whose volumes on the Harmonists make them probably the best documented German immigration group to America. See D. F. Durnbaugh's "Radical Pietism as the Foundation of German-American Communitarian Settlements" with a basic Harmonist bibliogr. in this volume.

[3] Old Economy, now an hist. site of the Commonwealth of Pa., is well preserved and maintained.

[4] Arndt, *Georg Rapp's Separatists/Georg Rapps Separatisten, 1700-1803* (Worcester, 1980), 272ff.

[5] Ibid., 294ff.

[6] For the original texts of the extant travel songs see op. cit., 442ff. "They are folk poetry, and reflect the Harmonist view that everyone could write poetry," 441. With this characterization Arndt comes closer to the nature of Harmonist song production than Theodor Heuss who, an admirer of Rapp's economic achievements, finds the songs "disquieting, trite verses with gibberish of theosophy mixed in" (*Schattenbeschwörung—Randfiguren der Geschichte* (Tübingen, 1950), 2. Aufl., 96.

[7] Arndt, *Georg Rapp's Separatists*, 446f. All trans. of excerpts by E. Reichmann.

[8] Ibid., 448f.

[9] Ibid., 442.

Other Publications

Volume 1 (1989)
George Theodore Probst/Eberhard Reichmann
The Germans in Indianapolis, 1840-1918.
xii + 200 pp., illustrated. Index by Elfrieda Lang.

Volume 2 (1991)
Theodore Stempfel's 1898 Festschrift:
Fünfzig Jahre unermüdlichen deutschen Strebens in Indianapolis/
Fifty Years of Unrelenting German Aspirations in Indianapolis, 1848-1898.
Trans. & ed. by Giles R. Hoyt, Claudia Grossmann, Elfrieda Lang and
Eberhard Reichmann.
vii + 150 pp., illustrated. Index.

Volume 3 (1991)
Eberhard Reichmann, Editor
Hoosier German Tales—Small and Tall.
333 German-American anecdotes, legends, memoirs and jokes from oral and
written Indiana sources. English-language version with some bilingual
entries.
xx + 258 pp. ISBN 1-880788-00-4.

Volume 4 (1993)
Willi Paul Adams
The German-Americans. An Ethnic Experience.
Trans. & adapted from the German by LaVern J. Rippley and Eberhard
Reichmann.
46 pp., illustrated. ISBN 1-880788-01-2

Volume 5 (1994)
Don Heinrich Tolzmann, Editor
The Sioux Uprising in Minnesota, 1862: Jacob Nix's Eyewitness History.
German/English Edition. Trans. by Gretchen Steinhauser, Don Heinrich
Tolzmann, and Eberhard Reichmann.
xxii + 165 pp., illustrated. ISBN 1-880788-02-0

Volume 6 (1994)
James P. Ziegler, Editor
The German-language Press in Indiana. A Bibliography.
vii + 63 pp., illustrated. ISBN 1-880788-03-9.

Volume 7 (1995)
Gerard Wilk
Americans from Germany.
Reprint edition. Don Heinrich Tolzmann, Editor.
xii + 83 pp., illustrated. ISBN 1-880788-06-3.

Also available

*Witter's Deutsch-Englische Schreib- und Lese-Fibel/German-English Primer
(1881).*
Reprint Edition 1987. viii + 95 pp. Introduces old German script. No
knowledge of German required.

James Divita/Giles R. Hoyt, Editors.
German Influence on Religion in Indiana, in: *Studies in Indiana German
Americana,* No. 2 (1995), 94 pp. ISBN 1-880788-07-1.